Herb Schildt's C++
Programming Cookbook

H4

About the Author

Herbert Schildt is a leading authority on C++, C, Java, and C#, and is a master Windows programmer. His programming books have sold more than 3.5 million copies worldwide and have been translated into all major foreign languages. He is the author of numerous bestsellers on C++, including *C++: The Complete Reference*, *C++: A Beginner's Guide*, *C++ from the Ground Up*, and *STL Programming from the Ground Up*. His other bestsellers include *C#: The Complete Reference*, *Java: The Complete Reference*, *C: The Complete Reference*, and *Herb Schildt's Java Programming Cookbook*. Schildt holds both graduate and undergraduate degrees from the University of Illinois. He can be reached at his consulting office at (217) 586-4683. His website is **www.HerbSchildt.com**.

About the Technical Editor

Jim Keogh introduced PC programming nationally in his *Popular Electronics Magazine* column in 1982, four years after Apple Computer started in a garage.

He was a team member who built one of the first Windows applications by a Wall Street firm, featured by Bill Gates in 1986. Keogh has spent about two decades developing computer systems for Wall Street firms, such as Salomon, Inc. and Bear Stearns, Inc.

Keogh was on the faculty of Columbia University where he taught technology courses, including the Java Development lab. He developed and chaired the electronic commerce track at Columbia University. Keogh is presently on the faculty of New York University. He is the author of *J2EE: The Complete Reference*, *J2ME: The Complete Reference*, both published by McGraw-Hill, and more than 55 other titles, including five in the popular ...For Dummies series. His other books include *Linux Programming for Dummies*, *Unix Programming for Dummies*, *Java Database Programming for Dummies*, *Essential Guide to Networking*, *Essential Guide to Computer Hardware*, *The C++ Programmer's Notebook*, and *E-Mergers*.

Herb Schildt's C++ Programming Cookbook

Herb Schildt

New York Chicago San Francisco
Lisbon London Madrid Mexico City
Milan New Delhi San Juan
Seoul Singapore Sydney Toronto

The McGraw·Hill Companies

Library of Congress Cataloging-in-Publication Data

Schildt, Herbert.
  [C++ programming cookbook]
  Herb Schildt's C++ programming cookbook / Herb Schildt.
      p. cm.
  ISBN 978-0-07-148860-0 (alk. paper)
  1. C++ (Computer program language) I. Title. II. Title: C++
programming cookbook.
  QA76.73.C153S325 2008
  005.13'3—dc22

                                                              2008014989

McGraw-Hill books are available at special quantity discounts to use as premiums and sales promotions, or for use in corporate training programs. To contact a representative, please visit the Contact Us pages at www.mhprofessional.com.

Herb Schildt's C++ Programming Cookbook

1234567890 DOC DOC 0198

ISBN: 978-0-07-148860-0
MHID: 0-07-148860-X

Sponsoring Editor
  Wendy Rinaldi

Editorial Supervisor
  Patty Mon

Project Manager
  Vasundhara Sawhney,
  International Typesetting
  and Composition

Acquisitions Coordinator
  Mandy Canales

Technical Editor
  Jim Keogh

Copy Editor
  Lisa McCoy

Proofreader
  Andrea Fox

Indexer
  Sheryl Schildt

Production Supervisor
  Jean Bodeaux

Composition
  International Typesetting
  and Composition

Illustration
  International Typesetting
  and Composition

Art Director, Cover
  Jeff Weeks

Cover Designer
  12E Design

Contents

Preface

Over the years, friends and readers have asked me to write a programming cookbook, sharing some of the techniques and approaches that I use when I program. From the start, I liked the idea, but was unable to make time for it in my very busy writing schedule. As many readers know, I write extensively about several facets of programming, with a special focus on C++, Java, and C#. Because of the rapid revision cycles of those languages, I spend nearly all of my available time updating my books to cover the latest versions. Fortunately, early in 2007, a window of opportunity opened and I was finally able to devote time to the cookbook. The two most requested cookbooks were ones for Java and C++. I began with Java, with the result being my Java programming cookbook. As soon as I finished the Java book, I moved on to C++. The result is, of course, this book. I must admit that both projects were among my most enjoyable.

Based on the format of a traditional food cookbook, this book distills the essence of many general-purpose C++ techniques into a collection of step-by-step *recipes*. Each recipe describes a set of key ingredients, such as classes, functions, and headers. It then shows the steps needed to assemble those ingredients into a code sequence that achieves the desired result. This organization makes it easy to find the technique in which you are interested and then put that technique *into action*.

Actually, "into action" is an important part of this book. I believe that good programming books contain two elements: solid theory and practical application. In the recipes, the step-by-step instructions and discussions supply the theory. To put that theory into practice, each recipe includes a complete code example. The examples demonstrate in a concrete, unambiguous way how the recipes can be applied. In other words, the examples eliminate the "guess work" and save you time.

Although no cookbook can include every recipe that one might desire (there is a nearly unbounded number of possible recipes), I tried to span a wide range of topics. My criteria for including a recipe are discussed in detail in Chapter 1, but briefly, I included recipes that would be useful to many programmers and that answered frequently asked questions. Even with these criteria, it was difficult to decide what to include and what to leave out. This was the most challenging part of writing this book. Ultimately, it came down to experience, judgment, and intuition. Hopefully, I have included something to satisfy every programmer's taste!

HS

Example Code on the Web

The source code for all of the examples in this book is available free-of-charge on the Web at www.mhprofessional.com.

More from Herbert Schildt

Herb Schildt's C++ Programming Cookbook is just one of Herb's many programming books. Here are some others that you will find of interest.

To learn more about C++, you will find these books especially helpful:

C++: The Complete Reference
C++: A Beginner's Guide
C++ from the Ground Up
STL Programming from the Ground Up
The Art of C++

To learn about Java, we recommend:

Java: The Complete Reference
Java: A Beginner's Guide
The Art of Java
Swing: A Beginner's Guide
Herb Schildt's Java Programming Cookbook

To learn about C#, we suggest the following Schildt books:

C#: The Complete Reference
C#: A Beginner's Guide

If you want to learn about the C language, then the following title will be of interest:

C: The Complete Reference

When you need solid answers fast, turn to Herbert Schildt, the recognized authority on programming.

Overview

This book is a collection of techniques that show how to perform various programming tasks in C++. As the title implies, it uses the well-known "cookbook" format. Each "recipe" illustrates how to accomplish a specific operation. For example, there are recipes that read bytes from a file, reverse a string, sort the contents of a container, format numeric data, and so on. In the same way that a recipe in a food cookbook describes a set of ingredients and a sequence of instructions necessary to prepare a dish, each technique in this book describes a set of key program elements and the sequence of steps necessary to use them to accomplish a programming task.

Ultimately, the goal of this book is to save you time and effort during program development. Many programming tasks consist of a set of standard functions and classes, which must be applied in a specific sequence. The trouble is that sometimes you don't know which functions to use or what classes are appropriate. Instead of having to wade through reams of documentation and online tutorials to determine how to approach some task, you can look up its recipe. Each recipe shows one way to craft a solution, describing the necessary elements and the order in which they must be used. With this information, you can design a solution that fits your specific need.

What's Inside

No cookbook is exhaustive. The author of a cookbook must make choices about what is and isn't included. The same is true for this cookbook. In choosing the recipes for this book, I focused on four main topic areas: string handling, the Standard Template Library (STL), I/O, and formatting data. These are core topics that relate to a wide range of programmers. They are also very large topics, which required many pages to explore in depth. As a result, each of these topics became the basis for one or more chapters. It is important to state, however, that the content of those chapters is not limited to only those topics. As most readers know, just about everything in C++ is interrelated. In the process of creating recipes for one aspect of C++, several others, such as localization, dynamic allocation, or operator overloading, are often involved. Thus, recipes for the preceding topics often illustrate other C++ techniques.

In addition to the recipes related to the main topic areas, I had several others that I wanted to include but for which an entire chapter was not feasible. I grouped those recipes into the final chapter. Several of these recipes focus on overloading C++'s more specialized operators, such as [ ], –>, **new**, and **delete**. Others illustrate the use of the **auto_ptr** and **complex** classes or show how to create a conversion function, a copy constructor, or an explicit constructor. There is also a recipe that demonstrates runtime type ID.

Of course, choosing the topics was only the beginning of the selection process. Within each category, I had to decide what to include and what not to include. In general, I included a recipe if it met the following two criteria.

1. The technique is useful to a wide range of programmers.

2. It provides an answer to a frequently asked programming question.

The first criterion is largely self-explanatory. I included recipes that describe how to accomplish a set of tasks that would commonly be encountered when creating C++ applications. Some of the recipes illustrate a general concept that can be adapted to solve several different types of problems. For example, Chapter 2 shows a recipe that searches for a substring within a string. This general procedure is useful in several contexts, such as finding an e-mail address or a telephone number within a sentence, or extracting a keyword from a database query. Other recipes describe more specific, yet widely used techniques. For example, Chapter 6 shows how to format the time and date.

The second criterion is based on my experience as the author of programming books. Over the many years that I have been writing, I have been asked hundreds and hundreds of "how to" questions by readers. These questions come from all areas of C++ programming and range from the very easy to the quite difficult. I have found, however, that a central core of questions occurs again and again. Here is one example: "How do I format a number so that it has two decimal places?" Here is another: "How do I create a function object?" There are many others. These same types of questions also occur frequently on various programmer forums on the Web. I used these commonly asked "how to" questions to guide my selection of recipes.

The recipes in this book span various skill levels. Some illustrate basic techniques, such as reading bytes from a file or overloading the << operator to output objects of a class that you create. Others are more advanced, such as using the localization library to format monetary values, tokenizing a string, or overloading the [ ] operator. Thus, the level of difficulty of an individual recipe can range from relatively easy to significantly advanced. Of course, most things in programming are easy once you know how to do them, but difficult when you don't. Therefore, don't be surprised if some recipe seems obvious. It just means that you already know how to accomplish that task.

How the Recipes Are Organized

Each recipe in this book uses the same format, which has the following parts:

- A table of key ingredients used by the recipe.
- A description of the problem that the recipe solves.
- The steps necessary to complete the recipe.
- An in-depth discussion of the steps.
- A code example that puts the recipe into action.
- Options and alternatives that suggest other ways to craft a solution.

A recipe begins by describing the task to accomplish. The key ingredients used by the recipe are shown in a table. These include the functions, classes, and headers required to create a solution. Of course, putting a recipe into practice may imply the use of additional elements, but the key ingredients are those that are fundamental to the task at hand.

Each recipe then presents step-by-step instructions that summarize the procedure. These are followed by an in-depth discussion of the steps. In many cases, the summary will be sufficient, but the details are there if you need them.

Next, a code example is presented that shows the recipe in action. All code examples are presented in their entirety. This avoids ambiguity and lets you clearly see precisely what is happening without having to fill in additional details yourself. Occasionally, a bonus example is included that further illustrates how a recipe can be applied.

Each recipe concludes with a discussion of various options and alternatives. This section is especially important because it suggests different ways to implement a solution or other ways to think about the problem.

A Few Words of Caution

There are a few important points that you should keep in mind when you use this book. First, a recipe shows *one way* to craft a solution. Other ways may (and often do) exist. Your specific application may require an approach that is different from the one shown. The recipes in this book can serve as starting points, they can help you choose a general approach to a solution, and they can spur your imagination. However, in all cases, you must determine what is and what isn't appropriate for your application.

Second, it is important to understand that the code examples are *not* optimized for performance. They are optimized for *clarity and ease of understanding*. Their purpose is to clearly illustrate the steps of the recipe. In many cases, you will have little trouble writing tighter, more efficient code. Furthermore, the examples are exactly that: examples. They are simple uses that do not necessarily reflect the way that you will write code for your own application. In all circumstances, you must create your own solution that fits the needs of your application.

Third, each code example contains error handling that is appropriate for that specific example, but may not be appropriate in other situations. In all cases, you must properly handle the various errors and exceptions that can result when adapting a recipe for use in your own code. Let me state this important point again: When implementing a solution, you must provide error handling appropriate to your application. You cannot simply assume that the way that errors or exceptions are handled (or not handled) by an example is sufficient or adequate for your use. Typically, additional error handling will be required in real-world applications.

C++ Experience Required

This book is for every C++ programmer, whether beginner or experienced pro. However, it does assume that you know the fundamentals of C++ programming, including the C++ keywords and syntax, and have a general familiarity with the core library functions and classes. You should also be able to create, compile, and run C++ programs. None of these things are taught by this book. (This book is about applying C++ to a variety of real-world programming problems. It is not about teaching the fundamentals of the C++ language.) If you need to improve your C++ skills, I recommend my books *C++: The Complete Reference, C++ From the Ground Up,* and *C++: A Beginner's Guide.* All are published by McGraw-Hill, Inc.

What Version of C++?

The code and discussions in this book are based on the ANSI/ISO International Standard for C++. Unless explicitly stated otherwise, no non-standard extensions are used. As a result, the majority of techniques presented here are portable and can be used with any C++ compiler that adheres to the International Standard for C++. The code in this book was developed and tested with Microsoft's Visual C++. Both Visual Studio and Visual C++ Express (which is available free of charge from Microsoft) were used.

> **NOTE**   *At the time of this writing, the International Standard for C++ is in the process of being updated. Many new features are being contemplated. However, none of them are formally part of C++ at this time and are, therefore, not used in this book. Of course, future editions of this book may make use of these new features.*

Two Coding Conventions

Before moving on to the recipes, there are two issues to discuss that relate to how the code in this book is written. The first relates to returning a value from **main( )**. The second concerns the use of **namespace std**. The following explains the decisions that I made relating to these two features.

Returning a Value from main( )

The code examples in this book always explicitly return an integer value from **main( )**. By convention, a return value of zero indicates successful termination. A non-zero return value indicates some form of error.

Explicitly returning a value from **main( )** is not technically necessary, however, because in the words of the International Standard for C++:

> "If control reaches the end of main without encountering a return statement, the effect is that of executing return 0;"

For this reason, you will occasionally find code that does not explicitly return a value from **main( )**, relying instead upon the implicit return value of zero. But this *is not* the approach used by this book.

Instead, all of the **main( )** functions in this book explicitly return a value because of two reasons. First, some compilers issue a warning when a non-**void** method fails to explicitly return a value. To avoid this warning, **main( )** must include a **return** statement. Second, it just seems good practice to explicitly return a value, given that **main( )** is declared with an **int** return type!

Using Namespace std?

One of the problems that a writer of a C++ book faces is whether or not to use the line:

```
using namespace std;
```

near the top of each program. This statement brings the contents of the **std** namespace into view. The **std** namespace contains the C++ standard library. Thus, by using the **std** namespace, the standard library is brought into the global namespace, and names such as **cout** can be referred to directly, rather than as **std::cout**.

The use of

```
using namespace std;
```

is both very common and occasionally controversial. Some programmers dislike it, suggesting that it defeats the point of packaging the standard library into the **std** namespace and invites conflicts with third-party code, especially in large projects. While this is true, others point out that in short programs (such as the examples shown in this book) and in small projects, the convenience it offers easily offsets the remote chance of conflicts, which seldom (if ever) occur in these cases. Frankly, in programs for which the risk of conflicts is essentially zero, having to always write **std::cout**, **std::cin**, **std::ofstream**, **std::string**, and so on *is* tedious. It also makes the code more verbose.

The foregoing debate notwithstanding, this book uses

```
using namespace std;
```

in the example programs for two reasons. First, it makes the code shorter, which means that more code can fit on a line. In a book, line-length is limited. Not having to constantly use **std::** shortens lines, which means that more code can fit on a single line without causing the line to break. The fewer broken lines, the easier the code is to read. Second, it makes the code examples less verbose, which enhances their clarity on the printed page. It has been my experience that **using namespace std** is very helpful when presenting example programs shown in a book. However, its use in the examples is *not* meant as an endorsement of the technique in general. You must decide what is appropriate for your own programs.

CHAPTER 2

String Handling

There is almost always more than one way to do something in C++. This is one reason why C++ is such a rich and powerful language. It lets the programmer choose the best approach for the task at hand. Nowhere is this multifaceted aspect of C++ more evident than in strings. In C++, strings are based on two separate but interrelated subsystems. One type of string is inherited from C. The other is defined by C++. Together, they provide the programmer with two different ways to think about and handle sequences of characters.

The first type of string supported by C++ is the *null-terminated string*. This is a **char** array that contains the characters that comprise a string, followed by a null. The null-terminated string is inherited from C and it gives you low-level control over string operations. As a result, the null-terminated string offers a very efficient way in which to handle character sequences. C++ also supports wide-character, null-terminated strings, which are arrays of type **wchar_t**.

The second type of string is an object of type **basic_string**, which is a template class defined by C++. Therefore, **basic_string** defines a unique type whose sole purpose is to represent sequences of characters. Because **basic_string** defines a class type, it offers a high-level approach to working with strings. For example, it defines many member functions that perform various string manipulations, and several operators are overloaded for string operations. There are two specializations of **basic_string** that are defined by C++: **string** and **wstring**. The **string** class operates on characters of type **char**, and **wstring** operates on characters of type **wchar_t**. Thus, **wstring** encapsulates a wide-character string.

As just explained, both null-terminated strings and **basic_string** support strings of types **char** and **wchar_t**. The main difference between strings based on **char** and those based on **wchar_t** is the size of the character. Otherwise, the two types of strings are handled in essentially the same way. For the sake of convenience and because **char**-based strings are, by far, the most common, they are the type of strings used in the recipes in this chapter. However, the same basic techniques can be adapted to wide-character strings with little effort.

The topic of C++ strings is quite large. Frankly, it would be easy to fill an entire book with recipes about them. Thus, limiting the string recipes to a single chapter presented quite a challenge. In the end, I selected recipes that answer common questions, illustrate key aspects of each string type, or demonstrate general principles that can be adapted to a wide variety of uses.

Here are the recipes contained in this chapter:

- Perform Basic Operations on Null-Terminated Strings
- Search a Null-Terminated String
- Reverse a Null-Terminated String
- Ignore Case Differences When Comparing Null-Terminated Strings
- Create a Search-and-Replace Function for Null-Terminated Strings
- Categorize Characters Within a Null-Terminated String
- Tokenize a Null-Terminated String
- Perform Basic Operations on **string** Objects
- Search a **string** Object
- Create a Search-and-Replace Function for **string** Objects
- Operate on **string** Objects Through Iterators
- Create Case-Insensitive Search and Search-and-Replace Functions for **string** Objects
- Convert a **string** Object into a Null-Terminated String
- Implement Subtraction for **string** Objects

NOTE *In-depth coverage of null-terminated strings and the **string** class is found in my book* C++: The Complete Reference.

Overview of Null-Terminated Strings

The type of string most commonly used in a C++ program is the null-terminated string. As mentioned, a null-terminated string is an array of **char** that ends with a null character. Thus, a null-terminated string *is not* a unique type of its own. Rather, it is a *convention* that is recognized by all C++ programmers. The null-terminated string was defined by the C language and is still widely used by C++ programmers. It is also commonly referred to as a *char * string*, or sometimes as a *C string*. Although null-terminated strings are familiar territory to most C++ programmers, it is still useful to review their key attributes and capabilities.

There are two main reasons why null-terminated strings are widely used in C++. First, all string literals are represented as null-terminated strings. Therefore, whenever you create a string literal, you are creating a null-terminated string. For example, in the statement

```
const char *ptr = "Hello";
```

the literal "Hello" is a null-terminated string. This means that it is a **char** array that contains the characters **Hello** and is terminated by a null. In this statement, a pointer to the array is assigned to **ptr**. As a point of interest, notice that **ptr** is specified as **const**. Standard C++ specifies that string literals are arrays of type **const char**. Therefore, it is best to use a **const char *** pointer to point to one. However, the current standard also defines an automatic (but deprecated) conversion to **char ***, and it is quite common to see code in which the **const** is omitted.

The second reason why null-terminated strings are widely used is efficiency. Using an array terminated by a null to hold a string allows many string operations to be implemented in a streamlined fashion. (Essentially, null-terminated string operations are simply specialized array operations.) For example, here is one way to write the standard library function **strcpy( )**, which copies the contents of one string to another.

```
// One way to implement the standard strcpy() function.
char *strcpy(char *target, const char *source) {
  char *t = target;

  // Copy the contents of source into target.
  while(*source) *target++ = *source++;

  // Null-terminate the target.
  *target = '\0';

  // Return pointer to the start of target.
  return t;
}
```

Pay special attention to this line:

```
while(*source) *target++ = *source++;
```

Because the source string ends with a null character, a very efficient loop can be created that simply copies characters until the character pointed to by **source** is null. Recall that in C++, any non-zero value is true, but zero is false. Since the null character is zero, the **while** loop stops when the null terminator is encountered. Loops like the one just shown are common when working with null-terminated strings.

The standard C++ library defines several functions that operate on null-terminated strings. These require the header **<cstring>**. These functions will, no doubt, be familiar to many readers. Furthermore, the recipes in this chapter fully explain the string functions that they employ. However, it is still helpful to briefly list the commonly used null-terminated string functions.

Function	Description
char *strcat(char *str1, const char *str2)	Concatenates the string pointed to by str2 to the end of the string pointed to by str1. Returns str1. If the strings overlap, the behavior of **strcat( )** is undefined.
char *strchr(const char *str, int ch)	Returns a pointer to the first occurrence of the low-order byte of ch in the string pointed to by str. If no match is found, a null pointer is returned.
int strcmp(const char *str1, const char str2)	Lexicographically compares the string pointed to by str1 with the string pointed to by str2. Returns less than zero if str1 is less than str2, greater than zero if str1 is greater than str2, and zero if the two strings are the same.

Function	Description
char *strcpy(char *target, const char *source)	Copies the string pointed to by source to the string pointed to by target. Returns target. If the strings overlap, the behavior of **strcpy( )** is undefined.
size_t strcspn(const char *str1, const char *str2)	Returns the index of the first character in the string pointed to by str1 that matches any character in the string pointed to by str2. If no match is found, the length of str1 is returned.
size_t strlen(const char *str)	Returns the number of characters in the string pointed to by str. The null terminator is not counted.
char *strncat(char *str1, const char *str2, size_t count)	Concatenates not more than count characters from the string pointed to by str2 to the end of str1. Returns str1. If the strings overlap, the behavior of **strncat( )** is undefined.
int strncmp(const char *str1, const char *str2, size_t count)	Lexicographically compares not more than the first count characters in the string pointed to by str1 with the string pointed to by str2. Returns less than zero if str1 is less than str2, greater than zero if str1 is greater than str2, and zero if the two strings are the same.
char *strncpy(char *target, const char *source, size_t count)	Copies not more than count characters from the string pointed to by source to the string pointed to by target. If source contains less than count characters, null characters will be appended to the end of target until count characters have been copied. However, if source is longer than count characters, the resultant string will not be null-terminated. Returns target. If the strings overlap, the behavior of **strcnpy( )** is undefined.
char *strpbrk(const char *str1, const char *str2)	Returns a pointer to the first character in the string pointed to by str1 that matches any character in the string pointed to by str2. If no match is found, a null pointer is returned.
char *strrchr(const char *str, int ch)	Returns a pointer to the last occurrence of the low-order byte of ch in the string pointed to by str. If no match is found, a null pointer is returned.
size_t strspn(const char *str1, const char *str2)	Returns the index of the first character in the string pointed to by str1 that does not match any of the characters in the string pointed to by str2.
char *strstr(const char *str1, const char *str2)	Returns a pointer to the first occurrence of the string pointed to by str2 in the string pointed to by str1. If no match is found, a null pointer is returned.
char *strtok(char *str, const char *delims)	Returns a pointer to the next token in the string pointed to by str. The characters in the string pointed to by delims specify the delimiters that determine the boundaries of a token. A null pointer is returned when there is no token to return. To tokenize a string, the first call to **strtok( )** must have str point to the string to be tokenized. Subsequent calls must pass a null pointer to str.

Notice that several of the functions, such as **strlen( )** and **strspn( )**, use the type **size_t**. This is some form of unsigned integer and it is defined by **<cstring>**.

The **<cstring>** header also defines several functions that begin with the "mem" prefix. These functions operate on characters, but do not use the null-terminator convention. They are sometimes useful when manipulating strings and can also be used for other purposes. The functions are **memchr( )**, **memcmp( )**, **memcpy( )**, **memmove( )**, and **memset( )**. The first three operate similar to **strchr( )**, **strcmp( )**, and **strcpy( )**, respectively, except that they take an extra parameter that specifies the number of characters on which to operate. The **memset( )** function sets a block of memory to a specified value. The **memmove( )** function moves a block of characters. Unlike **memcpy( )**, **memmove( )** can be used to move characters in overlapping arrays. It is the only "mem" function used in this chapter and is shown here:

    void *memmove(void *target, const void *source, size_t count)

It copies *count* characters from the array pointed to by *source* into the array pointed to by *target*. It returns *target*. As mentioned, the copy takes place correctly, even if the arrays overlap. However, in this case, the array pointed to by *source* may be modified (even though *source* is specified as **const**).

NOTE *Microsoft's Visual C++ "deprecates" (no longer recommends the use of) several standard string functions, such as strcpy( ), for security reasons. For example, Microsoft recommends using strcpy_s( ) instead. However, these alternatives are not defined by Standard C++ and are non-standard. Therefore, this book will use the functions specified by the International Standard for C++.*

Overview of the string Class

Although null-terminated strings are very efficient, they do suffer from two problems. First, they do not define a type. That is, representing a string as an array of characters terminated by a null is a *convention*. Although this convention is well understood and widely recognized, it is not a data type in the normal sense. (In other words, the null-terminated string is not part of C++'s type system.) As a result, null-terminated strings cannot be manipulated by operators. For example, you *cannot* concatenate two null-terminated strings by using the + operator or use = to assign one null-terminated string to another. Therefore, the following sequence won't work:

```
// This sequence is in error.
char strA[] = "alpha";
char strB[] = "beta";
char strC[10] = strA + strB; // Oops! Won't work!
```

Instead, you must use calls to library functions to perform these operations, as shown next:

```
// This sequence works.
char strA[] = "alpha";
char strB[] = "beta";
char strC[10];

strcpy(strC, strA);
strcat(strC, strB);
```

This corrected sequence uses **strcpy( )** and **strcat( )** to assign **strC** a string that contains the concatenation of **strA** and **strB**. Although it does achieve the desired result, manipulating strings through the use of functions rather than operators makes even the most rudimentary operations a bit clumsy.

The second problem with null-terminated strings is the ease with which errors can be created. In the hands of an inexperienced or careless programmer, it is very easy to overrun the end of the array that holds a string. Because C++ provides no boundary-checking on array (or pointer) operations, there is nothing that prevents the end of an array from being exceeded. For example, the standard **strcpy( )** function has no way to know if the target array is being exceeded. Therefore, if the source string contains more characters than the target array can hold, the target array will be overrun. In the best case, an array overrun simply crashes the program. However, in the worst case, it results in a security breach based on the now notorious "buffer overrun" attack.

Because of the desire to integrate strings into the overall C++ type system and to prevent array overruns, a string data type was added to C++. The string type is based on the template class **basic_string**, which is declared in the **<string>** header. As mentioned, there are two specializations of this class: **string** and **wstring**, which are also declared in **<string>**. The **string** class is for **char**-based strings. The **wstring** class is for wide character strings based on **wchar_t**. Other than the type of characters, the two specializations work essentially the same. Since **char**-based strings are, by far, the most commonly used, the following discussion and all of the recipes use **string**, but most of the information can be readily adapted to **wstring**.

The **string** class creates a dynamic data type. This means that a **string** instance can grow as needed during runtime to accommodate an increase in the length of the string. Not only does this eliminate the buffer overrun problem, but it also frees you from having to worry about specifying the correct length for a string. The **string** class handles this for you automatically.

The **string** class defines several constructors and many functions. Here are three commonly used constructors:

```
string(const Allocator &alloc = Allocator( ) )
string(const char *str, const Allocator &alloc = Allocator( ) )
string(const string &str, size_type start_idx = 0, size_type num = npos,
        const Allocator &alloc = Allocator( ) )
```

The first form creates an empty **string** object. The second creates a **string** object from the null-terminated string pointed to by *str*. This form lets you create a **string** from a null-terminated string. The third form creates a **string** from another **string**. The string being created contains *num* characters from *str*, beginning at the index specified by *start_idx*. Frequently, in the third constructor, the parameters *start_idx* and *num* are allowed to default. In this case, *start_idx* contains zero (indicating the start of the string) and *num* contains the value of **npos**, which (in this case) indicates the length of the longest possible string. In all cases, notice that the constructors allow an allocator to be specified. This is an object of type **Allocator** and it provides memory allocation for the string. Most often, this argument is allowed to default, which results in the default allocator being used.

Here is the way the constructors look when the argument defaults are used, which is often the case:

```
string( )
string(const char *str)
string (const string &str)
```

These all use the default allocator. The first creates an empty string. The second and third create a string that contains *str*.

The **string** class defines many functions, with most having several overloaded forms. Thus, a full description of each **string** function is not practical. Instead, the individual recipes describe in detail the functions that they employ. However, to give you an idea of the power available within **string**, here is a list of its core functions, grouped into categories.

The following functions search the contents of a string:

find	Returns the index at which the first occurrence of a substring or character is found within the invoking string. Returns **npos** if no match is found.
rfind	Returns the index at which the last occurrence of a substring or character is found within the invoking string. Returns **npos** if no match is found.
find_first_of	Searches the invoking string for the first occurrence of any character contained within a second string and returns the index within the invoking string at which the match is found. Returns **npos** if no match is found.
find_last_of	Searches the invoking string for the last occurrence of any character contained within a second string and returns the index within the invoking string at which the match is found. Returns **npos** if no match is found.
find_first_not_of	Searches the invoking string for the first occurrence of any character *not* contained within a second string and returns the index within the invoking string at which the mismatch is found. Returns **npos** if no match is found.
find_last_not_of	Searches the invoking string for the last occurrence of any character *not* contained within a second string and returns the index within the invoking string at which the mismatch is found. Returns **npos** if no match is found.

The next set of string functions alters the contents of a string:

append	Appends a string to the end of the invoking string.
assign	Assigns a new string to the invoking string.
clear	Removes all characters from the invoking string.
copy	Copies a range of characters from the invoking string into an array.
erase	Removes one or more characters from the invoking string.
insert	Inserts a string, substring, or one or more characters into the invoking string.
push_back	Adds a character to the end of the invoking string.
replace	Replaces a portion of the invoking string.
resize	Shortens or lengthens the invoking string. When shortening, characters may be lost.
swap	Exchanges two strings.

The next functions return information about a **string** object:

capacity	Returns the number of characters that the invoking string can hold without more memory being allocated.
c_str	Returns a pointer to a null-terminated string that contains the same characters as those contained in the invoking string.
data	Returns a pointer to an array that contains the characters in the invoking string. This array is not null-terminated.
empty	Returns true if the invoking string is empty.
length	Returns the number of characters currently held in the invoking string.
max_size	Returns the maximum size of a string.
size	Same as length.

The next set of functions supports iterators:

begin	Returns an iterator to the start of the string.
end	Returns an iterator to the location that is one past the end of the string.
rbegin	Returns a reverse iterator to the end of the string.
rend	Returns a reverse iterator to the location that is one before the start of the string.

The next two functions obtain a substring or a character from a string:

at	Returns a reference to the character at a specified index within the invoking string.
substr	Returns a string that is a substring of the invoking string. The starting index and number of characters in the substring are specified.

In addition to the functions just shown, there are two more. You can compare two strings by calling **compare( )**. You can cause a string to allocate sufficient memory to hold a specific number of characters by calling **reserve( )**. Because a **string** is a dynamic data structure, pre-allocating memory in advance prevents the need for costly reallocations as the string grows in length. Of course, this is helpful only if you know in advance the size of the largest string.

The **string** class also defines several types, including **size_type**, which is some form of unsigned integer that is capable of holding a value equal to the length of the largest string supported by the implementation. The type of character held by a string is defined by **value_type**. The **string** class also declares several iterator types, including **iterator** and **reverse_iterator**.

The **string** class declares a **static const** variable, called **npos**, of type **size_type**. This value is then initialized to –1. This results in **npos** containing the largest unsigned value that **size_type** can represent. Thus, in all cases, **npos** represents a value that is at least one larger than the size of the longest string. The **npos** variable is typically used to indicate the "end of string" condition. For example, if a search fails, **npos** is returned. It is also used to request that some operation take place through the end of a string.

A number of operators have been overloaded to apply to string objects. They are shown here:

Operator	Meaning
=	Assignment
+	Concatenation
+=	Concatenation assignment
==	Equality
!=	Inequality
<	Less than
<=	Less than or equal to
>	Greater than
>=	Greater than or equal to
[ ]	Subscripting
<<	Output
>>	Input

These operators allow the use of **string** objects in expressions and eliminate the need for calls to functions like **strcpy( )**, **strcat( )**, or **strcmp( )**, which are required for null-terminated strings. For example, you can use a relational operator such as < to compare two **string** objects, assign one **string** object to another by use of the = operator, and concatenate two string objects with the + operator.

In general, you can mix **string** objects with null-terminated strings within an expression, as long as the desired outcome is a **string** object. For example, the + operator can be used to concatenate a **string** object with another **string** object or a **string** object with a C-style string. That is, the following variations are supported:

    string + string
    string + C-string
    C-string + string

Also, you can use the = to assign a null-terminated string to a **string** object or compare a **string** object with a null-terminated string by use of the relational operators.

There is another important aspect to the **string** class: It is also an STL-compatible container. The **string** class supports iterators and functions such as **begin( )**, **end( )**, and **size( )**, which must be implemented by all containers. Because **string** is a container, it is compatible with the other standard containers, such as **vector**. It can also be operated on by the STL algorithms. This gives you extraordinary power and flexibility when handling strings.

Taken as a whole, the **string** class makes string handling exceedingly convenient and trouble-free. You can perform most common string operations through operators, and **string**'s rich assortment of member functions make tasks such as searching, replacing, and comparing strings easy and relatively error-free. You don't need to worry about overrunning an array, for example, when you assign one string to another. In general, the **string** type offers safety and convenience that far exceeds that of null-terminated strings.

Despite the advantages of the **string** class, null-terminated strings are still widely used in C++. One reason (as explained earlier) is that string literals are null-terminated strings. Another reason is that all of the power of **string** comes at a price. In some cases, operations on **string** objects are slower than operations on null-terminated strings. Therefore, for applications in which high performance is a principal concern and the benefits of **string** are not needed, null-terminated strings are still a good choice. It is important to state, however, that for many other uses, the **string** class is the best choice.

String Exceptions

Although string handling via **string** avoids many of the mishaps that are common with null-terminated strings, it is still possible to generate errors. Fortunately, when an error occurs when manipulating a **string**, an exception results, rather than a program crash or a security breach. This gives you a chance to rectify the error, or at least perform an orderly shutdown.

There are two exceptions that can be generated when working with **string** objects. The first is **length_error**. This exception is thrown when an attempt is made to create a string that is longer than the longest possible string. This could happen in a number of different cases, such as when concatenating strings or inserting one substring into another. The length of the longest possible string is found by calling the **max_size( )** function. The second exception is **out_of_range**. It is thrown when an argument is out of range. Both of these exceptions are declared in **<stdexcept>**. Because none of the examples in this chapter generate these exceptions, the examples do not explicitly handle them. However, in your own applications, you might need to do so.

Perform Basic Operations on Null-Terminated Strings

Key Ingredients		
Headers	**Classes**	**Functions**
<cstring>		char *strcat(char *str1, const char *str2)
		int strcmp(const char *str1, const char *str2)
		char *strcpy(char *target, const char *source)
		size_t strlen(const char *str)

This recipe shows how to perform the following basic null-terminated string operations:

- Obtain the length of a string.
- Copy a string.

- Concatenate one string to the end of another.
- Compare two strings.

These are the operations that are commonly needed whenever null-terminated strings are used in a C++ program. They will be familiar to many readers—especially those who have a background in C programming. We begin with them because they illustrate fundamental concepts related to working with null-terminated strings. They also illustrate why you must be careful to avoid buffer overrun errors when using null-terminated strings.

Step-by-Step

To perform the basic null-terminated string operations involves these steps:

1. Include the header **<cstring>**.
2. To obtain the length of a string, call **strlen( )**.
3. To copy one string to another, call **strcpy( )**.
4. To concatenate one string to the end of another, call **strcat( )**.
5. To compare two strings, call **strcmp( )**.

Discussion

The functions that support null-terminated strings are declared in the header **<cstring>**. Thus, a program that uses these (or the other functions that operate on null-terminated strings) must include this header.

To obtain the length of a null-terminated string, call **strlen( )**, shown here:

size_t strlen(const char *str)

It returns the number of characters in the string pointed to by str. As explained in the overview, a null-terminated string is simply an array of characters that is terminated with a null. The value returned by **strlen( )** does not include the null terminator. Thus, the string **"test"** has a length of 4. Understand, however, that the array that will hold **"test"** must be at least five characters long so that there is room for the null terminator. The type **size_t** is some form of unsigned integer that is capable of representing the result of the **sizeof** operations. Thus, it is a type that is capable of representing the length of the longest string.

To copy one null-terminated string to another, use **strcpy( )**, shown next:

char *strcpy(char *target, const char *source)

This function copies the characters in the string pointed to by source into the array pointed to by target. The result is null-terminated. In all cases, you must ensure that the array pointed to by target is large enough to hold the characters pointed to by source. If you don't, the copy will overwrite the end of the target array. This will corrupt your program and is one way that the notorious "buffer overrun attack" can be generated. The function returns target.

To concatenate one null-terminated string to the end of another, call **strcat( )**:

char *strcat(char *str1, const char *str2)

This function copies the characters in the string pointed to by *str2* to the end of the string pointed to by *str1*. The resulting string is null-terminated. It is imperative that the array pointed to by *str1* be large enough to hold the resulting string. If it isn't, an array overrun will occur. This will also corrupt your program and is another way that a buffer overrun attack can occur. The function returns *str1*.

You can lexicographically compare (compare using dictionary order) two strings using **strcmp( )**, shown next:

  int strcmp(const char *str1, const char *str2)

It returns zero if the two strings are the same. Otherwise, it returns less than zero if the string pointed to by *str1* is less than the string pointed to by *str2* and greater than zero if the string pointed to by *str1* is greater than the string pointed to by *str2*. The comparison is case-sensitive.

Example

The following example shows **strcpy( )**, **strcat( )**, **strcmp( )**, and **strlen( )** in action:

```
// Demonstrate the basic null-terminated string functions.
#include <iostream>
#include <cstring>

using namespace std;

int main() {
  char strA[7] = "Up";
  char strB[5] = "Down";
  char strC[5] = "Left";
  char strD[6] = "Right";

  cout << "Here are the strings: " << endl;
  cout << "strA: " << strA << endl;
  cout << "strB: " << strB << endl;
  cout << "strC: " << strC << endl;
  cout << "strD: " << strD << "\n\n";

  // Display the length of strA.
  cout << "Length of strA is " << strlen(strA) << endl;

  // Concatenate strB with strA.
  strcat(strA, strB);
  cout << "strA after concatenation: " << strA << endl;
  cout << "Length of strA is now " << strlen(strA) << endl;

  // Copy strC into strB.
  strcpy(strB, strC);
  cout << "strB now holds: " << strB << endl;

  // Compare strings.
  if(!strcmp(strB, strC))
    cout << "strB is equal to strC\n";
```

```
    int result = strcmp(strC, strD);
    if(!result)
      cout << "strC is equal to strD\n";
    else if(result < 0)
      cout << "strC is less than strD\n";
    else if(result > 0)
      cout << "strC is greater than strD\n";

    return 0;
}
```

The output is shown here:

```
Here are the strings:
strA: Up
strB: Down
strC: Left
strD: Right

Length of strA is 2
strA after concatenation: UpDown
Length of strA is now 6
strB now holds: Left
strB is equal to strC
strC is less than strD
```

Notice how the array that holds **strA** was declared to be larger than needed to hold its initial string. This extra room allows it to accommodate the concatenation of **strB**. Also, notice how **strB** and **strC** are the same size. This makes it possible to copy the contents of **strC** into **strB**. Remember, in all cases, the array that receives the result of a string copy or concatenation must be large enough. For example, in the preceding program, attempting to copy **strD** into **strC** would cause an error, because **strC** is only five elements long, but **strD** requires six elements (five for the characters in Right and one for the null terminator).

Options and Alternatives

In cases in which you do not know at compile time whether the length of the target array is sufficient to hold the result of a string copy or concatenation, you will need to confirm that fact at runtime prior to attempting the operation. One way to do this is to use **sizeof** to determine the size of the target array. For example, assuming the preceding example program, here is one way to add a "safety check" that ensures that **strA** is large enough to hold the concatenation of both **strA** and **strB**:

```
if(sizeof(strA) > strlen(strA) + strlen(strB)) strcat(strA, strB);
```

Here, the size of the target array is obtained by calling **sizeof** on the array. This returns the length of the array in bytes, which for arrays of type **char** equals the number of characters in the array. This value must be greater than the sum of the two strings that will be concatenated. (Remember, one extra character is needed to hold the null terminator.) By using this approach, you ensure that the target array will not be overrun.

> **NOTE** *The preceding technique for preventing an array overrun works for* **char** *strings, not for* **wchar_t** *strings. For* **wchar_t** *strings, you will need to use an expression like*
> ```
> if(sizeof(strA) > wcslen(strA)*sizeof(wchar_t) +
>     wcslen(strB)*sizeof(wchar_t)) // ...
> ```
> *This takes into consideration the size of a wide character.*

Sometimes you may want to operate on only a portion of a string, rather than the entire string. For example, you might want to copy just part of one string to another or compare only a portion of two strings. C++ includes functions that handle these types of situations. They are **strncpy( )**, **strncat( )**, and **strncmp( )**. Each is described next.

To copy only a portion of one string to another, use **strncpy( )**, shown here:

char *strncpy(char *target, const char *source, size_t count)

This function copies not more than *count* characters from *source* to *target*. If *source* contains less than *count* characters, null characters will be appended to the end of *target* until *count* characters have been copied. However, if the string pointed to by *source* is longer than *count* characters, the resultant string pointed to by *target* will not be null-terminated. It returns *target*.

You can concatenate only a portion of a string to another by calling **strncat( )**, shown next:

char *strncat(char *str1, const char *str2, size_t count)

It concatenates not more than *count* characters from the string pointed to by *str2* to the end of *str1*. It returns *str1*.

To compare a portion of one string to another, use **strncmp( )**, shown next:

int strncmp(const char *str1, const char *str2, size_t count)

The **strncmp( )** function compares not more than the first *count* characters in the string pointed to by *str1* with the string pointed to by *str2*. It returns less than zero if *str1* is less than *str2*, greater than zero if *str1* is greater than *str2*, and zero if the two strings are the same.

Search a Null-Terminated String

Key Ingredients		
Headers	**Classes**	**Functions**
<cstring>		char *strchr(const char *str, int ch)
		char *strpbrk(const char *str1, const char *str2)
		char *strstr(const char *str1, const char *str2)

Another common part of string handling involves searching. Here are three examples. You might want to know whether a string contains the substring ".com" or ".net" when processing an Internet address. You might want to find the first period in a file name so that you can separate the file's name from its extension. You might want to scan a billing log for occurrences of the string "Past Due" so that you can count the number of past due accounts. To handle these types of tasks, C++ provides functions that search a null-terminated string. This recipe demonstrates several of them. Specifically, it shows how to search a string for a specific character, for any of a set of characters, or for a substring.

Step-by-Step

To search a string involves the following steps:

1. To search for a specific character, call **strchr( )**.
2. To search for any of a set of characters, call **strpbrk( )**.
3. To search for a substring, call **strstr( )**.

Discussion

To find the first occurrence of a given character within a string, call **strchr( )**, shown here:

char *strchr(const char *str, int ch)

It returns a pointer to the first occurrence of the low-order byte of ch in the string pointed to by str. If no match is found, a null pointer is returned.

To find the first occurrence of any character within a set of characters, call **strpbrk( )**, shown next:

char *strpbrk(const char *str1, const char *str2)

This function returns a pointer to the first character in the string pointed to by str1 that matches *any character* in the string pointed to by str2. If no match is found, a null pointer is returned.

To find the first occurrence of a given substring within a string, call **strstr( )**, shown here:

char *strstr(const char *str1, const char *str2)

It returns a pointer to the first occurrence of the string pointed to by str2 within the string pointed to by str1. If no match is found, a null pointer is returned.

Example

The following example demonstrates **strchr( )**, **strpbrk( )**, and **strstr( )**:

```
// Search a null-terminated string.
#include <iostream>
#include <cstring>

using namespace std;

int main() {

  const char *url = "HerbSchildt.com";
  const char *url2 = "Apache.org";
```

```
const char *emailaddr = "Herb@HerbSchildt.com";

const char *tld[] = { ".com", ".net", ".org" };

const char *p;

// First, determine if url and url2 contain .com, .net, or .org.
for(int i=0; i < 3; i++) {
  p = strstr(url, tld[i]);
  if(p) cout << url << " has top-level domain " << tld[i] << endl;

  p = strstr(url2, tld[i]);
  if(p) cout << url2 << " has top-level domain " << tld[i] << endl;
}

// Search for a specific character.
p = strchr(emailaddr, '@');
if(p) cout << "Site name of e-mail address is: " << p+1 << endl;

// Search for any of a set of characters. In this case,
// find the first @ or period.
p = strpbrk(emailaddr, "@.");

if(p) cout << "Found " << *p << endl;

return 0;
}
```

The output is shown here:

```
HerbSchildt.com has top-level domain .com
Apache.org has top-level domain .org
Site name of e-mail address is: HerbSchildt.com
Found @
```

Options and Alternatives

In addition to the search functions used by this recipe, there are several others supported by C++. Two that are especially helpful in some cases are **strspn( )** and **strcspn( )**. They are shown here:

> size_t strspn(const char *str1, const char *str2)
> size_t strcspn(const char *str1, const char *str2)

The **strspn( )** function returns the index of the first character in the string pointed to by *str1* that *does not* match any of the characters in the string pointed to by *str2*. The **strcspn( )** function returns the index of the first character in the string pointed to by *str1* that matches any character in the string pointed to by *str2*.

You can find the last occurrence of a character within a null-terminated string by calling **strrchr( )**:

> char *strrchr(const char *str, int ch)

It returns a pointer to the last occurrence of the low-order byte of *ch* in the string pointed to by *str*. If no match is found, a null pointer is returned.

The **strtok( )** function is also used to search a string. It is described in its own recipe. See *Tokenize a Null-Terminated String*.

Reverse a Null-Terminated String

Key Ingredients		
Headers	**Classes**	**Functions**
<cstring>		size_t strlen(char *str)

This recipe shows how to perform one simple, yet useful task. It reverses a null-terminated string. Although reversing a string is an easy operation for the experienced programmer, it is a common source of questions from beginners. For this reason alone it merits inclusion in this book. However, there are several other reasons to include this recipe. First, there are many ways to reverse a string, and each variation illustrates a different technique for handling a null-terminated string. Second, the basic mechanism used to reverse a string can be adapted to other types of string manipulations. Finally, it demonstrates in very practical terms how handling null-terminated strings often relies on fairly low-level, hands-on code. Often, such code can be highly efficient, but it requires more work than using the **string** class.

The recipe shown here reverses the string in place. This means that the original string is modified. This is often what is needed. However, a variation that creates a reverse copy of the string is shown in the *Options and Alternatives* section for this recipe.

Step-by-Step

There are many ways to approach the task of reversing a string. This recipe uses a simple, yet effective method that is based on swapping end-to-end corresponding characters in the string. It puts this code inside a function called **revstr( )**.

1. Create a function called **revstr( )** that has this prototype:

   ```
   void revstr(char *str);
   ```

   The string to be reversed is passed to **str**.

2. Inside **revstr( )**, create a **for** loop that controls two variables that will be used to index the array that holds the string. Initialize the first variable to zero and increment it each time through the loop. Initialize the second variable to the index of the last character in the string and decrement it with each iteration. This value is obtained by calling **strlen( )**.

3. With each pass through the loop, swap the characters at the two indexes.

4. Stop the loop when the first index is equal to or greater than the second index. At this point, the string has been reversed.

Discussion

As most readers know, when an array name is used by itself, without an index, it represents a pointer to the array. Therefore, when you pass an array to a function, you are actually passing only a pointer to that array. This means that a function that will receive a null-terminated string as an argument must declare its parameter to be of type **char ***. This is why the **str** parameter to **revstr( )** is declared as **char *str**.

Although **str** is a pointer, it can be indexed like an array, using the normal array-indexing syntax. To reverse the contents of the string, create a **for** loop that controls two variables, which serve as indexes into the string. One index starts at zero and indexes from the beginning of the string. The other index starts at the last character in the string. Each time through the loop, the characters at the specified indexes are exchanged. Then, the first index is incremented and the second index is decremented. When the indexes converge (that is, when the first index is equal to or greater than the second index), the string is reversed. Here is one way to write this loop:

```
int i, j;
char t;

for(i = 0, j = strlen(str)-1; i < j; ++i, --j) {
  // Exchange corresponding characters, front to back.
  t = str[i];
  str[i] = str[j];
  str[j] = t;
}
```

Notice that the index of the last character in the string is obtained by subtracting one from the value returned by **strlen( )**. Its prototype is shown here:

size_t strlen(const char *str)

The **strlen( )** function returns the length of a null-terminated string, which is the number of characters in the string. However, the null terminator is not counted. Since array indexing in C++ begins at zero, 1 must be subtracted from this value to obtain the index of the last character in the string.

Example

Putting together the pieces, here is one way to write the **revstr( )** function:

```
// Reverse a string in place.
void revstr(char *str) {
  int i, j;
  char t;

  for(i = 0, j = strlen(str)-1; i < j; ++i, --j) {
    // Exchange corresponding characters, front to back.
    t = str[i];
    str[i] = str[j];
    str[j] = t;
  }
}
```

The following program shows **revstr( )** in action:

```
// Reverse a string in place.
#include <iostream>
#include <cstring>


using namespace std;

void revstr(char *str);

int main() {
  char str[] = "abcdefghijklmnopqrstuvwxyz";

  cout << "Original string: " << str << endl;

  revstr(str);

  cout << "Reversed string: " << str << endl;

  return 0;
}

// Reverse a string in place.
void revstr(char *str) {
  int i, j;
  char t;

  for(i = 0, j = strlen(str)-1; i < j; ++i, --j) {
    t = str[i];
    str[i] = str[j];
    str[j] = t;
  }
}
```

The output is shown here:

```
Original string: abcdefghijklmnopqrstuvwxyz
Reversed string: zyxwvutsrqponmlkjihgfedcba
```

Options and Alternatives

Although reversing a null-terminated string is a simple task, it does allow a number of interesting variations. For example, the approach used in the recipe relies on array indexing, which is probably the clearest way to implement this function. It may not be, however, the most efficient. One alternative is to use pointers rather than array indexing. Depending upon what compiler you are using (and what optimizations are turned on), pointer operations can be faster than array indexing. Also, many programmers simply prefer the use of pointers rather than array indexing when cycling through an array in a strictly sequential fashion. Whatever the reason, the pointer version is easy to implement. Here is one way to rework **revstr( )** so that it substitutes pointer operations for array indexing:

```
// Reverse a string in place. Use pointers rather than array indexing.
void revstr(char *str) {
  char t;

  char *inc_p = str;
  char *dec_p = &str[strlen(str)-1];

  while(inc_p <= dec_p) {
    t = *inc_p;
    *inc_p++ = *dec_p;
    *dec_p-- = t;
  }
}
```

One of the more interesting approaches to reversing a string makes use of recursion. Here is one implementation:

```
// Reverse a string in place by using recursion.
void revstr_r(char *str) {
  revstr_recursive(str, 0, strlen(str)-1);
}

// This function is called with a pointer to the string to reverse
// and the beginning and ending indexes of the characters to reverse.
// Thus, its first call passes zero for start and strlen(str)-1 for
// end. The position of the null terminator does not change.
void revstr_recursive(char *str, int start, int end) {
  if(start < end)
    revstr_recursive(str, start+1, end-1);
  else
    return;

  char t = str[start];
  str[start] = str[end];
  str[end] = t;
}
```

Notice that **revstr_r( )** calls **revstr_recursive( )** to actually reverse the string. This lets **revstr_r( )** be called with just a pointer to the string. Notice how the recursive calls reverse the string. When **start** is less than **end**, a recursive call to **revstr_recursive( )** is made, with the beginning index incremented by one and the ending index decremented by one. When these two indexes meet, the **return** statement is executed. This causes the recursive calls to begin returning, with corresponding characters being exchanged. As a point of interest, the same general technique can be used to reverse the contents of any type of array. Its use on a null-terminated string is simply a special case.

The last alternative presented here works differently from the previous approaches because it creates a copy of the original string that contains the reverse of the original string. Thus, it leaves the original string unchanged. This technique is useful when the original string must not be modified.

```
// Make a reverse copy of a string.
void revstrcpy(char *rstr, const char *orgstr) {

  rstr += strlen(orgstr);
  *rstr-- = '\0';

  while(*orgstr)  *rstr-- = *orgstr++;
}
```

This function is passed a pointer to the original string in **orgstr** and a pointer to a **char** array that will receive the reversed string in **rstr**. Of course, the array pointed to by **rstr** must be large enough to hold the reversed string plus the null terminator. Here is an example of how **revstrcpy( )** can be called:

```
char str[5] = "abcd";
char rev[5];

revstrcpy(rev, str);
```

After the call, **rev** will contain the characters dcba and **str** will be unaltered.

Ignore Case Differences When Comparing Null-Terminated Strings

Key Ingredients		
Headers	**Classes**	**Functions**
<cctype>		int tolower(int *ch*)

The standard **strcmp( )** function is case-sensitive. Therefore, the two strings "test" and "Test" compare as different. Although a case-sensitive comparison is often what is needed, there are times when a case-insensitive approach is required. For example, if you are alphabetizing a list of entries for the index of a book, some of those entries might be proper nouns, such as the name of a person. Despite the case differences, you want the alphabetical order to be preserved. For example, you want "Stroustrup" to come after "class". The trouble is that the lowercase letters are represented by values that are 32 greater than the uppercase letters. Therefore, performing a case-sensitive comparison on "Stroustrup" and "class" yields a result that puts "class" after "Stroustrup". To solve this problem, you must use a comparison function that ignores case differences. This recipe shows one way to do this.

Step-by-Step

One way to ignore case differences when comparing null-terminated strings is to create your own version of the **strcmp( )** function. This is quite easy to do, as this recipe shows. The key is to convert each set of characters to the same case and then compare the two. This recipe converts each character to lowercase using the standard function **tolower( )**, but the conversion to uppercase would work just as well.

1. Create a function called **strcmp_ign_case( )** that has this prototype:

   ```
   int strcmp_ign_case(const char *str1, const char *str2);
   ```

2. Inside **strcmp_ign_case( )**, compare each corresponding character in the two strings. To do this, set up a loop that iterates as long as the null terminator of one of the strings has not been reached.

3. Inside the loop, first convert each character to lowercase by calling **tolower( )**. Then compare the two characters. Continue comparing characters until the end of one of the strings is reached or the two characters differ. Notice that **tolower( )** requires the header **<cctype>**.

4. When the loop stops, return the result of subtracting the last character compared from the second string from the last character compared from the first string. This causes the function to return less than zero if *str1* is less than *str2*, zero if the two are equal (in this case, the terminating null of *str2* is subtracted from the terminating null of *str1*), or greater than zero if *str1* is greater than *str2*.

Discussion

The standard function **tolower( )** was originally defined by C and is supported by C++ in a couple of different ways. The version used here is declared within the header **<cctype>**. It converts uppercase to lowercase based on the character set defined by the current locale. It is shown here:

   int tolower(int *ch*)

It returns the lowercase equivalent of *ch*, which must be an 8-bit value. Non-alphabetical characters are returned unchanged.

To compare two null-terminated strings independently of case differences, you must compare corresponding characters in the strings after normalizing them to a common case. In this recipe, the characters are converted to lowercase. Here is an example of a loop that compares characters in two strings but ignores case differences:

```
while(*str1 && *str2) {
  if(tolower(*str1) != tolower(*str2))
    break;

  ++str1;
  ++str2;
}
```

Notice that the loop will stop when the end of either string is reached or when a mismatch is encountered.

When the loop ends, you must return a value that indicates the outcome of the comparison. This is easy to do. Simply return the result of subtracting the last character pointed to by **str2** from the last character pointed to by **str1**, as shown here:

```
return tolower(*str1) - tolower(*str2);
```

This returns zero if the null terminator of both strings has been encountered, indicating equality. Otherwise, if the character pointed to by **str1** is less than the one pointed to by **str2**, a negative value is returned, indicating that the first string is less than the second. If the character pointed to by **str1** is greater than the character pointed to by **str2**, a positive value is returned, indicating that the first string is greater than the second. Thus, it produces the same outcome as **strcmp( )**, but in a case-insensitive manner.

Example

Putting it all together, here is one way to implement a case-insensitive string comparison function called **strcmp_ign_case( )**:

```
// A simple string comparison function that ignores case differences.
int strcmp_ign_case(const char *str1, const char *str2) {

  while(*str1 && *str2) {
    if(tolower(*str1) != tolower(*str2))
      break;

    ++str1;
    ++str2;
  }

  return tolower(*str1) - tolower(*str2);
}
```

The following program puts the **string_ign_case( )** function into action:

```
// Ignore case differences when comparing strings.
#include <iostream>
#include <cctype>

using namespace std;

int strcmp_ign_case(const char *str1, const char *str2);
void showresult(const char *str1, const char *str2, int result);

int main() {
  char strA[]= "tesT";
  char strB[] = "Test";
  char strC[] = "testing";
  char strD[] = "Tea";

  int result;

  cout << "Here are the strings: " << endl;
  cout << "strA: " << strA << endl;
  cout << "strB: " << strB << endl;
  cout << "strC: " << strC << endl;
  cout << "strD: " << strD << "\n\n";
```

```
  // Compare strings ignoring case.
  result = strcmp_ign_case(strA, strB);
  showresult(strA, strB, result);

  result = strcmp_ign_case(strA, strC);
  showresult(strA, strC, result);

  result = strcmp_ign_case(strA, strD);
  showresult(strA, strD, result);

  result = strcmp_ign_case(strD, strA);
  showresult(strD, strA, result);

  return 0;
}

// A simple string comparison function that ignores case differences.
int strcmp_ign_case(const char *str1, const char *str2) {

  while(*str1 && *str2) {
    if(tolower(*str1) != tolower(*str2))
      break;

    ++str1;
    ++str2;
  }

  return tolower(*str1) - tolower(*str2);
}

void showresult(const char *str1, const char *str2, int result) {
  cout << str1 << " is ";

  if(!result)
    cout << "equal to ";
  else if(result < 0)
    cout << "less than ";
  else
    cout << "greater than ";

  cout << str2 << endl;
}
```

The output is shown here:

```
Here are the strings:
strA: tesT
strB: Test
strC: testing
strD: Tea

tesT is equal to Test
tesT is less than testing
tesT is greater than Tea
Tea is less than tesT
```

Options and Alternatives

As explained, the version of **tolower( )** declared in **<cctype>** converts characters based on the current locale. Frankly, this is often what you want, so it makes a good (and convenient) choice in most cases. However, **tolower( )** is also declared within **<locale>**, which declares the members of C++'s localization library. (Localization aids in the creation of code that can be easily internationalized.) Here is this version of **tolower( )**:

> template <class charT> charT tolower(charT *ch*, const locale &*loc*)

This version of **tolower( )** makes it possible to specify a different locale when converting the case of a letter. For example:

```
char ch;
//...
locale loc("French");
cout << tolower(ch, loc);
```

This call to **tolower( )** uses the locale information compatible with French.

Although there is no advantage to doing so, it is also possible to convert each character in the string to uppercase (rather than lowercase) to eliminate case differences. This is done via the **toupper( )** function, shown here:

> int toupper(int *ch*)

It works just like **tolower( )**, except that it converts characters to uppercase.

Create a Search-and-Replace Function for Null-Terminated Strings

Key Ingredients		
Headers	**Classes**	**Functions**
<ccstring>		char *strncpy(char *target*, const char *source*, int *count*)
		void *memmove(void *target*, const void *source*, size_t *count*)

When working with strings, it is not uncommon to need to substitute one substring for another. This operation involves two steps. First, you must find the substring to replace, and second, you must replace it with the new substring. This process is commonly referred to as "search and replace." This recipe shows one way to accomplish this for null-terminated strings.

There are various ways to implement a "search-and-replace" function. This recipe uses an approach in which the replacement takes place on the original string, thus modifying it. Two other approaches are described in the *Options and Alternatives* section for this recipe.

Step-by-Step

One way to implement a "search-and-replace" function for a null-terminated string involves the following steps. It creates a function called **search_and_replace( )** that replaces the first occurrence of one substring with another.

1. Create a function called **search_and_replace( )** that has this prototype:

```
bool search_and_replace(char *orgstr, int maxlen,
                        const char *oldsubstr, const char *newsubstr);
```

   A pointer to the original string is passed via **orgstr**. The maximum number of characters that **orgstr** can hold is passed in **maxlen**. A pointer to the substring to search for is passed through **oldsubstr**, and a pointer to the replacement is passed in **newsubstr**. The function will return true if a substitution has been made. That is, it returns true if the string originally contained at least one occurrence of **oldsubstr**. It returns false if no substitution takes place.

2. Search for a substring by calling **strstr( )**. It returns a pointer to the beginning of the first matching substring or a null pointer if no match is found.

3. If the substring is found, shift the remaining characters in the string as needed to create a "hole" in the string that is exactly the size of the replacement substring. This can be most easily done by calling **memmove( )**.

4. Using **strncpy( )**, copy the replacement substring into the "hole" in the original string.

5. Return true if a substitution was made and false if the original string is unchanged.

Discussion

To find a substring within a string, use the **strstr( )** function, shown here:

char *strstr(const char *str1, const char *str2)

It returns a pointer to the start of the first occurrence of the string pointed to by *str2* in the string pointed to by *str1*. If no match is found, a null pointer is returned.

Conceptually, when one substring is replaced by another, the old substring must be removed and its replacement inserted. In practice, there is no need to actually remove the old substring. Instead, you can simply overwrite the old substring with the new one. However, you must prevent the remaining characters in the string from being overwritten when the new substring is longer than the old substring. You must also ensure that there is no gap when the new substring is shorter than the old substring. Therefore, unless the new substring is the same size as the old one, you will need to move the remaining characters in the original string up or down so that you create a "hole" in the original string that is the same size as the new substring. An easy way to accomplish this is to use **memmove( )**, shown here:

void *memmove(void *target, const void *source, size_t count)

It copies *count* characters from the array pointed to by *source* into the array pointed to by *target*. It returns *target*. The copy takes place correctly even if the arrays overlap. This means that it can be used to move characters up or down in the same array.

After you have created the properly sized "hole" in the string, you can copy the new substring into the hole by calling **strncpy( )**, shown here:

char *strncpy(char *_target_, const char *_source_, size_t _count_)

This function copies not more than _count_ characters from _source_ to _target_. If the string pointed to by _source_ contains less than _count_ characters, null characters will be appended to the end of _target_ until _count_ characters have been copied. However, if the string pointed to by _source_ is longer than _count_ characters, the resultant string will not be null-terminated. It returns _target_. If the two strings overlap, the behavior of **strncpy( )** is undefined.

Have **search_and_replace( )** return true when a substitution takes place and false if the substring is not found or if the modified string exceeds the maximum permissible length of the resulting string.

Example

Here is one way to implement the **search_and_replace( )** function. It replaces the first occurrence of **oldsubstr** with **newsubstr**.

```
// Replace the first occurrence of oldsubstr with newsubstr
// in the string pointed to by str. This means that the string
// pointed to by str is modified by this function.
//
// The maximum size of the resulting string is passed in maxlen.
// This value must be less than the size of the array that holds
// str in order to prevent an array overrun.
//
// It returns true if a replacement was made and false otherwise.
bool search_and_replace(char *str, int maxlen,
                        const char *oldsubstr, const char *newsubstr) {

  // Don't allow the null terminator to be substituted.
  if(!*oldsubstr) return false;

  // Next, check that the resulting string has a length
  // less than or equal to the maximum number of characters allowed
  // as specified by maxlen. If the maximum is exceeded, the
  // function ends by returning false.
  int len = strlen(str) - strlen(oldsubstr) + strlen(newsubstr);
  if(len > maxlen) return false;

  // See if the specified substring is in the string.
  char *p = strstr(str, oldsubstr);

  // If the substring is found, replace it with the new one.
  if(p) {

    // First, use memmove() to move the remainder of the
    // string so that the new substring can replace the old one.
    // In other words, this step either increases or decreases
    // the size of the "hole" that the new substring will fill.
    memmove(p+strlen(newsubstr), p+strlen(oldsubstr),
            strlen(p)-strlen(oldsubstr)+1);
```

```
      // Now, copy substring into str.
      strncpy(p, newsubstr, strlen(newsubstr));

      return true;
  }

  // Return false if no replacement was made.
  return false;
}
```

Notice that the function will not put more than **maxlen** characters into **str**. The **maxlen** parameter is used to prevent array overruns. You must pass it a value that is, at most, one less than the size of the array pointed to by **str**. It must be one less than the size of the array because you must allow room for the null terminator.

The following program shows the **search_and_replace( )** function in action:

```
// Implement "search and replace" for null-terminated strings.
#include <iostream>
#include <cstring>

using namespace std;

bool search_and_replace(char *orgstr, int maxlen,
                        const char *oldsubstr, const char *newsubstr);

int main() {

  char str[80] = "alpha beta gamma alpha beta gamma";

  cout << "Original string: " << str << "\n\n";

  cout << "First, replace all instances of alpha with epsilon.\n";

  // Replace all occurrences of alpha with epsilon.
  while(search_and_replace(str, 79, "alpha", "epsilon"))
    cout << "After a replacement: " << str << endl;

  cout << "\nNext, replace all instances of gamma with zeta.\n";

  // Replace all occurrences of gamma with zeta.
  while(search_and_replace(str, 79, "gamma", "zeta"))
    cout << "After a replacement: " << str << endl;

  cout << "\nFinally, remove all occurrences of beta.\n";

  // Replace all occurrences of beta with a null string.
  // This has the effect of removing beta from the string.
  while(search_and_replace(str, 79, "beta", ""))
    cout << "After a replacement: " << str << endl;

  return 0;
}
```

```
// Replace the first occurrence of oldsubstr with newsubstr
// in the string pointed to by str. This means that the string
// pointed to by str is modified by this function.
//
// The maximum size of the resulting string is passed in maxlen.
// This value must be less than the size of the array that holds
// str in order to prevent an array overrun.
//
// It returns true if a replacement was made and false otherwise.
bool search_and_replace(char *str, int maxlen,
                        const char *oldsubstr, const char *newsubstr) {

  // Don't allow the null terminator to be substituted.
  if(!*oldsubstr) return false;

  // Next, check that the resulting string has a length
  // less than or equal to the maximum number of characters allowed
  // as specified by maxlen. If the maximum is exceeded, the
  // function ends by returning false.
  int len = strlen(str) - strlen(oldsubstr) + strlen(newsubstr);
  if(len > maxlen) return false;

  // See if the specified substring is in the string.
  char *p = strstr(str, oldsubstr);

  // If the substring is found, replace it with the new one.
  if(p) {

    // First, use memmove() to move the remainder of the
    // string so that the new substring can replace the old one.
    // In other words, this step either increases or decreases
    // the size of the "hole" that the new substring will fill.
    memmove(p+strlen(newsubstr), p+strlen(oldsubstr),
            strlen(p)-strlen(oldsubstr)+1);

    // Now, copy substring into str.
    strncpy(p, newsubstr, strlen(newsubstr));

    return true;
  }

  // Return false if no replacement was made.
  return false;
}
```

The output is shown here:

```
Original string: alpha beta gamma alpha beta gamma

First, replace all instances of alpha with epsilon.
After a replacement: epsilon beta gamma alpha beta gamma
After a replacement: epsilon beta gamma epsilon beta gamma
```

```
Next, replace all instances of gamma with zeta.
After a replacement: epsilon beta zeta epsilon beta gamma
After a replacement: epsilon beta zeta epsilon beta zeta

Finally, remove all occurrences of beta.
After a replacement: epsilon  zeta epsilon beta zeta
After a replacement: epsilon  zeta epsilon  zeta
```

Options and Alternatives

As it is written, the **search_and_replace( )** function substitutes a substring within the original string. This means that the original string is modified. However, it is possible to take a different approach in which the original string is left unchanged and the substituted string is returned in another array. One way to do this is to pass a pointer to a string into which the result is copied. This technique leaves the original string unchanged. This alternative is shown here:

```cpp
// This replaces the first occurrence of oldsubstr with newsubstr.
// The resulting string is copied into the string passed in
// resultstr. This means that the original string is unchanged.
// The result string must be large enough to hold the
// string that results after replacing oldsubstr with newsubstr.
// The maximum number of characters to copy into resultstr
// is passed in maxlen. It returns true if a replacement was made
// and false otherwise.
bool search_and_replace_copy(const char *orgstr, char *resultstr, int maxlen,
                    const char *oldsubstr, const char *newsubstr) {

  // Don't allow the null terminator to be substituted.
  if(!*oldsubstr) return false;

  // Next, check that the resulting string has a length
  // less than the maximum number of characters allowed
  // as specified by maxlen. If the maximum is exceeded,
  // the function ends by returning false.
  int len = strlen(orgstr) - strlen(oldsubstr) + strlen(newsubstr);
  if(len > maxlen) return false;

  // See if the specified substring is in the string.
  const char *p = strstr(orgstr, oldsubstr);

  // If the substring is found, replace it with the new one.
  if(p) {

    // Copy first part of original string.
    strncpy(resultstr, orgstr, p-orgstr);

    // Null-terminate the first part of resultstr so that it
    // can be operated on by the other string functions.
    *(resultstr + (p-orgstr)) = '\0';
```

```
    // Substitute the new substring.
    strcat(resultstr, newsubstr);

    // Add the remainder of the original string,
    // skipping over the old substring that was replaced.
    strcat(resultstr, p+strlen(oldsubstr));

    return true;
  }

  // Return false if no replacement was made.
  return false;
}
```

The comments give a "play-by-play" description of how **search_and_replace_copy( )** works. Here is a synopsis. The function begins by finding the first occurrence in **orgstr** of the substring passed in **oldsubstring**. It then copies the original string (**orgstr**) into the result string (**resultstr**) up to the point at which the substring was found. Next, it copies the replacement substring into **resultstr**. Finally, it copies the remainder of **orgstr** into **resultstr**. Thus, on return, **resultstr** contains a copy of **orgstr**, with the only difference being the substitution of **newsubstr** for **oldsubstr**. To prevent array overruns, **search_and_replace_copy( )** will copy only up to **maxlen** characters into **resultstr**. Therefore, the array pointed to by **resultstr** must be at least **maxlen**+1 characters long. The extra character leaves room for the null terminator.

Another alternative that is useful in some cases is to have the **search_and_replace( )** function dynamically allocate a new string that holds the resulting string and return a pointer to it. This approach offers one big advantage: You don't need to worry about array boundaries being overrun because you can allocate a properly sized array. This means that you don't need to know the size of the resulting string in advance. The main disadvantage is that you must remember to delete the dynamically allocated string when it is no longer needed. Here is one way to implement such an approach:

```
// Replace the first occurrence of oldsubstr with newsubstr
// in str. Return a pointer to a new string that contains
// the result. The string pointed to by str is unchanged.
// Memory for the new string is dynamically allocated and must be
// released when it is no longer needed. If no substitution is made,
// a null pointer is returned. This function throws bad_alloc if
// a memory allocation failure occurs.
char *search_and_replace_alloc(const char *str, const char *oldsubstr,
                               const char *newsubstr) throw(bad_alloc) {

  // Don't allow the null terminator to be substituted.
  if(!*oldsubstr) return 0;


  // Allocate an array that is large enough to hold the resulting string.
  int size = strlen(str) + strlen(newsubstr) - strlen(oldsubstr) + 1;
  char *result = new char[size];
```

```
const char *p = strstr(str, oldsubstr);

if(p) {

  // Copy first part of original string.
  strncpy(result, str, p-str);

  // Null-terminate the first part of result so that
  // it can be operated on by other string functions.
  *(result+(p-str)) = '\0';

  // Substitute the new substring.
  strcat(result, newsubstr);

  // Add the remainder of the original string.
  strcat(result, p+strlen(oldsubstr));
} else {
  delete [] result; // release the unused memory
  return 0;
}

  return result;
}
```

Notice that **search_and_replace_alloc( )** throws **bad_alloc** if the allocation of the temporary array fails. Remember, memory is finite and it is possible to run out. This is especially true for embedded systems. Therefore, the caller of this version may need to handle this exception. For example, here is the basic framework that you can use to call **search_and_replace_alloc( )**:

```
char *ptr;
try {
  ptr = search_and_replace_alloc(str, old, new)
} catch(bad_alloc exc) {
  // Take appropriate action here.
}

if(ptr) {
  // Use the string...

  // Delete the memory when no longer needed.
  delete [] ptr;
}
```

Categorize Characters Within a Null-Terminated String

Key Ingredients		
Headers	**Classes**	**Functions**
<cctype>		int isalnum(int *ch*)
		int isalpha(int *ch*)
		int iscntrl(int *ch*)
		int isdigit(int *ch*)
		int isgraph(int *ch*)
		int islower(int *ch*)
		int isprint(int *ch*)
		int ispunct(int *ch*)
		int isspace(int *ch*)
		int isupper(int *ch*)
		int isxdigit(int *ch*)

Sometimes you will want to know what sorts of characters a string contains. For example, you might want to remove all whitespace (spaces, tabs, and newlines) from a file or display non-printing characters using some type of visual representation. To perform these tasks implies that you can categorize characters into different types, such as alphabetical, control, digits, punctuation, and so on. Fortunately, C++ makes it very easy to accomplish this by using one or more standard functions that determine a character's category.

Step-by-Step

The character functions make it quite easy to categorize a character. It involves these steps:

1. All of the character categorization functions are declared in **<cctype>**. Therefore, it must be included in your program.
2. To determine if a character is a letter or digit, call **isalnum( )**.
3. To determine if a character is a letter, call **isalpha( )**.
4. To determine if a character is a control character, call **iscntrl( )**.
5. To determine if a character is a digit, call **isdigit( )**.
6. To determine if a character is visible (excluding the space), call **isgraph( )**.
7. To determine if a character is a lowercase letter, call **islower( )**.
8. To determine if a character is printable (including the space), call **isprint( )**.
9. To determine if a character is punctuation, call **ispunct( )**.
10. To determine if a character is whitespace, call **isspace( )**.
11. To determine if a character is an uppercase letter, call **isupper( )**.
12. To determine if a character is a hexadecimal digit, call **isxdigit( )**.

Discussion

The character categorization functions were originally defined by C and are supported by C++ in a couple of different ways. The versions used here are declared within the header **<cctype>**. They all categorize characters based on the current locale.

All of the **is...** functions work in essentially the same way. Each is briefly described here:

int isalnum(int *ch*)	Returns non-zero if *ch* is either a letter or a digit, and zero otherwise.
int isalpha(int *ch*)	Returns non-zero if *ch* is a letter and zero otherwise.
int iscntrl(int *ch*)	Returns non-zero if *ch* is a control character and zero otherwise.
int isdigit(int *ch*)	Returns non-zero if *ch* is a digit and zero otherwise.
int isgraph(int *ch*)	Returns non-zero if *ch* is a printable character other than a space and zero otherwise.
int islower(int *ch*)	Returns non-zero if *ch* is a lowercase letter and zero otherwise.
int isprint(int *ch*)	Returns non-zero if *ch* is printable (including a space) and zero otherwise.
int ispunct(int *ch*)	Returns non-zero if *ch* is punctuation and zero otherwise.
int isspace(int *ch*)	Returns non-zero if *ch* is whitespace (including spaces, tabs, newlines) and zero otherwise.
int isupper(int *ch*)	Returns non-zero if *ch* is an uppercase letter and zero otherwise.
int isxdigit(int *ch*)	Returns non-zero if *ch* is a hexadecimal digit (0-9, A-F, or a-f) and zero otherwise.

Most of the functions are self-explanatory. However, notice the **ispunct( )** function. It returns true for any character that is punctuation. This is defined as any character that is not a letter, a digit, or a space. Therefore, operators such as + and / are categorized as punctuation.

Example

The following example shows the **isalpha( )**, **isdigit( )**, **isspace( )**, and **ispunct( )** functions in action. They are used to count the number of letters, spaces, and punctuation contained within a string.

```
// Count spaces, punctuation, digits, and letters.
#include <iostream>
#include <cctype>

using namespace std;

int main() {

  const char *str = "I have 30 apples and 12 pears. Do you have any?";
  int letters = 0, spaces = 0, punct = 0, digits = 0;

  cout << str << endl;
```

```
  while(*str) {
    if(isalpha(*str)) ++letters;
    else if(isspace(*str)) ++spaces;
    else if(ispunct(*str)) ++punct;
    else if(isdigit(*str)) ++digits;

    ++str;
  }

  cout << "Letters: " << letters << endl;
  cout << "Digits: " << digits << endl;
  cout << "Spaces: " << spaces << endl;
  cout << "Punctuation: " << punct << endl;

  return 0;
}
```

The output is shown here:

```
I have 30 apples and 12 pears. Do you have any?
Letters: 31
Digits: 4
Spaces: 10
Punctuation: 2
```

Bonus Example: Word Count

There is one well-known application in which the character categorization functions are used: a word-count utility. As a result, a word-count program makes the quintessential example for functions such as **isalpha( )** and **ispunct( )**. The following example creates a very simple version of the word-count utility. The actual counting is handled by the **wordcount( )** function. It is passed a pointer to a string. It then counts the words, lines, spaces, and punctuation in the string and returns the result.

This version of **wordcount( )** uses a fairly simple strategy: It counts only whole words that consist solely of letters. This means that a hyphenated word counts as two separate words. As a result, the sequence "null-terminated" counts as two words. Furthermore, a word must not contain any digits. For example, the sequence "testing123testing" will count as two words. The **wordcount( )** function does, however, allow one non-letter character to be in a word: the apostrophe. This allows it to support possessives (such as Tom's) and contractions (such as it's). Each is counted as one word.

```
// Count words, lines, spaces, and punctuation.
#include <iostream>
#include <cctype>

using namespace std;

// A structure to hold the word-count statistics.
struct wc {
  int words;
  int spaces;
```

```
  int punct;
  int lines;

  wc() {
    words = punct = spaces = lines = 0;
  }
};

wc wordcount(const char *str);

int main() {

  const char *test = "By supplying a string class and also "
              "supporting null-terminated strings,\nC++ "
              "offers a rich programming environment for "
              "string-intensive tasks.\nIt's power programming.";


  cout << "Given: " << "\n\n";
  cout << test << endl;
  wc wcd = wordcount(test);

  cout << "\nWords: " << wcd.words << endl;
  cout << "Spaces: " << wcd.spaces << endl;
  cout << "Lines: " << wcd.lines << endl;
  cout << "Punctuation: " << wcd.punct << endl;

  return 0;
}

// A very simple "word count" function.
// It counts the words, lines, spaces, and punctuation in
// a string and returns the result in a wc structure.
wc wordcount(const char *str) {
  wc data;

  // If the string is not null, then it contains at least one line.
  if(*str) ++data.lines;

  while(*str) {

    // Check for a word.
    if(isalpha(*str)) {
      // Start of word found. Now, look for the end of the word.
      // Allow apostrophes in words, as in "it's."
      while(isalpha(*str) || *str == '\'') {
        if(*str == '\'') ++data.punct;
        ++str;
      }
      data.words++;
    }
    else {
      // Count punctuation, spaces (including newlines), and lines.
```

```
      if(ispunct(*str)) ++data.punct;
      else if(isspace(*str)) {
        ++data.spaces;
        // If there is any character after the newline, increment
        // the line counter.
        if(*str == '\n' && *(str+1)) ++data.lines;
      }
      ++str;
    }
  }

  return data;
}
```

The output is shown here:

```
Given:

By supplying a string class and also supporting null-terminated strings,
C++ offers a rich programming environment for string-intensive tasks.
It's power programming.

Words: 24
Spaces: 21
Lines: 3
Punctuation: 8
```

There are a couple of points of interest in this program. First, notice that the **wordcount( )** function returns the results in an object of type **wc**, which is a **struct**. I used a **struct** rather than a **class** because **wc** is, essentially, a data-only object. Although **wc** does contain a default constructor (which performs a simple initialization), it defines no member functions or parameterized constructors. Thus, I felt that **struct** better fit its purpose (which is to hold data) than did **class**. In general, I like to use **class** when there are member functions. I like to use **struct** for objects that simply house data. Of course, in C++, both create a class type and there is no hard and fast rule in this regard.

Second, the line count is incremented when a newline character is found only if that newline is not immediately followed by the terminating null. This check is handled by this line:

```
if(*str == '\n' && *(str+1)) ++data.lines;
```

Basically, this ensures that the number of lines of text that one would see is equal to the line count returned by the function. This prevents a completely empty final line from being counted as a line. Of course, the line may still appear blank if all it contains is spaces.

Options and Alternatives

As mentioned, the character categorization functions defined in **<cctype>** operate relative to the default locale. Additional versions of these functions are also supported by **<locale>** and they allow you to specify a locale.

Tokenize a Null-Terminated String

Key Ingredients		
Headers	Classes	Functions
<cstring>		char *strtok(char *str, const char *delimiters);

Tokenizing a string is one programming task that just about every programmer will face at one time or another. *Tokenizing* is the process of reducing a string into its individual parts, which are called *tokens*. Thus, a token represents the smallest indivisible element that can be meaningfully extracted from a string.

Of course, what constitutes a token depends on what type of input is being processed and for what purpose For example, if you want to obtain the words in a sentence, then a token is a set of characters surrounded by either whitespace or punctuation. For example, given the sentence:

I like apples, pears, and grapes.

The individual tokens are

I	like	apples
pears	and	grapes

Each token is delimited by the whitespace and/or punctuation that separates one from another. When tokenizing a string that contains a list of key/value pairs organized like this:

key=value, key=value, key=value, ...

The tokens are the *key* and the *value*. The = sign and the comma are separators that delimit the tokens. For example, given

price=10.15, quantity=4

The tokens are

price	10.15	quantity	4

The point is that what constitutes a token will change, depending on the circumstance. However, the general process of tokenizing a string is the same in all cases.

Because tokenizing a string is both an important and common task, C++ provides built-in support for it through the **strtok( )** function. This recipe shows how to use it.

Step-by-Step

To use **strtok( )** to tokenize a string involves these steps:

1. Create a string that contains the characters that separate one token from another. These are the token delimiters.

2. To obtain the first token in the string, call **strtok( )** with a pointer to the string to be tokenized and a pointer to the string that contains the delimiters.

3. To obtain the remaining tokens in the string, continue calling **strtok( )**. However, pass a null pointer for the first argument. You can change the delimiters as needed.

4. When **strtok( )** returns null, the string has been fully tokenized.

Discussion

The **strtok( )** function has the following prototype:

char *strtok(char *str, const char *delimiters)

A pointer to the string from which one or more tokens will be obtained is passed in str. A pointer to the string that contains the characters that delimit a token is passed in delimiters. Thus, delimiters contains the characters that divide one token from another. A null pointer is returned if there are no more tokens in str. Otherwise, a pointer to a string that contains the next token is returned.

Tokenizing a string is a two-step process. The first call to **strtok( )** passes a pointer to the string to be tokenized. Each subsequent call to **strtok( )** passes a null pointer to str. This causes **strtok( )** to continue tokenizing the string from the point at which the previous token was found. When no more tokens are found, a null pointer is returned.

One useful aspect of **strtok( )** is that you can change the delimiters as needed during the tokenization process. For example, consider a string that contains key/value pairs organized like this

count = 10, max = 99, min = 12, name = "Tom Jones, jr.", ...

To read most of the keys and values in this string, the following delimiter set can be used:

" =,"

However, to read a quoted string that can consist of any character, including commas, this delimiter is needed:

"\""

Because **strtok( )** lets you change delimiter sets "on the fly," you can specify which delimiters are needed at any point in time. This technique is illustrated by the following example.

Example

The following example shows how to use **strtok( )** to tokenize a null-terminated string:

```
// Demonstrate strtok().
#include <iostream>
#include <cstring>

using namespace std;
```

```cpp
int main() {

  // First, use strtok() to tokenize a sentence.

  // Create a string of delimiters for simple sentences.
  char delims[] = "., ?;!";

  char str[] = "I like apples, pears, and grapes. Do you?";

  char *tok;

  cout << "Obtain the words in a sentence.\n";

  // Pass the string to be tokenized and get the first token.
  tok = strtok(str, delims);

  // Get all remaining tokens.
  while(tok) {
    cout << tok << endl;

    // Each subsequent call to strtok() is passed NULL
    // for the first argument.
    tok  = strtok(NULL, delims);
  }

  // Now, use strtok() to extract keys and values stored
  // in key/value pairs within a string.
  char kvpairs[] = "count=10, name=\"Tom Jones, jr.\", max=100, min=0.01";

  // Create a list of delimiters for key/value pairs.
  char kvdelims[] = " =,";

  cout << "\nTokenize key/value pairs.\n";

   // Get the first key.
  tok = strtok(kvpairs, kvdelims);

  // Get all remaining tokens.
  while(tok) {
    cout << "Key: " << tok << " ";

    // Get a value.

    // First, if the key is name, the value will be
    // a quoted string.
    if(!strcmp("name", tok)) {
      // Notice that this call uses only quotes as a delimiter.
      // This lets it read a quoted string that contains any character.
      tok = strtok(NULL, "\"");
    }
    else {
      // Otherwise, read a simple value.
      tok  = strtok(NULL, kvdelims);
```

```
    }
    cout << "Value: " << tok << endl;

    // Get the next key.
    tok = strtok(NULL, kvdelims);
  }

  return 0;
}
```

The output is shown here:

```
Obtain the words in a sentence.
I
like
apples
pears
and
grapes
Do
you

Tokenize key/value pairs.
Key: count Value: 10
Key: name Value: Tom Jones, jr.
Key: max Value: 100
Key: min Value: 0.01
```

Pay special attention to the way that key/value pairs are read. The delimiters used to read a simple value differ from the delimiters used to read a quoted string. Furthermore, the delimiters are changed during the tokenization process. As explained, when tokenizing a string, you can change the delimiter set as needed.

Options and Alternatives

Although **strtok( )** is simple to use, and quite effective when applied in situations for which it is well suited, its use is inherently limited. The main trouble is that **strtok( )** tokenizes a string based on a set of delimiters, and once a delimiter has been encountered, it is lost. This makes it difficult to use **strtok( )** to tokenize a string in which the delimiters might also be tokens. For example, consider the following simple C++ statement:

    x = count+12;

To parse this statement, the + must be handled as both a delimiter that terminates **count** and as a token that indicates addition. The trouble is that there is no easy way to do this using **strtok( )**. To obtain **count**, the + must be in the set of delimiters. However, once the + has been encountered, it is consumed. Thus, it cannot also be read as a token. A second problem with **strtok( )** is that errors in the format of the string being tokenized are difficult to detect—at least until the end of the string is prematurely reached.

Because of the problems with applying **strtok( )** to a wide range of cases, other approaches to tokenization are often used. One such approach is to write your own "get token" function. This gives you full control over the tokenization process and lets you easily return tokens based on context rather than delimiters. A simple example of such an approach is shown here. The custom get token function is called **gettoken( )**. It tokenizes a string into the following token types:

- Alphanumeric strings, such as count, indx27, or OverFlow.
- Unsigned integer numbers, such as 2, 99, or 0.
- Punctuation, which includes operators, such as + and /.

Thus, **gettoken( )** can be used to tokenize very simple expressions, such as

x = count+12;

or

while(x<9) x = x − w;

The **gettoken( )** function is used much like **strtok( )**. On the first call, pass a pointer to the string to be tokenized. On subsequent calls, pass a null pointer. It returns a pointer to the next token in the string. It returns a null pointer when there are no more tokens. To tokenize a new string, simply start the process over by passing a pointer to the new string. The simple **gettoken( )** function, along with a **main( )** function to demonstrate its use, is shown here:

```
// Demonstrate a custom gettoken() function that can
// return the tokens that comprise very simple expressions.
#include <iostream>
#include <cstring>
#include <cctype>

using namespace std;

const char *gettoken(const char *str);

int main() {
  char sampleA[] = "max=12+3/89; count27 = 19*(min+floor);";
  char sampleB[] = "while(i < max) i = counter * 2;";
  const char *tok;

  // Tokenize the first string.
  tok = gettoken(sampleA);
  cout << "Here are the tokens in: " << sampleA << endl;
  while(tok) {
    cout << tok << endl;
    tok = gettoken(NULL);
  }
  cout << "\n\n";

  // Restart gettoken() by passing the second string.
  tok = gettoken(sampleB);
  cout << "Here are the tokens in: " << sampleB << endl;
  while(tok) {
    cout << tok << endl;
```

```
    tok  = gettoken(NULL);
  }

  return 0;
}

// A very simple custom gettoken() function. The tokens are comprised
// of alphanumeric strings, numbers, and single-character punctuation.
// Although this function is quite limited, it demonstrates the basic
// framework that can be expanded and enhanced to obtain other types
// of tokens.
//
// On the first call, pass a pointer to the string to be tokenized.
// On subsequent calls, pass a null pointer.
// It returns a pointer to the current token, or a null
// pointer if there are no more tokens.
#define MAX_TOK_SIZE 128
const char *gettoken(const char *str) {
  static char token[MAX_TOK_SIZE+1];
  static const char *ptr;
  int count; // holds the current character count
  char *tokptr;

  if(str) {
    ptr = str;
  }

  tokptr = token;
  count = 0;

  while(isspace(*ptr)) ptr++;

  if(isalpha(*ptr)) {
    while(isalpha(*ptr) || isdigit(*ptr)) {
      *tokptr++ = *ptr++;
      ++count;
      if(count == MAX_TOK_SIZE) break;
    }
  } else if(isdigit(*ptr)) {
    while(isdigit(*ptr)) {
      *tokptr++ = *ptr++;
      ++count;
      if(count == MAX_TOK_SIZE) break;
    }
  } else if(ispunct(*ptr)) {
    *tokptr++ = *ptr++;
  } else return NULL;

  // Null-terminate the token.
  *tokptr = '\0';

  return token;
}
```

The output from the program is shown here:

```
Here are the tokens in: max=12+3/89; count27 = 19*(min+floor);
max
=
12
+
3
/
89
;
count27
=
19
*
(
min
+
floor
)
;


Here are the tokens in: while(i < max) i = counter * 2;
while
(
i
<
max
)
i
=
counter
*
2
;
```

The operation of **gettoken( )** is straightforward. It simply examines the next character in the input string and then reads the type of token that starts with that type of character. For example, if the token is a letter, then **gettoken( )** reads an alphanumeric token. If the next character is a digit, then **gettoken( )** reads an integer. If the next character is punctuation, then the token consists of that character. Notice that **gettoken( )** does not let the length of a token exceed the maximum token length as specified by **MAX_TOK_SIZE**. Also, notice that **gettoken( )** *does not* modify the input string. This differs from **strtok( )**, which does modify the input string. Finally, notice that the pointer returned by **gettoken( )** is **const**. This means that it can't be used to modify the static array **token**. Finally, although **gettoken( )** is very simple, it can be easily adapted and enhanced to fit other, more sophisticated situations.

Perform Basic Operations on string Objects

Key Ingredients		
Headers	**Classes**	**Functions**
<string>	string	size_type capacity( ) const
		string &erase(size_type *indx* = 0, size_type *len* = npos)
		string &insert(size_type *indx*, const string &*str*)
		size_type max_size( ) const
		char &operator[ ](size_type *indx*)
		string &operator=(const string &*str*)
		void push_back (const char *ch*)
		void reserve(size_type *num* = 0)
		size_type size( ) const;
		string substr(size_type *indx* = 0, size_type *len* = npos) const
<string>		string operator+(const string &*leftop*, const string &*rightop*)
		bool operator==(const string &*leftop*, const string &*rightop*)
		bool operator<=(const string &*leftop*, const string &*rightop*)
		bool operator>(const string &*leftop*, const string &*rightop*)

As explained at the start of this chapter, C++ provides two ways of handling strings. The first is the null-terminated string (also called a C-string). The null-terminated string was inherited from C and is still widely used in C++ programming. It is also the type of string used in the preceding recipes. The second type of string is an object of the template class **basic_string**. This class is defined by C++ and is part of the standard C++ class library. The remaining recipes in this chapter use **basic_string**.

Strings of type **basic_string** have several advantages over null-terminated strings. Here are some of the most important:

- **basic_string** defines a data type. (Recall that a null-terminated string is simply a convention.)

- **basic_string** encapsulates the character sequence that forms the string, thus preventing improper operations. When using **basic_string**, it is not possible to generate an array overrun, for example.

- **basic_string** objects are dynamic. They grow as needed to accommodate the size of the string that is being held. Therefore, it is not necessary to know in advance how large a string is needed.

- **basic_string** defines operators that manipulate strings. This streamlines many types of string handling.

- **basic_string** defines a complete set of member functions that simplify working with strings. You seldom have to write your own function to perform some string manipulation.

There are two built-in specializations of **basic_string**: **string** (which is for characters of type **char**) and **wstring** (which is for wide characters). For convenience, all of the recipes in this book use **string**, but most of the information is applicable to any type of **basic_string**.

This recipe demonstrates several of the basic operations that can be applied to objects of type **string**. It shows how to construct a **string**. It then demonstrates several of its operators and member functions. It also demonstrates how **string** objects adjust their size at runtime to accommodate an increase in the size of the character sequence.

Step-by-Step

To perform the basic **string** operations involves these steps:

1. The **string** class is declared within the header **<string>**. Thus, **<string>** must be included in any program that uses **string**.

2. Create a **string** by using one of its constructors. Three are demonstrated in this recipe. The first creates an empty **string**, the second creates a **string** initialized by a **string** literal, and the third creates a **string** that is initialized by another **string**.

3. To obtain the length of the longest possible string, call **max_size( )**.

4. To assign one string to another, use the = operator.

5. To concatenate two **string** objects, use the + operator.

6. To lexicographically compare two **string** objects, use the relational operators, such as > or ==.

7. To obtain a reference to a character at a specified index, use the [ ] indexing operator.

8. To obtain the number of characters currently held by a **string**, call **size( )**.

9. To obtain the current capacity of a **string**, call **capacity( )**.

10. To specify a capacity, call **reserve( )**.

11. To remove all or part of the characters from a **string**, call **erase( )**.

12. To add a character to the end of a string, call **push_back( )**.

13. To obtain a substring, call **substr( )**.

Discussion

The **string** class defines several constructors. The ones used by this recipe are shown here:

explicit string(const Allocator &*alloc* = Allocator( ))
string(const char *str*, const Allocator &*alloc* Allocator( ))

```
string(const string &str, size_type indx = 0,
        size_type len=npos, const Allocator &alloc Allocator( ))
```

The first constructor creates an empty string. The second creates a string that is initialized by the null-terminated string pointed to by *str*. The third creates a string that is initialized by a substring of *str* that begins at *indx* and runs for *len* characters. Although these look a bit intimidating, they are easy to use. Generally, the allocator (which controls how memory is allocated) is allowed to default. This means that normally you won't specify an allocator when creating a **string**. For example, the following creates an empty string and a string · initialized with a string literal:

```
string mystr; // empty string
string mystr2("Hello"); // string initialized with the sequence Hello
```

In the third constructor, the defaults for both *indx* and *len* are typically used, which means that the string contains a complete copy of *str*.

Although **string** objects are dynamic, growing as needed at runtime, there is still a maximum length that a string can have. Although this maximum is typically quite large, it may be useful to know it in some cases. To obtain the maximum string length, call **max_size( )**, shown here:

```
size_type max_size( ) const
```

It returns the length of the longest possible string. ·

You can assign one **string** to another by using the = operator. This operator is implemented as a member function. It has several forms. Here is one used by this recipe:

```
string &operator=(const string &str)
```

It assigns the character sequence in *str* to the invoking **string**. It returns a reference to the invoking object. Other versions of the assignment operator let you assign a null-terminated string or a character to a **string** object.

You can concatenate one **string** with another by using the + operator. It is defined as a non-member function. It has several forms. Here is the one used by this recipe:

```
string operator+(const string &leftop, const string &rightop)
```

It concatenates *rightop* to *leftop* and returns a **string** object that contains the result. Other versions of the concatenation operator let you concatenate a **string** object with a null-terminated string or with a character.

You can insert one string into another by using the **insert( )** function. It has several forms. The one used here is:

```
string &insert(size_type indx, const string &str)
```

It inserts *str* into the invoking string at the index specified by *indx*. It returns a reference to the invoking object.

All of the relational operators are defined for the **string** class by non-member operator functions. They perform lexicographical comparisons of the character sequences contained within two strings. Each operator has several overloaded forms. The operators used here are ==, <=, and >, but all of the relational operators work in the same basic way. Here are the versions of these operators that are used in this recipe:

bool operator==(const string &*leftop*, const string &*rightop*)
bool operator<=(const string &*leftop*, const string &*rightop*)
bool operator>(const string &*leftop*, const string &*rightop*)

In all cases, *leftop* refers to the left operand and *rightop* refers to the right operand. The result of the comparison is returned. Other versions of these operators let you compare a **string** object with a null-terminated string.

You can obtain a reference to a specific element in a **string** by using the array indexing operator [ ]. It is implemented as a member function, as shown here:

char &operator[ ](size_type *indx*)

It returns a reference to the character at the zero-based index specified by *indx*. For example, given a **string** object called **mystr**, the expression **mystr[2]** returns a reference to the third character in **mystr**. A **const** version is also available.

The number of characters contained in the string can be obtained by calling **size( )**, shown here:

size_type size( ) const

It returns the number of characters currently in the string. As explained in the overview at the start of this chapter, **size_type** is a **typedef** that represents some form of unsigned integer.

The number of characters that a **string** object can hold is not predetermined. Instead, a **string** object will grow as needed to accommodate the size of the string that it needs to encapsulate. However, all **string** objects begin with an initial capacity, which is the maximum number of characters that can be held before more memory needs to be allocated. The capacity of a **string** object can be determined by calling **capacity( )**, shown here:

size_type capacity( ) const

It returns the current capacity of the invoking **string**.

The capacity of a **string** object can be important because memory allocations are costly in terms of time. If you know in advance the number of characters that a **string** will hold, then you can set the capacity to that amount, thereby eliminating a memory reallocation. To do this, call **reserve( )**, shown next:

void reserve(size_type *num* = 0)

It sets the capacity of the invoking **string** so that it is equal to at least *num*. If *num* is less than or equal to the number of characters in the string, then the call to **reserve( )** is a request to reduce the capacity to equal the size. This request can be ignored, however.

You can remove one or more characters from a string by calling **erase( )**. There are three versions of **erase( )**. The one used by this recipe is shown here:

string &erase(size_type *indx* = 0, size_type *len* = npos)

Beginning at *indx*, it removes *len* characters from the invoking object. It returns a reference to the invoking object.

One of the more interesting **string** member functions is **push_back( )**. It adds a character to the end of the string:

void push_back (const char *ch*)

It adds *ch* to the end of the invoking string. It is quite useful when you want to create a queue of characters.

You can obtain a portion of a string (i.e., a substring) by calling **substr( )**, shown here:

string substr(size_type *indx* = 0, size_type *len* = npos) const

It returns a substring of *len* characters, beginning at *indx* within the invoking **string**.

Example
The following example illustrates several of the fundamental string operations:

```
// Demonstrate the basic string operations.
#include <iostream>
#include <string>

using namespace std;

int main()
{
  // Create some string objects. Three are initialized
  // using the string literal passed as an argument.
  string str1("Alpha");
  string str2("Beta");
  string str3("Gamma");
  string str4;

  // Output a string via cout.
  cout << "Here are the original strings:\n";
  cout << "  str1: " << str1 << endl;
  cout << "  str2: " << str2 << endl;
  cout << "  str3: " << str3 << "\n\n";

  // Display the maximum string length.
  cout << "The maximum string length is: " << str1.max_size()
       << "\n\n";

  // Display the size of str1.
  cout << "str1 contains " << str1.size() << " characters.\n";

  // Display the capacity of str1.
  cout << "Capacity of str1: " << str1.capacity() << "\n\n";

  // Display the characters in a string one at a time
  // by using the indexing operator.
  for(unsigned i = 0; i < str1.size(); ++i)
    cout << "str1[i]: " << str1[i] << endl;
  cout << endl;

  // Assign one string to another.
  str4 = str1;
  cout << "str4 after being assigned str1: " << str4 << "\n\n";
```

```cpp
  // Concatenate two strings.
  str4 = str1 + str3;
  cout << "str4 after begin assigned st1+str3: " << str4 << "\n\n";

  // Insert one string into another.
  str4.insert(5, str2);
  cout << "str4 after inserting str2: " << str4 << "\n\n";

  // Obtain a substring.
  str4 = str4.substr(5, 4);
  cout << "str4 after being assigned str4.substr(5, 3): "
       << str4 << "\n\n";

  // Compare two strings.
  cout << "Compare strings.\n";
  if(str3 > str1) cout << "str3 > str1\n";
  if(str3 == str1+str2)
    cout << "str3 == str1+str2\n";
  if(str1 <= str2)
    cout << "str1 <= str2\n\n";

  // Create a string object using another string object.
  cout << "Initialize str5 with the contents of str1.\n";
  string str5(str1);
  cout << "str5: " << str5 << "\n\n";

  // Erase str4.
  cout << "Erasing str4.\n";
  str4.erase();
  if(str4.empty()) cout << "str4 is now empty.\n";
  cout << "Size and capacity of str4 is " << str4.size() << " "
       << str4.capacity() << "\n\n";

  // Use push_back() to add characters to str4.
  for(char ch = 'A'; ch <= 'Z'; ++ch)
    str4.push_back(ch);
  cout << "str4 after calls to push_back(): " << str4 << endl;
  cout << "Size and capacity of str4 is now " << str4.size() << " "
       << str4.capacity() << "\n\n";

  // Set the capacity of str4 to 128.
  cout << "Setting the capacity of str4 to 128\n";
  str4.reserve(128);
  cout << "Capacity of str4 is now: " << str4.capacity() << "\n\n";

  // Input a string via cin.
  cout << "Enter a string: ";
  cin >> str1;
  cout << "You entered: " << str1 << "\n\n";

  return 0;
}
```

The output is shown here:

```
Here are the original strings:
  str1: Alpha
  str2: Beta
  str3: Gamma

The maximum string length is: 4294967294

str1 contains 5 characters.
Capacity of str1: 15

str1[i]: A
str1[i]: l
str1[i]: p
str1[i]: h
str1[i]: a

str4 after being assigned str1: Alpha

str4 after being assigned st1+str3: AlphaGamma

str4 after inserting str2: AlphaBetaGamma

str4 after being assigned str4.substr(5, 3): Beta

Compare strings.
str3 > str1
str1 <= str2

Initialize str5 with the contents of str1.
str5: Alpha

Erasing str4.
str4 is now empty.
Size and capacity of str4 is 0 15

str4 after calls to push_back(): ABCDEFGHIJKLMNOPQRSTUVWXYZ
Size and capacity of str4 is now 26 31

Setting the capacity of str4 to 128
Capacity of str4 is now: 143

Enter a string: test
You entered: test
```

Perhaps the most important thing to notice in the example is that the size of the strings is not specified. As explained, **string** objects are automatically sized to hold the string that they are given. Thus, when assigning or concatenating strings, the target string will grow as needed to accommodate the size of the new string. It is not possible to overrun the end of the string. This dynamic aspect of **string** objects is one of the ways in which they are better than standard null-terminated strings, which *are* subject to boundary overruns. (As mentioned in the overview, an attempt to create a **string** that exceeds the longest possible string results in a **length_error** being thrown. Thus, it is not possible to overrun a **string**.)

There is one other important thing to notice in the sample run. When the capacity of **str4** is increased by calling **reserve( )** with an argument of 128, the actual capacity becomes 143. Remember, a call to **reserve( )** causes the capacity to be increased to *at least* the specified value. The implementation is free to set it to a higher value. This might happen because allocations might be more efficient in blocks of a certain size, for example. (Of course, because of differences between compilers, you might see a different capacity value when you run the sample program. Such differences are to be expected.)

Options and Alternatives

Even for the basic string operations, **string** offers many alternatives. Several are mentioned here.

As explained, to obtain the number of characters currently held by a string, you can call **size( )**. However, you can also call **length( )**. It returns the same value and works the same way. In essence, **size( )** and **length( )** are simply two different names for the same function. The reason for the two names is historical. The **size( )** method must be implemented by all STL containers. Although not always thought of as part of the STL, **string** meets all of the STL requirements for a container and is compatible with the STL. Part of those requirements is that a container must provide a **size( )** function. Therefore, **size( )** became part of **string**.

The **insert( )** function has several additional forms. For example, you can insert a portion of one **string** into another, one or more characters into a **string**, or a null-terminated string into a **string**.

The **erase( )** function has two additional forms that let you remove characters referred to by an iterator (see *Operate on* **string** *Objects Through Iterators*).

Although using the indexing operator [ ] is more straightforward, you can also obtain a reference to a specific character by calling the **at( )** method. It is shown here as it is implemented for **string**:

    char &at(size_type *indx*)

It returns a reference to the character at the zero-based index specified by *indx*. A **const** version is also available.

As the recipe shows, you can perform simple assignments and concatenations using the = and + operators defined for **string**. In cases in which more sophisticated assignments or concatenations are needed, **string** supplies the **assign( )** and **append( )** functions. These functions have many forms that allow you to assign or append portions of a string, all or part of a null-terminated string, or one or more characters. There are also forms that support iterators. Although there are far too many to describe in this recipe, here is an example of each:

    string &assign(const string &*str*, size_type *indx*, size_type *len*)
    string &append(const string &*str*, size_type *indx*, size_type *len*)

This version of **assign( )** assigns a substring of *str* to the invoking string. The substring begins at *indx* and runs for *len* characters. This version of **append( )** appends a substring of *str* onto the end of the invoking string. The substring begins at *indx* and runs for *len* characters. Both functions return a reference to the invoking object.

The relational operators are the easiest way to compare one string with another. In addition to the forms used in the recipe, other versions of these operators let you compare a **string** object with a null-terminated string. To provide added flexibility, **string** also supplies the **compare( )** function, which lets you compare portions of two strings. Here is one example. It compares a string with a substring of the invoking string.

int compare(size_type *indx*, size_type *len*, const string &*str*) const

This function compares *str* to the substring within the invoking string that begins at *indx* and is *len* characters long. It returns less than zero if the sequence in the invoking string is less than *str*, zero if the two sequences are equal, and greater than zero if the sequence in the invoking string is greater than *str*.

You can remove all characters from a **string** in two ways. First, as the recipe shows, you can use the **erase( )** function, allowing the arguments to default. Alternatively, you can call **clear( )**, which is shown here:

void clear( )

Search a string Object

Key Ingredients

Headers	Classes	Functions
<string>	string	size_type find(const char *str, size_type *indx* = 0) const
		size_type find(const string &str, size_type *indx* = 0) const
		size_type find_first_of(const char *str, size_type *indx* = 0) const
		size_type find_first_of(const string &str, size_type *indx* = 0) const
		size_type find_first_not_of(const char *str, size_type *indx* = 0) const
		size_type find_last_of(const char *str, size_type *indx* = npos) const
		size_type find_last_not_of(const char *str, size_type *indx* = npos) const
		size_type rfind(const char *str, size_type *indx* = npos) const

The **string** class defines a powerful assortment of functions that search a string. These functions let you find:

- The first occurrence of a substring or character.
- The last occurrence of a substring or character.
- The first occurrence of any character in a set of characters.
- The last occurrence of any character in a set of characters.
- The first occurrence of any character that is not part of a set of characters.
- The last occurrence of any character that is not part of a set of characters.

This recipe demonstrates their use.

Step-by-Step

Searching a **string** involves these steps:

1. To find the first occurrence of a sequence or character, call **find( )**.
2. To find the last occurrence of a sequence or character, call **rfind( )**.
3. To find the first occurrence of any character in a set of characters, call **find_first_of( )**.
4. To find the last occurrence of any character in a set of characters, call **find_last_of( )**.
5. To find the first occurrence of any character that is not part of a set of characters, call **find_first_not_of( )**.
6. To find the last occurrence of any character that is not part of a set of characters, call **find_last_not_of( )**.

Discussion

All of the search functions have four forms, which allow you to specify the objective of the search as a **string**, a null-terminated string, a portion of a null-terminated string, or a character. The forms used by the examples in this recipe are described here.

The **find( )** function finds the first occurrence of a substring or character within another string. Here are the forms used in this recipe or by the Bonus Example:

```
size_type find(const string &str, size_type indx = 0) const
size_type find(const char *str, size_type indx = 0) const
```

Both return the index of the first occurrence of *str* within the invoking string. The *indx* parameter specifies the index at which the search will begin within the invoking string. In the first form, *str* is a reference to a **string**. In the second form, *str* is a pointer to a null-terminated string. If no match is found, **npos** is returned.

The **rfind( )** function finds the last occurrence of a substring or character within another string. The form used here is:

```
size_type rfind(const char *str, size_type indx = npos) const
```

It returns the index of the last occurrence of *str* within the invoking string. The *indx* parameter specifies the index at which the search will begin within the invoking string. If no match is found, **npos** is returned.

To find the first occurrence of any character within a set of characters, call **find_first_of( )**. Here are the forms used in this recipe or by the Bonus Example:

size_type find_first_of(const string &*str*, size_type *indx* = 0) const
size_type find_first_of(const char **str*, size_type *indx* = 0) const

Both return the index of the first character within the invoking string that matches any character in *str.* The search begins at index *indx.* **npos** is returned if no match is found. The difference between the two is simply the type of *str,* which can be either a **string** or a null-terminated string.

To find the first occurrence of any character that is not part of a set of characters, call **find_first_not_of( )**. Here are the forms used in this recipe or by the Bonus Example:

size_type find_first_not_of(const string &*str*, size_type *indx* = 0) const
size_type find_first_not_of(const char **str*, size_type *indx* = 0) const

Both return the index of the first character within the invoking string that does *not* match any character in *str.* The search begins at index *indx.* **npos** is returned if no match is found. The difference between the two is simply the type of *str,* which can be either a **string** or a null-terminated string.

To find the last occurrence of any character within a set of characters, call **find_last_of( )**. The form used here is:

size_type find_last_of(const char **str*, size_type *indx* = npos) const

It returns the index of the last character within the invoking string that matches any character in *str.* The search begins at index *indx.* **npos** is returned if no match is found.

To find the last occurrence of any character that is not part of a set of characters, call **find_last_not_of( )**. The form used by this recipe is:

size_type find_last_not_of(const char **str*, size_type *indx* = npos) const

It returns the index of the last character within the invoking string that does *not* match any character in *str.* The search begins at index *indx.* **npos** is returned if no match is found.

NOTE *As just described, the value **npos** is returned by the **find...** functions when no match is found. The **npos** variable is of type **string::size_type**, which is some form of unsigned integer. However, **npos** is initialized to –1. This causes **npos** to contain its largest possible unsigned value. Microsoft currently recommends that if you will be comparing the value of some variable to **npos**, then that variable should be declared to be of type **string::size_type**, rather than **int** or **unsigned**, to ensure that the comparison is handled correctly in all cases. This is the approach used in these recipes. However, it is not uncommon to see code in which **npos** is declared as an **int** or **unsigned**.*

Example

The following example shows the search functions in action:

```
// Search a string.
#include <iostream>
#include <string>

using namespace std;
```

```cpp
void showresult(string s, string::size_type i);

int main()
{
  string::size_type indx;

  // Create a string.
  string str("one two three, one two three");
  string str2;

  cout << "String to be searched: " << str << "\n\n";

  cout << "Searching for the first occurrence of 'two'\n";
  indx = str.find("two");
  showresult(str, indx);

  cout << "Searching for the last occurrence of 'two'\n";
  indx = str.rfind("two");
  showresult(str, indx);

  cout << "Searching for the first occurrence of t or h\n";
  indx = str.find_first_of("th");
  showresult(str, indx);

  cout << "Searching for the last occurrence of t or h\n";
  indx = str.find_last_of("th");
  showresult(str, indx);

  cout << "Searching for the first occurrence of any character other "
       << "than o, n, e, or space\n";
  indx = str.find_first_not_of("one ");
  showresult(str, indx);

  cout << "Searching for the last occurrence of any character other "
       << "than o, n, e, or space\n";
  indx = str.find_last_not_of("one ");
  showresult(str, indx);

  return 0;
}

// Display the results of the search.
void showresult(string s, string::size_type i) {

  if(i == string::npos) {
    cout << "No match found.\n";
    return;
  }

  cout << "Match found at index " << i << endl;

  cout << "Remaining string from point of match: "
       << s.substr(i) << "\n\n";
}
```

The output is shown here:

```
String to be searched: one two three, one two three

Searching for the first occurrence of 'two'
Match found at index 4
Remaining string from point of match: two three, one two three

Searching for the last occurrence of 'two'
Match found at index 19
Remaining string from point of match: two three

Searching for the first occurrence of t or h
Match found at index 4
Remaining string from point of match: two three, one two three

Searching for the last occurrence of t or h
Match found at index 24
Remaining string from point of match: hree

Searching for the first occurrence of any character other than o, n, e, or space
Match found at index 4
Remaining string from point of match: two three, one two three

Searching for the last occurrence of any character other than o, n, e, or space
Match found at index 25
Remaining string from point of match: ree
```

Bonus Example: A Tokenizer Class for string Objects

The C++ standard library contains the function **strtok( )**, which can be used to tokenize a null-terminated string (see *Tokenize a Null-Terminated String*). However, the **string** class does not define a corresponding equivalent. Fortunately, it is quite easy to create one. Before beginning, it is important to state that there are several different ways to approach this task. This example shows just one of many.

The following program creates a class called **tokenizer** that encapsulates tokenization. To tokenize a string, first construct a **tokenizer**, passing the string as an argument. Next, call **get_token( )** to obtain the individual tokens in the string. The delimiters that define the boundaries of each token are passed to **get_token( )** as a string. The delimiters can be changed with each call to **get_token( )**. The **get_token( )** function returns an empty string when there are no more tokens to return. Notice that **get_token( )** makes use of the **find_first_of( )** and **find_first_not_of( )** functions.

```cpp
// Create a class called tokenizer that tokenizes a string.
#include <iostream>
#include <string>

using namespace std;

// The tokenizer class is used to tokenize a string.
// Pass the constructor the string to be tokenized.
// To obtain the next token, call get_token(),
// passing in a string that contains the delimiters.
```

```cpp
class tokenizer {
  string s;
  string::size_type startidx;
  string::size_type endidx;

public:
  tokenizer(const string &str) {
    s = str;
    startidx = 0;
  }

  // Return a token from the string.
  string get_token(const string &delims);
};

// Return a token from the string. Return an
// empty string when no more tokens are found.
// Pass the delimiters in delims.
string tokenizer::get_token(const string &delims) {

  // Return an empty string when there are no more
  // tokens to return.
  if(startidx == string::npos) return string("");

  // Beginning at startidx, find the next delimiter.
  endidx = s.find_first_of(delims, startidx);

  // Construct a string that contains the token.
  string tok(s.substr(startidx, endidx-startidx));

  // Find the start of the next token. This is a
  // character that is not a delimiter.
  startidx = s.find_first_not_of(delims, endidx);

  // Return the next token.
  return tok;
}

int main()
{
  // Strings to be tokenized.
  string strA("I have four, five, six tokens. ");
  string strB("I might have more tokens!\nDo You?");

  // This string contains the delimiters.
  string delimiters(" ,.!?\n");

  // This string will hold the next token.
  string token;

  // Create two tokenizers.
  tokenizer tokA(strA);
  tokenizer tokB(strB);
```

```
  // Display the tokens in strA.
  cout << "The tokens in strA:\n";
  token = tokA.get_token(delimiters);
  while(token != "") {
    cout << token << endl;
    token = tokA.get_token(delimiters);
  }
  cout << endl;

  // Display the tokens in strB.
  cout << "The tokens in strB:\n";
  token = tokB.get_token(delimiters);
  while(token != "") {
    cout << token << endl;
    token = tokB.get_token(delimiters);
  }

  return 0;
}
```

Here is the output:

```
The tokens in strA:
I
have
four
five
six
tokens

The tokens in strB:
I
might
have
more
tokens
Do
You
```

There is one easy enhancement that you might want to try making to **tokenize**: a **reset( )** function. This function could be called to enable a string to be retokenized from the start. This is easy to do. Simply set **startidx** to zero, as shown here:

```
void reset() { startidx = 0; }
```

Options and Alternatives

As mentioned, each of the **find...** functions has four forms. For example, here are all of the forms of **find( )**:

size_type find(const string &*str*, size_type *indx* = 0) const
size_type find(const char *str*, size_type *indx* = 0) const
size_type find(const char *str*, size_type *indx*, size_type *len*) const
size_type find(char *ch*, size_type *indx* = 0) const

The first two forms were described earlier. The third form searches for the first occurrence of the first *len* characters of *str*. The fourth form searches for the first occurrence of *ch*. In all cases, the search begins at the index specified by *indx* within the invoking **string**, and the index at which a match is found is returned. If no match is found, **npos** is returned. The other **find...** functions have similar forms.

As mentioned in the overview at the start of this chapter, the **string** class fulfills the general requirements for being an STL-compatible container. This means that it can be operated on by the algorithms declared in **<algorithm>**. Therefore, a **string** object can be searched by using the search algorithms, such as **search( )**, **find( )**, **find_first_of( )**, and so on. The one advantage that the algorithms offer is the ability to supply a user-defined predicate that lets you specify when one character in the string matches another. This feature is used by the recipe *Create Case-Insensitive Search and Search-and-Replace Functions for string Objects* to implement a search function that ignores case differences. (The STL and algorithms are covered in depth in Chapters 3 and 4.)

Create a Search-and-Replace Function for string Objects

Key Ingredients		
Headers	Classes	Functions
<string>	string	size_type find(const string &str, size_type *indx* = 0) const
		string &replace(size_type *indx*, size_type *len*, const string &str)

The **string** class provides very rich support for the replacement of one substring with another. This operation is provided by the **replace( )** function, of which there are ten forms. These ten forms give you great flexibility in specifying how the replacement process will take place. For example, you can specify the replacement string as a **string** object or as a null-terminated string. You can specify what part of the invoking string is replaced by specifying indexes or through the use of iterators. This recipe makes use of **replace( )** along with the **find( )** function demonstrated by the preceding recipe to implement a search-and-replace function for **string** objects. As you will see, because of the support that **string** provides through **find( )** and **replace( )**, the implementation of search-and-replace is straightforward. It is also a much cleaner implementation than is the same function implemented for null-terminated strings. (See *Create a Search-and-Replace Function for Null-Terminated Strings*.)

Step-by-Step

To create a search-and-replace function for **string** objects involves these steps:

1. Create a function called **search_and_replace( )** that has this prototype:

   ```
   bool search_and_replace(string &str, const string &oldsubstr,
                           const string &newsubstr);
   ```

   The string to be changed is passed via **str**. The substring to replace is passed in **oldsubstr**. The replacement is passed in **newsubstr**.

2. Use the **find( )** function to find the first occurrence of **oldsubstr**.

3. Use the **replace( )** function to substitute **newsubstr**.

4. Return true if a replacement was made and false otherwise.

Discussion

The **find( )** method is described by the preceding recipe and that discussion is not repeated here.

   Once the substring has been found, it can be replaced by calling **replace( )**. There are ten forms of **replace( )**. The one used by this recipe is shown here:

   string &replace(size_type *indx*, size_type *len*, const string &*str*)

Beginning at *indx* within the invoking string, this version replaces up to *len* characters with the string in *str*. The reason that it replaces "up to" *len* characters is that it is not possible to replace past the end of the string. Thus, if *len* + *indx* exceeds the total length of the string, then only those characters from *indx* to the end will be replaced. The function returns a reference to the invoking string.

Example

Here is one way to implement the **search_and_replace( )** function:

```
// In the string referred to by str, replace oldsubstr with newsubstr.
// Thus, this function modifies the string referred to by str.
// It returns true if a replacement occurs and false otherwise.
bool search_and_replace(string &str, const string &oldsubstr,
                        const string &newsubstr) {
  string::size_type startidx;

  startidx = str.find(oldsubstr);

  if(startidx != string::npos) {
    str.replace(startidx, oldsubstr.size(), newsubstr);
    return true;
  }

  return false;
}
```

If you compare this version of **search_and_replace( )** with the one created for null-terminated strings, you will see that this version is substantially smaller and simpler. There are two reasons for this. First, because objects of type **string** are dynamic, they can grow or shrink as needed.

Therefore, it is easy to replace one substring with another. There is no need to worry about overrunning an array boundary when the length of the string is increased, for example. Second, **string** supplies a **replace( )** function that automatically handles the removal of the old substring and the insertion of the new substring. This does not need to be handled manually, as is the case when inserting into a null-terminated string.

The following example shows the **search_and_replace( )** function in action.

```cpp
// Implement search-and-replace for string objects.
#include <iostream>
#include <string>

using namespace std;

bool search_and_replace(string &str, const string &oldsubstr,
                        const string &newsubstr);

int main()
{

  string str = "This is a test. So is this.";

  cout << "Original string: " << str << "\n\n";

  cout << "Replacing 'is' with 'was':\n";

  // The following replaces is with was. Notice that
  // it passes string literals for the substrings.
  // These are automatically converted into string objects.
  while(search_and_replace(str, "is", "was"))
   cout << str << endl;

  cout << endl;

  // Of course, you can explicitly pass string objects, too.
  string oldstr("So");
  string newstr("So too");
  cout << "Replace 'So' with 'So too'" << endl;
  search_and_replace(str, oldstr, newstr);
  cout << str << endl;

  return 0;
}

// In the string referred to by str, replace oldsubstr with newsubstr.
// Thus, this function modifies the string referred to by str.
// It returns true if a replacement occurs and false otherwise.
bool search_and_replace(string &str, const string &oldsubstr,
                        const string &newsubstr) {
  string::size_type startidx;

  startidx = str.find(oldsubstr);
```

```
  if(startidx != string::npos) {
    str.replace(startidx, oldsubstr.size(), newsubstr);
    return true;
  }

  return false;
}
```

The output is shown here:

```
Original string: This is a test. So is this.

Replacing 'is' with 'was':
Thwas is a test. So is this.
Thwas was a test. So is this.
Thwas was a test. So was this.
Thwas was a test. So was thwas.

Replace 'So' with 'So too'
Thwas was a test. So too was thwas.
```

Options and Alternatives

The **replace( )** function has several other forms. Three more commonly used forms are described here. All return a reference to the invoking string.

The following form of **replace( )** takes a null-terminated string as the replacement string:

string &replace(size_type *indx*, size_type *len*, const char **str*)

Beginning at *indx* within the invoking string, it replaces up to *len* characters with the string in *str*.

To replace a substring with a portion of another string, use this form:

string &replace(size_type *indx1*, size_type *len1*, const string &*str*,
                size_type *indx2*, size_type *len2*)

It replaces up to *len1* characters in the invoking string, beginning at *indx1*, with the *len2* characters from the string in *str*, beginning at *indx2*.

The next form of **replace( )** operates on iterators:

string &replace(iterator *start*, iterator *end*, const string &*str*)

The range specified by *start* and *end* is replaced with the characters in *str*.

The **search_and_replace( )** function operates in a case-sensitive manner. It is possible to perform a case-insensitive search-and-replace, but it takes a little work. One way is to implement a case-insensitive search function that uses the standard **search( )** STL algorithm. This algorithm lets you specify a binary predicate that can be tailored to test two characters for equality in a case-independent manner. You can then use this function to find the location of the substring to be removed. To see this approach in action, see *Create Case-Insensitive Search and Search-and-Replace Functions for* **string** *Objects*.

Operate on string Objects Through Iterators

Key Ingredients		
Headers	Classes	Functions
<string>	string	iterator begin( )
		iterator end( )
		reverse_iterator rbegin( )
		reverse_iterator rend( )
		iterator erase(iterator *start*, iterator *end*)
		template <class InIter>
		void insert(iterator *itr*, InIter *start*,
		InIter *end*)
		string &replace(iterator *start*,
		iterator *end*,
		const char **str*)
<algorithm>		template <class InIter, class T>
		InIter find(InIter *start*,
		InIter *end*,
		const T &*val*)
		template <class InIter, class OutIter,
		class Func>
		OutIter transform(InIter *start*,
		InIter *end*,
		OutIter *result*,
		Func *unaryFunc*)

This recipe shows how to use iterators with objects of type **string**. As most readers will know, iterators are objects that act much like pointers. They give you the ability to refer to the contents of a container by using a pointer-like syntax. They are also the mechanism that lets different types of containers be handled in the same way and enables different types of containers to exchange data. They are one of C++'s most powerful concepts.

As explained in the overview of **string** near the start of this chapter, **basic_string** fulfills the basic requirements of a container. Therefore, the **string** specialization of **basic_string** is, essentially, a container for characters. One of the requirements of all containers is that they support iterators. By supporting iterators, **string** gains three important benefits:

1. Iterators can streamline some types of **string** operations.
2. Iterators enable **string** objects to be operated on by the various STL algorithms.
3. Iterators enable **string** to be compatible with other STL containers. For example, through iterators, you can copy the characters in a **string** into a **vector** or construct a **string** from characters stored in a **deque**.

The **string** class supports all basic iterator operations. It also provides versions of several of the functions, such as **insert( )** and **replace( )**, that are designed to work through iterators. This recipe demonstrates the basic iterator operations and three iterator-enabled functions, and shows how iterators enable **string** to be integrated into the overall framework of the STL.

NOTE *For a detailed discussion of iterators, see Chapter 3, which presents STL-based recipes.*

Step-by-Step

To operate on a string through iterators involves these steps:

1. Declare a variable that will hold an iterator. To do this, you must use one of the iterator types defined by **string**, such as **iterator** or **reverse_iterator**.

2. To obtain an iterator to the start of a string, call **begin( )**.

3. To obtain an iterator to the end of a string, call **end( )**.

4. To obtain a reverse iterator to the start of the reversed string, call **rbegin( )**.

5. To obtain a reverse iterator to the end of the reversed string, call **rend( )**.

6. You can cycle through the characters in a string through an iterator in much the same way that you can use a pointer to cycle through the elements of an array.

7. You can create a **string** object that is initialized with the characters pointed to by a range of iterators. Among other uses, this lets you construct a **string** that contains elements from another type of container, such as a **vector**.

8. Many of the functions defined by **string** define versions that operate through iterators. The ones demonstrated by this recipe are **erase( )**, **insert( )**, and **replace( )**. They enable you to remove, insert, or replace characters within a string given iterators to the endpoints of the characters.

9. Because the STL algorithms work through iterators, you can use any of the algorithms on objects of type **string**. Two are demonstrated here: **find( )** and **transform( )**. They require the **<algorithm>** header.

Discussion

A general overview of iterators is presented in Chapter 3, and that information is not repeated here. However, it is useful to review a few key points. First, the object pointed to by an iterator is accessed via the * operator in just the way that the * is used to access the object pointed to by a pointer. As it applies to **string**, the object pointed to by an iterator is a **char** value. Second, when an iterator is incremented, it points to the next object in the container. When it is decremented, it points to the previous object. For **string**, this means that the iterator points to the next or previous character.

There are two basic styles of iterators supported by **string**: forward and reverse. When incremented, a forward iterator moves towards the end of the string and when decremented, it moves towards the start of the string. A reverse iterator works oppositely. When a reverse iterator is incremented, it moves towards the start of the string and when decremented, it moves towards the end of the string. Of these two basic iterators, the **string** class declares four basic types of iterators that have the following type names:

iterator	Forward-moving iterator that can read and write what it points to.
const_iterator	Forward-moving iterator that is read-only.
reverse_iterator	Reverse-moving iterator that can read and write what it points to.
const_reverse_iterator	Reverse-moving iterator that is read-only.

This recipe uses only **iterator** and **reverse_iterator**, but the other two work in the same way, except that the object to which they point cannot be written.

In the discussions that follow, the generic type names **InIter** and **OutIter** are used by some of the functions. In this book, **InIter** is an iterator type that is, at minimum, capable of read operations. **OutIter** is an iterator type that is, at minimum, capable of write operations. (Other types of iterators are discussed in Chapter 3.)

To declare an iterator to a **string**, use one of the aforementioned types. For example:

```
string::iterator itr;
```

declares a non-**const** forward iterator that can be used with a **string** object.

To obtain an iterator to the start of a string (which is the first character in the string), call **begin( )**. To obtain an iterator that points *one past* the end of the string, call **end( )**. Thus, the last character in the string is at **end( )** −1. These functions are shown here:

iterator begin( )
iterator end( )

The advantage to having **end( )** return an iterator to one past the last character is that very efficient loops can be written that cycle through all the characters in a string. Here is an example:

```
string::iterator itr;
for(itr = str.begin(); itr != str.end(); ++itr) {
  // ...
}
```

When **itr** equals **end( )**, all of the characters in **str** have been examined.

When using a reverse iterator, you can obtain a reverse iterator to the last character in the string by calling **rbegin( )**. To obtain a reverse iterator to one before the first character in the string, call **rend( )**. They are shown here:

reverse_iterator rbegin( )
reverse_iterator rend( )

A reverse iterator is used in just the same way that you use a regular iterator. The only difference is that it moves through the string in the reverse direction.

The **string** class provides a constructor that lets you create a string that is initialized by characters pointed to by iterators. It is shown here:

template <class InIter> string(InIter *start*, InIter *end*,
                       const Allocator &*alloc* = Allocator( ))

The range of characters is specified by *start* and *end*. The type of these iterators is specified by the generic type **InIter**, which indicates that the iterators must support read operations. However, they do not have to be of type **string::iterator**. This means that you can use this constructor to create a string that contains characters from another container, such as a **vector**.

Several of **string**'s functions have overloaded forms that use iterators to access the contents of the string. Three representative ones are used by this recipe: **insert( )**, **erase( )**, and **replace( )**. The versions used by this recipe are shown here:

iterator erase(iterator *start*, iterator *end*)
string &replace(iterator *start*, iterator *end*, const char **str*)
template <class InIter>
    void insert(iterator *itr*, InIter *start*, InIter *end*)

The **erase( )** method removes the characters in the range pointed to by *start* to *end*. It returns an iterator to the character that follows the last character removed. The **replace( )** function replaces the characters in the range specified by *start* and *end* with *str*. It returns a reference to the invoking object. (Other iterator-enabled versions of **replace( )** let you pass a **string** to *str*.) The **insert( )** method inserts the characters in the range pointed to by *start* and *end* immediately before the element specified by *itr*. In **insert( )**, notice that *start* and *end* are of the generic type **InIter**, which means that the iterators must support read operations. All **string** iterator types satisfy this constraint. So do many other iterators. Thus, you can insert characters from another type of container into a **string**. This is one of the advantages of iterators.

Because the STL algorithms work through iterators, you can use these algorithms on **string**s. The STL algorithms are declared in **<algorithm>**, and they perform various operations on containers. This recipe demonstrates the use of two algorithms, **find( )** and **transform( )**, which are shown here:

template <class InIter, class T>
    InIter find(InIter *start*, InIter *end*, const T &*val*)

template <class InIter, class OutIter, class Func>
    OutIter transform(InIter *start*, InIter *end*, OutIter *result*, Func *unaryFunc*)

The **find( )** algorithm searches the range pointed to by *start* and *end* for the value specified by *val*. It returns an iterator to the first occurrence of the element or to *end* if the value is not in the sequence. The **transform( )** algorithm applies a function to a range of elements specified by *start* and *end*, putting the outcome in *result*. The function to be applied is specified by *unaryFunc*. This function receives a value from the sequence and must return its transformation. Thus, both the parameter type and the return type must be compatible with the type of objects stored in the container, which in the case of **string** is **char**. The **transform( )** algorithm returns an iterator to the end of the resulting sequence. Notice that result is of type **OutIter**, which means that it must support write operations.

Example

The following example shows how to use iterators with **string** objects. It also demonstrates iterator versions of **string**'s member functions **insert( )**, **replace( )**, and **find( )**. The STL algorithms **find( )** and **transform( )** also are used.

```cpp
// Demonstrate iterators with strings.
#include <iostream>
#include <string>
#include <cctype>
#include <algorithm>
#include <vector>

using namespace std;

int main()
{
  string strA("This is a test.");

  // Create an iterator to a string.
  string::iterator itr;

  // Use an iterator to cycle through the characters
  // of a string.
  cout << "Display a string via an iterator.\n";
  for(itr = strA.begin(); itr != strA.end(); ++itr)
    cout << *itr;
  cout << "\n\n";

  // Use a reverse iterator to display the string in reverse.
  cout << "Display a string in reverse using a reverse iterator.\n";
  string::reverse_iterator ritr;
  for(ritr = strA.rbegin(); ritr != strA.rend(); ++ritr)
    cout << *ritr;
  cout << "\n\n";

  // Insert into a string via an iterator.

  // First, use the STL find() algorithm to obtain
  // an iterator to the start of the first 'a'.
  itr = find(strA.begin(), strA.end(), 'a');

  // Next, increment the iterator so that it points to the
  // character after 'a', which in this case is a space.
  ++itr;

  // Insert into str by using the iterator version of insert().
  cout <<"Insert into a string via an iterator.\n";
  string strB(" bigger");
  strA.insert(itr, strB.begin(), strB.end());
  cout << strA << "\n\n";

  // Now, replace 'bigger' with 'larger'.
  cout << "Replace bigger with larger.\n";
  itr = find(strA.begin(), strA.end(), 'b');
  strA.replace(itr, itr+6, "larger");
  cout << strA << "\n\n";
```

```
  // Now, remove ' larger'.
  cout << "Remove ' larger'.\n";
  itr = find(strA.begin(), strA.end(), 'l');
  strA.erase(itr, itr+7);
  cout << strA << "\n\n";

  // Use an iterator with the STL transform() algorithm to convert
  // a string to uppercase.
  cout << "Use the STL transform() algorithm to convert a "
       << "string into uppercase.\n";
  transform(strA.begin(), strA.end(), strA.begin(), toupper);
  cout << strA << "\n\n";

  // Create a string from a vector<char>.
  vector<char> vec;
  for(int i=0; i < 10; ++i)
    vec.push_back('A'+i);

  string strC(vec.begin(), vec.end());
  cout << "Here is strC, which is constructed from a vector:\n";
  cout << strC << endl;

  return 0;
}
```

The output is shown here:

```
Display a string via an iterator.
This is a test.

Display a string in reverse using a reverse iterator.
.tset a si sihT

Insert into a string via an iterator.
This is a bigger test.

Replace bigger with larger.
This is a larger test.

Remove ' larger'.
This is a test.

Use the STL transform() algorithm to convert a string into uppercase.
THIS IS A TEST.

Here is strC, which is constructed from a vector:
ABCDEFGHIJ
```

Options and Alternatives

As mentioned, several of the member functions defined by **string** have forms that operate on or return iterators. In addition to **insert( )**, **erase( )**, and **replace( )** used by this recipe,

string provides iterator-enabled versions of the **append( )** and **assign( )** functions. They are shown here:

> template<class InIter> string &append(InIter *start*, InIter *end*)
> template<class InIter> string &assign(InIter *start*, InIter *end*)

This version of **append( )** adds the sequence specified by *start* and *end* onto the end of the invoking string. This version of **assign( )** assigns the sequence specified by *start* and *end* to the invoking string. Both return a reference to the invoking string.

Create Case-Insensitive Search and Search-and-Replace Functions for string Objects

Key Ingredients		
Headers	**Classes**	**Functions**
<cctype>		int tolower(int *ch*)
<string>	string	iterator begin( )
		iterator end( )
		string &replace(iterator *start*, iterator *end*, const string &*newsubtr*)
<algorithm>		template <class ForIter1, class ForIter2, class BinPred> ForItrer1 search(ForIter1 *start1*, ForIter1 *end1*, ForIter2 *start2*, ForIter2 *end2*, BinPred *pfn*)

Although **string** is very powerful, it does not directly support two very useful functions. The first is a search function that ignores case differences. As virtually all readers know, case-insensitive searching is both a common and valuable feature in many contexts. For example, when searching a document for occurrences of the word "this", you usually want to find "This", too. The second function is a case-insensitive search-and-replace function, which replaces one substring with another independently of case differences. You could use such a function, for example, to replace all instances of "www" or "WWW" with the words "World Wide Web" in a single step. Whatever the purpose, it is easy to create case-insensitive search-and-replace functions that operate on **string** objects. This recipe shows one way.

The functions developed by this recipe rely on iterators to access the characters within a string. Because **string** is an STL-compatible container, it provides support for iterators. This support is particularly important because it enables a **string** to be operated on by the STL algorithms. This ability significantly expands the ways in which strings can be manipulated.

It also enables you to create streamlined solutions to what would otherwise be more challenging tasks. (See the preceding recipe for information on using iterators with **string**.)

Step-by-Step

One way to create a search function that ignores case differences involves these steps:

1. Create a comparison function called **comp_ign_case( )** that performs a case-insensitive comparison of two **char** values. Here is its prototype:

   ```
   bool comp_ign_case(char x, char y);
   ```

   Have the function return true if the two characters are equal and false otherwise.

2. Create a function called **search_ign_case( )** that has this prototype:

   ```
   string::iterator search_ign_case(string &str, const string &substr);
   ```

   The string to be searched is passed in **str**. The substring to search for is passed in **substr**.

3. Inside **search_ign_case( )**, use the STL algorithm **search( )** to search a string for a substring. This algorithm searches one sequence for an occurrence of another. The sequences are specified by ranges of iterators. Specify the **comp_ign_case( )** function created in Step 1 as the binary predicate that determines when one character equals another. This enables **search( )** to ignore case differences when searching. Note that **search( )** is declared in the **<algorithm>** header, which must be included.

4. Have **search_ign_case( )** return an iterator to the start of the first match or **str.end( )** if no match is found.

To create a search-and-replace function that ignores case differences, follow these steps:

1. You will need the **search_ign_case( )** function described by the preceding steps. Therefore, if you have not yet created **search_ign_case( )**, you must do so at this time.

2. Create a function called **search_and_replace_ign_case( )** that has this prototype:

   ```
   bool search_and_replace_ign_case(string &str, const string &oldsubstr,
                                     const string &newsubstr);
   ```

   The string to be modified is passed in **str**. The sequence to be replaced is passed in **oldsubstr**. The string to substitute is passed in **newsubstr**.

3. Use **search_ign_case( )** to find the first occurrence of **oldsubstr** within **str**.

4. Use the iterator version of **string**'s **replace( )** function to replace the first occurrence of **oldsubstr** with **newsubstr**.

5. Have **search_and_replace_ign_case( )** return true if the replacement is made and false if **str** did not contain an occurrence of **oldsubstr**.

Discussion

Before you can use the **search( )** algorithm to perform a case-insensitive search, you must create a function that compares two **char** values in a case-independent manner. It must return true if the characters are equal and false otherwise. In the language of the STL, such a function is called a *binary predicate*. (See Chapter 3 for a discussion of binary predicates.)

This function is used by the **search( )** algorithm to compare two elements. By having this function ignore case differences, the search will be conducted independently of case. Here is one way to code this function:

```
bool comp_ign_case(char x, char y) {
  return tolower(x) == tolower(y);
}
```

Notice that this uses the standard **tolower( )** function to obtain the lowercase equivalent of each character. (See *Ignore Case Differences When Comparing Null-Terminated Strings* for details on **tolower( )**.) By converting each argument to lowercase, case differences are eliminated.

To find a substring, call the **search( )** algorithm. The version used by this recipe is shown here:

> template <class ForIter1, class ForIter2, class BinPred>
> ForItrer1 search(ForIter1 *start1*, ForIter1 *end1*,
> ForIter2 *start2*, ForIter2 *end2*,
> BinPred *pfn*)

It searches for an occurrence of the sequence specified by *start2* and *end2* within the range of the sequence specified by *start1* and *end1*. In this book, the generic type names **ForIter1** and **ForIter2** indicate iterators that have read/write capabilities and that can move in the forward direction. The binary predicate *pfn* determines when two elements are equal. (In this book, the generic type name **BinPred** indicates a binary predicate.) For the purposes of this recipe, pass **comp_ign_case** to this parameter. If a match is found, the function returns an iterator to the start of the matching sequence. Otherwise, *end1* is returned.

The **search_and_replace_ign_case( )** function uses the iterator returned by **search_ign_case( )** to find the location at which to substitute one substring for another. To handle the actual replacement, you can use this version of **string**'s **replace( )** function, which operates through iterators:

> string &replace(iterator *start*, iterator *end*, const string &*newsubstr*)

It replaces the range specified by *start* and *end* with *newsubstr*. Thus, the invoking string is modified. It returns a reference to the invoking string.

Example

Here is one way to create the **search_ign_case( )** function. It uses **comp_ign_case( )** to determine when two characters are equal.

```
// Ignore case when searching for a substring.
// The string to search is passed in str. The substring to search
// for is passed in substr. It returns an iterator to the start of
// the match or str.end() if no match is found.
//
// Notice that it uses the search() algorithm and specifies the
// binary predicate comp_ign_case().
string::iterator search_ign_case(string &str, const string &substr) {
  return search(str.begin(), str.end(),
                substr.begin(), substr.end(),
                comp_ign_case);
}
```

As the comments indicate, **search_ign_case( )** finds (independently of case differences) the first occurrence of **substr** and returns an iterator to the start of the matching sequence. It returns **str.end( )** if no match is found.

Here is one way to implement **search_and_replace_ign_case( )**. Notice that it uses **search_ign_case( )** to find the substring to replace.

```
// This function replaces the first occurrence of oldsubstr with
// newsubstr in the string passed in str. It returns true if a
// replacement occurs and false otherwise.
//
// Notice that this function modifies the string referred to by str.
// Also notice that it uses search_ign_case() to find the substring
// to replace.
bool search_and_replace_ign_case(string &str, const string &oldsubstr,
                       const string &newsubstr) {
  string::iterator startitr;

  startitr = search_ign_case(str, oldsubstr);

  if(startitr != str.end()) {
    str.replace(startitr, startitr+oldsubstr.size(), newsubstr);
    return true;
  }

  return false;
}
```

This function replaces the first occurrence of **oldsubstr** with **newsubstr**. It returns true if a replacement occurs (that is, if **str** contains **oldsubstr**) and false otherwise. As the comments indicate, this function modifies **str** in the process. It uses **search_ign_case( )** to find the first occurrence of **oldsubstr**. Therefore, the search is performed independently of case differences.

The following example shows both **search_ign_case( )** and **search_and_replace_ign_case( )** in action:

```
// Implement case-insensitive search and search-and-replace
// for string objects.
#include <iostream>
#include <string>
#include <cctype>
#include <algorithm>

using namespace std;

bool comp_ign_case(char x, char y);
string::iterator search_ign_case(string &str, const string &substr);
bool search_and_replace_ign_case(string &str, const string &oldsubstr,
                       const string &newsubstr);

int main()
{
  string strA("This is a test of case-insensitive searching.");
  string strB("test");
```

```
  string strC("TEST");
  string strD("testing");

  cout << "First, demonstrate search_ign_case().\n";
  cout << "String to be searched:\n" << strA << "\n\n";

  cout << "Searching for " << strB << ". ";
  if(search_ign_case(strA, strB) != strA.end())
    cout << "Found!\n";

  cout << "Searching for " << strC << ". ";
  if(search_ign_case(strA, strC) != strA.end())
    cout << "Found!\n";

  cout << "Searching for " << strD << ". ";
  if(search_ign_case(strA, strD) != strA.end())
    cout << "Found!\n";
  else
    cout << "Not Found.\n";

  // Use the iterator returned by search_ign_case() to display
  // the remainder of the string.
  cout << "\nRemainder of string after finding 'of':\n";
  string::iterator itr = search_ign_case(strA, "of");
  while(itr != strA.end())
    cout << *itr++;
  cout << "\n\n";

  // Now, demonstrate search and replace.
  strA = "Alpha Beta Gamma alpha beta gamma";
  cout << "Now demonstrate search_and_replace_ign_case().\n";
  cout << "String that will receive replacements:\n" << strA << "\n\n";
  cout << "Replacing all occurrences of alpha with zeta:\n";
  while(search_and_replace_ign_case(strA, "alpha", "zeta"))
    cout << strA << endl;

  return 0;
}

// Ignore case when searching for a substring.
// The string to search is passed in str. The substring to search
// for is passed in substr. It returns an iterator to the start of
// the match or str.end() if no match is found.
//
// Notice that it uses the search() algorithm and specifies the
// binary predicate comp_ign_case().
string::iterator search_ign_case(string &str, const string &substr) {
  return search(str.begin(), str.end(),
                substr.begin(), substr.end(),
                comp_ign_case);
}

// Ignore case when comparing two characters for equality.
```

```
// Return true if the characters are equal, independently
// of case differences.
bool comp_ign_case(char x, char y) {
  return tolower(x) == tolower(y);
}

// This function replaces the first occurrence of oldsubstr with
// newsubstr in the string passed in str. It returns true if a
// replacement occurs and false otherwise.
//
// Note that this function modifies the string referred to by str.
// Also note that it uses search_ign_case() to find the substring
// to replace.
bool search_and_replace_ign_case(string &str, const string &oldsubstr,
                      const string &newsubstr) {
  string::iterator startitr;

  startitr = search_ign_case(str, oldsubstr);

  if(startitr != str.end()) {
    str.replace(startitr, startitr+oldsubstr.size(), newsubstr);
    return true;
  }

  return false;
}
```

The output is shown here:

```
First, demonstrate search_ign_case().
String to be searched:
This is a test of case-insensitive searching.

Searching for test. Found!
Searching for TEST. Found!
Searching for testing. Not Found.

Remainder of string after finding 'of':
of case-insensitive searching.

Now demonstrate search_and_replace_ign_case().
String that will receive replacements:
Alpha Beta Gamma alpha beta gamma

Replacing all occurrences of alpha with zeta:
zeta Beta Gamma alpha beta gamma
zeta Beta Gamma zeta beta gamma
```

Options and Alternatives

Although I personally favor implementing a case-insensitive search through the use of the
STL **search( )** algorithm as this recipe does, there is another approach. You can implement

such a search function yourself, working character by character and manually attempting to find a matching substring. Here is one way to do this:

```
// Implement search_ign_case() manually.
// Like the original version, the string to search is passed in str
// and the substring to search for is passed in substr.
// It returns an iterator to the start of the match or str.end()
// if no match is found.
string::iterator search_ign_case(string &str, const string &substr) {
  string::iterator start1, found_at;
  string::const_iterator start2;

  // If the string to match is null, return an iterator to
  // the start of str.
  if(substr.begin() == substr.end()) return str.begin();

  start1 = found_at = str.begin();
  while(start1 != str.end()) {
    start2 = substr.begin();
    while(tolower(*start1) == tolower(*start2)) {
      ++start1;
      ++start2;
      if(start2 == substr.end()) return found_at;
      if(start1 == str.end()) return str.end();
    }

    ++found_at;
    start1 = found_at;
  }
  return str.end();
}
```

As you can see, the manual approach involves much more code. Furthermore, developing and testing this function takes more time than does using the STL **search( )** algorithm. Finally, no attempt was made to optimize the preceding code. Optimization also takes a significant amount of time. For these reasons, I prefer the STL algorithms over a "home grown" approach in most cases.

The **tolower( )** function converts characters based on the current locale. To compare characters for a different locale, you can use a version of **tolower( )** that is declared within **<locale>**.

Although there is no advantage to doing so, it is also possible to convert each character in the string to uppercase (rather than lowercase) to eliminate case differences. This is done via the **toupper( )** function, shown here:

   int toupper(int *ch*)

It works just like **tolower( )**, except that it converts characters to uppercase.

Convert a string Object into a Null-Terminated String

Key Ingredients		
Headers	**Classes**	**Functions**
<string>	string	const char *c_str( ) const

The **string** class provides easy mechanisms that convert a null-terminated string into a **string** object. For example, you can construct a string that is initialized with a null-terminated string. You can also assign a null-terminated string to a **string** object. Unfortunately, the reverse procedure is not quite as easy. The reason is that a null-terminated string is not a data type, but a convention. This means that you cannot initialize a null-terminated string with a **string** or assign a **string** to a **char *** pointer, for example. However, **string** does provide the **c_str( )** function that converts a **string** object into a null-terminated string. This recipe shows the process.

Step-by-Step

To obtain a null-terminated string that contains the same character sequence as that encapsulated by a **string** object, follow these steps:

1. Create an array of **char** that is large enough to hold the characters contained in the **string** object, plus the null terminator. This can be a statically declared array or an array that is dynamically allocated via **new**.
2. To obtain a pointer to a null-terminated string that corresponds to the string contained in a **string** object, call **c_str( )**.
3. Copy the null-terminated string obtained in Step 2 into the array created in Step 1.

Discussion

To obtain a null-terminated string representation of the character sequence stored in a **string** object, call **c_str( )**, shown here:

    const char *c_str( ) const

Although the character sequence in a **string** is not necessarily null-terminated, the pointer returned by a call to **c_str( )** is guaranteed to point to a null-terminated character array that contains the same sequence. Notice, however, that the returned pointer is **const**. Thus, it cannot be used to modify the string. Furthermore, this pointer is valid only until a non-**const** member function is called on the same **string** object. As a result, you will usually want to copy the null-terminated string into another array.

Example

The following example shows how to convert a string object into a null-terminated string:

```
// Convert a string object into a null-terminated string.
#include <iostream>
#include <string>
```

```
#include <cstring>

using namespace std;

int main()
{
  string str("This is a test.");
  char cstr[80];

  cout << "Here is the original string:\n";
  cout << str << "\n\n";

  // Obtain a pointer to the string.
  const char *p = str.c_str();

  cout << "Here is the null-terminated version of the string:\n";
  cout << p << "\n\n";


  // Copy the string into a statically allocated array.
  //
  // First, confirm that the array is long enough
  // to hold the string.
  if(sizeof(cstr) < str.size() + 1) {
    cout << "Array is too small to hold the string.\n";
    return 0;
  }
  strcpy(cstr, p);
  cout << "Here is the string copied into cstr:\n" << cstr << "\n\n";


  // Next,copy the string into a dynamically allocated array.
  try {
    // Dynamically allocate the array.
    char *p2 = new char[str.size()+1];

    // Copy the string into the array.
    strcpy(p2, str.c_str());

    cout << "String after being copied into dynamically-allocated array:\n";
    cout << p2 << endl;

    delete [] p2;
  } catch(bad_alloc ba) {
    cout << "Allocation Failure\n";
    return 1;
  }

  return 0;
}
```

The output is shown here:

```
Here is the original string:
This is a test.
```

Here is the null-terminated version of the string:
This is a test.

Here is the string copied into cstr:
This is a test.

String after being copied into dynamically-allocated array:
This is a test.

Options and Alternatives

As explained, the **c_str( )** function returns a pointer to a null-terminated array of **char**. If you only need access to the characters that comprise the sequence encapsulated by a string, without the null terminator, then you can use the **data( )** function. It returns a pointer to an array of **char** that contains the characters, but that array is not null-terminated. It is shown here:

        const char *data( ) const

Because a **const** pointer is returned, you cannot use it to modify the underlying characters in the array. If you want to modify the character sequence, copy it into another array.

    Although the pointer returned by **c_str( )** is **const**, it is possible to override this by using a **const_cast**, as shown here:

```
char *p = const_cast<char *> (str.c_str());
```

After this statement executes, it would be possible to modify the character sequence pointed to by **p**. *However, doing this is not recommended!* Changing the character sequence controlled by a **string** object from code outside the object could easily cause the object to become corrupted, possibly leading to a program crash or a security breach. Therefore, changes to a **string** object must always take place through **string** member functions. You should never attempt to change the underlying sequence through a pointer returned by **c_str( )** or **data( )**. If you see a construct like this, you should consider it invalid code and take steps to remedy the situation.

Implement Subtraction for string Objects

Key Ingredients		
Headers	**Classes**	**Functions**
<string>	string	string &erase(size_type *indx* = 0, size_type *len* = npos)
		size_type find(const string &*str*, size_type *indx* = 0) const

As you know, the + operator is overloaded for objects of type **string**, and it concatenates two strings and returns the result. However, the – operator is not overloaded for **string**. Some programmers find this a bit surprising because, intuitively, one would expect the – operator to be used to remove a substring from a string, as illustrated by this sequence:

```
string strA("one two three");
string strB;
strB = strA – "two";
```

At this point, one would expect **strB** to contain the sequence "one three", which is the original sequence with the word "two" removed. Of course, this is not possible using only the operators defined for **string** by the standard library, because subtraction is not one of them. Fortunately, it is quite easy to remedy this situation, as this recipe shows.

To support substring subtraction, this recipe implements both the – and the –= operators for objects of type **string**. Each removes the first occurrence of the string on the left from the string on the right. In the case of –, the result is returned but neither operand is modified. For –=, the substring is removed from the left operand. Thus, the left operand is modified.

Step-by-Step

To overload **operator–( )** for objects of type **string** involves these steps:

1. Create a version of **operator–( )** that has the following prototype:

   ```
   string operator-(const string &left, const string &right);
   ```

   When one string is subtracted from another, the string on the left will be referred to by **left** and the string on the right will be referred to by **right**.

2. Inside **operator–( )**, create a string that will hold the result of the subtraction, and initialize that string with the character sequence in **left**.

3. Use **find( )** to find the first occurrence of **right** in the result string.

4. If a matching substring is found, use **erase( )** to remove the substring from the result string.

5. Return the resulting string.

To overload **operator–=( )** for objects of type **string** involves these steps:

1. Create a version of **operator–=( )** that has the following prototype:

   ```
   string operator-=(string &left, const string &right);
   ```

   Here, the string on the left will be referred to by **left** and the string on the right will be referred to by **right**. Furthermore, **left** will receive the result of the subtraction.

2. Inside **operator–( )**, use **find( )** to find the first occurrence of **right** in the string referred to by **left**.

3. If a matching substring is found, use **erase( )** to remove the substring from **left**. This results in **left** being modified.

4. Return **left**.

Discussion

When binary operators are overloaded by non-member functions, the operand on the left is always passed in the first parameter and the operand on the right is always passed in the second parameter. Therefore, given an **operator–( )** function with this prototype:

```
string operator-(const string &left, const string &right);
```

the expression

```
strA - strB
```

causes a reference to **strA** to be passed to **left** and a reference to **strB** to be passed to **right**. Furthermore, given an **operator–=( )** function with this prototype:

```
string operator-=(string &left, const string &right)
```

The statement

```
strA -= strB;
```

causes a reference to **strA** to be passed to **left** and a reference to **strB** to be passed to **right**.

Although there is no mechanism that enforces it, usually it is better to overload operators in a manner consistent with their normal meaning and effects. Therefore, typically, when a binary operator such as – is overloaded, the result is returned but neither operand is modified. This is in keeping with the normal usage of the – in expressions such as 10–3. In this case, the result is 7, but neither 10 nor 3 is modified. Of course, the situation is different for the –= operation. In this case, the operand on the left receives the outcome of the operation. Therefore, typically, an overloaded **operator–=( )** modifies the left operand. This recipe follows these conventions.

The actual process of removing the first occurrence of a substring is quite easy, involving only two main steps. First, **string**'s **find( )** function is called to locate the start of the first match. The **find( )** function is detailed in *Search a string Object*, but here is a brief summary. The **find( )** function has several forms. The one used here is:

size_type find(const string &*str*, size_type *indx* = 0) const

It returns the index of the first occurrence of *str* within the invoking string. The search begins at the index specified by *indx*. **npos** is returned if no match is found.

Assuming a match is found, the substring is removed by calling **erase( )**. This function is discussed in *Perform Basic Operations on string Objects*. Here is a quick recap. The **erase( )** function has three forms. The one used by this recipe is shown here:

string &erase(size_type *indx* = 0, size_type *len* = npos)

Beginning at *indx*, it removes *len* characters from the invoking string. It returns a reference to the invoking string.

When implementing **operator–( )**, neither operand should be modified. Therefore, a temporary string that will hold the result of the subtraction must be used. Initialize this string with the character sequence in the left operand. Then, remove the substring specified by the right operand. Finally, return the result.

When implementing **operator−=( )**, the left operand must contain the result of the subtraction. Therefore, remove the substring specified by the right operand from the string referred to by the left operand. Even though the left operand contains the result, you should also return the resulting string. This enables the −= operator to be used as part of a larger expression.

Example

Here is one way to implement **operator−( )** and **operator−=( )** for objects of type **string**:

```
// Overload - (subtraction) for string objects so that it removes
// the first occurrence of the substring on the right from the
// string on the left and returns the result. Neither
// operand is modified.  If the substring was not found, the
// result contains the same string as the left operand.
string operator-(const string &left, const string &right) {
  string::size_type i;
  string result(left);

  i = result.find(right);
  if(i != string::npos)
    result.erase(i, right.size());

  return result;
}

// Overload -= for string objects. It removes the first
// occurrence of the substring on the right from the string
// on the left. Thus, the string referred to by left is modified.
// The resulting string is also returned.
string operator-=(string &left, const string &right) {
  string::size_type i;

  i = left.find(right);
  if(i != string::npos)
    left.erase(i, right.size());

  return left;
}
```

The following example shows these operators in action:

```
// Implement operator-() and operator-=() for strings.
#include <iostream>
#include <string>

using namespace std;

string operator-(const string &left, const string &right);
string operator-=(string &left, const string &right);

int main()
{
```

```
  string str("This is a test.");
  string res_str;

  cout << "Contents of str: " << str << "\n\n";

  // Subtract "is" from str and put the result in res_str.
  res_str = str - "is";
  cout << "Result of str - \"is\": " << res_str << "\n\n";

  // Use -= to subtract "is" from res_str. This puts the result
  // back into res_str.
  res_str -= "is";
  cout << "Result of res_str -= \"is\": " << res_str << "\n\n";
  cout << "Here is str again: " << str
       << "\nNotice that str is unchanged by the preceding "
       << "operations." << "\n\n";

  cout << "Here are some more examples:\n\n";

  // Attempt to subtract "xyz". This causes no change.
  res_str = str - "xyz";
  cout << "Result of str - \"xyz\": " << res_str << "\n\n";

  // Remove the last three characters from str.
  res_str = str - "st.";
  cout << "Result of str - \"st.\": " << res_str << "\n\n";

  // Remove a null string, which results in no change.
  res_str = str - "";
  cout << "Result of str - \"\": " << res_str << "\n\n";

  return 0;
}

// Overload - (subtraction) for string objects so that it removes
// the first occurrence of the substring on the right from the
// string on the left and returns the result. Neither
// operand is modified.  If the substring was not found, the
// result contains the same string as the left operand.
string operator-(const string &left, const string &right) {
  string::size_type i;
  string result(left);

  i = result.find(right);
  if(i != string::npos)
    result.erase(i, right.size());

  return result;
}

// Overload -= for string objects. It removes the first
// occurrence of the substring on the right from the string
// on the left. Thus, the string referred to by left is modified.
```

```
// The resulting string is also returned.
string operator-=(string &left, const string &right) {
  string::size_type i;

  i = left.find(right);
  if(i != string::npos)
    left.erase(i, right.size());

  return left;
}
```

The output is shown here:

```
Contents of str: This is a test.

Result of str - "is": Th is a test.

Result of res_str -= "is": Th  a test.

Here is str again: This is a test.
Notice that str is unchanged by the preceding operations.

Here are some more examples:

Result of str - "xyz": This is a test.

Result of str - "st.": This is a te

Result of str - "": This is a test.
```

Options and Alternatives

The versions of **operator–( )** and **operator–=( )** described by the recipe remove only the first occurrence of the substring on the right from the string on the left. However, with a bit of work, you can change their operation so that they remove all occurrences of the substring. Here is one approach:

```
// Overload - (subtraction) for string objects so that it removes
// ALL occurrences of the substring on the right from the
// string on the left. The result is returned. Neither operand
// is modified.
string operator-(const string &left, const string &right) {
  string::size_type i;
  string result(left);

  if(right != "") {
    do {
      i = result.find(right);
      if(i != string::npos)
        result.erase(i, right.size());
    } while(i != string::npos);
  }
```

```
    return result;
}

// Overload -= for string objects so that it removes
// ALL occurrences of the substring on the right from the string
// on the left. The result is contained in the string referred
// to by the left operand. Thus, the left operand is modified.
// The resulting string is also returned.
string operator-=(string &left, const string &right) {
  string::size_type i;

  if(right != "") {
    do {
      i = left.find(right);
      if(i != string::npos)
        left.erase(i, right.size());
    } while(i != string::npos);
  }

  return left;
}
```

Another option that you may find helpful in some cases is to implement string subtraction so that it operates independently of case differences. To do this, use the approach described in *Create Case-Insensitive Search and Search-and-Replace Functions for **string** Objects* to perform a case-insensitive search to find the substring to remove.

CHAPTER 3

Working with STL Containers

This is the first of two chapters that present recipes that use the Standard Template Library (STL). Two chapters are needed because the STL is an extraordinarily large and important part of C++. Not only does it provide off-the-shelf solutions to some of programming's most challenging problems, it also redefines the way in which one approaches many common tasks. For example, instead of having to provide your own code for a linked list, you can use the STL's **list** class. If your program needs to associate a key with a value and provide a means of finding that value given the key, it can use the **map** class. Because the STL provides solid, debugged implementations of the most commonly used "data engines," you can use one whenever it is needed, without going through the time and trouble to develop your own.

This chapter starts with an overview of the STL and then presents recipes that demonstrate the core of the STL: its containers. In the process, it shows how iterators are used to access and cycle through the contents of a container. The following chapter shows how to use algorithms and several other key components of the STL.

Here are the recipes contained in this chapter:

- Basic Sequence Container Techniques
- Use **vector**
- Use **deque**
- Use **list**
- Use the Sequence Container Adaptors: **stack**, **queue**, and **priority_queue**
- Store User-Defined Objects in a Container
- Basic Associative Container Techniques
- Use **map**
- Use **multimap**
- Use **set** and **multiset**

NOTE *For an in-depth description of the STL, see my book* STL Programming from the Ground Up. *Much of the overview and descriptions in this chapter are adapted from that work. The STL also receives extensive coverage in my book* C++: The Complete Reference.

STL Overview

At its core, the Standard Template Library is a sophisticated set of template classes and functions that implements many popular and commonly used data structures and algorithms. For example, it includes support for vectors, lists, queues, and stacks. It also supplies many algorithms—such as sorting, searching, and merging—that operate on them. Because the STL is constructed from template classes and functions, the data structures and algorithms can be applied to nearly any type of data. This is, of course, part of its power.

The STL is organized around three foundational items: *containers, algorithms,* and *iterators.* Put simply, algorithms act on containers through iterators. More than anything else, the design and implementation of these features determine the nature of the STL. In addition to containers, algorithms, and iterators, the STL relies on several other standard elements for support: *allocators, adaptors, function objects, predicates, binders,* and *negators.* A brief description of each follows.

Containers

As the name implies, a container is an object that can hold other objects. There are several different types of containers. For example, the **vector** class defines a dynamic array, **deque** creates a double-ended queue, and **list** provides a linked list. These containers are called *sequence containers* because in STL terminology, a sequence is a linear list. The STL also defines *associative containers,* which allow efficient retrieval of values based on keys. Thus, the associative containers store key/value pairs. A **map** is an example. It stores key/value pairs in which each key is unique. This makes it easy to retrieve a specific value given its key.

Algorithms

Algorithms act on containers. Their capabilities include initializing, sorting, searching, merging, replacing, and transforming the contents of a container. Many algorithms operate on a *range* of elements within a container.

Iterators

Iterators are objects that act, more or less, like pointers. They give you the ability to cycle through the contents of a container in much the same way that you would use a pointer to cycle through an array. There are five types of iterators:

Iterator	Access Allowed
Random Access	Store and retrieve values. Elements may be accessed randomly.
Bidirectional	Store and retrieve values. Forward- and backward-moving.
Forward	Store and retrieve values. Forward-moving only.
Input	Retrieve, but not store, values. Forward-moving only.
Output	Store, but not retrieve, values. Forward-moving only.

In general, an iterator that has greater access capabilities can be used in place of one that has lesser capabilities. For example, a forward iterator can be used in place of an input iterator.

Iterators are handled just like pointers. You can increment and decrement them. You can apply the * and –> operators to them. Iterators are declared using the **iterator** type defined by the various containers.

The STL also supports reverse iterators. Reverse iterators are either bidirectional or random-access iterators that move through a sequence in the reverse direction. Thus, if a reverse iterator points to the end of a sequence, incrementing that iterator will cause it to point to one element before the end.

All iterators must support the types of pointer operations allowed by their category. For example, an input iterator class must support –>, ++, *, ==, and !=. Further, the * operator cannot be used to assign a value. By contrast, a random-access iterator must support –>, +, ++, –, ––, *, <, >, <=, >=, –=, +=, ==, !=, and [ ]. Also, the * must allow assignment. The operations that are supported for each type of iterator are shown here:

Iterator	Operations Supported
Random Access	*, –>, =, +, –, ++, – –, [ ], <, >, <=, >=, –=, +=, ==, !=
Bidirectional	*, –>, =, ++, – –, ==, !=
Forward	*, –>, =, ++, ==, !=
Input	*, –>, =, ++, ==, !=
Output	*, =, ++

When referring to the various iterator types in template descriptions, this book will use the following terms:

Term	Represents
BiIter	Bidirectional iterator
ForIter	Forward iterator
InIter	Input iterator
OutIter	Output iterator
RandIter	Random-access iterator

Allocators

Each container has defined for it an *allocator*. Allocators manage memory allocation for a container. The default allocator is an object of class **allocator**, but you can define your own allocators, if needed, for specialized applications. For most uses, the default allocator is sufficient.

Function Objects

Function objects are instances of classes that define **operator( )**. There are several predefined function objects, such as **less( )**, **greater( )**, **plus( )**, **minus( )**, **multiplies( )**, and **divides( )**. Perhaps the most widely used function object is **less( )**, which determines when one object is less than another. Function objects can be used in place of function pointers in the

STL algorithms. Function objects increase the efficiency of some types of operations and provide support for certain operations that would not otherwise be possible using only a function pointer.

Adaptors

In the most general sense, an *adaptor* transforms one thing into another. There are container adaptors, iterator adaptors, and function adaptors. An example of a container adaptor is **queue**, which adapts the **deque** container for use as a standard queue.

Predicates

Several of the algorithms and containers use a special type of function called a *predicate*. There are two variations of predicates: unary and binary. A unary predicate takes one argument. A binary predicate has two arguments. These functions return true/false results, but the precise conditions that make them return true or false are defined by you. In this book, when a unary predicate function is required, it will be notated using the type **UnPred**. When a binary predicate is required, the type **BinPred** will be used. In a binary predicate, the arguments are always in the order of *first, second*. For both unary and binary predicates, the arguments will contain values of the type of objects being stored by the container.

Some algorithms use a special type of binary predicate that compares two elements. *Comparison functions* return true if their first argument is less than their second. In this book, comparison functions will be notated using the type **Comp**.

Binders and Negators

Two other entities that populate the STL are binders and negators. A *binder* binds an argument to a function object. A *negator* returns the complement of a predicate. Both increase the versatility of the STL.

The Container Classes

At the core of the STL are its containers. They are shown in Table 3-1. Also shown are the headers necessary to use each container. As one might expect, each container has different capabilities and attributes.

Containers are implemented using template classes. For example, the template specification for the **deque** container is shown here. All containers use similar specifications.

template <class T, class Allocator = allocator<T> > class deque

Here, the generic type **T** specifies the type of objects held by the **deque**. The allocator used by the **deque** is specified by **Allocator**, which defaults to the standard allocator class. For the vast majority of applications, you will simply use the default allocator, and that is what all of the code in this chapter does. However, it is possible to define your own allocator class if a special allocation scheme is ever needed. If you are not familiar with default arguments in templates, just remember that they work in much the same way as default arguments in functions. If the generic type argument is not specified explicitly when an object is created, then the default type is used.

Container	Description	Required Header
deque	A double-ended queue.	<deque>
list	A linear list.	<list>
map	Stores key/value pairs in which each key is associated with only one value.	<map>
multimap	Stores key/value pairs in which one key may be associated with two or more values.	<map>
multiset	A set in which each element is not necessarily unique.	<set>
priority_queue	A priority queue.	<queue>
queue	A queue.	<queue>
set	A set in which each element is unique.	<set>
stack	A stack.	<stack>
vector	A dynamic array.	<vector>

TABLE 3-1   Containers Defined by the STL

Each container class includes several **typedef**s that create a set of standard type names. Several of these **typedef** names are shown here:

size_type	Some type of unsigned integer.
reference	A reference to an element.
const_reference	A **const** reference to an element.
iterator	An iterator.
const_iterator	A **const** iterator.
reverse_iterator	A reverse iterator.
const_reverse_iterator	A **const** reverse iterator.
value_type	The type of value stored in a container. Same as **T** for sequence containers.
allocator_type	The type of the allocator.
key_type	The type of a key.

As mentioned, there are two broad categories of containers: sequence and associative. The sequence containers are **vector**, **list**, and **deque**. The associative containers are **map**, **multimap**, **set**, and **multiset**. The sequence containers operate on sequences, which are essentially linear lists of objects. The associative containers operate on lists of keys. Associative containers that implement maps operate on key/value pairs and allow the retrieval of a value given its key.

The **stack**, **queue**, and **priority_queue** classes are called *container adaptors* because they use (i.e., adapt) one of the sequence containers to hold their elements. Thus, one of the sequence containers underlies the functionality provided by **stack**, **queue**, and **priority_queue**. From the programmer's perspective, the container adaptors look and act like the other containers.

Common Functionality

The STL specifies a set of requirements that all containers must satisfy. By specifying a common functionality, the STL ensures that all containers can be acted on by algorithms and that all containers can be used in a well-understood, consistent manner that is independent of the details of each container implementation. This is another major strength of the STL.

All containers must support the assignment operator. They must also support all of the logical operators. In other words, all containers must support these operators:

=, ==, <, <=, !=, >, >=

All containers must supply a constructor that creates an empty container and a copy constructor. They must supply a destructor that releases all memory used by the container and calls the destructor for every element in the container.

All containers must also support iterators. Among other advantages, this ensures that all containers can be operated on by algorithms.

All containers must provide the following functions:

iterator begin( )	Returns an iterator to the first element in the container.
const_iterator begin( ) const	Returns a **const** iterator to the first element in the container.
bool empty( ) const	Returns true if the container is empty.
iterator end( )	Returns an iterator to one past the last element in the container.
const_iterator end( ) const	Returns a **const** iterator to one past the last element in the container.
size_type max_size( ) const	Returns the maximum number of elements that the container can hold.
size_type size( ) const	Returns the number of elements currently stored in the container.
void swap(*ContainerType* c)	Exchanges the contents of two containers.

A container that supports bidirectional access to its elements is called a *reversible container*. In addition to the basic container requirements, a reversible container must also provide reverse iterators and the following functions:

reverse_iterator rbegin( )	Returns a reverse iterator to the last element in the container.
const_reverse_iterator rbegin( ) const	Returns a **const** reverse iterator to the last element in the container.
reverse_iterator rend( )	Returns a reverse iterator to one before the first element in the container.
const_reverse_iterator rend( ) const	Returns a **const** reverse iterator to one before the first element in the container.

Sequence Container Requirements

In addition to the functionality common to all containers, a sequence container adds the following functions:

void clear( )	Removes all elements in the container.
iterator erase(iterator *i*)	Removes the element pointed to by *i*. Returns an iterator to the element after the one removed.
iterator erase(iterator *start*, iterator *end*)	Removes elements in the range specified by *start* and *end*. Returns an iterator to the element that follows the last element removed.
iterator insert(iterator *i*, const T &*val*)	Inserts *val* immediately before the element specified by *i*. Returns an iterator to the element.
void insert(iterator *i*, size_type *num*, const T &*val*)	Inserts *num* copies of *val* immediately before the element specified by *i*.
template <class InIter> void insert(iterator *i*, InIter *start*, InIter *end*)	Inserts the sequence defined by *start* and *end* immediately before the element specified by *i*.

The STL also defines a set of functions for sequence containers that are optional, but often implemented. These are shown here:

reference at(size_type *idx*)	Returns a reference to the element specified by *idx*.
const_reference at(size_type *idx*) const	Returns a **const** reference to the element specified by *idx*.
reference back( )	Returns a reference to the last element in the container.
const_reference back( ) const	Returns a **const** reference to the last element in the container.
reference front( )	Returns a reference to the first element in the container.
const_reference front( ) const	Returns a **const** reference to the first element in the container.
reference operator[ ](size_type *idx*)	Returns a reference to the element specified by *idx*.
const_reference operator[ ](size_type *idx*) const	Returns a **const** reference to the element specified by *idx*.
void pop_back( )	Removes the last element in the container.
void pop_front( )	Removes the first element in the container.
void push_back(const T &*val*)	Adds an element with the value specified by *val* to the end of the container.
void push_front(const T &*val*)	Adds an element with the value specified by *val* to the beginning of the container.

Sequence containers must also supply constructors that enable a container to be initialized by elements specified by a pair of iterators or with a specified number of a specified element. Of course, a sequence container is free to supply additional functionality.

Associative Container Requirements

In addition to the functionality required of all containers, associative containers have several other requirements. First, all associative containers must support the following functions:

void clear( )	Removes all elements from the container.
size_type count(const key_type &k) const	Returns the number of times k occurs in the container.
void erase(iterator i)	Removes the element pointed to by i.
void erase(iterator start, iterator end)	Removes the elements in the range start to end.
size_type erase(const key_type &k)	Removes elements that have keys with the value k. Returns the number of elements that have been removed.
pair<iterator, iterator> equal_range(const key_type &k)	Returns a pair of iterators that point to the upper bound and the lower bound in the container for the specified key.
pair<const_iterator, const_iterator> equal_range(const key_type &k) const	Returns a pair of **const** iterators that point to the upper bound and the lower bound in the container for the specified key.
iterator find(const key_type &k)	Returns an iterator to the specified key. If the key is not found, then an iterator to the end of the container is returned.
const_iterator find(const key_type &k) const	Returns a **const** iterator to the specified key. If the key is not found, then an iterator to the end of the container is returned.
pair<iterator, bool> insert(const value_type &val)	Inserts val into the container. If the container requires unique keys, then val is inserted only if it does not already exist. If the element is inserted, **pair<iterator, true>** is returned. Otherwise, **pair<iterator, false>** is returned.
iterator insert(iterator start, const value_type &val)	Inserts val. The search for the proper insertion point begins at the element specified by start. For containers that require unique keys, elements are inserted only if they do not already exist. An iterator to the element is returned.
template <class InIter> void insert(InIter start, InIter end)	Inserts a range of elements. For containers that require unique keys, elements are inserted only if they do not already exist.
key_compare key_comp( ) const	Returns the function object that compares two keys.
iterator lower_bound(const key_type &k)	Returns an iterator to the first element with a key equal to or greater than k.
const_iterator lower_bound(const key_type &k) const	Returns a **const** iterator to the first element with a key equal to or greater than k.

iterator upper_bound(const key_type &k)	Returns an iterator to the first element with a key greater than *k*.
const_iterator upper_bound(const key_type &k) const	Returns a **const** iterator to the first element with a key greater than *k*.
value_compare value_comp( ) const	Returns the function object that compares two values.

Notice that some of the functions return a **pair** object. This is a class that encapsulates two objects. For associative containers that are maps, **value_type** represents a **pair** that encapsulates a key and value. The **pair** class is explained in detail in *Basic Associative Container Techniques*.

Associative containers must supply constructors that enable a container to be initialized by elements specified by a pair of iterators. They must also support constructors that let you specify the comparison function used to compare two keys. Of course, an associative container is free to supply additional functionality.

Performance Issues

There is one other important aspect to the STL that adds to its power and general applicability: performance guarantees. Although a compiler manufacturer is free to implement the underlying mechanism used by each container and algorithm in its own way, all implementations must conform to the performance guarantees specified by the STL. The following general performance categories are defined:

constant

linear

logarithmic

Since different containers store their contents differently, they will have different performance guarantees. For example, insertion into the middle of a **vector** takes linear time. By contrast, insertion into a **list** takes constant time. Different algorithms might also behave differently. For example, the **sort( )** algorithm executes proportional to N log N, but the **find( )** algorithm runs in linear time.

In some cases, an operation will be said to take *amortized constant time*. This is the term used to describe a situation in which an operation usually takes constant time, but occasionally requires longer. (For example, insertions onto the end of a vector normally occur in constant time, but if more memory must be allocated, then the insertion requires linear time.) If the longer operation is rare enough, then it can be thought of as being amortized over a number of shorter operations.

In general, the STL specification requires that the containers and algorithms be implemented using techniques that ensure (loosely speaking) optimal runtime performance. This is important because it guarantees to you, the programmer, that the STL building blocks meet a certain level of efficiency no matter what implementation of the STL you are using. Without such a guarantee, the performance of STL-based code would depend entirely upon each individual implementation and could vary widely.

Basic Sequence Container Techniques

Key Ingredients		
Headers	**Classes**	**Functions**
<vector>	vector	iterator begin( )
		void clear( )
		bool empty( ) const
		iterator end( )
		iterator erase(iterator *i*)
		iterator insert(iterator *i*, const T &*val*)
		reverse_iterator rbegin( )
		reverse_iterator rend( )
		size_type size( ) const
		void swap(vector<T, Allocator> &*ob*)
<vector>		template <class T, class Allocator>
		bool operator==(const vector<T, Allocator>
		&*leftop*,
		const vector<T, Allocator>
		&*rightop*)
		template <class T, class Allocator>
		bool operator<(const vector<T, Allocator>
		&*leftop*,
		const vector<T, Allocator>
		&*rightop*)
		template <class T, class Allocator>
		bool operator>(const vector<T, Allocator>
		&*leftop*,
		const vector<T, Allocator>
		&*rightop*)

All sequence containers share a common functionality. For example, all allow you to add elements to the container, remove elements from the container, or cycle through the container via an iterator. All support the assignment operator and the logical operators, and all sequence containers are constructed in the same way. This recipe describes this common functionality, showing the basic techniques that apply to all sequence containers.

This recipe shows how to:

- Create a sequence container.
- Add elements to the container.
- Determine the size of the container.
- Use an iterator to cycle through the container.

- Assign one container to another.
- Determine when one container is equivalent to another.
- Remove elements from the container.
- Exchange the elements in one container with another.
- Determine if a container is empty.

This recipe uses the **vector** container class, but only those methods common to all sequence containers are employed. Therefore, the same general principles can be applied to any sequence container type.

Step-by-Step

To create and use a sequence container involves these steps:

1. Create an instance of the desired container. In this recipe, **vector** is used, but any other sequence container could be substituted.
2. Add elements to the container by calling **insert( )**.
3. Obtain the number of elements in the container by calling **size( )**.
4. Determine if the container is empty (i.e., contains no elements) by calling **empty( )**.
5. Remove elements from the container by calling **erase( )**.
6. Remove all elements from a container by calling **clear( )**.
7. Obtain an iterator to the start of the sequence by calling **begin( )**. Obtain an iterator to one past the end of the sequence by calling **end( )**.
8. For reversible sequence containers, obtain a reverse iterator to the end of the sequence by calling **rbegin( )**. Obtain a reverse iterator to one before the start of the sequence by calling **rend( )**.
9. Cycle through the elements in the container via an iterator.
10. Exchange the contents of one container with another via **swap( )**.
11. Determine when one container is equal to, less than, or greater than another.

Discussion

Although the internal operation of the STL is quite sophisticated, using the STL is actually quite easy. In many ways, the hardest part of using the STL is deciding what type of container to use. Each offers certain benefits and trade-offs. For example, **vector** is very good when a random-access, array-like object is required and not too many insertions or deletions are required. A **list** offers low-cost insertion and deletion, but trades away speedy look-ups. A double-ended queue is supported by **deque**. This recipe uses **vector** to demonstrate the basic sequence container operations, but the program will work with either **list** or **deque**. This is one of the major advantages of the STL; all sequence containers support a base level of common functionality.

The template specification for **vector** is shown here:

template <class T, class Allocator = allocator<T> > class vector

Here, **T** is the type of data being stored and **Allocator** specifies the allocator, which defaults to the standard allocator. To use **vector**, you must include the header **<vector>**.

The **vector** class supports several constructors. The two used in this recipe are those required by all sequence containers. They are shown here:

explicit vector(const Allocator &*alloc* = Allocator( ))

vector(const vector<T, Allocator> &*ob*)

The first form constructs an empty vector. The second form is **vector**'s copy constructor.

After a container has been created, objects can be added to it. One way to do this that works for all sequence containers is to call **insert( )**. All sequence containers support at least three versions of **insert( )**. The one used here is:

iterator insert(iterator *i*, const T &*val*)

It inserts *val* into the invoking container at the point specified by *i*. It returns an iterator to the inserted element. A sequence container will automatically grow as needed when elements are added to it.

You can remove one or more elements from a sequence container by calling **erase( )**. It has at least two forms. The one used by this recipe is shown here:

iterator erase(iterator *i*)

It removes the element pointed to by *i*. It returns an iterator to the element after the one removed. To remove all elements in a container, call **clear( )**. It is shown here:

void clear( )

You can determine the number of elements in a container by calling **size( )**. To determine if a container is empty, call **empty( )**. Both functions are shown here:

bool empty( ) const

size_type size( ) const

You can obtain an iterator to the start of the sequence by calling **begin( )**. An iterator to one past the last element in the sequence is obtained by calling **end( )**. These functions are shown here:

iterator begin( )

iterator end( )

There are also **const** versions of these functions.

To declare a variable that will be used as an iterator, you must specify the iterator type of the container. For example, this declares an iterator that can point to elements within a **vector<double>**:

```
vector<double>::iterator itr;
```

It is useful to emphasize that **end( )** *does not* return an iterator that points to the last element in a container. Instead, it returns an iterator that points to *one past* the last element.

Thus, the last element in a container is pointed to by **end( )** – 1. This feature lets you write very efficient algorithms that cycle through all of the elements of a container, including the last one, using an iterator. When the iterator has the same value as the one returned by **end( )**, you know that all elements have been accessed. For example, here is a loop that cycles through all elements in a sequence container called **cont**:

```
for(itr = cont.begin(); itr != cont.end(); ++itr) // ...
```

The loop runs until **itr** equals **cont.end( )**. Thus, all elements in **cont** will have been processed.

As explained, a reversible container is one in which the elements can be traversed in reverse order (back to front). All of the built-in sequence containers are reversible. For a reversible container, you can obtain a reverse iterator to the end of the sequence by calling **rbegin( )**. An iterator to one before the first element in the sequence is obtained by calling **rend( )**. These functions are shown here:

reverse_iterator rbegin( )

reverse_iterator rend( )

There are also **const** versions of these functions. A reverse iterator is declared just like a regular iterator. For example,

```
vector<double>::reverse_iterator ritr;
```

You can use a reverse iterator to cycle through a vector in reverse order. For example, given a reverse iterator called **ritr**, here is a loop that cycles through all elements in a reversible sequence container called **cont** from back to front:

```
for(ritr = cont.rbegin(); ritr != cont.rend(); ++ritr) // ...
```

The reverse iterator **ritr** starts at the element pointed to by **rbegin( )**, which is the last element in the sequence. It runs until it equals **rend( )**, which points to an element that is one before the start of the sequence. (It is sometimes helpful to think of **rbegin( )** and **rend( )** returning iterators to the start and end of a reversed sequence.) Each time a reverse iterator is incremented, it points to the previous element. Each time it is decremented, it points to the next element.

The contents of two sequence containers can be exchanged by calling **swap( )**. Here is the way that it is defined for **vector**:

void swap(vector<T, Allocator> &*ob*)

The contents of the invoking container are exchanged with those specified by *ob*.

Example
The following example demonstrates the basic sequence container operations:

```
// Demonstrate the basic sequence container operations.
//
// This example uses vector, but the same techniques can be
// applied to any sequence container.
```

```cpp
#include <iostream>
#include <vector>

using namespace std;

void show(const char *msg, vector<char> vect);

int main() {
  // Declare an empty vector that can hold char objects.
  vector<char> v;

  // Declare an iterator to a vector<char>.
  vector<char>::iterator itr;

  // Obtain an iterator to the start of v.
  itr = v.begin();

  // Insert characters into v. An iterator to the inserted
  // object is returned.
  itr = v.insert(itr, 'A');
  itr = v.insert(itr, 'B');
  v.insert(itr, 'C');

  // Display the contents of v.
  show("The contents of v: ", v);

  // Declare a reverse iterator.
  vector<char>::reverse_iterator ritr;

  // Use a reverse iterator to show the contents of v in reverse.
  cout << "Here is v in reverse: ";
  for(ritr = v.rbegin(); ritr != v.rend(); ++ritr)
    cout << *ritr << " ";
  cout << "\n\n";

  // Create another vector that is the same as the first.
  vector<char> v2(v);
  show("The contents of v2: ",v2);
  cout << "\n";

  // Show the size of v, which is the number of elements
  // currently held by v.
  cout << "Size of v is " << v.size() << "\n\n";

  // Compare two containers.
  if(v == v2) cout << "v and v2 are equivalent.\n\n";

  // Insert more characters into v and v2. This time,
  // insert them at the end.
  cout << "Insert more characters into v and v2.\n";
  v.insert(v.end(), 'D');
  v.insert(v.end(), 'E');
  v2.insert(v2.end(), 'X');
  show("The contents of v: ", v);
```

```
    show("The contents of v2: ", v2);
    cout << "\n";

    // Determine if v is less than v2. This is a
    // lexicographical compare. Therefore, the first
    // non-matching element determines which
    // container is less than another.
    if(v < v2) cout << "v is less than v2.\n\n";

    // Now, insert Z at the start of v.
    cout << "Insert Z at the start of v.\n";
    v.insert(v.begin(), 'Z');
    show("The contents of v: ", v);
    cout << "\n";

    // Now, compare v to v2 again.
    if(v > v2) cout << "Now, v is greater than v2.\n\n";

    // Remove the first element from v2.
    v2.erase(v2.begin());
    show("v2 after removing the first element: ", v2);
    cout << "\n";

    // Create another vector.
    vector<char> v3;
    v3.insert(v3.end(), 'X');
    v3.insert(v3.end(), 'Y');
    v3.insert(v3.end(), 'Z');
    show("The contents of v3: ", v3);
    cout << "\n";

    // Exchange the contents of v and v3.
    cout << "Exchange v and v3.\n";
    v.swap(v3);
    show("The contents of v: ", v);
    show("The contents of v3: ", v3);
    cout << "\n";

    // Clear v.
    v.clear();
    if(v.empty()) cout << "v is now empty.";

    return 0;
}

// Display the contents of a vector<char> by using
// an iterator.
void show(const char *msg, vector<char> vect) {
    vector<char>::iterator itr;

    cout << msg;
    for(itr=vect.begin(); itr != vect.end(); ++itr)
        cout << *itr << " ";
    cout << "\n";
}
```

The output is shown here:

```
The contents of v: C B A
Here is v in reverse: A B C

The contents of v2: C B A

Size of v is 3

v and v2 are equivalent.

Insert more characters into v and v2.
The contents of v: C B A D E
The contents of v2: C B A X

v is less than v2.

Insert Z at the start of v.
The contents of v: Z C B A D E

Now, v is greater than v2.

v2 after removing the first element: B A X

The contents of v3: X Y Z

Exchange v and v3.
The contents of v: X Y Z
The contents of v3: Z C B A D E

v is now empty.
```

Although much of the program is self-explanatory, there are several points of interest that warrant closer examination. First, notice that no allocator is specified when the containers in the program (**v**, **v2**, and **v3**) are declared. As explained, for most uses of the STL, the default allocator is the right choice.

Next, notice how the iterator **itr** is declared by this statement:

```
vector<char>::iterator itr;
```

This declares an iterator that can be used with objects of type **vector<char>**. Each container class creates a **typedef** for **iterator**. Iterators to other types of vectors or other containers are declared in the same general way. For example,

```
vector<double>::iterator itrA;
deque<string>::iterator itrB;
```

Here, **itrA** is an iterator that can be used on **vector<double>** containers, and **itrB** applies to containers of type **deque<string>**. In general, you must declare an iterator in a way that matches both the type of the container and the type of objects contained in the container. The same goes for reverse iterators.

Next, an iterator to the start of the container is obtained by calling **begin( )**, and then the following set of calls to **insert( )** puts elements into **v**:

```
itr = v.insert(itr, 'A');
itr = v.insert(itr, 'B');
v.insert(itr, 'C');
```

Each call inserts the value immediately before the element pointed to by the iterator passed in **itr**. An iterator to the inserted item is returned. Thus, these three calls cause **v** to contain the sequence CBA.

Now, look at the **show( )** function. It is used to display the contents of a **vector<char>**. Pay special attention to the following loop:

```
for(itr=vect.begin(); itr != vect.end(); ++itr)
  cout << *itr << " ";
```

It cycles through the vector passed to **vect**, beginning with the first element and stopping when the last element has been encountered. Remember, **end( )** returns an iterator that points one element past the end of the container. Therefore, when **itr** equals **vect.end( )**, the end of the container has been reached. These types of loops are extremely common when working with the STL. Also, notice how **itr** is dereferenced via the * operator in just the same way you would dereference a pointer. In general, iterators work like pointers and are handled in essentially the same way.

Next, in **main( )**, notice how the reverse iterator **ritr** is used to cycle through the contents of **v** in reverse order. A reverse iterator works just like a normal iterator, except that it accesses the elements of the container in reverse order.

Now, notice how two containers are compared by use of the == and < operators. For sequence containers, comparisons are conducted using a lexicographical comparison of the elements. Although the term "lexicographical" literally means "dictionary order," its meaning is generalized as it relates to the STL. For container comparisons, two containers are equal if they contain the same number of elements, in the same order, and all corresponding elements are equal. Otherwise, the result of a lexicographical comparison is based on the first non-matching elements. For example, given these two sequences:

seq1: 7, 8, 9

seq2: 7, 8, 11

seq1 is less than seq2 because the first mismatch is 9 and 11, and 9 is less than 11. Because the comparison is lexicographical, seq1 is still less than seq2, even if the length of seq1 is increased to 7, 8, 9, 10, 11, 12. The first non-matching elements (in this case, 9 and 11) determine the outcome.

Options and Alternatives

In addition to the version of **insert( )** used in this recipe, all sequence containers support the two forms shown here:

void insert(iterator *i*, size_type *num*, const T &*val*)

template <class InIter> void insert(iterator *i*, InIter *start*, InIter *end*)

The first form inserts *num* copies of *val* immediately before the element specified by *i*. The second form inserts the sequence that runs from *start* to *end*–1 immediately before the element specified by *i*. Notice that *start* and *end* do not need to point into the invoking container. Thus, this form can be used to insert elements from one container into another. Furthermore, the containers do not need to be of the same kind. As long as the elements are compatible, you can insert elements from a **deque** into a **list**, for example.

There is a second form of **erase( )** that is supported by all sequence containers. It is shown here:

iterator erase(iterator *start*, iterator *end*)

This version removes elements in the range *start* to *end*–1 and returns an iterator to the element after the last element removed.

In addition to the ==, <, and > operators, all sequence containers support the <=, >=, and != logical operators.

You can find the maximum number of elements that a container can hold by calling **max_size( )**, shown here:

size_type max_size( ) const

Understand that the maximum size will vary, depending on the type of data the container holds. Also, different types of containers may (probably will) have differing maximum capacities.

As mentioned, the preceding example works for all sequence containers. To prove this, try substituting **list** or **deque** for **vector**. As you will see, the program produces the same output as before. Of course, choosing the right container is an important part of using the STL successfully. Remember, different containers have different performance guarantees. For example, inserting an element into the middle of a **deque** takes linear time. Inserting into a **list** takes constant time. Inserting into the middle of a **vector** uses linear time, but inserting on the end can occur in constant time (if no reallocation is required). In general, if there is no compelling reason to choose one container over another, the **vector** is usually the best choice because it implements what is, in essence, a dynamic array (see *Use vector*).

In some cases, you will want to use one of the sequence container adaptors, such as **queue**, **stack**, or **priority_queue**, that provides a specific functionality that you desire. For example, if you want a container that implements a classic stack, then use **stack**. For a single-ended queue, use **queue**. For a queue that is ordered according to priority, use **priority_queue**.

Use vector

Key Ingredients		
Headers	**Classes**	**Functions**
<vector>	vector	template <class InIter> void assign(InIter *start*, InIter *end*) reference at(size_type *i*) reference back( ) size_type capacity( ) const reference front( ) reference operator[ ](size_type *i*) void pop_back( ) void push_back(const T &*val*) void reserve(size_type *num*) void resize(size_type *num*, T *val* = T( ))

This recipe demonstrates **vector**, which is probably the most widely used sequence container because it implements a dynamic array. Unlike a static array, whose dimensions are fixed at compile time, a dynamic array can grow as needed during program execution. This makes **vector** an excellent choice for situations in which you need an array but don't know in advance how large it needs to be. Even though the array created by **vector** is dynamic, its elements can still be accessed using the normal array-subscripting operator [ ]. This makes it easy to drop **vector** into situations that would otherwise require an array.

NOTE   *The focus of this recipe is on the attributes and features of **vector** that make it unique. See Basic Sequence Container Techniques for information that applies to all sequence containers.*

Step-by-Step

Using **vector** involves the following steps:

1. Create a **vector** instance of the desired type and initial size.
2. Assign or obtain values to elements via the subscripting operator.
3. Use the **at( )** function as an alternative to the subscripting operator.
4. Add elements to the vector using either **insert( )** or **push_back( )**.
5. Remove elements from the end by calling **pop_back( )**.
6. Obtain a reference to the first element in the vector by calling **front( )**.

7. Obtain a reference to the last element in the vector by calling **back( )**.

8. Assign a range of elements to a vector by calling **assign( )**.

9. To obtain the current capacity of a vector, call **capacity( )**. To specify a capacity, call **reserve( )**.

10. To change the size of a vector, call **resize( )**.

Discussion

The template specification for **vector** is shown here:

template <class T, class Allocator = allocator<T> > class vector

Here, **T** is the type of data being stored and **Allocator** specifies the allocator, which defaults to the standard allocator. To use **vector**, you must include the **<vector>** header.
Here are **vector**'s constructors:

explicit vector(const Allocator &*alloc* = Allocator( ))

explicit vector(size_type *num*, const T &*val* = T ( ),
        const Allocator &*alloc* = Allocator( ))

vector(const vector<T, Allocator> &*ob*)

template <class InIter> vector(InIter *start*, InIter *end*,
        const Allocator &*alloc* = Allocator( ))

The first form constructs an empty vector. The second form constructs a vector that has *num* elements with the value *val*. The third form is **vector**'s copy constructor. The fourth form constructs a vector that contains the elements in the range *start* to *end*–1. The allocator used by the vector is specified by *alloc,* which is typically allowed to default.
   The **vector** class supports random-access iterators, and the [ ] is overloaded. This allows a **vector** object to be indexed like an array.
   The **vector** class implements all required sequence container functions and operations, such as **erase( )**, **insert( )**, **swap( )**, and the logical operators. It also provides all functions required for a reversible container. It supplies most of the optional sequence container functions. The only optional functions that it does not implement are **push_front( )** and **pop_front( )**.
   The elements within a vector can be accessed in two ways. First, and most convenient, is through the use of the [ ] subscripting operator. It is shown here:

reference operator[ ](size_type *i*)

It returns a reference to the element at the index specified by *i*. The **reference** type is a **typedef** for **T &**. (A **const** version of the function is also supplied that returns a **const_reference**.) This operator can be used to set or get the value at a specified index. Of course, the index you specify must be within the current range of the vector. Like arrays, indexing begins at zero.
   Another way to access the elements in a vector is to use the **at( )** method. It is shown here:

reference at(size_type *i*)

It returns a reference to the element at the index specified by *i*. (A **const** version of the function is also supplied that returns a **const_reference**.) This reference can be used to set or get the value at a specified index. Of course, the index you specify must be within the current range of the **vector**. Like the [ ] operator, indexing using **at( )** also begins at zero.

Although the [ ] operator is more convenient to use, the **at( )** function does offer one benefit. If an attempt is made to access an element that is outside the current bounds of the **vector**, **at( )** will throw an **out_of_range** exception. Thus, it provides bounds checking. The [ ] does not.

Although all vectors have an initial size (which can be zero), it is possible to increase that size by adding elements to the vector. There are two easy ways to do this: insert elements using the **insert( )** function and add elements to the end by calling **push_back( )**. The **insert( )** function is described in *Basic Sequence Container Techniques* and is not described further here. The **push_back( )** function is shown here:

   void push_back(const T &*val*)

It adds an element with the value specified by *val* to the end of the vector. The vector is automatically increased in size to accommodate the addition.

The complement to **push_back( )** is **pop_back( )**. It removes an element from the end of the vector. It is shown here:

   void pop_back( )

After **pop_back( )** executes, the size of the vector is reduced by one.

You can obtain a reference to the last element in the vector by calling **back( )**. A reference to the first element is returned by **front( )**. These functions are shown here:

   reference back( )

   reference front( )

The **vector** class also supplies **const** versions of these functions.

The iterator type provided by **vector** is random-access. This means that an integer value can be added to or subtracted from an iterator, enabling the iterator to point to any arbitrary element within the container. It also allows an iterator to traverse a vector in either the forward or reverse direction. The **vector** class defines two iterator types: forward and reverse iterators. Forward iterators are objects of type **iterator** or **const_iterator**. Reverse iterators are of type **reverse_iterator** or **const_reverse_iterator**.

A forward iterator to the start of a vector is obtained by calling **begin( )**, and an iterator to the end of the vector is obtained by calling **end( )**. A reverse iterator to the end of the vector is obtained by calling **rbegin( )**. A reverse iterator to one before the start of a vector is obtained by calling **rend( )**. These functions and the basic procedure required to cycle through a sequence container are described in *Basic Sequence Container Techniques*.

You can assign a new set of values to a vector by using the **assign( )** function. It has two forms. The one used by this recipe is shown here:

   template <class InIter> void assign(InIter *start*, InIter *end*)

It replaces the entire contents of the invoking vector with the values specified in the range *start* to *end*–1. Notice that *start* and *end* can be any type of input iterator. This means that you can use **assign( )** to assign values from another vector or any other type of container. The only rule is that the values must be compatible with the invoking object.

All vectors are created with an initial *capacity*. This is the number of elements that the vector can hold before more memory needs to be allocated. You can obtain the current capacity by calling **capacity( )**, shown here:

size_type capacity( ) const

It is important not to confuse capacity with size. The size of a vector, which is available by calling the standard container function **size( )**, is the number of elements that it currently holds. Capacity is how many it can hold before a reallocation must occur.

You can reserve memory for a specific number of elements by calling **reserve( )**, shown here:

void reserve(size_type *num*)

The **reserve( )** function reserves memory for at least the number of elements specified by *num*. In other words, its sets the capacity of the invoking **vector** equal to or greater than *num*. (Thus, a compiler is free to adjust the capacity upward in the interest of efficiency.) Since increasing the capacity may cause a memory reallocation, it might invalidate any pointers or references to elements within the vector. If you know in advance that a vector will be holding a specific number of elements, then using **reserve( )** will prevent unnecessary reallocations, which are costly in terms of time.

You can change the size of a vector by calling **resize( )**, shown here:

void resize(size_type *num*, T *val* = T( ))

It sets the size of the vector to that specified by *num*. If the size of the vector is increased, then elements with the value specified by *val* are added to the end. Notice that *val* defaults to the default value of the **T**. If the vector is decreased in size, then elements are removed from the end.

The **vector** class has the following performance characteristics. Inserting or deleting elements at the end of a vector takes place in amortized constant time. When occurring at the beginning or in the middle, insertions or deletions take place in linear time. As just explained, it is possible to reserve additional space in a vector by using the **reserve( )** function. By pre-allocating extra memory, you will prevent reallocations from occurring. Thus, if you manage your vectors correctly, most insertions can occur in constant time.

Access of an element via the subscripting operator takes place in constant time. In general, element access in a vector is faster than it is with any other sequence containers defined by the STL. This is why **vector** is used for dynamic arrays.

In all cases, when an insertion occurs, references and iterators to elements after the point of the insertion will be invalid. However, in some cases, including those in which the element is added to the end via a call to **push_back( )**, all references and iterators to elements may be invalid. This situation occurs only if the vector needs to allocate more memory. In this case, a *reallocation* occurs, and the contents of the vector may have to be moved to a new location. If the vector is physically moved, previous iterators and references are no longer valid. Thus, for all practical purposes, it is best to assume that iterators and references are not valid after insertions. When an element is deleted from a vector, iterators and references to elements that are after the point of the erasure are invalid.

Example

The following example shows **vector** in action:

```
// Demonstrate vector.

#include <iostream>
#include <vector>

using namespace std;

void show(const char *msg, vector<int> vect);

int main() {

  // Declare a vector that has an initial capacity of 10.
  vector<int> v(10);

  // Assign its elements some values. Notice how this is
  // done using the standard array-subscripting syntax.
  // Notice that the number of elements in the vector is
  // obtained by calling size().
  for(unsigned i=0; i < v.size(); ++i) v[i] = i*i;

  show("Contents of v: ", v);

  // Compute the average of the values. Again, notice
  // the use of the subscripting operator.
  int sum = 0;
  for(unsigned i=0; i < v.size(); ++i) sum += v[i];
  double avg = sum / v.size();
  cout << "The average of the elements is " << avg << "\n\n";

  // Add elements to the end of v.
  v.push_back(100);
  v.push_back(121);

  show("v after pushing elements onto the end: ", v);
  cout << endl;

  // Now use pop_back() to remove one element.
  v.pop_back();
  show("v after back-popping one element: ", v);
  cout << endl;

  cout << "The first and last element in v as"
       << " pointed to by begin() and end()-1:\n"
       << *v.begin() << ", " << *(v.end()-1) << "\n\n";

  cout << "The first and last element in v as"
       << " pointed to by rbegin() and rend()-1:\n"
       << *v.rbegin() << ", " << *(v.rend()-1) << "\n\n";

  // Declare an iterator to a vector<int>.
  vector<int>::iterator itr;
```

```
  // Now, declare reverse iterator to a vector<int>
  vector<int>::reverse_iterator ritr;

  // Cycle through v in the forward direction using an iterator.
  cout << "Cycle through the vector in the forward direction:\n";
  for(itr = v.begin(); itr != v.end(); ++itr)
    cout << *itr << " ";
  cout << "\n\n";
  cout << "Now, use a reverse iterator to cycle through in the"
       << " reverse direction:\n";

  // Cycle through v in the reverse direction using a reverse_iterator.
  for(ritr = v.rbegin(); ritr != v.rend(); ++ritr)
    cout << *ritr << " ";
  cout << "\n\n";

  // Create another vector that contains a subrange of v.
  vector<int> v2(v.begin()+2, v.end()-4);

  // Display the contents of v2 by using an iterator.
  show("v2 contains a subrange of v: ", v2);
  cout << endl;

  // Change the values of some of v2's elements.
  v2[1] = 100;
  v2[2] = 88;
  v2[4] = 99;
  show("After the assignments, v2 now contains: ", v2);
  cout << endl;

  // Create an empty vector and then assign it a sequence
  // that is the reverse of v.
  vector<int> v3;
  v3.assign(v.rbegin(), v.rend());
  show("v3 contains the reverse of v: ", v3);
  cout << endl;

  // Show the size and capacity of v.
  cout << "Size of v is " << v.size() << ". The capacity is "
       << v.capacity() << ".\n";

  // Now, resize v.
  v.resize(20);
  cout << "After calling resize(20), the size  of v is "
       << v.size() << " and the capacity is "
       << v.capacity() << ".\n";

   // Now, reserve space for 50 elements.
   v.reserve(50);
   cout << "After calling reserve(50), the size of v is "
        << v.size() << " and the capacity is "
        << v.capacity() << ".\n";

  return 0;
}
```

```
// Display the contents of a vector<int>.
void show(const char *msg, vector<int> vect) {
  cout << msg;
  for(unsigned i=0; i < vect.size(); ++i)
    cout << vect[i] << " ";
  cout << "\n";
}
```

The output is shown here:

```
Contents of v: 0 1 4 9 16 25 36 49 64 81
The average of the elements is 28

v after pushing elements onto the end: 0 1 4 9 16 25 36 49 64 81 100 121

v after back-popping one element: 0 1 4 9 16 25 36 49 64 81 100

The first and last element in v as pointed to by begin() and end()-1:
0, 100

The first and last element in v as pointed to by rbegin() and rend()-1:
100, 0

Cycle through the vector in the forward direction:
0 1 4 9 16 25 36 49 64 81 100

Now, use a reverse iterator to cycle through in the reverse direction:
100 81 64 49 36 25 16 9 4 1 0

v2 contains a subrange of v: 4 9 16 25 36

After the assignments, v2 now contains: 4 100 88 25 99

v3 contains the reverse of v: 100 81 64 49 36 25 16 9 4 1 0

Size of v is 11. The capacity is 15.
After calling resize(20), the size  of v is 20 and the capacity is 22.
After calling reserve(50), the size of v is 20 and the capacity is 50.
```

Most of the program is self-explanatory, but a couple of points merit further discussion. First, notice that the subscripting operator is used to assign a value to an element of a vector or to obtain the current value of an element. Thus, it works in the same way that it does when applied to an array. A key point to understand is that you can only use subscripting to access an existent element. For example, in the program, **v** initially has 10 elements. Therefore, you cannot assign a value to **v[15]**, for example. If you need to expand a vector after it is created, you should use either the **push_back( )** method, which adds a value to the end, or the **insert( )** method, which can be used to insert one or more elements anywhere in the sequence.

Secondly, notice that reverse iterators are used in two places: first, to cycle through a vector in the reverse direction, and second, in the call to **assign( )** to assign **v3** a sequence that is the reverse of the one that is in **v**. It is this second use that is of most interest. By using a reverse iterator, it is possible to obtain a reversed sequence in one step, rather than the two steps that would be required if the sequence were first copied as-is and then reversed. Reverse iterators can often streamline operations that would otherwise be somewhat cumbersome.

Options and Alternatives

There is another form of **assign( )** that lets you assign a value to a vector. It is shown here:

> void assign(size_type *num*, const T& *val*)

This version removes any elements previously held by the vector and then assigns *num* copies of *val* to the vector. This version of **assign( )** is useful when you want to re-initialize a vector to a known value, for example.

The **vector** container *does not* store elements in sorted order. However, it is possible to sort a vector by using the **sort( )** algorithm. See *Sort a Container* in Chapter 4.

In some cases, the **deque** container is a good alternative to **vector**. It has similar capabilities, such as allowing its elements to be accessed via the subscripting operator, but it has different performance characteristics. See *Use deque* for details.

The STL also contains a specialization of **vector** for **bool** values: **vector<bool>**. It includes all of the functionality of **vector** and adds these two members:

void flip( )	Reverses all bits in the vector.
static void swap(reference *i*, reference *j*)	Exchanges the bits specified by *i* and *j*.

By specializing for **bool**, **vector** can pack true/false values into individual bits. The **vector<bool>** specialization defines a class called **reference**, which is used to emulate a reference to a bit.

Use deque

Key Ingredients

Headers	Classes	Functions
<deque>	deque	template <class InIter> void assign(InIter *start*, InIter *end*) reference at(size_type *i*) reference back( ) reference front( ) reference operator[ ](size_type *i*) void pop_back( ) void pop_front( ) void push_back(const T &*val*) void push_front(const T &*val*) void resize(size_type *num*, T *val* = T( ))

Perhaps the second most commonly used container is **deque**. There are two reasons for this. First, **deque** supports all of the optional functions defined for sequence containers. This makes it the STL's most full-featured sequence container. Second, **deque** is the default container that underlies the **queue** and **stack** container adaptors. (The default container used by **priority_queue** is **vector**). This recipe shows how to put **deque** into action.

NOTE   *The focus of this recipe is on the attributes and features of **deque** that make it unique. See* Basic Sequence Container Techniques *for information that applies to all sequence containers.*

Step-by-Step

To use a **deque** involves these steps:

1. Create a **deque** instance of the desired type and initial size.
2. Assign or obtain values to elements via the subscripting operator.
3. Use the **at( )** function as an alternative to the subscripting operator.
4. Add elements to the deque using either **insert( )**, **push_back( )**, or **push_front( )**.
5. Remove elements from the end by calling **pop_back( )**. Remove elements from the front by calling **pop_front( )**.
6. Obtain a reference to the first element in the deque by calling **front( )**.
7. Obtain a reference to the last element in the deque by calling **back( )**.
8. Assign a range of elements to a deque by calling **assign( )**.
9. To change the size of a deque, call **resize( )**.

Discussion

The template specification for **deque** is:

    template <class T, class Allocator = allocator<T> > class deque

Here, **T** is the type of data stored in the deque and **Allocator** specifies the allocator, which defaults to the standard allocator. To use **deque**, you must include the **<deque>** header.
  Here are **deque**'s constructors:

    explicit deque(const Allocator &alloc = Allocator( ))
    explicit deque(size_type num, const T &val = T ( ),
        const Allocator &alloc = Allocator( ))
    deque(const deque<T, Allocator> &ob)
    template <class InIter> deque(InIter start, InIter end,
        const Allocator &alloc = Allocator( ))

The first form constructs an empty deque. The second form constructs a deque that has *num* elements with the value *val*. The third form constructs a deque that contains the same elements as *ob*. This is **deque**'s copy constructor. The fourth form constructs a deque that contains the elements in the range *start* to *end*–1. The allocator used by the deque is specified by *alloc* and is typically allowed to default.

The **deque** container supports random-access iterators, and the [ ] is overloaded. This means that a **deque** object can be indexed like an array. It also means that a deque can be traversed in both the forward and reverse directions by use of an iterator.

The **deque** container provides all required sequence container functions, including those for a reversible container, and all optional sequence container functions. This makes **deque** the most general-purpose container.

Although **deque** and **vector** have different performance characteristics, they offer nearly identical functionality. For example, the standard sequence functions implemented by **deque**, such as **insert( )**, **erase( )**, **begin( )**, **end( )**, **rbegin( )**, **rend( )**, **operator[ ]( )**, **front( )**, **back( )**, **push_back( )**, and so on, work in **deque** just like they work in **vector**. The **resize( )** function provided by **deque** also works like the one provided by **vector**. Because a detailed discussion of these standard methods is presented in *Use vector*, those discussions are not duplicated here. (Note, however, that **deque** does not support the **capacity( )** and **reserve( )** methods defined for **vector**. They are not needed by **deque**.)

The **deque** class does support two functions not provided by **vector**: **push_front( )** and **pop_front( )**. They are shown here:

void push_front(const T &*val*)

void pop_front( )

The **push_front( )** function adds an element with the value specified by *val* to the start of the container. The container is automatically increased in size to accommodate the addition. The **pop_front( )** function removes an element from the start of the container.

The **deque** class has the following performance characteristics. Pushing or popping elements from either end of a **deque** takes place in constant time. When occurring in the middle, insertions or erasures of elements take place in linear time. Access of an element via the subscripting operator takes place in constant time. Since adding or deleting elements from the ends of a deque are quite efficient, deques make an excellent choice when these types of operations will occur frequently. The ability to make efficient additions to the start of the deque is one of the principal differences between **vector** and **deque**.

An insertion into the middle of a **deque** container invalidates all iterators and references to the contents of that container. Because **deque** is typically implemented as a double-ended dynamic array, an insertion implies that existing elements will be "spread apart" to accommodate the new elements. Thus, if an iterator is pointing to an element prior to an insertion, there is no guarantee that it will be pointing to the same element after the insertion. The same applies to references.

An insertion at the head or the tail of a **deque** invalidates iterators, but not references. An erasure to the middle invalidates both iterators and references. An erasure limited to either end invalidates only those iterators and references that point to the elements that are being erased.

Example

The following example shows **deque** in action. For comparison purposes, it reworks the example used for **vector**, substituting **deque** for **vector** throughout. Because **vector** and **deque** are very similar in the features that each provides, most of the two programs are the same. Of course, the calls to **capacity( )** and **reserve( )** that are in the **vector** version have been removed because these functions are not supported by **deque**. Also, the functions **push_front( )** and

pop_front( ) have been added. As explained, these functions are provided by **deque** but not **vector**.

```
// Demonstrate deque.

#include <iostream>
#include <deque>

using namespace std;

void show(const char *msg, deque<int> q);

int main() {

  // Declare a deque that has an initial capacity of 10.
  deque<int> dq(10);

  // Assign its elements some values. Notice how this is
  // done using the standard array-subscripting syntax.
  // Notice that the number of elements in the deque is
  // obtained by calling size().
  for(unsigned i=0; i < dq.size(); ++i) dq[i] = i*i;

  show("Contents of dq: ", dq);

  // Compute the average of the values. Again, notice
  // the use of the subscripting operator.
  int sum = 0;
  for(unsigned i=0; i < dq.size(); ++i) sum += dq[i];
  double avg = sum / dq.size();
  cout << "The average of the elements is " << avg << "\n\n";

  // Add elements to the end of dq.
  dq.push_back(100);
  dq.push_back(121);

  show("dq after pushing elements onto the end: ", dq);
  cout << endl;

  // Now use pop_back() to remove one element.
  dq.pop_back();
  show("dq after back-popping one element: ", dq);
  cout << endl;

  cout << "The first and last element in dq as"
       << " pointed to by begin() and end()-1:\n"
       << *dq.begin() << ", " << *(dq.end()-1) << "\n\n";

  cout << "The first and last element in dq as"
       << " pointed to by rbegin() and rend()-1:\n"
       << *dq.rbegin() << ", " << *(dq.rend()-1) << "\n\n";

  // Declare an iterator to a deque<int>.
```

```
    deque<int>::iterator itr;
    // Now, declare reverse iterator to a deque<int>
    deque<int>::reverse_iterator ritr;

    // Cycle through dq in the forward direction using an iterator.
    cout << "Cycle through the deque in the forward direction:\n";
    for(itr = dq.begin(); itr != dq.end(); ++itr)
      cout << *itr << " ";
    cout << "\n\n";
    cout << "Now, use a reverse iterator to cycle through in the"
         << " reverse direction:\n";

    // Cycle through dq in the reverse direction using a reverse_iterator.
    for(ritr = dq.rbegin(); ritr != dq.rend(); ++ritr)
      cout << *ritr << " ";
    cout << "\n\n";

    // Create another deque that contains a subrange of dq.
    deque<int> dq2(dq.begin()+2, dq.end()-4);

    // Display the contents of dq2 by using an iterator.
    show("dq2 contains a subrange of dq: ", dq2);
    cout << endl;

    // Change the values of some of dq2's elements.
    dq2[1] = 100;
    dq2[2] = 88;
    dq2[4] = 99;
    show("After the assignments, dq2 now contains: ", dq2);
    cout << endl;

    // Create an empty deque and then assign it a sequence
    // that is the reverse of dq.
    deque<int> dq3;
    dq3.assign(dq.rbegin(), dq.rend());
    show("dq3 contains the reverse of dq: ", dq3);
    cout << endl;

    // Push an element onto the front of dq.
    dq.push_front(-31416);
    show("dq after call to push_front(): ", dq);
    cout <<endl;

    // Now, clear dq by popping elements one at a time.
    cout << "Front popping elements from dq.\n";
    while(dq.size() > 0) {
      cout << "Popping: " << dq.front() << endl;
      dq.pop_front();
    }
    if(dq.empty()) cout << "dq is now empty.\n";

    return 0;
}
```

```
// Display the contents of a deque<int>.
void show(const char *msg, deque<int> q) {
  cout << msg;
  for(unsigned i=0; i < q.size(); ++i)
    cout << q[i] << " ";
  cout << "\n";
}
```

The output is shown here:

```
Contents of dq: 0 1 4 9 16 25 36 49 64 81
The average of the elements is 28

dq after pushing elements onto the end: 0 1 4 9 16 25 36 49 64 81 100 121

dq after back-popping one element: 0 1 4 9 16 25 36 49 64 81 100

The first and last element in dq as pointed to by begin() and end()-1:
0, 100

The first and last element in dq as pointed to by rbegin() and rend()-1:
100, 0

Cycle through the deque in the forward direction:
0 1 4 9 16 25 36 49 64 81 100

Now, use a reverse iterator to cycle through in the reverse direction:
100 81 64 49 36 25 16 9 4 1 0

dq2 contains a subrange of dq: 4 9 16 25 36

After the assignments, dq2 now contains: 4 100 88 25 99

dq3 contains the reverse of dq: 100 81 64 49 36 25 16 9 4 1 0

dq after call to push_front(): -31416 0 1 4 9 16 25 36 49 64 81 100

Front popping elements from dq.
Popping: -31416
Popping: 0
Popping: 1
Popping: 4
Popping: 9
Popping: 16
Popping: 25
Popping: 36
Popping: 49
Popping: 64
Popping: 81
Popping: 100
dq is now empty.
```

Options and Alternatives

Although the functions **push_front( )** and **pop_front( )** enable you to use deque as a first-in, last-out stack, the STL offers a better approach. The container adaptor **stack** provides a stack implementation that implements the FILO stack and provides the classic **push( )** and **pop( )** functions. Along the same lines, although you could use a **deque** to create a first-in, first-out queue by using the **push_front( )** and **pop_back( )** functions, the **queue** container adaptor is a better choice. By default, both **stack** and **queue** use a **deque** container to hold the elements. (See *Use the Sequence Container Adaptors: stack, queue, and priority_queue.*)

Like **vector**, **deque** also offers another form of **assign( )** that lets you assign a value to a deque. It is shown here:

void assign(size_type *num*, const T& *val*)

This version removes any elements previously held by the container and then assigns *num* copies of *val* to it. You might use this version of **assign( )** to reinitialize a deque to a known value, for example.

Like **vector**, **deque** *does not* store elements in sorted order. However, it is possible to sort a deque by using the **sort( )** algorithm. See *Sort a Container* in Chapter 4.

As explained, **vector** and **deque** are very similar. For some uses, such as when few insertions (especially insertions into the middle) are needed, a vector will be more efficient than a deque and makes a better choice. (See *Use vector* for details.)

Use list

Key Ingredients		
Headers	**Classes**	**Functions**
<list>	list	void merge(list<T, Allocator> &*ob*)
		void push_back(const T &*val*)
		reverse_iterator rbegin( )
		void remove(const T &*val*)
		void reverse( )
		void sort( )
		void splice(iterator *i*, list<T, Allocator> &*ob*)
		void unique( )

The **list** class implements a bidirectional sequence container that is most often implemented as a doubly linked list. Unlike the other two sequence containers **vector** and **deque**, which support random access, **list** can be accessed only sequentially. However, since **list**s are bidirectional, they can be accessed front to back or back to front. The **list** class offers the same benefits associated with any doubly linked list: fast insertion and deletion times.

Of course, access to a specific element in the list is a slower operation. A **list** is particularly useful when elements will be frequently added to or removed from the middle of the container and random access to elements is not required. This recipe demonstrates the key aspects of **list**.

NOTE *The focus of this recipe is on the attributes and features of **list** that make it unique. See* Basic Sequence Container Techniques *for information that applies to all sequence containers.*

Step-by-Step

To use **list** involves the following steps:

1. Create a **list** instance of the desired type.
2. Add elements to the list by calling **insert( )**, **push_front( )**, or **push_back( )**.
3. Delete an element at the end of the list by calling **pop_back( )**. Delete an element from the start of the list by calling **pop_front( )**.
4. Sort a list by calling **sort( )**.
5. Merge two ordered lists by calling **merge( )**.
6. Join one list to another by calling **splice( )**.
7. Delete a specific element or elements from the list by calling **remove( )**.
8. Remove duplicate elements by calling **unique( )**.
9. Reverse the list by calling **reverse( )**.

Discussion

The template specification for **list** is:

template <class T, class Allocator = allocator<T> > class list

Here, **T** is the type of data being stored and **Allocator** specifies the allocator, which defaults to the standard allocator. To use **list**, you must include the **<list>** header.

The **list** class has the following constructors:

explicit list(const Allocator &*alloc* = Allocator( ))

explicit list(size_type *num*, const T &*val* = T ( ),
        const Allocator &*alloc* = Allocator( ))

list(const list<T, Allocator> &*ob*)

template <class InIter> list(InIter *start*, InIter *end*,
        const Allocator &*alloc* = Allocator( ))

The first form constructs an empty list. The second form constructs a list that has *num* elements with the value *val*. The third form is **list**'s copy constructor. The fourth form constructs a list that contains the elements in the range *start* to *end*–1. The allocator used by **list** is specified by *alloc*, which is typically allowed to default.

The **list** class supports bidirectional iterators. Thus, the container can be accessed through an iterator in both the forward and reverse directions. However, random-access operations are not supported. Thus, the **at( )** function is not provided and the [ ] operator is not overloaded.

In addition to the required sequence and reversible sequence container functions, **list** implements the following optional ones: **front( )**, **back( )**, **push_front( )**, **push_back( )**, **pop_front( )**, and **pop_back( )**. These functions are described in the overview and in *Basic Sequence Container Techniques*. (Additional discussions are found in *Use vector* and *Use deque*.) The only optional functions that it does not implement are **at( )** and **operator[ ]( )**.

The **list** class adds several functions of its own, including **merge( )**, **reverse( )**, **unique( )**, **remove( )**, **remove_if( )**, and **sort( )**. These functions duplicate the functionality provided by the standard algorithms of the same names. They are defined by **list** because they have been specially optimized for operation on objects of type **list** and offer a high-performance alternative to the standard algorithms.

You can add elements to a list by using the standard sequence container functions **insert( )**, **push_front( )**, and **push_back( )**. You can remove elements from a list by calling the standard sequence container functions **erase( )**, **clear( )**, **pop_back( )**, and **pop_front( )**.

The **list** class supports both forward and reverse iterators. Like the other sequence containers, these are objects of type **iterator** and **reverse_iterator**. The functions **begin( )** and **end( )** return iterators to the beginning and the end of the list. The functions **rbegin( )** and **rend( )** return reverse iterators to the end and one before the beginning, respectively. These functions and the techniques required to use them to cycle through a container are described in *Basic Sequence Container Techniques*.

The contents of a list are not automatically ordered. However, some operations, such as merging, require an ordered list. To sort a list, call the **sort( )** function. It has two versions. The one used by this recipe is shown here:

    void sort( )

After a call to **sort( )**, the list will be sorted in ascending order based on the natural ordering of the elements. (The second version lets you specify a comparison function that will be used to determine the ordering of the elements. See the *Options and Alternatives* section in this recipe for details.)

A particularly powerful function implemented by **list** is **merge( )**. It combines two ordered lists, which must be sorted using the same criteria. During a merge, each element of the source list is inserted into its proper location in the target list. Thus, the result is an ordered list that contains all of the elements of the two original lists. The **merge( )** function has two versions. The one used by this recipe is shown here:

    void merge(list<T, Allocator> &ob)

It merges the ordered list passed in *ob* with the ordered invoking list. The result is ordered. After the merge, the list contained in *ob* is empty.

An operation related to merging is splicing, which is performed by the **splice( )** function. When a splice occurs, the source list is inserted as a unit into the target list. No element-by-element integration of the two lists takes place, and there is no requirement that either list be sorted. A splice is essentially just a "cut and paste" operation. There are three versions of **splice( )**. The one used by this recipe is shown here:

    void splice(iterator *i*, list<T, Allocator> &*ob*)

The contents of *ob* are inserted into the invoking list at the location pointed to by *i*. After the operation, *ob* is empty. A splice can take place at any point in the target sequence: at the front, the middle, or the end. When a splice is at the front of a list, the spliced sequence is inserted before **begin( )**. When a splice occurs at the end, the spliced sequence is inserted before **end( )**.

    You can remove a specific element from a list using **remove( )**, shown here:

    void remove(const T &*val*)

It removes elements with the value *val* from the invoking list. If no element matches *val*, then the list is unchanged. At first glance, **remove( )** may seem redundant because **list** also defines the **erase( )** function. However, this is not the case. The difference lies in the fact that **erase( )** requires iterators to the element(s) to be deleted. The **remove( )** function automatically searches the list for the specified element.

    Another way to remove elements from a list is through the use of the **unique( )** function, which deletes duplicate consecutive elements. It has two forms. The one used by this recipe is shown here:

    void unique( )

It removes duplicate elements from the invoking list. Therefore, the resulting list contains no consecutive duplicate elements. If the initial list is ordered, then after applying **unique( )**, each element will be unique.

    To reverse a list, use the **reverse( )** function, shown here:

    void reverse( )

It reverses the entire contents of the invoking list.

    The **list** class has the following performance characteristics. Inserting or deleting elements in a list takes place in constant time. It doesn't matter where in the list the insertion or deletion will occur. Since **list** is usually implemented as a linked list, an insertion or deletion involves only the rearrangement of the links and not a shifting of elements or the reallocation of memory.

    Unlike **vector** and **deque**, insertion into a list invalidates no iterators or references to elements. A deletion invalidates only those iterators or references to the deleted elements. The fact that these operations do not affect the validity of iterators or references to existing elements makes the **list** class especially useful for those applications in which non-volatile iterators and/or references are desired.

Example

The following example demonstrates **list**:

```
// Demonstrate list

#include <iostream>
#include <list>
```

```cpp
using namespace std;

void show(const char *msg, list<char> lst);

int main() {

  // Declare two lists.
  list<char> lstA;
  list<char> lstB;

  // Use push_back() to give the lists some elements.
  lstA.push_back('A');
  lstA.push_back('F');
  lstA.push_back('B');
  lstA.push_back('R');

  lstB.push_back('X');
  lstB.push_back('A');
  lstB.push_back('F');

  show("Original contents of lstA: ", lstA);
  show("Original contents of lstB: ", lstB);
  cout << "Size of lstA is " << lstA.size() << endl;
  cout << "Size of lstB is "<< lstB.size() << endl;
  cout << endl;

  // Sort lstA and lstB
  lstA.sort();
  lstB.sort();

  show("Sorted contents of lstA: ", lstA);
  show("Sorted contents of lstB: ", lstB);
  cout << endl;

  // Merge lstB into lstA.
  lstA.merge(lstB);
  show("lstA after merge: " , lstA);
  if(lstB.empty()) cout << "lstB is now empty().\n";
  cout << endl;

  // Remove duplicates from lstA.
  lstA.unique();
  show("lstA after call to unique(): ", lstA);
  cout << endl;

  // Give lstB some new elements.
  lstB.push_back('G');
  lstB.push_back('H');
  lstB.push_back('P');

  show("New contents of lstB: ", lstB);
  cout << endl;
```

```
  // Now, splice lstB into lstA.
  list<char>::iterator itr = lstA.begin();
  ++itr;
  lstA.splice(itr, lstB);
  show("lstA after splice: ", lstA);
  cout << endl;

  // Remove A and H.
  lstA.remove('A');
  lstA.remove('H');
  show("lstA after removing A and H: ", lstA);
  cout << endl;

  return 0;
}

// Display the contents of a list<char>.
void show(const char *msg, list<char> lst) {
  list<char>::iterator itr;

  cout << msg;

  for(itr = lst.begin(); itr != lst.end(); ++itr)
    cout << *itr << " ";

  cout << "\n";
}
```

The output is shown here:

```
Original contents of lstA: A F B R
Original contents of lstB: X A F
Size of lstA is 4
Size of lstB is 3

Sorted contents of lstA: A B F R
Sorted contents of lstB: A F X

lstA after merge: A A B F F R X
lstB is now empty().

lstA after call to unique(): A B F R X

New contents of lstB: G H P

lstA after splice: A G H P B F R X

lstA after removing A and H: G P B F R X
```

Options and Alternatives

The **list** container gives you detailed control over several of its operations because a number of functions let you specify comparison functions or predicates that govern their outcomes. They are described here.

When sorting a **list** instance, there is a second form of **sort( )** that lets you specify a comparison function that will be used to determine when one element is greater than another. This version of **sort( )** is shown here:

template <class Comp> void sort(Comp *cmpfn*)

Here, *cmpfn* specifies a pointer to a function that takes two arguments, which must be of the same type as the elements of the invoking container. To sort in ascending order, the function must return true when the first argument is less than the second argument. However, you can specify any sorting criteria you want. For example, you can sort the list in reverse order by reversing the comparison. Here is a reverse-comparison function that can be used to reverse-sort the lists in the preceding program:

```
// A reverse comparison function.
bool revcomp(char a, char b) {
  if(b < a) return true;
  else return false;
}
```

Notice that the operands are reversed in the < operation. This causes the function to return true if **b** is less than **a**, which causes the list to be sorted in descending order. (Normally, the comparison **a < b** would be used, which would cause the sorted outcome to be in ascending order.) Here is how to use this function to reverse-sort **lstA**:

```
lstA.sort(revcomp);
```

Another place that you can specify a comparison function when working with **list** is with this version of the **merge( )** function:

template <class Comp> void merge(<list<T, Allocator> &*ob*, Comp *cmpfn*)

In this version, the ordered list passed in *ob* is merged with the ordered invoking list based on the ordering specified by the *cmpfn* function. After the merge, the list contained in *ob* is empty. Normally, the same comparison function used to sort a list is also used to merge lists. Of course, special uses in which this is not the case are possible.

As explained, you can remove a specific element by calling **remove( )**. However, you can also remove elements that satisfy a certain condition by using **remove_if( )**, shown here:

template <class UnPred> void remove_if(UnPred *pr*)

This function removes elements for which the unary predicate *pr* is true. If no element satisfies the predicate, then the list is unchanged. You might use **remove_if( )** to remove all elements from a list that satisfy some general condition. For example, assuming the preceding program, you could use this predicate to remove all elements that are between A and G, inclusive:

```
bool mypred(char ch) {
  if(ch <= 'G' && ch >= 'A') return true;
  return false;
}
```

Therefore, to remove all letters A through G from **lstA**, you would use this call to **remove_if( )**:

```
lstA.remove_if(mypred);
```

The version of **unique( )** used by the recipe removes adjacent duplicate elements. There is a second form that lets you specify a binary predicate that defines what constitutes a duplicate element. (In other words, the predicate determines when two elements are equal.) This form of **unique( )** is shown here:

template <class BinPred> void unique(BinPred *pr*)

This form uses *pr* to determine when one element is the same as another. This means that you could use a criterion other than bitwise equality. For example, if a list is storing name and contact information, then you might specify that two elements are the same if their e-mail addresses match. Alternatively, you might specify a predicate that normalizes each element before comparing. For example, assuming the preceding program, the following predicate will return true if two elements are the same letter, independently of case differences. Therefore, given the sequence, XxABcdEe, it will remove the duplicate X and E.

```
bool ign_case_pred(char a, char b) {
  if(tolower(a) == tolower(b)) return true;
  else return false;
}
```

To use **ign_case_pred( )**, call **unique( )** as shown here:

```
lstA.unique(ign_case_pred);
```

As mentioned, **list** supports bidirectional iterators. This means that a list can be traversed in either the forward or reverse direction. Therefore, assuming the preceding example, the following fragment uses a **reverse_iterator** to display the contents of **lstA** from back to front:

```
list<char>::reverse_iterator ritr;
for(ritr = lstA.rbegin(); ritr != lstA.rend(); ++ritr)
  cout << *ritr << " ";
```

Use the Sequence Container Adaptors: stack, queue, and priority_queue

Key Ingredients		
Headers	**Classes**	**Functions**
<stack>	stack	bool empty( ) const
		void pop( )
		void push(const value_type &*val*)
		size_type size( ) const
		value_type &top( )
<queue>	queue	value_type &back( )
		bool empty( ) const
		value_type &front( )
		void pop( )
		void push(const value_type &*val*)
		size_type size( ) const
<queue>	priority_queue	bool empty( ) const
		void pop( )
		void push(const value_type &*val*)
		size_type size( ) const
		const value_type &top( ) const

The STL provides three container adaptors, called **stack, queue**, and **priority_queue**. They utilize one of the sequence containers as the underlying container, adapting it to their own special purposes. In essence, a container adaptor is simply a tightly controlled interface to another container. Although the container adaptors are built on one of the sequence containers, they are, themselves, also containers and you use them much like you use the other containers. It's just that access to their elements is restricted. This recipe demonstrates their use.

Before we begin, an important point needs to be made. The container adaptors *do not* support all of the functionality of their underlying containers. The manipulations allowed by an adaptor are a highly restricted subset of what the base container supports. While the precise restrictions differ from adaptor to adaptor, there is one difference that is shared by all: Iterators are not supported. If the adaptors supported iterators, then it would be a trivial matter to circumvent the data structure defined by the adaptor (such as a stack) and access its elements out of order.

Step-by-Step

To use the sequence container adaptors involves these steps:

1. Create an instance of the container adaptor, selecting the one suited to your application.

2. Use the functions defined by the adaptor to insert, access, and remove elements from the container. Each adaptor defines its own set of these functions. For example, to push an element onto a **stack**, call **push( )**. To obtain the next element from a **queue**, call **front( )**.

Discussion

The **stack** class supports a last-in, first-out (LIFO) stack. Its template specification is shown here:

    template <class T, class Container = deque<T> > class stack

Here, **T** is the type of data being stored and **Container** is the type of container used to hold the stack, which by default is **deque**.

The **stack** adaptor has the following constructor:

    explicit stack(const Container &*cnt* = Container( ))

The **stack( )** constructor creates an empty stack. To use a stack, include the **<stack>** header. The underlying container is held in a protected object called **c** of type **Container**.

In general, **stack** can adapt any container that supports the following operations:

    back( )
    pop_back( )
    push_back( )

Thus, you can also use a **list** or a **vector** as a container for a stack.

The **stack** class defines the functions shown here. Notice that elements in a stack can be accessed only in last-in, first-out order. This enforces its stack-like nature.

Member	Description
bool empty( ) const	Returns true if the invoking stack is empty and false otherwise.
void pop( )	Removes the top of the stack.
void push(const value_type &*val*)	Pushes an element onto the stack.
size_type size( ) const	Returns the number of elements currently in the stack.
value_type &top( ) cont value_type &top( ) const	Returns a reference to the top of the stack.

The **queue** class supports a normal first-in, first-out (FIFO) queue. Elements are inserted into a queue on one end and removed from the other. Elements cannot be accessed in any other fashion. The **queue** template specification is shown here:

    template <class T, class Container = deque<T> > class queue

Here, **T** is the type of data being stored and **Container** is the type of container used to hold the queue, which by default is a **deque**. The underlying container is held in a protected object called **c** of type **Container**.

The **queue** adaptor has the following constructor:

explicit queue(const Container &*cnt* = Container( ))

The **queue( )** constructor creates an empty queue. To use a queue, include the **<queue>** header.

In general, **queue** can adapt any container that supports the following operations:

back( )
front( )
pop_front( )
push_back( )

Thus, you can also use **list** as a container for a queue. However, you cannot use **vector** because **vector** does not provide the **pop_front( )** function.

The **queue** adaptor defines the functions shown here. As you can see, they restrict **queue** to providing only first-in, first-out access to its elements.

Member	Description
value_type &back( ) const value_type &back( ) const	Returns a reference to the last element in the queue.
bool empty( ) const	Returns true if the invoking queue is empty and false otherwise.
value_type &front( ) const value_type &front( ) const	Returns a reference to the first element in the queue.
void pop( )	Removes the first element in the queue.
void push(const value_type &*val*)	Adds an element with the value specified by *val* to the end of the queue.
size_type size( ) const	Returns the number of elements currently in the queue.

The **priority_queue** class supports a single-ended priority queue. A priority queue arranges its contents in order of their priority. The **priority_queue** template specification is shown here:

template <class T, class Container = vector<T>,
        class Comp = less<typename Container::value_type> >
        class priority_queue

Here, **T** is the type of data being stored. **Container** is the type of container used to hold the priority queue, which by default is a **vector**. The underlying container is held in a protected object called **c** of type **Container**. **Comp** specifies the comparison function object that determines when one member is lower in priority than another. This object is held in a protected member called **comp** of type **Compare**.

The **priority_queue** adaptor has the following constructors:

explicit priority_queue(const Comp &*cmpfn* = Comp( ),
        Container &*cnt* = Container( ))

template <class InIter> priority_queue(InIter *start*, InIter *end*,
        const Comp &*cmpfn* = Comp( ),
        Container &*cnt* = Container( ))

The first **priority_queue( )** constructor creates an empty priority queue. The second creates a priority queue that contains the elements specified by the range *start* to *end*–1. To use **priority_queue**, include the **<queue>** header.

In general, **priority_queue** can adapt any container that supports the following operations:

front( )

pop_back( )

push_back( )

The container must also support random-access iterators. Thus, you can also use a **deque** as a container for a priority queue. However, you cannot use **list** because **list** does not support random-access iterators.

The first **priority_queue** class defines the functions shown here. The elements in a **priority_queue** can be accessed only in the order of their priority.

Member	Description
bool empty( ) const	Returns true if the invoking priority queue is empty and false otherwise.
void pop( )	Removes the first element in the priority queue.
void push(const value_type &*val*)	Adds an element to the priority queue.
size_type size( ) const	Returns the number of elements currently in the priority queue.
const value_type &top( ) const	Returns a reference to the element with the highest priority. The element is not removed.

Example

The following example shows all three container adaptors in action:

```
// Demonstrate the sequence container adaptors.

#include <iostream>
#include <string>
#include <queue>
#include <stack>

using namespace std;
```

```cpp
int main()
{
  // Demonstrate queue.
  queue<string> q;

  cout << "Demonstrate a queue for strings.\n";

  cout << "Pushing one two three four\n";
  q.push("one");
  q.push("two");
  q.push("three");
  q.push("four");

  cout << "Now, retrieve those values in FIFO order.\n";
  while(!q.empty()) {
    cout << "Popping ";
    cout << q.front() << "\n";
    q.pop();
  }
  cout << endl;

  // Demonstrate priority_queue.
  priority_queue<int> pq;

  cout << "Demonstrate a priority_queue for integers.\n";

  cout << "Pushing 1, 3, 4, 2.\n";
  pq.push(1);
  pq.push(3);
  pq.push(4);
  pq.push(2);

  cout << "Now, retrieve those values in priority order.\n";
  while(!pq.empty()) {
    cout << "Popping ";
    cout << pq.top() << "\n";
    pq.pop();
  }
  cout << endl;

  // Finally, demonstrate stack.
  stack<char> stck;

  cout << "Demonstrate a stack for characters.\n";

  cout << "Pushing  A, B, C, and D.\n";
  stck.push('A');
  stck.push('B');
  stck.push('C');
  stck.push('D');

  cout << "Now, retrieve those values in LIFO order.\n";
  while(!stck.empty()) {
```

```
    cout << "Popping: ";
    cout << stck.top() << "\n";
    stck.pop();
  }

  return 0;
}
```

The output is shown here:

```
Demonstrate a queue for strings.
Pushing one two three four
Now, retrieve those values in FIFO order.
Popping one
Popping two
Popping three
Popping four

Demonstrate a priority_queue for integers.
Pushing 1, 3, 4, 2.
Now, retrieve those values in priority order.
Popping 4
Popping 3
Popping 2
Popping 1

Demonstrate a stack for characters.
Pushing A, B, C, and D.
Now, retrieve those values in LIFO order.
Popping: D
Popping: C
Popping: B
Popping: A
```

Bonus Example: Use stack to Create a Four-Function Calculator

Stacks are one of computing's most useful data structures. At the machine level, they provide the mechanism by which a subroutine can be called. At the program level, stacks are used to solve several common problems. For example, many AI-based searching routines rely on stacks. Also, many types of tree traversals employ a stack. One interesting use of a stack is in a postfix-style calculator. When using this type of calculator, you first enter the operands and then the operation that you want applied. For example, to add 10 to 12, you first enter 10, then 12, then +. As each operand is entered, it is pushed onto the stack. When an operator is entered, the top two elements are popped, the operation is performed, and the result is pushed onto the stack. The following program uses the **stack** class to implement such a calculator.

```
// A four-function postfix calculator.
#include <iostream>
#include <stack>
#include <string>
#include <cmath>
```

```
using namespace std;

int main()
{
  stack<double> stck;
  double a, b;
  string s;

  do {
    cout << ": ";
    cin >> s;
    switch(s[0]) {
      case 'q': // quit the calculator
        break;
      case '.': // show top-of-stack
        cout << stck.top() << "\n";
        break;
      case '+': // add
        if(stck.size() < 2) {
          cout << "Operand Missing\n";
          break;
        }

        a = stck.top();
        stck.pop();
        b = stck.top();
        stck.pop();
        cout << a+b << "\n";
        stck.push(a+b);
        break;
      case '-': // subtract
        // See if user entered a negative number.
        if(s.size() != 1) {
          // Push value onto the stack.
          stck.push(atof(s.c_str()));
          break;
        }

        // otherwise, is a subtraction
        if(stck.size() < 2) {
          cout << "Operand Missing\n";
          break;
        }

        a = stck.top();
        stck.pop();
        b = stck.top();
        stck.pop();
        cout << b-a << "\n";
        stck.push(b-a);
        break;
      case '*': // multiply
        if(stck.size() < 2) {
```

```
          cout << "Operand Missing\n";
          break;
        }

      a = stck.top();
      stck.pop();
      b = stck.top();
      stck.pop();
      cout << a*b << "\n";
      stck.push(a*b);
      break;
    case '/': // divide
      if(stck.size() < 2) {
        cout << "Operand Missing\n";
        break;
      }

      a = stck.top();
      stck.pop();
      b = stck.top();
      stck.pop();
      cout << b/a << "\n";
      stck.push(b/a);
      break;
    default:
      // push value onto the stack
      stck.push(atof(s.c_str()));
      break;
    }
  } while(s != "q");

  return 0;
}
```

A sample run is shown here:

```
: 10
: 2
: /
5
: -1
: *
-5
: 2.2
: +
-2.8
: 4
: 5
: 6
: +
11
: +
15
: q
```

For the most part, the operation of the calculator is intuitive, but there are a couple of points to keep in mind. First, to see the value on the top of the stack, enter a period. This means that you will need to precede values that are less than 1 with a leading zero, as in 0.12, for example. Second, notice that when an entry begins with a minus sign, if its length is longer than 1, it is assumed that the user is entering a negative number and not requesting a subtraction.

Options and Alternatives

As long as the container meets the requirements specified by the adaptor, any container can be used as the underlying container. To use a different container, simply specify its class name when creating an instance of the adaptor. For example, the following creates a **queue** that adapts **list** rather than **deque**:

```
queue<char, list<char> > q;
```

Since **q** uses **list** as its underlying container, it will be subject to all of **list**'s benefits and disadvantages. Usually, the default container is your best choice, but you *do* have a choice. You could even use your own custom container as the basis for a **queue**. The same general principle applies to the other container adaptors, too.

One other point: Notice that there is a space between the two closing angle brackets that end the preceding declaration. Because of a quirk in the C++ syntax, this space is necessary. Without it, the compiler will mistake two closing angle brackets as a right shift (>>) and not as nested template terminators. Forgetting this space is a common error, which can be hard to find since your program looks correct.

Store User-Defined Objects in a Container

Key Ingredients		
Headers	**Classes**	**Functions**
	user-defined	bool operator<(*user-type a*, *user-type b*)
		bool operator==(*user-type a*, *user-type b*)

An STL container can be used to store objects of classes that you create. However, these classes must meet a minimal set of requirements. This recipe describes those requirements and demonstrates their implementation. It creates a class called **part** that encapsulates the name and number associated with some part, such as a nail or a bolt. However, the same basic approach can be used to store any type of object within any type of container.

Step-by-Step

To enable objects of a class that you create to be stored in a sequence container involves the following steps:

1. The class must have a publicly accessible copy constructor.
2. The class must provide a publicly accessible destructor.
3. The class must provide a publicly accessible assignment operator.
4. In some cases, the class must provide a publicly accessible default constructor.
5. In some cases, the class must provide a publicly accessible **operator==( )** function.
6. In some cases, the class must provide a publicly accessible **operator<( )** function.

To enable objects of a class that you create to be stored in an associative container involves the following steps:

1. All of the requirements described for a sequence container must be met.
2. The class *must* provide a publicly accessible **operator<( )** function because all associative containers are sorted.

Discussion

For all containers, if an object is to be stored in a container, then its class must provide the following publicly accessible functions:

- Copy constructor
- Destructor
- **operator==( )**

Depending upon the specific usage, a publicly accessible default (parameterless) constructor and **operator==( )** are often needed. A key point to understand, however, is that the default copy constructor, parameterless constructor, destructor, and assignment operator provided automatically by a class satisfy this requirement. Therefore, you don't always need to explicitly declare these items.

In order to use a sequence container, such as **vector**, with certain algorithms, such as **sort( )**, your class must provide an **operator<( )** function that compares two objects. Some other algorithms, such as **find( )**, require that an **operator==( )** function be provided that determines when one object equals another.

In order for an object to be stored in an associative container, such as **set** or **multiset**, you must provide an **operator<( )**. Sets are ordered by using the < operator. It is also used by the **find( )**, **upper_bound( )**, **lower_bound( )**, and **equal_range( )** functions.

Example

The following example creates a class called **part** that encapsulates the name and number of a part. Notice that **operator<( )** and **operator==( )** are defined. The < operator enables a container that stores **part** objects to be operated on by algorithms that require comparisons. The program demonstrates this by sorting the vector using the **sort( )** algorithm The == operator enables the equality of two **part** objects to be determined by algorithms such as **find( )**, which is also used by the program. (Recipes that describe the STL algorithms are presented in Chapter 4.)

```cpp
// Store user-defined objects in a vector.
//
// The objects being stored are instances of the
// part class. The operator<() and operator==() are
// defined for part objects. This lets the objects
// be operated on by various algorithms, such as
// sort() and find().
#include <iostream>
#include <vector>
#include <algorithm>
#include <string>

using namespace std;


// This class stores information on parts.
class part {
  string name;
  unsigned number;
public:
  // Default constructor.
  part() { name  = ""; number = 0; }

  // Construct a complete part object.
  part(string n, unsigned num) {
    name = n;
    number = num;
  }

  // Accessor functions for part data.
  string get_name() { return name; }
  unsigned get_number() { return number; }
};

void show(const char *msg, vector<part> vect);

// Compare objects using part number.
bool operator<(part a, part b)
{
  return a.get_number() < b.get_number();
}

// Check for equality based on part number.
bool operator==(part a, part b)
{
  return a.get_number() == b.get_number();
}

int main()
{
  vector<part> partlist;
```

```
  // Initialize the parts list.
  partlist.push_back(part("flange", 9324));
  partlist.push_back(part("screw", 8452));
  partlist.push_back(part("bolt", 6912));
  partlist.push_back(part("nail", 1274));

  // Display contents of the vector.
  show("Parts list unsorted:\n", partlist);
  cout << endl;

  // Use the sort() algorithm to sort the parts list.
  // This requires that operator<() be defined for part.
  sort(partlist.begin(), partlist.end());

  show("Parts list sorted by part number:\n", partlist);

  // Use the find() algorithm to find a part given its number.
  // This requires that operator==() be defined for part.
  cout << "Searching for part number 6912.\n";

  vector<part>::iterator itr;
  itr = find(partlist.begin(), partlist.end(), part("", 6912));
  cout << "Part found. Its name is " << itr->get_name() << ".\n";

  return 0;
}

// Display the contents of a vector<part>.
void show(const char *msg, vector<part> vect) {
  vector<part>::iterator itr;

  cout << msg;
  cout << "  Part#\t Name\n";
  for(itr=vect.begin(); itr != vect.end(); ++itr)
    cout << "  " << itr->get_number() << "\t "
         << itr->get_name() << endl;;
  cout << "\n";
}
```

The output is shown here:

```
Parts list unsorted:
  Part#    Name
  9324     flange
  8452     screw
  6912     bolt
  1274     nail


Parts list sorted by part number:
  Part#    Name
  1274     nail
```

```
6912    bolt
8452    screw
9324    flange
```

```
Searching for part number 6912.
Part found. Its name is bolt.
```

Options and Alternatives

An example that demonstrates storing a user-defined class object in a **set** is shown in *Use set and multiset*.

It has been my experience that there is some variation between compilers regarding precisely what a class must provide in order for objects of that class to be stored in a container and/or operated on by algorithms. The requirements described in this recipe are in accordance with those specified by the ANSI/ISO standard for C++. However, I have seen some cases in which additional requirements must be met. The discrepancies between implementations were greater in the past than they are today. Nevertheless, although this recipe describes general requirements that a class must meet in order to be stored in a container, they should be treated as guidelines (rather than hard and fast rules) that you may need to adjust to fit your specific situation.

Basic Associative Container Techniques

Key Ingredients		
Headers	**Classes**	**Functions**
<map>	map	iterator begin( )
		void clear( )
		bool empty( ) const
		iterator end( )
		size_type erase(const key_type &k)
		iterator find(const key_type &k)
		pair<iterator, bool> insert(const value_type &val)
		reverse_iterator rbegin( )
		reverse_iterator rend( )
		size_type size( ) const
		void swap(map<Key, T, Comp, Allocator> &ob)
<map>		template <class Key, class T, class Comp, class Allocator> bool operator==(const map<Key, T, Comp, Allocator> &leftop, const map<Key, T, Comp, Allocator> &rightop) template <class Key, class T, class Comp, class Allocator> bool operator<(const map<Key, T, Comp, Allocator> &leftop, const map<Key, T, Comp, Allocator> &rightop) template <class Key, class T, class Comp, class Allocator> bool operator>(const map<Key, T, Comp, Allocator> &leftop, const map<Key, T, Comp, Allocator> &rightop)
<utility>	pair	
<utility>		template <class Ktype, class Vtype> pair<Ktype, Vtype> make_pair(const Ktype &k, const Vtype &v)

All associative containers share common functionality, and all are handled in essentially the same way. This recipe uses this common functionality to demonstrate the basic techniques needed to create and use an associative container.

This recipe shows how to:

- Create an associative container.
- Create elements that consist of key/value pairs.
- Add elements to an associative container.
- Determine the size of the container.
- Use an iterator to cycle through the container.
- Assign one container to another.
- Determine when one container is equivalent to another.
- Remove elements from the container.
- Exchange the contents of one container with another.
- Determine if a container is empty.
- Find an element given its key.

This recipe uses the **map** class. In general, the techniques described here also apply to the other associative containers, such as **set**, defined by the STL. However, **map** stores key/value pairs in which the type of the key and the type of the value may differ. The **set** container stores objects in which the key and the value are part of the same object. Furthermore, **map** creates a container in which each key must be unique. A **multimap** container, by contrast, allows duplicate keys. Therefore, while the general principles shown here apply to any associative container, some adaptation will be needed, depending upon which associative container is used.

Step-by-Step

To create and use an associative container involves these steps:

1. Create an instance of the desired associative container. In this recipe, **map** is used.
2. Construct **pair** objects, which are the type of objects stored in a **map**.
3. Add elements to the container by calling **insert( )**.
4. Obtain the number of elements in the container by calling **size( )**.
5. Determine if the container is empty (i.e., it contains no elements) by calling **empty( )**.
6. Remove elements from the container by calling **erase( )**.
7. Remove all elements from a container by calling **clear( )**.
8. Find an element with a specified key by calling **find( )**.
9. Obtain an iterator to the start of the container by calling **begin( )**. Obtain an iterator to one past the end of the container by calling **end( )**.
10. Obtain a reverse iterator to the end of the container by calling **rbegin( )**. Obtain an iterator to one before the start of the container by calling **rend( )**.
11. Cycle through the elements in the container via an iterator.

12. Exchange the contents of one container with another via **swap( )**.

13. Determine when one associative container is equal to, less than, or greater than another.

Discussion

The STL supports two basic flavors of associative container: maps and sets. In a map, each element consists of a key/value pair and the type of the key can differ from the type of the value. In a set, the key and the value are embedded in the same object. Although both maps and sets operate in essentially the same way, a **map** is used by this recipe because it best demonstrates the essential techniques required to use any associative container.

The template specification for **map** is shown here:

template <class Key, class T, class Comp = less<Key>,
        class Allocator = allocator<T> > class map

Here, **Key** is the data type of the keys and **T** is the type of values being stored (mapped). The function that compares two keys is specified by **Comp**. Notice that this defaults to the **less** function object. The allocator is specified by **Allocator**, which defaults to the standard allocator.

A central aspect of an associative container is that it maintains an ordered collection of elements based on the value of the keys. The specific order is determined by the comparison function, which is **less** by default. This means that, by default, the elements in an associative container are stored in ascending key order. However, it is possible to specify a comparison object that stores the elements differently.

The **map** class supports three constructors. The two used in this recipe are shown here:

explicit map(const Comp &*cmpfn* = Comp( ), const Allocator &*alloc* = Allocator( ))

map(const map<Key, T, Comp, Allocator> &*ob*)

The first form constructs an empty map. The second form constructs a map that contains the same elements as *ob* and is **map**'s copy constructor. The *cmpfn* parameter specifies the comparison function used to order the map. In most cases, you can allow this to default. The *alloc* parameter specifies the allocator, which also is typically allowed to default. To use a map, you must include the **<map>** header.

The type of object held by a map is an instance of **pair**, which is a **struct** that encapsulates two objects. It is declared like this:

```
template <class Ktype, class Vtype> struct pair {
  typedef Ktype first_type;
  typedef Vtype second_type;
  Ktype first; // for map elements, contains the key
  Vtype second; // for map elements, contains the value

  // Constructors
  pair();
  pair(const Ktype &k, const Vtype &v);
  template<class A, class B> pair(const pair<A, B> &ob);
}
```

The **pair** class can be used to hold any pair of objects. However, when used to hold a key/value pair, the value in **first** contains the key and the value in **second** contains the value associated with that key. The **pair** class requires the **<utility>** header, which is automatically included by **<map>**.

You can construct a **pair** by using either one of **pair**'s constructors or by using the **make_pair( )** function, which is also declared in **<utility>**. It constructs a **pair** object based upon the types of the data used as parameters. The **make_pair( )** function is generic and has this prototype:

>   template <class *Ktype*, class *Vtype*>
>   pair<*Ktype*, *Vtype*> make_pair(const *Ktype* &*k*, const *Vtype* &*v*)

As you can see, it returns a **pair** object consisting of values of the types specified by *Ktype* and *Vtype*. The advantage of **make_pair( )** is that the types of the objects being stored are determined automatically by the compiler rather than being explicitly specified by you.

For **map**, the type **value_type** is a **typedef** for **pair<const Key, T>**. Therefore, a map holds instances of **pair**. Furthermore, the **iterator** type defined for **map** points to objects of type **pair<Key, T>**. Thus, when a **map** function returns an iterator, the key is available through the **first** field of **pair** and the value is obtained through **pair**'s **second** field.

After a map has been created, **pair** objects can be added to it. One way to do this that works for all associative containers is to call **insert( )**. All associative containers support at least three versions of **insert( )**. The one used here is:

>   pair<iterator, bool> insert(const value_type &*val*)

It inserts *val* into the invoking container at a point that maintains the ordering of the associative container. (Recall that **value_type** is a **type_def** for **pair<const Key, T>**.) The function returns a **pair** object that indicates the outcome of the operation. If *val* can be inserted, the **bool** value (which is in the **second** field) will be true, and false otherwise. The **iterator** value (which is in the **first** field) will point to the inserted element if successful or to an already existing element that uses the same key. The insertion operation will fail if an attempt is made to insert an element into a container that requires unique keys (such as **map** or **set**) and the container already contains the key. An associative container will automatically grow as needed when elements are added to it.

You can remove one or more elements from an associative container by calling **erase( )**. It has at least three forms. The one used by this recipe is shown here:

>   size_type erase(const key_type &*k*)

It removes from the container all elements that have keys with the value *k*. For associative containers that require unique keys, a call to **erase( )** removes only one element. It returns the number of elements removed, which will be either zero or one for a **map**.

You can remove all elements from an associative container by calling **clear( )**, shown here:

>   void clear( )

You can obtain an iterator to an element in an associative container that has a specified key by calling **find( )**, shown here:

>   iterator find(const key_type &*k*)

Here, *k* specifies the key. If the container contains an element that has a key equal to *k*, **find( )** returns an iterator to the first matching element. If the key is not found, then **end( )** is returned.

You can determine the number of elements in a container by calling **size( )**. To determine if a container is empty, call **empty( )**. Both functions are shown here:

bool empty( ) const

size_type size( ) const

You can obtain an iterator to the first element in the container by calling **begin( )**. Because associative containers are ordered, this will always be the first element as specified by the comparison function. An iterator to one past the last element in the sequence is obtained by calling **end( )**. These functions are shown here:

iterator begin( )

iterator end( )

To declare a variable that will be used as an iterator, you must specify the iterator type of the container. For example, this declares an iterator that can point to elements within a **map<string, int>**:

```
map<string,int>::iterator itr;
```

You can use iterators to cycle through the contents of an associative container. The process is similar to that used to cycle through the contents of a sequence container. The main difference is that for associative containers that store key/value pairs, the object pointed to by the iterator is a **pair**. For example, assuming a properly declared iterator called **itr**, here is a loop that displays all keys and values in a **map** called **mymap**:

```
for(itr=mymap.begin(); itr != mymap.end(); ++itr)
   cout << "Key: " << itr->first << ", Value:" << itr->second << endl;
```

The loop runs until **itr** equals **mymap.end( )**, thus ensuring that all elements are displayed. Remember: **end( )** *does not* return a pointer to the last element in a container. Instead, it returns a pointer *one past* the last element. Thus, the last element in a container is pointed to by **end( )** –1.

As explained in the overview, a reversible container is one in which the elements can be traversed in reverse order (back to front). All of the built-in associative containers are reversible. When using a reversible container, you can obtain a reverse iterator to the end of the container by calling **rbegin( )**. A reverse iterator to one before the first element in the container is obtained by calling **rend( )**. These functions are shown here:

reverse_iterator rbegin( )

reverse_iterator rend( )

There are also **const** versions of these functions. A reverse iterator is declared just like a regular iterator. For example:

```
map<string,int>::reverse_iterator ritr;
```

You can use a reverse iterator to cycle through a map in reverse order. For example, given a reverse iterator called **ritr**, here is a loop that displays the keys and values for a map called **mymap**, from back to front:

```
for(ritr=mymap.rbegin(); ritr != mymap.rend(); ++ritr)
  cout << "Key: " << ritr->first << ", Value:" << ritr->second << endl;
```

The reverse iterator **ritr** starts at the element pointed to by **rbegin( )**, which is the last element in the container. It runs until it equals **rend( )**, which points to an element that is one before the start of the container. (It is sometimes helpful to think of **rbegin( )** and **rend( )** returning pointers to the start and end of a reversed container.) Each time a reverse iterator is incremented, it points to the previous element. Each time it is decremented, it points to the next element.

The contents of two associative containers can be exchanged by calling **swap( )**. Here is the way it is declared by **map**:

> void swap(map<Key, T, Comp, Allocator> &*ob*)

The contents of the invoking container are exchanged with those specified by *ob*.

Example

The following example uses **map** to demonstrate the basic associative container techniques:

```
// Demonstrate the basic associative container operations.
//
// This example uses map, but the same basic techniques can be
// applied to any associative container.

#include <iostream>
#include <string>
#include <map>

using namespace std;

void show(const char *msg, map<string, int> mp);

int main() {
  // Declare an empty map that holds key/value pairs
  // in which the key is a string and the value is an int.
  map<string, int> m;

  // Insert characters into m. An iterator to the inserted
  // object is returned.
  m.insert(pair<string, int>("Alpha", 100));
  m.insert(pair<string, int>("Gamma", 300));
  m.insert(pair<string, int>("Beta", 200));

  // Declare an iterator to a map<string, itr>.
  map<string, int>::iterator itr;

  // Display the first element in m.
```

```
itr = m.begin();
cout << "Here is the first key/value pair in m: "
     << itr->first << ", " << itr->second << endl;

// Display the last element in m.
itr = m.end();
--itr;
cout << "Here is the last key/value pair in m: "
     << itr->first << ", " << itr->second << "\n\n";

// Display the entire contents of m.
show("Entire contents of m: ", m);

// Show the size of m, which is the number of elements
// currently held by m.
cout << "Size of m is " << m.size() << "\n\n";

// Declare a reverse iterator to a map<string, itr>.
map<string, int>::reverse_iterator ritr;

// Now, show the contents of m in reverse order.
cout << "The contents of m in reverse:\n";

for(ritr=m.rbegin(); ritr != m.rend(); ++ritr)
  cout << "  " << ritr->first << ", " << ritr->second << endl;
cout << endl;

// Find an element given its key.
itr = m.find("Beta");
if(itr != m.end())
  cout << itr->first << " has the value " << itr->second << "\n\n";
else
  cout << "Key not found.\n\n";

// Create another map that is the same as the first.
map<string, int> m2(m);
show("Contents of m2: ", m2);

// Compare two maps.
if(m == m2) cout << "m and m2 are equivalent.\n\n";

// Insert more elements into m and m2.
cout << "Insert more elements into m and m2.\n";
m.insert(make_pair("Epsilon", 99));
m2.insert(make_pair("Zeta", 88));
show("Contents of m are now: ", m);
show("Contents of m2 are now: ", m2);

// Determine the relationship between m and m2. This is a
// lexicographical compare. Therefore, the first non-matching
// element in the container determines which
// container is less than the other.
if(m < m2) cout << "m is less than m2.\n\n";
```

```
   // Remove the Beta from m.
   m.erase("Beta");
   show("m after removing Beta: ", m);
   if(m > m2) cout << "Now, m is greater than m2.\n\n";

   // Exchange the contents of m and m2.
   cout << "Exchange m and m2.\n";
   m.swap(m2);
   show("Contents of m: ", m);
   show("Contents of m2: ", m2);

   // Clear m.
   m.clear();
   if(m.empty()) cout << "m is now empty.";

   return 0;
}

// Display the contents of a map<string, int> by using
// an iterator.
void show(const char *msg, map<string, int> mp) {
   map<string, int>::iterator itr;

   cout << msg << endl;
   for(itr=mp.begin(); itr != mp.end(); ++itr)
      cout << "   " << itr->first << ", " << itr->second << endl;
   cout << endl;
}
```

The output is shown here:

```
Here is the first key/value pair in m: Alpha, 100
Here is the last key/value pair in m: Gamma, 300

Entire contents of m:
  Alpha, 100
  Beta, 200
  Gamma, 300

Size of m is 3

The contents of m in reverse:
  Gamma, 300
  Beta, 200
  Alpha, 100

Beta has the value 200

Contents of m2:
  Alpha, 100
  Beta, 200
  Gamma, 300
```

```
m and m2 are equivalent.

Insert more elements into m and m2.
Contents of m are now:
  Alpha, 100
  Beta, 200
  Epsilon, 99
  Gamma, 300

Contents of m2 are now:
  Alpha, 100
  Beta, 200
  Gamma, 300
  Zeta, 88

m is less than m2.

m after removing Beta:
  Alpha, 100
  Epsilon, 99
  Gamma, 300

Now, m is greater than m2.

Exchange m and m2.
Contents of m:
  Alpha, 100
  Beta, 200
  Gamma, 300
  Zeta, 88

Contents of m2:
  Alpha, 100
  Epsilon, 99
  Gamma, 300

m is now empty.
```

Much of the program is self-explanatory, but there are a few aspects that warrant close examination. First, notice how a **map** object is declared by the following line:

```
map<string, int> m;
```

This declares a map called **m** that holds key/value pairs in which the key is of type **string** and the value is of type **int**. This means that the types of objects held by **m** are instances of **pair<string, int>**. Notice that the default comparison function **less** is used. This means that objects are stored in the map in ascending, sorted order. Also notice that the default allocator is used.

Next, key/value pairs are inserted in **m** by calling **insert( )**, as shown here:

```
m.insert(pair<string, int>("Alpha", 100));
m.insert(pair<string, int>("Gamma", 300));
m.insert(pair<string, int>("Beta", 200));
```

Because **m** uses the default comparison function, the contents are automatically sorted in ascending order based on the keys. Thus, the order of the keys in the map after the preceding calls to **insert( )** is Alpha, Beta, Gamma, as the output confirms.

Next, an iterator to the map is declared by the following line:

```
map<string, int>::iterator itr;
```

Because the iterator type must match exactly the container type, it is necessary to specify the same key and value types. For example, an iterator that contains key/value pairs of type **string/int** won't work with a map that contains key/value pairs of type **ofstream/string**.

The program then uses the iterator to display the first and last key/value pairs in the map by use of this sequence:

```
// Display the first element in m.
itr = m.begin();
cout << "Here is the first key/value pair in m: "
    << itr->first << ", " << itr->second << endl;

// Display the last element in m.
itr = m.end();
--itr;
cout << "Here is the last key/value pair in m: "
    << itr->first << ", " << itr->second << "\n\n";
```

As explained, the **begin( )** function returns an iterator to the first element in the container and **end( )** returns an iterator to one past the last element. This is why **itr** is decremented after the call to **end( )** so that the last element can be displayed. Recall that the type of object pointed to by a **map** iterator is an instance of **pair**. The key is contained in the **first** field and the value in the **second** field. Also notice how the **pair** fields are specified by applying the –> operator to **itr** in just the same way you would use –> with a pointer. In general, iterators work like pointers and are handled in essentially the same way.

Next, the entire contents of **m** are displayed by a call to **show( )**, which displays the contents of the **map<string, int>** that it is passed. Pay special attention to how the key/value pairs are displayed by the following **for** loop:

```
for(itr=mp.begin(); itr != mp.end(); ++itr)
  cout << "   " << itr->first << ", " << itr->second << endl;
```

Because **end( )** obtains an iterator that points one past the end of the container, the loop stops immediately after the last element has been displayed.

The program then displays the contents of **m** in reverse by using a reverse iterator and a loop that runs from **m.rbegin( )** to **m.rend( )**. As explained, a reverse iterator operates on the container back to front. Therefore, incrementing a reverse iterator causes it to point to the previous element in the container.

Pay special attention to how two containers are compared by use of the **==**, **<**, and **>** operators. For associative containers, comparisons are conducted using a lexicographical comparison of the elements, which in the case of **map**, are key/value pairs. Although the term "lexicographical" literally means "dictionary order," its meaning is generalized as it relates to the STL. For container comparisons, two containers are equal if they contain the same number of elements, in the same order, and all corresponding elements are equal. For associative containers that hold key/value pairs, this means that each element's key and value must match. If a mismatch is found, the result of a lexicographical comparison is based on the first non-matching elements. For example, assume one map contains the pair:

test, 10

and another contains:

test, 20

Even though the keys are the same, because the values differ, these two elements are not equivalent. Therefore, the first map will be judged to be less than the second.

One other point of interest is the sequence that finds an element given its key. It is shown here:

```
// Find an element given its key.
itr = m.find("Beta");
if(itr != m.end())
  cout << itr->first << " has the value " << itr->second << "\n\n";
else
  cout << "Key not found.\n\n";
```

The ability to find an element given its key is one of the defining aspects of associative containers. (They are called "associative containers" for a reason!) The **find( )** method searches the invoking container for a key that matches the one specified as an argument. If it is found, an iterator to the element is returned. Otherwise, **end( )** is returned.

Options and Alternatives

You can count the number of elements in an associative container that match a specified key by calling **count( )**, shown here:

size_type count(const key_type &*k*) const

It returns the number of times *k* occurs in the container. For containers that require unique keys, this will be either zero or one.

All associative containers let you determine a range of elements in which an element falls. This ability is supported by three functions: **lower_bound( )**, **upper_bound( )**, and **equal_range( )**. They are shown here. (There are also **const** versions of these functions.)

iterator lower_bound(const key_type &*k*)

iterator upper_bound(const key_type &*k*)

pair<iterator, iterator> equal_range(const key_type &*k*)

The **lower_bound( )** function returns an iterator to the first element in the container with a key equal to or greater than *k*. The **upper_bound( )** function returns an iterator to the first element in the container with a key greater than *k*. The **equal_range( )** function returns a pair of iterators that point to the upper bound and the lower bound in the container for a specified key by calling **equal_range( )**.

All associative containers support three forms of **insert( )**. One was described earlier. The other two versions of **insert( )** are shown here:

iterator insert(iterator *i*, const value_type &*val*)

template <class InIter> void insert(InIter *start*, InIter *end*)

The first form inserts *val* into the container. For associative containers that allow duplicates, this form of insert will always succeed. Otherwise, it will insert *val* only if its key is not already in the container. In either case, an iterator to the element with the same key is returned. The iterator specified by *i* indicates a good place to start the search for the proper insertion point. Because associative containers are sorted based on keys, supplying a good starting point can speed up insertions. The second form of **insert( )** inserts the range *start* to *end*–1. Whether duplicate keys will be inserted depends upon the container. In all cases, the resulting associative container will remain sorted based on keys.

In addition to the form of **erase( )** used by this recipe, all associative containers support two other forms. They are shown here:

void erase(iterator *i*)

void erase(iterator *start*, iterator *end*)

The first form removes the element pointed to by *i*. The second form removes the elements in the range *start* to *end*–1.

As mentioned, the STL supports two categories of associative containers: maps and sets. A map stores key/value pairs. A set stores objects in which the key and the value are the same. Within these two categories, there are two divisions: those associative containers that require unique keys and those that allow duplicate keys. The **map** and **set** containers require unique keys. The **multimap** and **multiset** containers allow duplicate keys. Because each associative container uses a different strategy, it is usually a simple matter to choose which is best for an application. For example, if you need to store key/value pairs and all keys are unique, use **map**. For maps that require duplicate keys, use **multimap**.

Use map

Key Ingredients		
Headers	**Classes**	**Functions**
<map>	map	iterator find(const key_type &*k*)
		pair<iterator, bool> insert(const value_type &*val*)
		T &operator[ ] (const key_type &*k*)
<utility>	pair	

This recipe describes what is probably the most widely used associative container: **map**. A map stores key/value pairs, and all keys must be unique. Therefore, given a key, you can easily find its value. This makes **map** especially useful for maintaining property lists, storing attribute and option settings, or anyplace else in which a value must be found through a key. For example, you might use **map** to create a contact list that uses a person's name for the key and a telephone number for the value. Such a map would let you easily retrieve a phone number given a name. A map is an ordered container, with the order based on the keys. By default, the keys are in ascending order, but it is possible to specify a different ordering.

NOTE *The basic mechanism required to use an associative container, including* **map***, was described in* Basic Associative Container Techniques. *The recipe given here focuses on those aspects of* **map** *that go beyond those general techniques.*

Step-by-Step

To use **map** involves these steps:

1. Create a **map** instance of the desired type.
2. Add elements to the map by calling **insert( )** or by using the subscripting operator.
3. Obtain or set the value of an element by using the subscripting operator.
4. Find a specific element in the map by calling **find( )**.

Discussion

The **map** class supports an associative container in which unique keys are mapped with values. In essence, a key is simply a name that you give to a value. Once a value has been stored, you can retrieve it by using its key. Thus, in its most general sense, a map is a list of key/value pairs.

The template specification for **map** is shown here:

template <class Key, class T, class Comp = less<Key>,
      class Allocator = allocator<pair<const Key, T> > > class map

Here, **Key** is the data type of the keys, **T** is the data type of the values being stored, and **Comp** is a function that compares two keys. The following constructors are defined for **map**:

explicit map(const Comp &*cmpfn* = Comp( ),
      const Allocator &*alloc* = Allocator( ))

map(const map<Key, T, Comp, Allocator> &*ob*)

template <class InIter> map(InIter *start*, InIter *end*,
      const Comp &*cmpfn* = Comp( ),
      const Allocator &*alloc* = Allocator( ))

The first form constructs an empty map. The second form constructs a map that contains the same elements as *ob* and is **map**'s copy constructor. The third form constructs a map that contains the elements in the range *start* to *end*–1. The function specified by *cmpfn*, if present, determines the ordering of the map. Most often, you will allow both *cmpfn* and *alloc* to default. To use **map**, you must include **<map>**.

The **map** class supports bidirectional iterators. Thus, the container can be accessed through an iterator in both the forward and reverse directions, but random-access operations are not supported. However, the [ ] operator is supported, but not in its traditional usage.

Key/value pairs are stored in a map as objects of type **pair**. (See *Basic Associative Container Techniques* for details on **pair**.) The iterator type defined by **map** points to objects of type **pair<const Key, T>**. Thus, when a **map** function returns an iterator, the key is available through the **first** member of **pair** and the value is obtained through **pair**'s **second** field.

The **map** class supports all of the standard functions specified for associative containers, such as **find( )**, **count( )**, **erase( )**, and so on. These are described in *Basic Associative Container Techniques*.

Elements can be added to a map in two ways. The first is by the **insert( )** function. The general operation of **insert( )** is described in *Basic Associative Container Techniques*. Here is a summary. All associative containers support at least three versions of **insert( )**. The one used by this recipe is:

pair<iterator, bool> insert(const value_type &*val*)

It inserts *val* into the invoking container at a point that maintains the ordering of the associative container. In **map**, **value_type** is a **type_def** for **pair<const Key, T>**. Thus, this version of **insert( )** inserts a key/value pair into the invoking map. It returns a **pair** object that indicates the outcome of the operation. As explained, **map** requires that all keys be unique. Therefore, if *val* contains a unique key, the insertion will be successful. In this case, the **bool** value of the returned **pair** object (which is in the **second** field) will be true. However, if the specified key already exists, then this value will be false. The **iterator** portion of the returned **pair** object (which is in the **first** field) will point to the inserted element if successful or to an already existing element that uses the same key.

The second way to add a key/value pair to a map involves the use of **operator[ ]( )**. You may be surprised by the way in which it works. Its prototype is shown here:

T &operator[](const key_type &*k*)

Notice that *k* (which receives the index value) is not an integer. Rather, it is an object that represents a key. This key is then used to find the value, and the function returns a reference to the value associated with the key. Thus, the subscripting operator is implemented by **map** so that it uses a key as the index and it returns the value associated with that key.

To best understand the effects of **operator[ ]( )**, it helps to work through an example. Consider a map called **phonemap** that contains key/value pairs consisting of a person's name and phone number. Also assume that there is an entry in the map that has the key "Tom," which has the value "555-0001." In this case, the following statement displays the phone number linked to "Tom":

```
cout << phonemap["Tom"];
```

Because "555-0001" is the value associated with "Tom", this statement displays 555-0001.

There is a very important aspect of the [ ] operator as it applies to **map** that greatly expands its power. Because of the way that [ ] is implemented, *it will always succeed*. If the key you are looking for is not in the map, it is automatically inserted, with its value being that of the type's default constructor (which is zero for the built-in types). Thus, any key that you search for will always be found!

As mentioned, the value returned by the [ ] operator is a reference to the value associated with the key used as the index. Thus, you can use the [ ] operator on the left side of an assignment to give an element a new value. For example:

```
phonemap["Tom"] = "555-1234";
```

This statement assigns the number 555-1234 to the key "Tom". If "Tom" is not currently in the map, it will first be automatically added (with a default value for the key) and then assigned the number 555-1234. If it did previously exist, then its value is simply changed to the new number.

One important point: Whether elements are added by calling **insert( )** or by using **operator[ ]( )**, the map is maintained in sorted order based on keys.

Because the **map** class supports bidirectional iterators, it can be traversed in both the forward and reverse directions through an iterator. Furthermore, the **map** class supports both the **iterator** and **reverse_iterator** types. (Corresponding **const** types are also provided.) Because **map** elements consist of **pair** objects, **map** iterators point to **pair** objects.

You can obtain an iterator to the first element in a map by calling **begin( )**. An iterator to one past the last element is obtained by calling **end( )**. You can obtain a reverse iterator to the end of the map by calling **rbegin( )** and a reverse iterator to the element that is one before the beginning of the map by calling **rend( )**. These functions and the technique used to cycle through an associative container by use of an iterator are described in *Basic Associative Container Techniques*.

You can obtain an iterator to a specific element by calling **find( )**, which is implemented like this for **map**:

```
iterator find(const key_type &k)
```

This function returns an iterator to the element whose key matches *k*. If the key is not found, then **end( )** is returned. A **const** version is also available. It is important to understand that unlike [ ], if the entry being sought is not found, **find( )** *will not* create the element.

The **map** class has the following performance characteristics. Maps are designed for the efficient storage of key/value pairs. In general, inserting or deleting elements in a map takes place in logarithmic time. There are two exceptions. First, an element that is inserted at a given location takes place in amortized constant time. Amortized constant time is also consumed when a specific element is deleted given an iterator to that element. Insertion into a map invalidates no iterators or references to elements. A deletion invalidates only iterators or references to the deleted elements.

Example

The following example shows **map** in action. It creates a container that works as a phone directory, in which a person's name is the key and the phone number is the value.

```
// Demonstrate map.
//
// This program creates a simple phone list in which
// a person's name is the key and the phone number is
```

```
// the value. Thus, you can look up a phone number
// given a name.

#include <iostream>
#include <string>
#include <map>
#include <utility>

using namespace std;

void show(const char *msg, map<string, string> mp);

int main() {
  map<string, string> phonemap;

  // Insert elements by using operator[].
  phonemap["Tom"] = "555-1234";
  phonemap["Jane"] = "314 555-6576";
  phonemap["Ken"] = "660 555-9843";

  show("Here is the original map: ", phonemap);
  cout << endl;

  // Now, change the phone number for Ken.
  phonemap["Ken"] = "415 997-8893";
  cout << "New number for Ken: " << phonemap["Ken"] << "\n\n";

  // Use find() to find a number.
  map<string, string>::iterator itr;
  itr = phonemap.find("Jane");
  if(itr != phonemap.end())
    cout << "Number for Jane is " << itr->second << "\n\n";

  // Cycle through the map in the reverse direction.
  map<string, string>::reverse_iterator ritr;
  cout << "Display phonemap in reverse order:\n";
  for(ritr = phonemap.rbegin(); ritr != phonemap.rend(); ++ritr)
   cout << "  " << ritr->first << ": " << ritr->second << endl;
  cout << endl;

  // Create a pair object that will contain the result
  // of a call to insert().
  pair<map<string, string>::iterator, bool> result;

  // Use insert() to add an entry.
  result = phonemap.insert(pair<string, string>("Jay", "555-9999"));
  if(result.second) cout << "Jay added.\n";
  show("phonemap after adding Jay: ", phonemap);

  // Duplicate keys are not allowed, as the following proves.
  result = phonemap.insert(pair<string, string>("Jay", "555-1010"));
  if(result.second) cout << "Duplicate Jay added! Error!";
  else cout << "Duplicate Jay not allowed.\n";
```

```
    show("phonemap after attempt to add duplicate Jay key: ", phonemap);

    return 0;
}

// Display the contents of a map<string, string> by using
// an iterator.
void show(const char *msg, map<string, string> mp) {
  map<string, string>::iterator itr;

  cout << msg << endl;

  for(itr=mp.begin(); itr != mp.end(); ++itr)
   cout << "  " << itr->first << ": " << itr->second << endl;

  cout << endl;
}
```

The output is shown here:

```
Here is the original map:
  Jane: 314 555-6576
  Ken: 660 555-9843
  Tom: 555-1234

New number for Ken: 415 997-8893

Number for Jane is 314 555-6576

Display phonemap in reverse order:
  Tom: 555-1234
  Ken: 415 997-8893
  Jane: 314 555-6576

Jay added.
phonemap after adding Jay:
  Jane: 314 555-6576
  Jay: 555-9999
  Ken: 415 997-8893
  Tom: 555-1234

Duplicate Jay not allowed.
phonemap after attempt to add duplicate Jay key:
  Jane: 314 555-6576
  Jay: 555-9999
  Ken: 415 997-8893
  Tom: 555-1234
```

In the program, notice how the [ ] operator is used. First, it adds elements to **phonemap** in the following statements:

```
phonemap["Tom"] = "555-1234";
phonemap["Jane"] = "314 555-6576";
phonemap["Ken"] = "660 555-9843";
```

When **phonemap** is created, it is initially empty. Therefore, when the preceding statements execute, there will be no elements in **phonemap** that have the specified keys. This causes the key and the value to be added. (In essence, a **pair** object that contains the key and value is automatically constructed and added to the map.)

The following use of [ ] changes the phone number associated with Ken:

```
phonemap["Ken"] = "415 997-8893";
```

Because the key "Ken" is already in the map, its entry is found and its value is set to the new phone number.

Options and Alternatives

As explained, **map** holds key/value pairs in which each key is unique. If you want to use a map that allows duplicate keys, use **multimap**. It is described by the next recipe.

As described in *Basic Associative Container Techniques*, all associative containers support two other forms of **insert( )** in addition to the one used by the recipe. One form is especially helpful when working with maps because it gives you a way to merge two maps. It is shown here:

template <class InIter> void insert(InIter *start*, InIter *end*)

This function inserts the elements in the range *start* to *end*–1 into the invoking map. Elements are inserted in such a way that the invoking map remains sorted. Of course, the types of the elements must match those stored in the invoking map and duplicate elements are not allowed. Here is an example of how this version of **insert( )** can be used. Assuming the preceding program, the following sequence creates a second telephone list called **friends** and then adds those numbers to **phonemap**:

```
map<string, string> friends;

friends["Larry"] = "555-4857";
friends["Cindy"] = "555-1101";
friends["Liz"]   = "555-0100";

// Insert the elements from friends into phonemap.
phonemap.insert(friends.begin(), friends.end());
```

After this sequence executes, **phonemap** will contain all of its original entries plus those contained in **friends**. The resulting **phonemap** remains in sorted order. The **friends** map will be unchanged.

Like all associative containers, **map** supplies three forms of **erase( )** that let you remove elements from a **map**. These are described in *Basic Associative Container Techniques*, but one merits a special mention. It is shown here:

size_type erase(const key_type &*k*)

This version of **erase( )** removes the element with the key passed in *k* and returns the number of elements removed. However, for **map**, it will never remove more than one element because duplicate elements are not allowed. Therefore, if the key specified by *k* exists in the invoking map, it will be removed and 1 will be returned. Otherwise, 0 is returned.

Use multimap

Key Ingredients		
Headers	**Classes**	**Functions**
<map>	multimap	size_type erase(const key_type &*k*)
		iterator insert(const value_type &*val*)
		iterator find(const key_type &*k*)
		iterator upper_bound(const key_type &*k*)
<utility>	pair	

A variation of **map** is **multimap**. Like **map**, **multimap** stores key/value pairs. However, in a multimap, the keys need not be unique. In other words, one key might be associated with two or more different values. Such a container is useful in two general types of situations. First, it helps in cases in which duplicate keys cannot be avoided. For example, an online phone directory might have two different numbers for the same person. By using **multimap**, a person's name can be used as a key that maps to both numbers. Second, it is well suited for situations in which a key describes a general relationship that exists between its values. For example, family members could be represented in a multimap that uses the last name of the family as the key. The values are the first names. With this approach, to find all members of the Jones family, you simply use Jones as the key.

NOTE *Aside from allowing duplicate keys,* ***multimap*** *works much like* ***map***, *which is described by the preceding recipe. It also supports all of the operations described in* Basic Associative Container Techniques. *This recipe focuses on the unique aspects of* ***multimap***.

Step-by-Step
To use **multimap** involves these steps:

1. Create a **multimap** instance of the desired type.
2. Add elements, which may include duplicate keys, to the multimap by calling **insert( )**.
3. Find all elements with a specified key by using **find( )** and **upper_bound( )**.
4. Remove all elements within a multimap that have the same key by using **erase( )**.

Discussion
The **multimap** template specification is shown here:

```
template <class Key, class T, class Comp = less<Key>,
        class Allocator = allocator<pair<const Key, T> > > class multimap
```

Here, **Key** is the data type of the keys, **T** is the data type of the values being stored (mapped), and **Comp** is a function that compares two keys. It has the following constructors.

explicit multimap(const Comp &*cmpfn* = Comp( ),
        const Allocator &*alloc* = Allocator( ))

multimap(const multimap<Key, T, Comp, Allocator> &*ob*)

template <class InIter> multimap(InIter *start*, InIter *end*,
        const Comp &*cmpfn* = Comp( ),
        const Allocator &*alloc* = Allocator( ))

The first form constructs an empty multimap. The second form is **multimap**'s copy constructor. The third form constructs a multimap that contains the elements in the range *start* to *end*–1. The function specified by *cmpfn* determines the ordering of the multimap. The allocator used by the multimap is specified by *alloc*. Typically, both *cmpfn* and *alloc* are allowed to default. To utilize **multimap**, you must include **<map>**.

The **multimap** class supports bidirectional iterators. Thus, the container can be accessed through an iterator in both the forward and reverse directions. Unlike **map**, **multimap** does not support the [ ] operator. (Since there is not a one-to-one mapping of keys to values, it is not possible to index a **multimap** object by using a key.)

In general, **multimap** is used like **map**. The primary difference is that duplicate keys are allowed. This difference has its greatest impact on two operations: inserting an element and finding an element. Each is examined, beginning with insertion.

You can add elements to a multimap by using the **insert( )** function. There are three versions of **insert( )**. The one used in this recipe is shown here:

iterator insert(const value_type &*val*)

It inserts *val* (which is a **pair** object) into the invoking multimap. (As with **map**, **value_type** is a **typedef** for **pair<const Key, T>**.) Because duplicate keys are allowed, *val* will always be inserted (until memory is exhausted, of course). The function returns an iterator that points to the inserted element. Therefore, **insert( )** always succeeds. This differs from the corresponding version of **insert( )** used by **map**, which fails if there is an attempt to insert a duplicate element.

Since the defining characteristic of **multimap** is its ability to store more than one value for any given key, this raises the obvious question: How do I find all values associated with a key? The answer is a bit more complicated than you might expect because the **find( )** function alone is insufficient to find multiple matches. Recall that **find( )** is a function that all associative containers must implement. It is defined like this for **multimap**:

iterator find(const key_type &*k*)

Here, *k* specifies the key. If the multimap contains an element that has a key equal to *k*, **find( )** returns an iterator to the first matching element. If the key is not found, then **end( )** is returned. (A **const** version of **find( )** is also supplied.)

Because **find( )** always returns an iterator to the *first matching key*, there is no way to make it move on to the next one. Instead, to obtain the next matching key, you must increment the iterator returned by **find( )**. The process stops when the last matching key has been found.

The end point is obtained through the use of the **upper_bound( )** function. Its non-**const** version is shown here:

iterator upper_bound(const key_type &*k*)

The **upper_bound( )** function returns an iterator to the first element in the container with a key greater than *k*. In other words, it returns an iterator to the element that comes after the ones with the key you specify. Therefore, assuming some multimap called **mm**, to find all matches for a given key, you will use a sequence like this:

```
itr = mm.find(key);
if(itr != end()) {
  do {
    // ...
    ++itr;
  } while(itr != mm.upper_bound(key));
}
```

First, an attempt is made to find an element that matches the specified key. If a match is found, then the **do** loop is entered. (Recall that **find( )** returns **end( )** if the key is not found.) Inside the loop, the iterator is incremented and its value is checked against the upper bound for the key. This process continues until **itr** points to the upper bound.

You can erase all elements that share a given key by using this form of **erase( )**:

size_type erase(const key_type &*k*)

It removes from the multimap elements that have keys with the value *k*. It returns the number of elements removed. Two other versions of **erase( )** are supported, which operate on iterators.

The **multimap** class has the same performance characteristics as **map**. In general, inserting or deleting elements in a map takes place in logarithmic time. The two exceptions are when an element is inserted at a given location and when a specific element is deleted given an iterator to that element. In these cases, amortized constant time is required. Insertion into a multimap invalidates no iterators or references to elements. A deletion invalidates only those iterators or references to the deleted elements.

Example

The following example demonstrates how **multimap** can be used to store key/value pairs in which duplicates might occur. It reworks the example program used by the preceding recipe so that it uses a multimap rather than a map to store the list of names and telephone numbers.

```
// Demonstrating a multimap.
//
// This program uses a multimap to store names and phone
// numbers. It allows one name to be associated with more
// than one phone number.

#include <iostream>
#include <map>
```

```cpp
#include <string>
using namespace std;

void shownumbers(const char *n, multimap<string, string> mp);

int main()
{
  multimap<string, string> phonemap;

  // Insert elements by using operator[].
  phonemap.insert(pair<string, string>("Tom", "Home: 555-1111"));
  phonemap.insert(pair<string, string>("Tom", "Work: 555-1234"));
  phonemap.insert(pair<string, string>("Tom", "Cell: 555-2224"));

  phonemap.insert(pair<string, string>("Jane", "Home: 314 555-6576"));
  phonemap.insert(pair<string, string>("Jane", "Cell: 314 555-8822"));

  phonemap.insert(pair<string, string>("Ken", "Home: 660 555-9843"));
  phonemap.insert(pair<string, string>("Ken", "Work: 660 555-1010"));
  phonemap.insert(pair<string, string>("Ken", "Cell: 217 555-9995"));

  // Show all phone numbers for Tom, Jane, and Ken
  shownumbers("Tom", phonemap);
  cout << endl;
  shownumbers("Jane", phonemap);
  cout << endl;
  shownumbers("Ken", phonemap);
  cout << endl;

  // Now remove all phone numbers for Ken:
  cout << "Removing all numbers for Ken.\n";
  int count = phonemap.erase("Ken");
  cout << count << " elements have been removed.\n\n";

  cout << "After removing Ken, attempt to find phone number fails:\n";
  shownumbers("Ken", phonemap);

  return 0;
}

// Show all numbers for a given name.
void shownumbers(const char *n, multimap<string, string> mmp) {
  multimap<string, string>::iterator itr;

  // Find the first matching key.
  itr = mmp.find(n);

  // If the key was found, then display all phone numbers
  // that have that key.
  if(itr != mmp.end()) {
    cout << "Here are the numbers for " <<  n << ": " << endl;
    do {
      cout << "   " << itr->second << endl;
```

```
      ++itr;
    } while (itr != mmp.upper_bound(n));
  }
  else
    cout << "No entry for " << n << " found.\n";
}
```

The output is shown here:

```
Here are the numbers for Tom:
  Home: 555-1111
  Work: 555-1234
  Cell: 555-2224

Here are the numbers for Jane:
  Home: 314 555-6576
  Cell: 314 555-8822

Here are the numbers for Ken:
  Home: 660 555-9843
  Work: 660 555-1010
  Cell: 217 555-9995

Removing all numbers for Ken.
3 elements have been removed.

After removing Ken, attempt to find phone number fails:
No entry for Ken found.
```

There are three important features of this program. First, notice how **insert( )** is used to insert elements with duplicate keys into **phonemap**, which in this program is a **multimap**. As explained, **insert( )** will always succeed (until memory is exhausted, of course) because **multimap** allows duplicate keys. Second, notice how all elements with a specific key are found. As explained in the preceding discussion, to find all matching entries for a given key, find the first key by calling **find( )**. Then, find subsequent matching keys by incrementing the iterator returned by **find( )** until it is equal to the upper bound, as obtained from **upper_bound( )**. Finally, notice how this call to **erase( )** removes all elements that have the key "Ken":

```
int count = phonemap.erase("Ken");
```

If you want to erase a specific element that has the key "Ken", then you will need to first find the entry that you want to erase and remove it using another form of **erase( )**. This procedure is described in the *Options and Alternatives* section for this recipe.

Options and Alternatives

As explained, this form of **erase( )** removes all elements that share the specified key:

```
size_type erase(const key_type &k)
```

It removes elements that have keys with the value k. If you want to remove one or more specific elements, then you will need to use one of the other forms of **erase( )**. Recall that all associative containers, including **multimap**, support the following additional forms of **erase( )**:

> void erase(iterator i)
>
> void erase(iterator $start$, iterator end)

The first form removes the element pointed to by i. The second form removes the elements in the range $start$ to end–1. You can use these forms to remove specific elements from a **multimap**. For example, assuming the preceding program, the following sequence removes the work phone number for Tom:

```
multimap<string, string>::iterator itr;

// Find the first matching key.
itr = phonemap.find("Tom");

// Now, search for the specific phone number to remove.
if(itr != phonemap.end()) {
  do {
    // If the entry contains the work phone, remove it.
    if(itr->second.find("Work") != string::npos) {
        phonemap.erase(itr);
        break;
      }

    ++itr;
  } while (itr != phonemap.upper_bound("Tom"));
}
```

This sequence works by finding the first matching element with the key "Tom". It then uses a loop that checks all elements with the key "Tom" to see if one of them contains the work phone number. In the list, work numbers are preceded by the substring "Work", so each value is checked to see if it contains the "Work" substring. If it does, the entry is removed and the loop terminates.

Sometimes, it's useful to know the start and end points of a set of elements that share a key. To accomplish this, use **equal_range( )**, shown here:

> pair<iterator, iterator> equal_range(const key_type &k)

It returns a **pair** object that contains iterators that point to the lower bound (in the **first** field) and the upper bound (in the **second** field) in the multimap for the specified key. (A **const** version of the function is also supplied.) Although all associative containers provide **equal_range( )**, it is most useful with those that allow duplicate keys. Recall that the lower bound is the first element that has a key that is equal to or greater than k, and the upper bound is the first element that has a key greater than k. Assuming the preceding program, here is an example that shows how **equal_range( )** can be used to display all phone numbers for Tom:

```
multimap<string, string>::iterator itr;
pair<multimap<string, string>::iterator,
     multimap<string, string>::iterator> pr;
```

```
pr = phonemap.equal_range("Tom");

itr = pr.first;

cout << "Here are the numbers for Tom:\n";
while(itr != pr.second) {
  cout << itr->second << endl;
  ++itr;
}
```

Use set and multiset

Key Ingredients		
Headers	**Classes**	**Functions**
<set>	set	size_type erase(const key_type &*val*)
		iterator find(const key_type &*val*)
		pair<iterator, bool>
		insert(const value_type &*val*)
<set>	multiset	size_type erase(const key_type &*val*)
		iterator find(const key_type &*val*)
		pair<iterator, bool>
		insert(const value_type &*val*)
		iterator upper_bound(const key_type &*val*)
		const

This recipe demonstrates **set** and **multiset**. The set containers are similar to maps, except that the key and the value are not separated from each other. That is, sets store objects in which the key is part of the value. In fact, if you use a set to store one of the built-in types, such as an integer, the key and value are one and the same. Sets provide very efficient containers when there is no need to separate the key from the data. The **set** container requires that all keys be unique. The **multiset** container allows duplicate keys. Aside from this difference, both **set** and **multiset** work in similar ways.

Because **set** and **multiset** store objects in which the key and the value are inseparable, you might initially think that applications for **set** and **multiset** are quite limited. In fact, when storing simple types, such as **int** or **char**, a **set** simply creates a sorted list. However, the power of sets becomes apparent when objects are stored. In this case, the object's key is determined by the < and/or == operator defined for the class. Therefore, the object's key might consist of only one part of the object. This means that **set** can provide a very efficient means to store objects that are retrieved based on the value of a field defined by the object. For example, you might use **set** to store objects that hold employee information, such as name, address, phone number, and an ID number. In this case, the ID number could be used as a key. Because the main use of **set** and **multiset** is to hold objects rather than simple values, this is the focus of this recipe.

NOTE *The techniques needed for **set** and **multiset** are similar to those used for **map** and **multimap**, and those discussions are not repeated here. For general information on using associative containers, see* Basic Associative Container Techniques. *Also see* Use **map** *and* Use **multimap** *for related information.*

Step-by-Step

To use **set** involves the following steps:

1. Create a **set** instance of the desired type.
2. Add elements to the set by calling **insert( )**. Each element's key must be unique.
3. Find a specific element in a set by calling **find( )**.
4. Remove an element with a specified key by calling **erase( )**.

To use **multiset** involves the following steps:

1. Create a **multiset** instance of the desired type.
2. Add elements to the set by calling **insert( )**. Duplicate keys are allowed.
3. Find all elements with a specified key by using **find( )** and **upper_bound( )**.
4. Remove all elements that have the same key by using **erase( )**.

Discussion

The **set** class supports a set in which unique keys are stored in ascending order. Its template specification is shown here:

```
template <class Key, class Comp = less<Key>,
          class Allocator = allocator<Key> > class set
```

Here, **Key** is the data type of the keys (which also contain the data) and **Comp** is a function that compares two keys. The **set** class has the following constructors:

```
explicit set(const Comp &cmpfn = Comp( ),
          const Allocator &alloc = Allocator( ) )

set(const set<Key, Comp, Allocator> &ob)

template <class InIter> set(InIter start, InIter end,
          const Comp &cmpfn = Comp( ),
          const Allocator &alloc = Allocator( ))
```

The first form constructs an empty set. The second form is **set**'s copy constructor. The third form constructs a set that contains the elements specified by the range *start* to *end*–1. The function specified by *cmpfn*, if present, determines the ordering of the set. By default, **less** is used. To use **set**, you must include **<set>**.

The **multiset** class supports a set in which duplicate keys are allowed. Its template specification is shown here:

template <class Key, class Comp = less<Key>,
        class Allocator = allocator<Key> > class multiset

Here, **Key** is the data of the keys and **Comp** is a function that compares two keys. The **multiset** class has the following constructors:

explicit multiset(const Comp &*cmpfn* = Comp( ),
        const Allocator &*alloc* = Allocator( ))

multiset(const multiset<Key, Comp, Allocator> &*ob*)

template <class InIter> multiset(InIter *start*, InIter *end*,
        const Comp &*cmpfn* = Comp( ),
        const Allocator &*alloc* = Allocator( ))

The first form constructs an empty multiset. The second form constructs a multiset that contains the same elements as *ob*. The third form constructs a multiset that contains the elements specified by the range *start* to *end*–1. The function specified by *cmpfn*, if present, determines the ordering of the set. By default, **less** is the comparison function. The header for **multiset** is also **<set>**.

Both **set** and **multiset** support bidirectional iterators. Thus, the containers can be accessed through an iterator in both the forward and reverse directions, but random-access operations are not supported.

The **insert( )**, **erase( )**, and **find( )** functions are described in *Basic Associative Container Techniques*. Here is a brief review of the forms used by this recipe. When used with **set**, this version of **insert( )**

pair<iterator, bool> insert(const value_type &*val*)

will fail if *val* contains a key that is already in the container. (In this case, false is returned in the **second** field of the **pair** object and an iterator to the previously existing element is returned in the **first** field.) When used with **multiset**, **insert( )** will always succeed. In both cases, when **insert( )** succeeds, the **first** field of the returned **pair** object will contain an iterator that points to the object inserted.

When used with **set**, this form of **erase( )**

size_type erase(const key_type &*val*)

removes the element whose key matches *val*. When used with **multiset**, it removes all elements whose keys match *val*. In both cases, the number of elements removed is returned.

The **find( )** function is shown next:

iterator find(const key_type &*val*)

For **set**, it returns an iterator to the element whose key matches *val*. For **multiset**, it returns an iterator to the first element whose key matches *val*. To find all elements with matching keys, use **upper_bound( )** to establish the upper limit. All elements between the one pointed to by **find( )** and the one pointed to by **upper_bound( )** will contain matching keys.

As explained in *Store User-Defined Objects in a Container*, in general, for an object to be stored in associative container, its class must overload the < operator. This is because associative containers are ordered by using the < operator. The < operator is also used by the **find( )**, **upper_bound( )**, **lower_bound( )**, and **equal_range( )** functions. Thus, the secret to using **set** to store class objects is to correctly overload **operator<( )**. Typically, the < operator is defined in such a way that only one member of the class is compared. This member, thus, forms the key, even though the entire class forms the element. In some cases, you will also need to define **operator==( )**.

NOTE *It has been my experience that there is some variation among compilers in precisely what operators and functions a class must define in order for instances of that class to be stored in a container. This is especially true for older compilers. As a result, you might find that additional operators need to be overloaded.*

Example

The following example shows **set** in action. It is used to store objects that contain employee information. The employee's ID is used as the key. Therefore, **operator<( )** is implemented so that it compares IDs. Notice that **operator==( )** is also implemented. This operator is not necessary for the following program, but is needed by some algorithms, such as **find( )**. Therefore, it is included for completeness. (Remember, depending upon implementation and use, other functions may need to be defined.)

```cpp
// Demonstrate set.
//
// This example stores objects that contain employee
// information. The employee's ID is used as the key.

#include <iostream>
#include <set>
#include <string>

using namespace std;

// This class stores employee information.
class employee {
  string name;
  string ID;
  string phone;
  string department;
public:
  // Default constructor.
  employee() { ID = name = phone = department = ""; }

  // Construct temporary object using only the ID, which is the key.
  employee(string id) { ID = id;
                        name = phone = department = ""; }

  // Construct a complete employee object.
  employee(string n, string id, string dept, string p)
```

```
    {
      name = n;
      ID = id;
      phone = p;
      department = dept;
    }

    // Accessor functions for employee data.
    string get_name() { return name; }
    string get_id() { return ID; }
    string get_dept() { return department; }
    string get_phone() { return phone; }

};

// Compare objects using ID.
bool operator<(employee a, employee b)
{
  return a.get_id() < b.get_id();
}

// Check for equality based on ID.
bool operator==(employee a, employee b)
{
  return a.get_id() == b.get_id();
}

// Create an inserter for employee.
ostream &operator<<(ostream &s, employee &o)
{
  s << o.get_name() << endl;
  s << "Emp#:  " << o.get_id() << endl;
  s << "Dept:  " << o.get_dept() << endl;
  s << "Phone: " << o.get_phone() << endl;

  return s;
}

int main()
{
  set<employee> emplist;

  // Initialize the employee list.
  emplist.insert(employee("Tom Harvy", "9423",
                          "Client Relations", "555-1010"));

  emplist.insert(employee("Susan Thomasy", "8723",
                          "Sales", "555-8899"));

  emplist.insert(employee("Alex Johnson", "5719",
                          "Repair", "555-0174"));

  // Create an iterator to the set.
  set<employee>::iterator itr = emplist.begin();
```

```
// Display contents of the set.
cout << "Current set: \n\n";
do {
  cout << *itr << endl;
  ++itr;
} while(itr != emplist.end());
cout << endl;

// Find a specific employee.
cout << "Searching for employee 8723.\n";
itr = emplist.find(employee("8723"));
if(itr != emplist.end()) {
  cout << "Found. Information follows:\n";
  cout << *itr << endl;
}

return 0;
}
```

The output is shown here:

```
Current set:

Alex Johnson
Emp#:  5719
Dept:  Repair
Phone: 555-0174

Susan Thomasy
Emp#:  8723
Dept:  Sales
Phone: 555-8899

Tom Harvy
Emp#:  9423
Dept:  Client Relations
Phone: 555-1010


Searching for employee 8723.
Found. Information follows:
Susan Thomasy
Emp#:  8723
Dept:  Sales
Phone: 555-8899
```

Bonus Example: Use multiset to Store Objects with Duplicate Keys

As explained, the difference between **set** and **multiset** is that a set must contain unique keys, but a multiset can store duplicate keys. In general, **multiset** is handled in the same way as **multimap**. For example, to find all elements with a given key, call **find( )** to obtain an iterator to the first matching key. Then increment that iterator to obtain the next element until the iterator is equal to the upper bound. (See *Use multimap* for a detailed description of this technique.) A similar mechanism is used to find a specific element. Find the first matching key. Then search for the specific element within the bounded range.

The following program demonstrates how a multiset can store elements with duplicate keys. It reworks the preceding example so that the key is the department rather than the ID. This means that **operator<( )** is changed to compare department names rather than IDs. The program then displays all employees in the Repair department. It ends by showing the information for Cary Linus in the Repair department.

```cpp
// Demonstrate multiset.
//
// This example stores objects that contain employee
// information. In this example, the department name
// is used as the key.

#include <iostream>
#include <set>
#include <string>

using namespace std;

// This class stores employee information.
class employee {
  string name;
  string ID;
  string phone;
  string department;
public:
  // Default constructor.
  employee() { ID = name = phone = department = ""; }

  // Construct temporary object using only the department,
  // which is the key.
  employee(string d) { department = d;
                       name = phone = ID = ""; }

  // Construct a complete employee object.
  employee(string n, string id, string dept, string p)
  {
    name = n;
    ID = id;
    phone = p;
    department = dept;
  }

  // Accessor functions for employee data.
  string get_name() { return name; }
  string get_id() { return ID; }
  string get_dept() { return department; }
  string get_phone() { return phone; }

};
```

```cpp
// Compare objects using department.
bool operator<(employee a, employee b)
{
  return a.get_dept() < b.get_dept();
}

// Create an inserter for employee.
ostream &operator<<(ostream &s, employee &o)
{
  s << o.get_name() << endl;
  s << "Emp#:  " << o.get_id() << endl;
  s << "Dept:  " << o.get_dept() << endl;
  s << "Phone: " << o.get_phone() << endl;

  return s;
}

int main()
{
  multiset<employee> emplist;

  // Initialize the employee list.
  emplist.insert(employee("Tom Harvy", "9423",
                          "Client Relations", "555-1010"));

  emplist.insert(employee("Susan Thomasy", "8723",
                          "Sales", "555-8899"));

  emplist.insert(employee("Alex Johnson", "5719",
                          "Repair", "555-0174"));

  emplist.insert(employee("Cary Linus", "0719",
                          "Repair", "555-0175"));

  // Declare an iterator to the multiset.
  multiset<employee>::iterator itr = emplist.begin();

  // Display contents of the multiset.
  cout << "Current set: \n\n";
  do {
    cout << *itr << endl;
    ++itr;
  } while(itr != emplist.end());
  cout << endl;

  // Find all employees in the Repair department.

  cout << "All employees in the Repair department:\n\n";
  employee e("Repair"); // temporary object that contains the Repair key.

  itr = emplist.find(e);
  if(itr != emplist.end()) {
    do {
```

```
      cout << *itr << endl;
      ++itr;
    } while(itr != emplist.upper_bound(e));
  }

  // Now find Cary Linus in Repair.
  cout << "Looking for Cary Linus in Repair:\n";
  itr = emplist.find(e);
  if(itr != emplist.end()) {
    do {
      if(itr->get_name() == "Cary Linus") {
        cout << "Found:\n";
        cout << *itr << endl;
        break;
      }
      ++itr;
    } while(itr != emplist.upper_bound(e));
  }

  return 0;
}
```

The output is shown here:

```
Current set:

Tom Harvy
Emp#:  9423
Dept:  Client Relations
Phone: 555-1010

Alex Johnson
Emp#:  5719
Dept:  Repair
Phone: 555-0174

Cary Linus
Emp#:  0719
Dept:  Repair
Phone: 555-0175

Susan Thomasy
Emp#:  8723
Dept:  Sales
Phone: 555-8899


All employees in the Repair department:

Alex Johnson
Emp#:  5719
Dept:  Repair
Phone: 555-0174
```

```
Cary Linus
Emp#:   0719
Dept:   Repair
Phone: 555-0175

Looking for Cary Linus in Repair:
Found:
Cary Linus
Emp#:   0719
Dept:   Repair
Phone: 555-0175
```

Options and Alternatives

Like all associative containers, both **set** and **multiset** define three versions of **erase( )**. One is described by the recipe. The other forms are shown here:

> void erase(iterator *i*)
>
> void erase(iterator *start*, iterator *end*)

The first form removes the element pointed to by *i*. The second form removes the elements in the range *start* to *end*–1. These forms are especially helpful when you want to remove a specific element from a multiset. As explained, the form of **erase( )** used by the recipe removes all elements whose keys match a specified key. Because a multiset allows more than one element to have the same key, if you want to remove a specific element, then you will need to find that element and remove it by using **erase(iterator)**. (See *Use multimap* for an example that uses this approach.)

The **set** and **multiset** containers also support the three standard forms of **insert( )**. These include the one used by the recipe and the two forms shown here:

> iterator insert(iterator *i*, const value_type &*val*)
>
> template <class InIter> void insert(InIter *start*, InIter *end*)

For **multiset**, the first form inserts *val* into the container. For **set**, *val* is inserted if it does not contain a duplicate key. In all cases, an iterator to the element with the same key is returned. The iterator specified by *i* indicates where to start the search for the proper insertion point. Because sets are sorted based on keys, you should try to use a value for *i* that is close to the insertion point. The second version inserts the elements in the range *start* to *end*–1. Of course, when used with **set**, elements with duplicate keys are not inserted.

When using a **multiset**, it is sometimes useful to know the start and end points of a range of elements that share a key. To accomplish this, use **equal_range( )**, shown here:

> pair<iterator, iterator> equal_range(const key_type &*k*)

It returns a **pair** object that contains iterators that point to the lower bound (in the **first** field) and the upper bound (in the **second** field) in the multiset for the specified key. (A **const** version of the function is also supplied.) Recall that the lower bound is the first element that has a key that is equal to or greater than *k*, and the upper bound is the first element that has a key greater than *k*. Thus, **equal_range( )** returns iterators to the range of elements that all share a common key.

If you want to store a set of bits, consider the **bitset** class. It uses the header **<bitset>** and it creates a specialized container for bit values. The **bitset** class is not, however, a fully formed container and is not part of the STL. For some applications, however, **bitset** might be a better choice than a full-featured, STL container.

Although **set** and **multiset** are very useful in some applications, I have come to prefer **map** and **multimap** for two reasons. First, they provide the quintessential implementations of containers that hold key/value pairs because the key is separate from the value. Second, the key can change without requiring a change to the implementation of **operator<( )** in the objects being stored. Of course, in all cases, you must use the container that provides the best fit for your application.

4

CHAPTER

Algorithms, Function Objects, and Other STL Components

At its foundation, the STL consists of containers, iterators, and algorithms. Two of these, containers and iterators, are the focus of Chapter 3. The primary focus of this chapter is algorithms. Because of the large number of algorithms, it is not possible to present a recipe for each one. Instead, the recipes show how to use algorithms to handle a variety of common STL programming situations. These recipes also form a representative sample of techniques that can be generalized to other algorithms. Therefore, if you don't find a recipe that directly describes what you want to do, you can probably adapt one. This chapter also includes recipes that demonstrate other key parts of the STL, including function objects, binders, and negators. There are also recipes that demonstrate a function adaptor, three iterator adaptors, and the stream iterators.

Here are the recipes contained in this chapter:

- Sort a Container
- Find an Element in a Container
- Use **search( )** to Find a Matching Sequence
- Reverse, Rotate, and Shuffle a Sequence
- Cycle Through a Container with **for_each( )**
- Use **transform( )** to Change a Sequence
- Perform Set Operations
- Permute a Sequence
- Copy a Sequence from One Container to Another
- Replace and Remove Elements in a Container
- Merge Two Sorted Sequences
- Create and Manage a Heap
- Create an Algorithm
- Use a Built-In Function Object

- Create a Custom Function Object
- Use a Binder
- Use a Negator
- Use the Pointer-to-Function Adaptor
- Use the Stream Iterators
- Use the Insert Iterator Adaptors

Algorithm Overview

Algorithms expand the power and reach of the STL by providing a common base of functionality that is available to all containers. They also offer ready-to-use solutions to several difficult programming tasks. For example, there are algorithms that search one sequence for an occurrence of another, that sort a sequence, or that apply a transformation to a sequence. In combination with containers and iterators, they define the essence of the STL.

Why Algorithms?

Algorithms are one of the three major components of the STL, and they offer functionality not provided by the containers themselves. As the preceding chapter has shown, the container classes include a number of functions that support a wide variety of operations. This fact gives rise to the following question: Why are separate algorithms needed? The answer to this question has three parts.

First, algorithms allow two different types of containers to be operated on at the same time. Because most algorithms operate through iterators, iterators to different types of containers can be used by the same algorithm. For example, the **merge( )** algorithm can be used to merge a **vector** with a **list**.

Second, algorithms contribute to the extensibility of the STL. Because an algorithm can operate on any type of container that meets its minimum requirements, it is possible to create new containers that can be manipulated by the standard algorithms. As long as a container supports iterators (which all containers must), it can be used by the STL algorithms. It is also possible to create new algorithms. As long as the new algorithm operates through iterators, it can be applied to any container.

Third, algorithms streamline the STL. Because they provide operations that can be applied to a wide range of containers, this functionality need not be duplicated by the member functions of each container. They also give you, the programmer, a consistent way to perform an operation that can be applied to any type of container.

Algorithms Are Template Functions

The STL algorithms are template functions. This means that they can be applied to any type of container. With very few exceptions, the algorithms operate through iterators. (The exceptions use reference parameters.) All of the STL algorithms require the header **<algorithm>**.

In the algorithm descriptions found throughout this chapter, the following generic iterator type names are used:

Generic Name	Represents
BiIter	Bidirectional iterator
ForIter	Forward iterator
InIter	Input iterator
OutIter	Output iterator
RandIter	Random-access iterator

Not all algorithms will work with all types of iterators. For example, the **sort( )** algorithm requires random-access iterators. This means that **sort( )** cannot be used on **list** containers, for example. (This is why **list** provides its own function to sort lists.) When choosing an algorithm, you must make sure that the container on which it will be operating provides the necessary iterators.

In addition to iterators, the algorithm prototypes often specify various other generic type names, which are used to represent predicates, comparison functions, etc. The ones used in this chapter are shown here:

T	Some type of data
Size	Some type of integer
Func	Some type of function
Generator	A function that generates objects
BinPred	Binary predicate
UnPred	Unary predicate
Comp	Comparison function

The Algorithm Categories

The STL defines a large number of algorithms, and it is common to group them by category. There are many ways to do this. One way is the categories used by the International Standard for C++, which are shown here:

- Non-modifying sequence operations
- Modifying sequence operations
- Sorting and related operations

Tables 4-1 through 4-3 show the algorithms that comprise each of these categories. The non-modifying sequence operations do not alter the containers upon which they operate. The modifying operations do. The sorting category includes the various sort algorithms as well as those algorithms that require a sorted sequence or that in one way or another order a sequence.

While the categories defined in the C++ Standard are useful, they each still contain a large number of algorithms. Another way to organize the algorithms is into smaller, functional groupings, such as those shown in Table 4-4.

Algorithm	Purpose
adjacent_find	Searches for adjacent matching elements within a sequence and returns an iterator to the first match.
count	Returns the number of elements in the sequence.
count_if	Returns the number of elements in the sequence that satisfy some predicate.
equal	Determines if two ranges are the same.
find	Searches a range for a value and returns an iterator to the first occurrence of the element.
find_end	Searches a range for a subsequence. It returns an iterator to the last occurrence of the subsequence within the range.
find_first_of	Finds the first element within a sequence that matches an element within a range.
find_if	Searches a range for an element for which a user-defined unary predicate returns true.
for_each	Applies a function to a range of elements.
mismatch	Finds the first mismatch between the elements in two sequences. Iterators to the two elements are returned.
search	Searches for a subsequence within a sequence.
search_n	Searches for a sequence of a specified number of similar elements.

TABLE 4-1   Non-Modifying Sequence Algorithms

Function Object Overview

Function objects are classes that define **operator( )**. A function object can often be used in place of a function pointer, such as when passing a predicate to an algorithm. Function objects offer more flexibility than do function pointers, and can be more efficient in some situations. Many built-in function objects, such as **less** and **minus**, are provided by the STL. You can also define your own.

There are two types of function objects: unary and binary. A unary function object requires one argument; a binary function object requires two. You must use the type of object required. For example, if an algorithm is expecting a binary function, you must pass it a binary function object.

The built-in binary function objects are shown here:

plus	minus	multiplies	divides	modulus
equal_to	not_equal_to	greater	greater_equal	less
less_equal	logical_and	logical_or		

Algorithm	Purpose
copy	Copies a sequence.
copy_backward	Same as **copy( )**, except that it moves the elements from the end of the sequence first.
fill	Fills a range with the specified value.
fill_n	Assigns a specific number of elements with a specified value.
generate	Assigns elements in a range the values returned by a generator function.
generate_n	Assigns a specified number of elements the values returned by a generator function.
iter_swap	Exchanges the values pointed to by its two iterator arguments.
partition	Arranges a sequence such that all elements for which a predicate returns true come before those for which the predicate returns false.
random_shuffle	Randomizes a sequence.
replace	Replaces elements in a sequence.
replace_copy	Replaces elements while copying.
replace_copy_if	While copying, replaces elements for which a user-defined unary predicate is true.
replace_if	Replaces elements for which a user-defined unary predicate is true.
remove	Removes elements from a specified range.
remove_copy	Removes and copies elements from a specified range.
remove_copy_if	While copying, removes elements from a specified range for which a user-defined unary predicate is true.
remove_if	Removes elements from a specified range for which a user-defined unary predicate is true.
reverse	Reverses the order of a range.
reverse_copy	Reverses the order of a range while copying.
rotate	Left-rotates the elements in a range.
rotate_copy	Left-rotates the elements in a range while copying.
stable_partition	Arranges a sequence such that all elements for which a predicate returns true come before those for which the predicate returns false. The partitioning is stable. This means that the relative ordering of the sequence is preserved.
swap	Exchanges two values.
swap_ranges	Exchanges elements in a range.
transform	Applies a function to a range of elements and stores the outcome in a new sequence.
unique	Eliminates duplicate elements from a range.
unique_copy	Eliminates duplicate elements from a range while copying.

TABLE 4-2   Modifying Sequence Operations

Algorithm	Purpose
binary_search	Performs a binary search on an ordered sequence.
equal_range	Returns a range in which an element can be inserted into a sequence without disrupting the ordering of the sequence.
includes	Determines if one sequence includes all of the elements in another sequence.
inplace_merge	Merges a range with another range. Both ranges must be sorted in increasing order. The resulting sequence is sorted.
lexicographical_compare	Lexicographically compares one sequence with another.
lower_bound	Finds the first point in the sequence that is not less than a specified value.
make_heap	Constructs a heap from a sequence.
max	Returns the maximum of two values.
max_element	Returns an iterator to the maximum element within a range.
merge	Merges two ordered sequences, placing the result into a third sequence.
min	Returns the minimum of two values.
min_element	Returns an iterator to the minimum element within a range.
next_permutation	Constructs the next permutation of a sequence.
nth_element	Arranges a sequence such that all elements less than a specified element E come before that element and all elements greater than E come after it.
partial_sort	Sorts a range.
partial_sort_copy	Sorts a range and then copies as many elements as will fit into a result sequence.
pop_heap	Exchanges the first and last−1 elements and then rebuilds the heap.
prev_permutation	Constructs the previous permutation of a sequence.
push_heap	Pushes an element onto the end of a heap.
set_difference	Produces a sequence that contains the difference between two ordered sets.
set_intersection	Produces a sequence that contains the intersection of two ordered sets.
set_symmetric_difference	Produces a sequence that contains the symmetric difference between two ordered sets.
set_union	Produces a sequence that contains the union of two ordered sets.
sort	Sorts a range.
sort_heap	Sorts a heap within a specified range.
stable_sort	Sorts a range. The sort is stable. This means that equal elements are not rearranged.
upper_bound	Finds the last point in a sequence that is not greater than some value.

TABLE 4-3   Sorting and Related Algorithms

Copying			
copy	copy_backward	iter_swap	fill
fill_n	swap	swap_ranges	
Searching Unsorted Sequences			
adjacent_find	equal	find	find_end
find_if	find_first_of	mismatch	search
search_n			
Replacing and Removing Elements			
remove	remove_if	remove_copy	remove_copy_if
replace	replace_if	replace_copy	replace_copy_if
unique	unique_copy		
Reordering a Sequence			
rotate	rotate_copy	random_shuffle	partition
reverse	reverse_copy	stable_partition	next_permutation
prev_permutation			
Sorting and Searching a Sorted Sequence			
nth_element	sort	stable_sort	partial_sort
partial_sort_copy	binary_search	lower_bound	upper_bound
equal_range			
Merging Sorted Sequences			
merge	inplace_merge		
Set Operations			
includes	set_difference	set_intersection	set_symmetric_difference
set_union			
Heap Operations			
make_heap	push_heap	pop_heap	sort_heap
Minimum and Maximum			
max	max_element	min	min_element
Transforming and Generating a Sequence			
generate	generate_n	transform	
Miscellaneous			
count	count_if	for_each	lexicographical_compare

TABLE 4-4   The STL Algorithms Organized by Functional Groupings

Here are the unary function objects:

logical_not	negate

All of the built-in function objects are template classes that overload **operator( )**. Because they are template classes, they can work on any type of data for which their associated operation is defined. The built-in function objects use the header **<functional>**.

Although it is certainly permissible to construct a function object in advance, often, you will construct a function object when it is passed to an algorithm. You do this by explicitly calling its constructor using the following general form:

func_ob<type>( )

For example,

```
sort(start, end, greater<int>())
```

constructs a **greater** object for use on operands of type **int** and passes it to the **sort( )** algorithm.

There is a special type of function object called a *predicate*. The defining characteristic of a predicate is that it returns a **bool** value. In other words, a predicate returns a true/false result. There are unary and binary predicates. A unary predicate takes one argument. A binary predicate takes two arguments. There is a special type of predicate that performs a less-than comparison, returning true only if the one element is less than another. Such a predicate is sometimes called a *comparison function.*

Binders and Negators Overview

As explained in the previous section, a binary function object takes two parameters. Normally, these parameters receive values from the sequence or sequences upon which the object is operating. There will be times, however, in which you will want one of the values to be bound to a specific value. For example, you might want to use **less** to compare elements from a sequence against a specified value. To handle this type of situation, you will use a *binder.* The STL provides two binders: **bind1st( )** and **bind2nd( )**. **bind1st( )** binds a value to the first argument of a binary function object. **bind2nd( )** binds a value to the second argument of a binary function object.

Related to a binder is the *negator.* The negators are **not1( )** and **not2( )**. They return the negation (i.e., the complement) of whatever predicate they modify.

Sort a Container

Key Ingredients		
Headers	**Classes**	**Functions**
<algorithm>		template<class RandIter> void sort(RandIter *start*, RandIter *end*)
		template<class RandIter, class Comp> void sort(RandIter *start*, RandIter *end*, Comp *cmpfn*)

One of the more common container operations is sorting. The reason for this is easy to understand: Sequence containers are not required to maintain their elements in sorted order. For example, neither **vector** nor **deque** maintain a sorted container. Therefore, if you want the elements of one of these containers to be in sorted order, you will need to sort it yourself. Fortunately, it is easy to sort one of these containers by using the **sort( )** algorithm. The container can be sorted in natural order or in an order determined by a comparison function. This recipe describes the process and offers three interesting alternatives.

Step-by-Step

To sort a container in natural order uses only one step:

1. Call the two-parameter form of **sort( )**, passing in iterators to the beginning and end of the range to be sorted.

To sort a container in an order determined by a comparison function that you provide involves these steps:

1. If you will be sorting based on a comparison function that you provide, create the comparison function.
2. Call the three-parameter form of **sort( )**, passing in iterators to the beginning and end of the sequence and to the comparison function.

Discussion

The STL provides several sorting algorithms. At the core is **sort( )**, shown here:

```
template <class RandIter>
  void sort(RandIter start, RandIter end)

template <class RandIter, class Comp>
  void sort(RandIter start, RandIter end, Comp cmpfn)
```

The **sort( )** algorithm sorts the range *start* through *end*–1. The second form allows you to pass a comparison function to *cmpfn* that determines when one element is less than another.

This function can be passed via a function pointer or as a function object, such as **greater( )**. (See *Use a Built-In Function Object* for a recipe that discusses the function objects. See *Create a Custom Function Object* for details on creating your own function object.)

Notice that **sort( )** requires random-access iterators. Only a few containers, such as **vector** and **deque**, support random-access iterators. Those containers, such as **list**, which do not, must provide their own sort routines.

It is important to understand that **sort( )** sorts the range specified by its arguments, which need not include the entire contents of the container. Thus, **sort( )** can be used to sort a subset of a container. To sort an entire container, you must specify **begin( )** and **end( )** as the starting and ending points.

Example

The following example shows both versions of **sort( )** in action. It creates a vector and then sorts it into natural order. It then uses the standard **greater( )** function object to sort the vector into descending order. Finally, it re-sorts the center 6 elements into natural order.

```
// Demonstrate the sort() algorithm

#include <cstdlib>
#include <iostream>
#include <vector>
#include <functional>
#include <algorithm>

using namespace std;

void show(const char *msg, vector<int> vect);

int main()
{
  vector<int> v(10);

  // Initialize v with random values.
  for(unsigned i=0; i < v.size(); i++)
    v[i] = rand() % 100;

  show("Original order:\n", v);
  cout << endl;

  // Sort the entire container.
  sort(v.begin(), v.end());

  show("Order after sorting into natural order:\n", v);
  cout << endl;

  // Now, sort into descending order by using greater().
  sort(v.begin(), v.end(), greater<int>());

  show("Order after sorting into descending order:\n", v);
  cout << endl;
```

```
  // Sort a subset of the container
  sort(v.begin()+2, v.end()-2);

  show("After sorting elements v[2] to v[7] into natural order:\n", v);

  return 0;
}

// Display the contents of a vector<int>.
void show(const char *msg, vector<int> vect) {
  cout << msg;
  for(unsigned i=0; i < vect.size(); ++i)
    cout << vect[i] << " ";
  cout << "\n";
}
```

The output is shown here:

```
Original order:
41 67 34 0 69 24 78 58 62 64

Order after sorting into natural order:
0 24 34 41 58 62 64 67 69 78

Order after sorting into descending order:
78 69 67 64 62 58 41 34 24 0

After sorting elements v[2] to v[7] into natural order:
78 69 34 41 58 62 64 67 24 0
```

Options and Alternatives

An interesting variation on sorting is found in **partial_sort( )**. It has the two versions shown here:

> template <class RandIter>
>   void partial_sort(RandIter *start*, RandIter *mid*, RandIter *end*)

> template <class RandIter, class Comp>
>   void partial_sort(RandIter *start*, RandIter *mid*, RandIter *end*, Comp *cmpfn*)

The **partial_sort( )** algorithm sorts elements from the range *start* to *end*–1. However, after execution, only elements in the range *start* to *mid*–1 will be in sorted order. The remainder is in an arbitrary order. Thus, **partial_sort( )** examines all elements from *start* to *end*, but orders only *mid–start* elements from the entire range, and these elements are all less than the remaining, unordered elements. You might use **partial_sort( )** to obtain the top 10 selling songs from the list of all songs provided by an online music service, for example. The second form allows you to specify a comparison function that determines when one element is less than another. Assuming the example program, the following fragment sorts the first five elements of **v**:

```
partial_sort(v.begin(), v.begin()+5, v.end());
```

After this statement executes, the first 5 elements in **v** will be in sorted order. The remaining elements will be in an unspecified order.

A useful variation on partial sorting is **partial_sort_copy( )**, which puts the sorted elements into another sequence. It has the following two versions:

    template <class InIter, class RandIter>
       RandIter partial_sort_copy(InIter *start*, InIter *end*,
                           RandIter *result_start*, RandIter *result_end*)

    template <class InIter, class RandIter, class Comp>
       RandIter partial_sort_copy(InIter *start*, InIter *end*,
                           RandIter *result_start*, RandIter *result_end*,
                           Comp *cmpfn*)

Both sort the range *start* to *end*–1 and then copy as many elements as will fit into the result sequence defined by *result_start* to *result_end*–1. An iterator to one past the last element copied into the resulting sequence is returned. The second form allows you to specify a comparison function that determines when one element is less than another.

Another sorting option is **stable_sort( )**, which provides a sort that does not rearrange equal elements. It has these two forms:

    template <class RandIter>
       void stable_sort(RandIter *start*, RandIter *end*)

    template <class RandIter, class Comp>
       void stable_sort(RandIter *start*, RandIter *end*, Comp *cmpfn*)

It sorts the range *start* through *end*–1, but equal elements are not rearranged. The second form allows you to specify a comparison function that determines when one element is less than another.

Find an Element in a Container

Key Ingredients		
Headers	**Classes**	**Functions**
<algorithm>		template <class InIter, class T> InIter find(InIter *start*, InIter *end*, 　　　　const T &*val*)
		template <class InIter, class UnPred> InIter find_if(InIter *start*, InIter *end*, 　　　　UnPred *pfn*)

Frequently, you will want to find a specific element within a container. For example, you might want to find an element so that it can be deleted, viewed, or updated with new information. Whatever the need, the STL provides several algorithms that in one way or another enable you to find a specific element within a container. This recipe looks at two: **find( )** and **find_if( )**, but several others are described in the *Options and Alternatives* section for this recipe. The principal advantage of **find( )** and **find_if( )** is that they do not require that the container be sorted. Thus, they work in all cases.

Step-by-Step

To use **find( )** to find an element within a container involves these steps:

1. Create an instance of the object that you want to find.
2. Call **find( )**, passing in iterators to the range to search and the object to find.

To use **find_if( )** to find an element within a container involves these steps:

1. Create a unary predicate that returns true when the desired object is found.
2. Call **find_if( )**, passing in iterators to the range to sort and the predicate from Step 1.

Discussion

Perhaps the most widely used search algorithms are **find( )** and its close relative, **find_if( )**. The **find( )** algorithm searches a range for the first occurrence of a specified element. It is shown here:

```
template <class InIter, class T>
  InIter find(InIter start, InIter end, const T &val)
```

It searches the range *start* to *end*–1 for the value specified by *val*. It returns an iterator to the first occurrence of the element or to *end* if *val* is not in the range.

The **find_if( )** algorithm searches a range for the first occurrence of an element that meets the conditions specified by a predicate. It is shown here:

```
template <class InIter, class UnPred>
  InIter find_if(InIter start, InIter end, UnPred pfn)
```

It searches the range *start* to *end*–1 for an element for which the unary predicate *pfn* returns true. It returns an iterator to the first element that satisfies *pfn*, or to *end* if *val* is not in the range. This algorithm is particularly useful when you want to search for an element that meets a certain criterion. For example, if a container holds a mailing list, you could use **find_if( )** to find addresses that have a specific postal code.

Both **find( )** and **find_if( )** can operate on an unsorted range. This means that they can be used on any type of container and there is no need for the container to be maintained in sorted order. They will also work with a sorted container, but better search algorithms exist for sorted containers. See the *Options and Alternatives* section in this recipe for examples.

Example

The following example illustrates both **find( )** and **find_if( )**. It uses a vector to hold strings. It then uses **find( )** to find the first string that matches "two". It then uses **find_if( )** to find a string that has 3 or fewer characters.

```
// Demonstrate the find() and find_if() algorithms.

#include <iostream>
#include <vector>
#include <algorithm>
#include <string>

using namespace std;

bool is_short_str(string str);

int main()
{
  vector<string> v;
  vector<string>::iterator itr;

  v.push_back("one");
  v.push_back("two");
  v.push_back("three");
  v.push_back("four");
  v.push_back("five");
  v.push_back("six");

  cout << "Contents of v: ";
  for(unsigned i=0; i < v.size(); ++i)
    cout << v[i] << " ";
  cout << "\n\n";

  // Find the element that contains "two".
  cout << "Searching for \"two\"\n";
  itr = find(v.begin(), v.end(), "two");
  if(itr != v.end()) {
    cout << "Found \"two\", Replacing with \"TWO\"\n";
    *itr = "TWO";
  }
  cout << endl;

  // Find all strings that are less than 4 characters long.
  cout << "Searching for all strings that have 3 or fewer characters.\n";
  itr = v.begin();
  do {
    itr = find_if(itr, v.end(), is_short_str);
    if(itr != v.end()) {
      cout << "Found " << *itr << endl;
      ++itr;
    }
  } while(itr != v.end());
```

```
  return 0;
}

// Return true if the string is 3 characters or less.
bool is_short_str(string str)
{
  if(str.size() <= 3) return true;
  return false;
}
```

The output is shown here:

```
Contents of v: one two three four five six

Searching for "two"
Found "two", Replacing with "TWO"

Searching for all strings that have 3 or fewer characters.
Found one
Found TWO
Found six
```

In the program, notice how **find_if( )** is used in a loop to enable all strings that have 3 or fewer characters to be found. Each search begins where the previous one left off. This is possible because **find_if( )** returns an iterator to the found element. This iterator can then be incremented and used to begin the next search. Remember, both **find( )** and **find_if( )** (and nearly all other algorithms) operate on a specified range of elements, rather than on the entire contents of the container. This makes these algorithms far more versatile than they would otherwise be.

Bonus Example: Extract Sentences from a Vector of Characters

Although the preceding example shows the mechanics of **find_if( )**, it does not show its full potential. By carefully crafting a predicate, you can use **find_if( )** to perform very sophisticated search operations. For example, your predicate can maintain state information that is used to find elements based on context. The following program presents a simple case study. It uses **find_if( )** to extract sentences from a vector of characters. It uses a predicate called **is_sentence_start( )** to find the start of each sentence. This function maintains state information that indicates when the end of a sentence has been reached.

```
// Extract sentences from a vector of chars with help from find_if().

#include <iostream>
#include <vector>
#include <algorithm>
#include <cstring>
#include <cctype>

using namespace std;

bool is_sentence_start(char ch);
```

```cpp
template<class InIter>
    void show_range(const char *msg, InIter start, InIter end);

int main()
{
  vector<char> v;
  vector<char>::iterator itr;
  const char *str = "This is a test? Yes, it is! This too.";

  for(unsigned i=0; i < strlen(str); i++)
    v.push_back(str[i]);

  show_range("Contents of v: ", v.begin(), v.end());
  cout << endl;

  // Find the beginning of all sentences.
  cout << "Use find_if() to display each sentence in v:\n";

  // itr_start will point to the start of a sentence and
  // itr_end will point to the start of the next sentence.
  vector<char>::iterator itr_start, itr_end;

  itr_start = v.begin();
  do {
    // Find start of a sentence.
    itr_start = find_if(itr_start, v.end(), is_sentence_start);

    // Find start of the next sentence.
    itr_end = find_if(itr_start, v.end(), is_sentence_start);

    // Show the sequence in between.
    show_range("", itr_start, itr_end);
  } while(itr_end != v.end());

  return 0;
}

// Return true if ch is the first letter in a sentence.
bool is_sentence_start(char ch) {
  static bool endofsentence = true;

  if(isalpha(ch) && endofsentence ) {
    endofsentence = false;
    return true;
  }

  if(ch=='.' || ch=='?' || ch=='!') endofsentence = true;
  return false;
}
```

```
// Show a range of elements.
template<class InIter>
    void show_range(const char *msg, InIter start, InIter end) {

  InIter itr;

  cout << msg;

  for(itr = start; itr != end; ++itr)
    cout << *itr;
  cout << endl;
}
```

The output is shown here:

```
Contents of v: This is a test? Yes, it is! This too.

Use find_if() to display each sentence in v:
This is a test?
Yes, it is!
This too.
```

Pay special attention to the way the predicate **is_sentence_start( )** works. It looks for the first letter after the end of a previous sentence. It uses a **static bool** called **endofsentence** to indicate that the end of a sentence has been found. The end of a sentence is assumed if a sentence-terminating character (a period, question mark, or exclamation mark) is encountered. In this case, **endofsentence** is set to true. When **endofsentence** is true, then the next letter in the sequence is assumed to be the start of the next sentence. When this occurs, **endofsentence** is set to false and **is_sentence_start( )** returns true. In all other cases, **is_sentence_start( )** returns false. Notice that **endofsentence** is true to begin with so that the first sentence is found.

Options and Alternatives

To search for a sequence of elements, rather than one specific value, use the **search( )** algorithm. It is described by the following recipe.

If you are operating on a sorted sequence, then you can use a binary search to find a value. In most cases, a binary search is much faster than a sequential search. It does, of course, require a sorted sequence. The prototypes for **binary_search( )** are shown here:

    template <class ForIter, class T>
        bool binary_search(ForIter *start*, ForIter *end*, const T &*val*)
    template <class ForIter, class T, class Comp>
        bool binary_search(ForIter *start*, ForIter *end*, const T &*val*, Comp *cmpfn*)

The **binary_search( )** algorithm performs a binary search on an ordered range *start* to *end*–1 for the value specified by *val*. It returns true if *val* is found and false otherwise. The first version compares the elements in the specified sequence for equality. The second version allows you to specify your own comparison function. When acting on random-access iterators, **binary_search( )** consumes logarithmic time. For other types of iterators, the number of comparisons is logarithmic, even though the time it takes to move between elements is not.

You might be surprised by the fact that **binary_search( )** returns a true/false result rather than an iterator to the element that it finds. One justification for this approach is based in the argument that a sorted sequence may contain two or more values that match the one being sought. Thus, there is little value in returning the first one found. While the validity of this argument has been a subject of debate, it is nevertheless the way that **binary_search( )** works.

To actually obtain an iterator to an element in a sorted sequence, you will use one of these algorithms: **lower_bound( )**, **upper_bound( )**, or **equal_range( )**. The prototypes for the non-predicate versions of these algorithms are shown here:

```
template <class ForIter, class T>
  pair<ForIter, ForIter> equal_range(ForIter start, ForIter end,
                                     const T &val)

template <class ForIter, class T>
  ForIter lower_bound(ForIter start, ForIter end, const T &val)

template <class ForIter, class T>
  ForIter upper_bound(ForIter start, ForIter end, const T &val)
```

The **lower_bound( )** algorithm returns an iterator to the first element that is equal to or greater than *val*, **upper_bound( )** returns an iterator one beyond the last matching element (in other words, the first element greater than *val*), and **equal_range( )** returns a pair of iterators that point to the lower and upper bounds. All of these algorithms operate in logarithmic time when acting upon random-access iterators because they, too, use a binary search to find their respective values. For other types of iterators, the number of comparisons is logarithmic, even though the time it takes to move between elements is not. In general, if you want to obtain an iterator to the first matching element in a sorted sequence, use **equal_range( )**. If the upper- and lower-bound iterators differ, then you know that at least one matching element has been found and the lower-bound iterator points to the first occurrence of the element.

Although finding a specific element is often what is needed, in some cases, you will want to find the first occurrence of any element from a set of elements. One way to do this is to use the **find_first_of( )** algorithm, shown here:

```
template <class ForIter1, class ForIter2>
  ForIter1 find_first_of(ForIter1 start1, ForIter1 end1,
                         ForIter2 start2, ForIter2 end2)

template <class ForIter1, class ForIter2, class BinPred>
  ForIter1 find_first_of(ForIter1 start1, ForIter1 end1,
                         ForIter2 start2, ForIter2 end2,
                         BinPred pfn)
```

It finds the first element within the range *start1* through *end1–1* that matches any element within the range *start2* through *end2–1*. It returns an iterator to the matching element or *end1* if no match is found. The second form lets you specify a binary predicate that determines when two elements are equal.

An interesting algorithm that will be helpful in some cases is **adjacent_find( )**. It searches for the first occurrence of a matching pair of adjacent elements. Its two versions are shown here:

template <class ForIter> ForIter adjacent_find(ForIter *start*, ForIter *end*)

template <class ForIter, class BinPred> ForIter adjacent_find(ForIter *start*, ForIter *end*, BinPred *pfn*)

The **adjacent_find( )** algorithm searches for adjacent matching elements within the range *start* through *end*–1. It returns an iterator to the first element of the first matching pair. It returns *end* if no adjacent matching elements are found. The second form lets you specify a binary predicate that determines when two elements are equal.

Another interesting variation on searching is the **mismatch( )** algorithm, which allows you to find the first mismatch between two sequences. Its prototypes are shown here:

template <class InIter1, class InIter2>
    pair<InIter1, InIter2> mismatch(InIter1 *start1*, InIter1 *end1*, InIter2 *start2*)

template <class InIter1, class InIter2, class BinPred>
    pair<InIter1, InIter2> mismatch(InIter1 *start1*, InIter1 *end1*,
                                    InIter2 *start2*, BinPred *pfn*)

The **mismatch( )** algorithm finds the first mismatch between the elements in the range *start1* to *end1*–1 and the one beginning with *start2*. Iterators to the two mismatching elements are returned. If no mismatch is found, then the iterators *last1* and *first2* + (*last1*–*first1*) are returned. Thus, it is the length of the first sequence that determines the number of elements tested. The second form allows you to specify a binary predicate that determines when one element is equal to another. (The **pair** template class contains two fields, called **first** and **second**, which hold the pair of iterators. See Chapter 3 for details.)

Use search( ) to Find a Matching Sequence

Key Ingredients		
Headers	**Classes**	**Functions**
<algorithm>		template <class ForIter1, class ForIter2> ForIter1 search(ForIter1 *start1*, ForIter1 *end1*, ForIter2 *start2*, ForIter2 *end2*)

The preceding recipe showed how to search for a specific element. This recipe shows how to search for a sequence of elements. Such a search is, obviously, quite useful in a variety of situations. For example, assume a **deque** that contains strings that indicate the success or failure of attempts to log into a network. You might want to search that container for occurrences in which an incorrect password was entered three times in row, which could indicate an attempted break-in. To do this, you need to search for a sequence of three failures. Finding a single failure is insufficient. The principal algorithm used to find a sequence is **search( )**, and it is demonstrated by this recipe.

Step-by-Step

To search for a sequence of elements involves these steps:

1. Define the sequence that you want to find.
2. Call **search( )**, passing in iterators to the start and end of the range to search and iterators to the start and end of the sequence to find.

Discussion

The **search( )** algorithm looks for a sequence of elements. It has two forms. The one used by this recipe is shown here:

```
template <class ForIter1, class ForIter2>
   ForIter1 search(ForIter1 start1, ForIter1 end1,
                   ForIter2 start2, ForIter2 end2)
```

The sequence being searched is defined by the range *start1* through *end1*–1. The subsequence being sought is specified by *start2* and *end2*–1. If the subsequence is found, an iterator to its beginning is returned. Otherwise, *end1* is returned.

There is no requirement that the sequence being searched and the sequence being sought must be stored in the same type of container. For example, you can look for a sequence in a list that matches a sequence from a vector. This is one of the advantages of the STL algorithms. Because they work through iterators, they can be applied to any container that supports the required iterator type, which is a forward iterator in this case.

Example

The following example shows **search( )** in action. It searches a **deque** that contains network log-in responses. It looks for a series of log-in attempts in which the incorrect password was entered three times in a row, which might indicate a possible break-in. For this example, assume that the network log can contain several different types of responses, such as log-in OK, connection failed, and so on. However, when an invalid password is entered, the following two responses are placed in the log:

```
invalid password
password reprompt
```

To look for possible break-in attempts, the program looks for cases in which these responses occur three times in a row. If it finds this sequence, it reports that a possible network break-in occurred.

> **NOTE** *Another example of the* **search( )** *algorithm is found in Chapter 2, in the recipe* Create Case-Insensitive Search and Search-and-Replace Functions for **string** Objects.

```cpp
// Demonstrate search().

#include <iostream>
#include <deque>
#include <algorithm>
#include <string>

using namespace std;

int main()
{
  deque<string> log;
  deque<string> break_in;
  deque<string>::iterator itr;

  // Create a sequence of three invalid password responses.
  break_in.push_back("invalid password");
  break_in.push_back("password reprompt ");
  break_in.push_back("invalid password");
  break_in.push_back("password reprompt ");
  break_in.push_back("invalid password");


  // Create some log entries.
  log.push_back("log-on OK");
  log.push_back("invalid password");
  log.push_back("password reprompt ");
  log.push_back("log-on OK");
  log.push_back("connection failed");
  log.push_back("log-on OK");
  log.push_back("log-on OK");
  log.push_back("invalid password");
  log.push_back("password reprompt ");
  log.push_back("invalid password");
  log.push_back("password reprompt ");
  log.push_back("invalid password");
  log.push_back("port conflict");
  log.push_back("log-on OK");

  cout << "Here is the log:\n";
  for(itr = log.begin(); itr != log.end(); ++itr)
    cout << *itr << endl;
  cout << endl;

  // See if an attempt was made to break in.
  itr = search(log.begin(), log.end(), break_in.begin(), break_in.end());

  if(itr != log.end())
    cout << "Possible attempted break-in found.\n";
  else
```

```
      cout << "No repeated password failures found.\n";

  return 0;
}
```

The output is shown here:

```
Here is the log:
log-on OK
invalid password
password reprompt
log-on OK
connection failed
log-on OK
log-on OK
invalid password
password reprompt
invalid password
password reprompt
invalid password
port conflict
log-on OK

Possible attempted break-in found.
```

It is important to understand that the call to **search( )** will succeed only if three invalid password responses occur in a row. To confirm this, try commenting out one of the calls to **log.push_back("password reprompt ")**. When the program is run, it will no longer find a matching sequence.

Options and Alternatives

There is a second form of **search( )** that lets you specify a binary predicate that determines when two elements are equal. It is shown here:

    template <class ForIter1, class ForIter2, class BinPred>
       ForIter1 search(ForIter1 *start1*, ForIter1 *end1*,
                ForIter2 *start2*, ForIter2 *end2*, BinPred *pfn*)

It works just like the first version, except that the binary predicate is passed in *pfn*.
    You can find the last occurrence of a sequence by calling **find_end( )**, shown here:

    template <class ForIter1, class ForIter2>
       ForIter1 find_end(ForIter1 *start1*, ForIter1 *end1*,
                ForIter2 *start2*, ForIter2 *end2*)

    template <class ForIter1, class ForIter2, class BinPred>
       ForIter1 find_end(ForIter1 *start1*, ForIter1 *end1*,
                ForIter2 *start2*, ForIter2 *end2*,
                BinPred *pfn*)

It works just like **search( )**, except that it finds the last, rather than the first, occurrence of the range specified by *start2* and *end2* within the range specified by *start1* and *end1*.

To search for a sequence of a specified length in which all values are the same, consider using **search_n( )**. It has the two forms shown here:

```
template <class ForIter1, class Size, class T>
    ForIter1 search_n(ForIter1 start, ForIter1 end,
                        Size num, const T &val)
```

```
template <class ForIter1, class Size, class T, class BinPred>
    ForIter1 search_n(ForIter1 start, ForIter1 end,
                        Size num, const T &val, binPred pfn)
```

Within the range *start* through *end*–1, **search_n( )** searches for a sequence of *num* elements that are equal to *val*. If the sequence is found, an iterator to its beginning is returned. Otherwise, *end* is returned. The second form lets you specify a binary predicate that determines when one element is equal to another.

Other algorithms that relate to searching for a sequence are **equal( )**, which compares two sequences for equality, and **mismatch( )**, which finds the first mismatch between two sequences.

Reverse, Rotate, and Shuffle a Sequence

Key Ingredients		
Headers	**Classes**	**Functions**
<algorithm>		template <class RandIter> void random_shuffle(RandIter *start*, RandIter *end*)
		template <class BiIter> void reverse(BiIter *start*, BiIter *end*)
		template <class ForIter> void rotate(ForIter *start*, ForIter *mid*, ForIter *end*)

This recipe demonstrates the use of three related algorithms: **reverse( )**, **rotate( )**, and **random_shuffle( )**. They relate to each other because each changes the order of the range to which it is applied. The **reverse( )** algorithm reverses the sequence, **rotate( )** rotates the sequence (that is, it takes an element off one end and puts it on the other), and **random_shuffle( )** randomizes the order of the elements.

Step-by-Step

To reverse, rotate, or shuffle a sequence involves these steps:

1. Reverse a sequence by calling **reverse( )**, specifying the endpoints of the range to reverse.

2. Rotate a sequence by calling **rotate( )**, specifying the endpoints of the range to rotate.

3. Randomize the order of elements within a sequence by calling **random_shuffle( )**, specifying the endpoints of the range to randomize.

Discussion

You can reverse the contents of a sequence by calling **reverse( )**. It has this prototype:

    template <class BiIter> void reverse(BiIter *start*, BiIter *end*)

The **reverse( )** algorithm reverses the order of the range *start* through *end*–1.

The **rotate( )** algorithm performs a left-rotate. A rotate is a shift in which the value shifted off one end is put onto the other end. The prototype for **rotate( )** is shown here:

    template <class ForIter>
        void rotate(ForIter *start*, ForIter *mid*, ForIter *end*)

The **rotate( )** algorithm left-rotates the elements in the range *start* through *end*–1 so that the element specified by *mid* becomes the new first element.

An algorithm that is particularly useful to programmers creating simulations is **random_shuffle( )**. It re-orders the elements in a sequence in some random way. It has the two versions shown here:

    template <class RandIter>
        void random_shuffle(RandIter *start*, RandIter *end*)

    template <class RandIter, class Generator>
        void random_shuffle(RandIter *start*, RandIter *end*, Generator *rand_gen*)

The **random_shuffle( )** algorithm randomizes the range *start* through *end*–1. In the second form, *rand_gen* specifies a custom random number generator. This function must have the following general form:

    rand_gen(*num*)

It must return a random number between zero and *num*. Notice that **random_shuffle( )** requires random-access iterators. This means that it can be used on containers such as **vector** and **deque**, but not on **list**, for example.

Example

The following example demonstrates **reverse( )**, **rotate( )**, and **random_shuffle( )**:

```
// Reverse, rotate, and shuffle a sequence.

#include <iostream>
#include <vector>
```

```
#include <algorithm>

using namespace std;

void show(const char *msg, vector<int> vect);

int main()
{
  vector<int> v;

  for(int i=0; i<10; i++) v.push_back(i);

  show("Original order: ", v);
  cout << endl;

  // Reverse v.
  reverse(v.begin(), v.end());
  show("After reversal: ", v);
  cout << endl;

  // Reverse again to restore original order.
  reverse(v.begin(), v.end());
  show("After second call to reverse(): ", v);
  cout << endl;

  // Rotate left one position.
  rotate(v.begin(), v.begin()+1, v.end());

  show("Order after rotating left one position:  ", v);
  cout << endl;

  // Now, rotate left two places.
  rotate(v.begin(), v.begin()+2, v.end());

  show("Order after rotating left two positions: ", v);
  cout << endl;

  // Randomize v.
  random_shuffle(v.begin(), v.end());
  show("After shuffle: ", v);

  return 0;
}

// Display the contents of a vector<int>.
void show(const char *msg, vector<int> vect) {
  cout << msg;
  for(unsigned i=0; i < vect.size(); ++i)
    cout << vect[i] << " ";
  cout << "\n";
}
```

The output is shown here:

```
Original order: 0 1 2 3 4 5 6 7 8 9

After reversal: 9 8 7 6 5 4 3 2 1 0

After second call to reverse(): 0 1 2 3 4 5 6 7 8 9

Order after rotating left one position:  1 2 3 4 5 6 7 8 9 0

Order after rotating left two positions: 3 4 5 6 7 8 9 0 1 2

After shuffle: 1 4 2 5 3 8 0 6 7 9
```

Bonus Example: Use Reverse Iterators to Perform a Right-Rotate

Although the STL supplies a left-rotate algorithm, it does not provide one that right-rotates. At first, this might seem like a serious flaw in the STL's design, or at least a troublesome omission. But neither is the case. To perform a right-rotate, use the **rotate( )** algorithm, but call it using reverse iterators. Since reverse iterators run backwards, the net effect of such a call is that a right-rotate is performed on the sequence! This technique is demonstrated by the following program.

```cpp
// Right-rotate a sequence by using reverse iterators with
// the rotate() algorithm.

#include <iostream>
#include <vector>
#include <algorithm>

using namespace std;

void show(const char *msg, vector<int> vect);

int main()
{
  vector<int> v;

  for(int i=0; i<10; i++) v.push_back(i);

  show("Original order: ", v);
  cout << endl;

  // Rotate right two positions using reverse iterators.
  rotate(v.rbegin(), v.rbegin()+2, v.rend());

  show("Order after two right-rotates: ", v);

  return 0;
}

// Display the contents of a vector<int>.
```

```
void show(const char *msg, vector<int> vect) {
  cout << msg;
  for(unsigned i=0; i < vect.size(); ++i)
    cout << vect[i] << " ";
  cout << "\n";
}
```

Here is the program's output:

```
Original order: 0 1 2 3 4 5 6 7 8 9

Order after two right-rotates: 8 9 0 1 2 3 4 5 6 7
```

As you can see, the original sequence was rotated right two positions.

As this application of **rotate( )** illustrates, part of the STL's power and elegance come from the subtleties of its design. By defining reverse iterators, the creators of the STL made it possible for several algorithms to operate in reverse order, thus reducing the need to explicitly define a backwards-running complement for each algorithm. While it certainly would have been possible to create a template library that did not include such things as reverse iterators, it is these types of constructs that streamline its design.

Options and Alternatives

There is a variation of **reverse( )** called **reverse_copy( )** that you might find useful in some cases. Instead of reversing the contents of the specified sequence in place, it copies the reversed sequence into another range. It has this prototype:

> template <class BiIter, class OutIter>
>   void reverse_copy(BiIter *start*, BiIter *end*, OutIter *result_start*)

It copies in reverse order the range *start* through *end*–1 into the sequence whose initial element is pointed to by *result_start*. The range pointed to by *result_start* must be at least as large as the range being reversed.

Similarly, there is a variation of **rotate( )** called **rotate_copy( )** that copies the rotated sequence into another range. It is shown here:

> template <class ForIter, class OutIter>
>   void rotate_copy(ForIter *start*, ForIter *mid*, ForIter *end*, OutIter *result_start*)

It copies the range *start* through *end*–1 into the range whose first element is pointed to by *result_start*. The range pointed to by *result_start* must be at least as large as the range being rotated. In the process, it left-rotates the elements so that the element specified by *mid* becomes the new first element. It returns an iterator to one past the end of the resulting range.

You can create permutations of a range by calling **next_permutation( )** or **prev_permutation( )**. These are described in *Permute a Sequence*.

Cycle Through a Container with for_each( )

Key Ingredients		
Headers	**Classes**	**Functions**
<algorithm>		template<class InIter, class Func> Func for_each(InIter *start*, InIter *end*, Func *fn*)

As most programmers know, cycling through the contents of a container is a very common activity. For example, to display the contents of a container, you will need to cycle through it from start to finish, displaying each element in turn. Cycling through a container can be performed in a variety of ways. For example, you can cycle through any type of container through the use of an iterator. Containers such as **vector** and **deque** allow you to cycle through their contents via the array subscripting operator. The **for_each( )** algorithm offers another approach. It cycles through a range of elements, applying a specific operation to each element. This recipe demonstrates its use.

Step-by-Step

To cycle through a range of elements by use of **for_each( )** involves these steps:

1. Create a function (or function object) that will be called for each element in the range.
2. Call **for_each( )**, passing in iterators to the beginning and end of the range to be processed and the function to be applied.

Discussion

The prototype for the **for_each( )** algorithm is shown here:

    template<class InIter, class Func>
       Func for_each(InIter *start*, InIter *end*, Func *fn*)

The **for_each( )** algorithm applies the function *fn* to the range of elements specified by *start* and *end*. Thus, *fn* is called once for each element in the range. **for_each( )** returns *fn*. You can pass either a function pointer or a function object to *fn*. In both cases, the *fn* must take one argument whose type is compatible with the type of the elements in the specified range. It can return a value. However, if *fn* does return a value, the value is ignored by **for_each( )**. Therefore, often, the return type of *fn* is **void**. However, a return value might be useful in situations other than in a call to the **for_each( )** algorithm. For example, *fn* could keep a count of the number of elements that it processes and return this count after the **for_each( )** algorithm returns.

Example

The following example shows **for_each( )** in action. It uses **for_each()** for two purposes. First, a call to **for_each( )** displays the contents of a container, one element at a time. It uses the **show( )** function to display each element. Second, it computes the summation of the elements in the container. In this case, **for_each( )** is passed a pointer to the **summation( )** function. Notice that this function returns the summation. This value is not used by **for_each( )**. Rather, it is obtained afterwards to obtain the sum of the elements.

```
// Demonstrate the for_each() algorithm.
#include <iostream>
#include <vector>
#include <algorithm>
using namespace std;

// Display an int value.
void show(int i) {
  cout << i << " ";
}

// Keep a running sum of the values passed to i.
int summation(int i) {
  static int sum = 0;

  sum += i;
  return sum;
}

int main()
{
  vector<int> v;
  int i;

  for(i=1; i < 11; i++) v.push_back(i);

  cout << "Contents of v: ";
  for_each(v.begin(), v.end(), show);
  cout << "\n";

  for_each(v.begin(), v.end(), summation);
  cout << "Summation of v: " << summation(0);

  return 0;
}
```

The output is shown here:

```
Contents of v: 1 2 3 4 5 6 7 8 9 10
Summation of v: 55
```

As explained in the discussion, the function passed to **for_each( )** must have one parameter, and the type of this parameter must be the same as the type of the elements in the container on which the **for_each( )** is used. In this example, because **v** is a vector of **int**, both **show( )** and **summation( )** have one **int** parameter. Each time one of these functions is called, it is passed an element from the specified range. It must be pointed out that the **summation( )** function is quite limited. A better way to implement it is as a function object, as is shown in *Create a Custom Function Object*.

Options and Alternatives

The International Standard for C++ categorizes **for_each( )** as a *non-modifying algorithm*. However, this label can be a bit misleading. For example, there is nothing that prevents the function passed to **for_each( )** from using a reference parameter and modifying the underlying element through the reference. In other words, a function applied to each element in a container could be declared like this:

void *fn*(*type &arg*)

In this case, *arg* is a reference parameter. Thus, the value pointed to by *arg* could be changed via an assignment, as shown here:

```
arg = newvalue;
```

For example, the following function will reverse the case of a character that it is passed, changing an uppercase letter to lowercase and a lowercase to uppercase. Notice that **ch** is passed by reference.

```
// Reverse the case of the character passed in ch.
void rev_case(char &ch) {
  if(islower(ch)) ch = toupper(ch);
  else ch = tolower(ch);
}
```

Therefore, assuming a vector called **v** that contains characters, the following call to **for_each( )** will modify **v** such that each character in the container has its case reversed:

```
for_each(v.begin(), v.end(), rev_case);
```

Although the preceding code works, I am uncomfortable with it for two reasons. First, as explained, the International Standard for C++ categorizes **for_each( )** as a non-modifying algorithm. While not technically breaking this rule (because the algorithm, *itself*, does not modify the sequence), changing the contents of the container as a side effect of the function passed to **for_each( )** seems inconsistent and misleading. Second, the STL offers a better way to modify a sequence that uses the **transform( )** algorithm, which is described in *Use transform( ) to Change a Sequence*.

The example program passed a function pointer to **for_each( )**, but you can also pass a function object. Recall that a function object is an instance of a class that implements **operator( )**. Function objects are described in detail in *Use a Built-In Function Object* and *Create a Custom Function Object*. For an example that uses a function object with **for_each( )**, see *Create a Custom Function Object*.

Use transform( ) to Change a Sequence

Key Ingredients		
Headers	**Classes**	**Functions**
<algorithm>		template <class InIter, class OutIter, class Func> OutIter transform(InIter *start*, InIter *end*, OutIter *result*, Func *unaryfunc*) template <class InIter1, class InIter2, class OutIter, class Func> OutIter transform(InIter1 *start1*, InIter1 *end1*, InIter2 *start2*, OutIter *result*, Func *binaryfunc*)

Sometimes, you will want to apply a transformation to all of the elements within a sequence and store the result. The best way to accomplish this is to use the **transform( )** algorithm. It has two forms. The first lets you apply a transformation to a range of elements from a single sequence. The second lets you apply a transformation to elements from two sequences. In both cases, the resulting sequence is stored. A key aspect of **transform( )** is that the resulting sequence can be the same as the input sequence or it can be a different sequence. Thus, **transform( )** can be used to change the elements in a sequence in place or to create a separate sequence that contains the result. This recipe shows the process.

Step-by-Step

To apply **transform( )** to the elements of a single range involves the following steps:

1. Create a function (or function object) that performs the desired transform. It must have a single parameter that receives an element from the input range.
2. Call **transform( )**, specifying the input range, the output range, and the transform function.

To apply **transform( )** to pairs of elements from two ranges involves the following steps:

1. Create a function (or function object) that performs the desired transform. It must have two parameters, with each receiving an element from an input range.
2. Call **transform( )**, specifying both input ranges, the output range, and the transform function.

Discussion

The **transform( )** algorithm has these two forms.

    template <class InIter, class OutIter, class Func)
        OutIter transform(InIter *start*, InIter *end*, OutIter *result*, Func *unaryfunc*)

    template <class InIter1, class InIter2, class OutIter, class Func)
        OutIter transform(InIter1 *start1*, InIter1 *end1*, InIter2 *start2*,
                        OutIter *result*, Func *binaryfunc*)

The **transform( )** algorithm applies a function to a range of elements and stores the outcome in *result*. The range pointed to by *result* must be at least as large as the range being transformed. In the first form, the range is specified by *start* and *end*. The function to be applied is specified by *unaryfunc*. It receives the value of an element in its parameter and it must return its transformation. In the second form of **transform( )**, the transformation is applied using a function that receives the value of an element from the sequence to be transformed (*start1* to *end1*) in its first parameter and an element from the second sequence (beginning at *start2*) as its second parameter. Both versions of **transform( )** return an iterator to the end of the resulting sequence.

A key aspect of **transform( )** is that it can be used to change the contents of a sequence in-place. Therefore, for the first form of **transform( )**, *result* and *start* can both specify the same element. For the second form, the result can be the same as either *start1* or *start2*.

There is one more important point about **transform( )**: The International Standard for C++ states that the transformation function (*unaryfunc* or *binaryfunc*) must not produce side effects.

Example

The following example shows both forms of **transform( )** in action. The first form is used to compute the reciprocals of a sequence of **double** values that are held in a vector. This transformation is applied twice. First, it stores the results back into the original sequence. The second time, it stores the results in another sequence. In both cases, the **reciprocal( )** function is passed to **transform( )**.

The second form of **transform( )** computes the midpoints between two integer values contained in two sequences. It stores the result in a third sequence. The **midpoint( )** function performs the midpoint computation, and it is the function that is passed to **transform( )**.

```
// Demonstrate the transform() algorithm.
//
// Both versions of transform() are used within
// the program. The first alters the sequence of doubles
// so that it contains reciprocal values. The second
// creates a sequence that contains the midpoints
// between the values in two other sequences.

#include <iostream>
#include <vector>
#include <algorithm>
```

```cpp
using namespace std;

double reciprocal(double val);
int midpoint(int a, int b);

template<class T> void show(const char *msg, vector<T> vect);

int main()
{
  int i;

  // First, demonstrate the single-sequence form of transform().
  vector<double> v;

  // Put values into v.
  for(i=1; i < 10; ++i) v.push_back((double)i);

  cout << "Demonstrate single-sequence form of transform().\n";
  show("Initial contents of v:\n", v);
  cout << endl;

  // Transform v by applying the reciprocal() function.
  // Put the result back into v.
  cout << "Compute reciprocals for v and store the results back in v.\n";
  transform(v.begin(), v.end(), v.begin(), reciprocal);

  show("Transformed contents of v:\n", v);

  // Transform v a second time, putting the result into a new sequence.
  cout << "Transform v again. This time, store the results in v2.\n";
  vector<double> v2(10);
  transform(v.begin(), v.end(), v2.begin(), reciprocal);

  show("Here is v2:\n", v2);
  cout << endl;

  // Now, demonstrate the two-sequence form of transform()
  cout << "Demonstrate double-sequence form of transform().\n";
  vector<int> v3, v4, v5(10);
  for(i = 0; i < 10; ++i) v3.push_back(i);
  for(i = 10; i < 20; ++i) if(i%2) v4.push_back(i); else v4.push_back(-i);

  show("Contents of v3:\n", v3);
  show("Contents of v4:\n", v4);
  cout << endl;

  cout << "Compute midpoints between v3 and v4 and store results in v5.\n";
  transform(v3.begin(), v3.end(), v4.begin(), v5.begin(), midpoint);

  show("Contents of v5:\n", v5);

  return 0;
}
```

```
// Display the contents of a vector<int>.
template<class T> void show(const char *msg, vector<T> vect) {
  cout << msg;
  for(unsigned i=0; i < vect.size(); ++i)
    cout << vect[i] << " ";
  cout << "\n";
}

// Return the whole-number midpoint between two values.
int midpoint(int a, int b) {
  return((a-b) / 2) + b;
}

// Return the reciprocal of a double.
double reciprocal(double val) {
  if(val == 0.0) return 0.0;
  return 1.0 / val; // return reciprocal
}
```

The output is shown here:

```
Demonstrate single-sequence form of transform().
Initial contents of v:
1 2 3 4 5 6 7 8 9

Compute reciprocals for v and store the results back in v.
Transformed contents of v:
1 0.5 0.333333 0.25 0.2 0.166667 0.142857 0.125 0.111111
Transform v again. This time, store the results in v2.
Here is v2:
1 2 3 4 5 6 7 8 9 0

Demonstrate double-sequence form of transform().
Contents of v3:
0 1 2 3 4 5 6 7 8 9
Contents of v4:
-10 11 -12 13 -14 15 -16 17 -18 19

Compute midpoints between v3 and v4 and store the results in v5.
Contents of v5:
-5 6 -5 8 -5 10 -5 12 -5 14
```

A key point illustrated by the program is that the function or function object used by **transform( )** must specify a parameter or parameters whose types are compatible with the types of the elements in the sequences. Also, it must return a compatible type.

Options and Alternatives

The ranges specified in the two-sequence version of **transform( )** do not need to be in separate containers. This is a common misconception. Instead, you can specify both ranges from the same container. For example, assuming the preceding program, the following computes the midpoints between the first and last five elements of **v3** and stores them in the first five elements of **v5**:

```
transform(v3.begin(), v3.begin()+5, v3.begin()+5, v5.begin(), midpoint);
```

As mentioned, it is possible to store the result back into one of the original sequences, thus allowing a sequence to be modified in-place. When using the two-sequence form of **transform( )**, the target sequence can be either of the input sequences. For example, this statement computes the midpoints for the sequences held in **v3** and **v4** and stores the result in **v4**:

```
transform(v3.begin(), v3.end(), v4.begin(), v4.begin(), midpoint);
```

This works because the values of each pair of elements are first obtained from each sequence and then passed to **midpoint( )**. The result is then stored in **v4**. Thus, the original values in **v4** are obtained before they are overwritten.

The preceding example passed function pointers to **transform( )**, but you can also use function objects. Function objects are described in detail in *Use a Built-In Function Object* and *Create a Custom Function Object*. For an example that uses a function object with **transform( )**, see *Create a Custom Function Object*.

If you want to perform a non-modifying operation on a sequence, consider using **for_each( )**. See *Cycle Through a Container with for_each( )*.

In some cases, you may want to generate a sequence of elements that are not transformations of another sequence. To do this, you can use the **generate( )** or **generate_n( )** algorithms. They are shown here:

> template <class ForIter, class Generator>
>   void generate(ForIter *start*, ForIter *end*, Generator *fngen*)

> template <class OutIter, class Size, class Generator>
>   void generate_n(OutIter *start*, Size *num*, Generator *fngen*)

The algorithms **generate( )** and **generate_n( )** assign values returned by a generator function to elements within a specified range. For **generate( )**, the range being assigned is specified by *start* and *end*. For **generate_n( )**, the range begins at *start* and runs for *num* elements. The generator function is passed in *fngen*. It has no parameters and it must return objects that are compatible with the type of the desired sequence. Here is a very simple example that demonstrates **generate( )**. It uses a function called **pow_of_two( )** to generate a sequence that contains powers of 2.

```
// Generate a sequence.
#include <iostream>
#include <vector>
#include <algorithm>

using namespace std;

double pow_of_two();
```

```
int main()
{
  vector<double> v(5);

  // Generate a sequence.
  generate(v.begin(), v.end(), pow_of_two);

  cout << "Powers of 2: ";
  for(unsigned i=0; i < v.size(); ++i)
    cout << v[i] << " ";

  return 0;
}

// A simple generator function that generates the powers of 2.
double pow_of_two() {
  static double val = 1.0;
  double t;

  t = val;
  val += val;

  return t;
}
```

The following output is displayed:

```
Powers of 2: 1 2 4 8 16
```

Perform Set Operations

Key Ingredients		
Headers	**Classes**	**Functions**
<algorithm>		template <class InIter1, class InIter2, class OutIter> OutIter set_union(InIter1 *start1*, InIter1 *end1*, InIter2 *start2*, InIter2 *end2*, OutIter *result*)
		template <class InIter1, class InIter2, class OutIter> OutIter set_difference(InIter1 *start1*, InIter1 *end1*, InIter2 *start2*, InIter2 *end2*, OutIter *result*)
		template <class InIter1, class InIter2, class OutIter> OutIter set_symmetric_difference(InIter1 *start1*, InIter1 *end1*, InIter2 *start2*, InIter2 *end2*, OutIter *result*)
		template <class InIter1, class InIter2, class OutIter> OutIter set_intersection(InIter1 *start1*, InIter1 *end1*, InIter2 *start2*, InIter2 *end2*, OutIter *result*)
		template <class InIter1, class InIter2> bool includes(InIter1 *start1*, InIter1 *end1*, InIter2 *start2*, InIter2 *end2*)

The STL provides five algorithms that perform set operations. Understand that these algorithms operate on any type of container; they are not for use only with the **set** or **multiset** classes. The one requirement is that the contents of the containers must be in sorted order. The set algorithms are **set_union( )**, **set_difference( )**, **set_symmetric_difference( )**, **set_intersection( )**, and **includes( )**. This recipe demonstrates their use.

Step-by-Step

To use the set algorithms involves these steps:

1. The two sequences that will participate in the set algorithms must be sorted. They must also both contain elements of the same or compatible types.

2. Obtain the union of two sets by calling **set_union( )**.

3. Obtain the difference between two sets by calling **set_difference( )**.

4. Obtain the symmetric difference between two sets by calling **set_symmetric_difference( )**.

5. Obtain the intersection of two sets by calling **set_intersection( )**.

6. Determine if one set includes all of another set by calling **includes( )**. This algorithm can be used to determine a subset relationship.

Discussion

To obtain the union of two sorted sets, use **set_union( )**. It has two forms. The one used by this recipe is shown here:

```
template <class InIter1, class InIter2, class OutIter>
  OutIter set_union(InIter1 start1, InIter1 end1,
          InIter2 start2, InIter2 end2, OutIter result)
```

It produces a sequence that contains the union of the two sets defined by the ranges *start1* through *end1*–1 and *start2* through *end2*–1. Thus, the resultant set contains those elements that are in both sets. The result is sorted and put into *result*. The input ranges must not overlap the resulting range. An iterator to the end of the resulting range is returned.

To obtain the difference between two sorted sets, use **set_difference( )**. It has two forms. The one used by this recipe is shown here:

```
template <class InIter1, class InIter2, class OutIter>
  OutIter set_difference(InIter1 start1, InIter1 end1,
          InIter2 start2, InIter2 end2, OutIter result)
```

The **set_difference( )** algorithm produces a sequence that contains the difference between the two sets defined by the ranges *start1* through *end1*–1 and *start2* through *end2*–1. That is, the set defined by *start2, end2* is removed from the set defined by *start1, end1*. The result is sorted and put into *result*. The input ranges must not overlap the resulting range. An iterator to the end of the resulting range is returned.

The symmetric difference of two ordered sets can be found using the **set_symmetric_difference( )** algorithm. It has two forms. The one used by this recipe is shown here:

```
template <class InIter1, class InIter2, class OutIter>
  OutIter set_symmetric_difference(InIter1 start1, InIter1 end1,
          InIter2 start2, InIter2 end2, OutIter result)
```

The **set_symmetric_difference( )** algorithm produces a sequence that contains the symmetric difference between the two ordered sets defined by the ranges *start1* through *end1*–1 and *start2* through *end2*–1. The symmetric difference of two sets contains only those elements that are not common to both sets. The result is sorted and put into *result*. The input ranges must not overlap the resulting range. An iterator to the end of the resulting range is returned.

The intersection of two sorted sets can be obtained by calling **set_intersection( )**. It has two forms. The one used by this recipe is shown here:

```
template <class InIter1, class InIter2, class OutIter>
   OutIter set_intersection(InIter1 start1, InIter1 end1,
               InIter2 start2, InIter2 end2, OutIter result)
```

The **set_intersection( )** algorithm produces a sequence that contains the intersection of the two sets defined by the ranges *start1* through *end1*–1 and *start2* through *end2*–1. These are the elements common to both the sets. The result is ordered and put into *result*. The input ranges must not overlap the resulting range. An iterator to the end of the resulting range is returned.

For all of the preceding algorithms, the range pointed to by *result* must be large enough to hold the elements that will be stored in it. The set algorithms overwrite the existing elements. They do not insert new elements.

To see if the entire contents of one sorted set is included in another, use **includes( )**. It has two forms. The one used by this recipe is shown here:

```
template <class InIter1, class InIter2>
   bool includes(InIter1 start1, InIter1 end1,
            InIter2 start2, InIter2 end2)
```

The **includes( )** algorithm determines if the range *start1* through *end1*–1 includes all of the elements in the range *start2* through *end2*–1. It returns true if the elements are all found and false otherwise. The **includes( )** algorithm can be used to determine if one set is a subset of another.

Remember, the set algorithms can be used with any sorted sequence, not just instances of **set** or **multiset**. However, in all cases, the sequence must be sorted.

Example

The following program demonstrates the set algorithms:

```
// Demonstrate the set algorithms.
//
// This program uses list, but any other sequence
// container could be used.

#include <iostream>
#include <list>
#include <algorithm>

using namespace std;

template<class InIter>
    void show_range(const char *msg, InIter start, InIter end);

int main()
{
  list<char> lst1, lst2, result(15), lst3;
  list<char>::iterator res_end;

  for(int i=0; i < 5; i++) lst1.push_back('A'+i);
  for(int i=3; i < 10; i++) lst2.push_back('A'+i);
```

```
  show_range("Contents of lst1: ", lst1.begin(), lst1.end());
  cout << endl;

  show_range("Contents of lst2: ", lst2.begin(), lst2.end());
  cout << endl;

  // Create the union of lst1 and lst2.
  res_end = set_union(lst1.begin(), lst1.end(),
                      lst2.begin(), lst2.end(),
                      result.begin());

  show_range("Union of lst1 and lst2: ", result.begin(), res_end);
  cout << endl;

  // Create a set that contains lst1 - lst2.
  res_end = set_difference(lst1.begin(), lst1.end(),
                           lst2.begin(), lst2.end(),
                           result.begin());

  show_range("lst1 - lst2: ", result.begin(), res_end);
  cout << endl;

  // Create the symmetric difference between lst1 and lst2.
  res_end = set_symmetric_difference(lst1.begin(), lst1.end(),
                                     lst2.begin(), lst2.end(),
                                     result.begin());

  show_range("Symmetric difference of lst1 and lst2: ",
             result.begin(), res_end);
  cout << endl;

  // Create the intersection of lst1 and lst2.
  res_end = set_intersection(lst1.begin(), lst1.end(),
                             lst2.begin(), lst2.end(),
                             result.begin());

  show_range("Intersection of lst1 and lst2: ", result.begin(), res_end);
  cout << endl;

  // Use includes() to check for subset.
  lst3.push_back('A');
  lst3.push_back('C');
  lst3.push_back('D');

  if(includes(lst1.begin(), lst1.end(),
              lst3.begin(), lst3.end()))
    cout << "lst3 is a subset of lst1\n";
  else
    cout << "lst3 is not a subset of lst1\n";

  return 0;
}
```

```
// Show a range of elements.
template<class InIter>
    void show_range(const char *msg, InIter start, InIter end) {

  InIter itr;

  cout << msg;

  for(itr = start; itr != end; ++itr)
    cout << *itr << " ";
  cout << endl;
}
```

This program generates the following output.

```
Contents of lst1: A B C D E

Contents of lst2: D E F G H I J

Union of lst1 and lst2: A B C D E F G H I J

lst1 - lst2: A B C

Symmetric difference of lst1 and lst2: A B C F G H I J

Intersection of lst1 and lst2: D E

lst3 is a subset of lst1
```

Options and Alternatives

All of the set algorithms provide a second form that lets you specify a comparison function, which determines when one element is less than another. You can use this function to specify the ordering of the input sequences and of the result. These forms are shown here:

```
template <class InIter1, class InIter2, class OutIter, class Comp>
    OutIter set_union(InIter1 start1, InIter1 end1,
            InIter2 start2, InIter2 end2, OutIter result, Comp cmpfn)

template <class InIter1, class InIter2, class OutIter, class Comp>
    OutIter set_difference(InIter1 start1, InIter1 end1,
            InIter2 start2, InIter2 end2,
            OutIter result, Comp cmpfn)

template <class InIter1, class InIter2, class OutIter, class Comp>
    OutIter set_symmetric_difference(InIter1 start1, InIter1 end1,
            InIter2 start2, InIter2 end2, OutIter result, Comp cmpfn)

template <class InIter1, class InIter2, class OutIter, class Comp>
    OutIter set_intersection(InIter1 start1, InIter1 end1,
            InIter2 start2, InIter2 end2,
            OutIter result, Comp cmpfn)
```

```
template <class InIter1, class InIter2, class Comp>
   bool includes(InIter1 start1, InIter1 end1,
                 InIter2 start2, InIter2 end2, Comp cmpfn)
```

For all, the ranges specified by *start1, end1* and *start2, end2* must be sorted in accordance with the comparison function passed in *cmpfn*, which determines when one element is less than another. The result will also be sorted according to *cmpfn*. Otherwise, these functions work like their previously described versions.

Permute a Sequence

Key Ingredients		
Headers	**Classes**	**Functions**

<algorithm>		template <class BIter>
		   bool next_permutation(BIter *start*,
		                         BIter *end*)

		template <class BIter>
		   bool prev_permutation(BIter *start*,
		                         BIter *end*)

Two of the more intriguing algorithms are **next_permutation( )** and **prev_permutation( )**. They are used to provide permutations of a sequence. They are often used in simulations and in testing. These algorithms require bidirectional iterators and can only be used on sequences that are capable of being sorted. This recipe demonstrates their use.

Step-by-Step

To permute a sequence involves these steps.

1. The sequence to be permuted must support bidirectional iterators and be capable of being sorted.

2. To obtain the next permutation, call **next_permutation( )**, specifying iterators to the beginning and end of the range to be permuted.

3. To obtain the previous permutation, call **prev_permutation( )**, specifying iterators to the beginning and end of the range to be permuted.

Discussion

You can generate a permutation of any sorted sequence by using the algorithms **next_permutation( )** and **prev_permutation( )**. Each has two forms. The ones used by this recipe are shown here:

```
template <class BiIter>
   bool next_permutation(BiIter start, BiIter end)
template <class BiIter>
   bool prev_permutation(BiIter start, BiIter end)
```

The **next_permutation( )** algorithm constructs the next permutation of the range *start* through *end*–1. The **prev_permutation( )** algorithm constructs the previous permutation of the range *start* through *end*–1. The permutations are generated assuming a sorted sequence represents the first permutation. If all permutations have been exhausted, both algorithms return false. In this case, **next_permutation( )** arranges the range into sorted ascending order and **prev_permutation( )** arranges the range into sorted descending order. Otherwise, both functions return true. Therefore, a loop that obtains all possible permutations will run until false is returned.

Example

The following example uses **next_permutation( )** to generate all possible permutations of the sequence ABC. It then uses **prev_permutation( )** to generate the permutations in reverse order.

```cpp
// Demonstrate next_permutation() and prev_permutation().

#include <iostream>
#include <vector>
#include <algorithm>

using namespace std;

int main()
{
  vector<char> v;
  unsigned i;

  // This creates the sorted sequence ABC.
  for(i=0; i<3; i++) v.push_back('A'+i);

  // Demonstrate next_permutation().
  cout << "All permutations of ABC by use of next_permutation():\n";
  do {
    for(i=0; i < v.size(); i++)
      cout << v[i];
    cout << "\n";
  } while(next_permutation(v.begin(), v.end()));

  // At this point, v has cycled back to containing ABC.

  cout << endl;

  // Demonstrate prev_permutation().

  // First, back up to the previous permutation.
  prev_permutation(v.begin(), v.end());
```

```
cout << "All permutations of ABC by use of prev_permutation():\n";
do {
  for(i=0; i<v.size(); i++)
    cout << v[i];
  cout << "\n";
} while(prev_permutation(v.begin(), v.end()));

return 0;
}
```

The output from the program is shown here:

```
All permutations of ABC by use of next_permutation():
ABC
ACB
BAC
BCA
CAB
CBA

All permutations of ABC by use of prev_permutation():
CBA
CAB
BCA
BAC
ACB
ABC
```

Options and Alternatives

Both the **next_permutation( )** and **prev_permutation( )** algorithms supply a second form that lets you specify a comparison function, which determines when one element is less than another. You can use this function to specify the ordering of the sequence. (In other words, this function determines the sorted order of the sequence.) These forms are shown here:

> template <class BiIter, class Comp>
>   bool next_permutation(BiIter *start*, BiIter *end*, Comp *cmpfn*)

> template <class BiIter, class Comp>
>   bool prev_permutation(BiIter *start*, BiIter *end*, Comp *cmpfn*)

The permutation order will be based on *cmpfn*. Otherwise, these functions work like their previously described versions.

The **next_permutation( )** and **prev_permutation( )** algorithms generate permutations in a well-defined order. In some situations, you might want to randomize the generation of permutations. One way to do this is with the **random_shuffle( )** algorithm. It randomizes a sequence. One of its forms is shown here:

> template <class RandIter> void random_shuffle(RandIter *start*, RandIter *end*)

It randomizes the range *start* through *end*–1. Assuming the previous example program, the following produces a random permutation of **v**:

```
random_shuffle(v.begin(), v.end());
```

There is also a second form of **random_shuffle( )** that lets you specify a custom random number generator. See *Reverse, Rotate, and Shuffle a Sequence.*

Copy a Sequence from One Container to Another

Key Ingredients		
Headers	**Classes**	**Functions**
<algorithm>		template <class InIter, class OutIter> OutIter copy(InIter *start*, InIter *end*, OutIter *result*)

Although conceptually simple, one of the most important STL algorithms is **copy( )**, which copies a sequence. It is so important because it gives you a way to copy elements from one container to another. Furthermore, the types of containers do not need to be the same. For example, using **copy( )**, you can copy elements from a **vector** to a **list**. Of course, what makes this possible is the fact that **copy( )** (like most of the STL algorithms) works through iterators. It has been said that iterators are the glue that binds the STL together. The **copy( )** algorithm illustrates this point, and this recipe shows how to put it into action.

Step-by-Step

To use **copy( )** to copy elements from one type of container to another involves these steps:

1. Confirm that the destination container is large enough to hold the elements that will be copied to it.
2. Call **copy( )** to copy the elements, specifying the range to be copied and an iterator to the start of the destination.

Discussion

The **copy( )** algorithm is shown here:

    template <class InIter, class OutIter>
        OutIter copy(InIter *start*, InIter *end*, OutIter *result*)

This algorithm copies the range *start* through *end*–1 into the target sequence, beginning at *result*. It returns a pointer to one past the end of the resulting sequence. Here is an important point: The copied elements *are not* added to the target container. Rather, they *overwrite* existing elements. Therefore, the target container pointed to by *result* must be large enough to hold the elements being copied. The **copy( )** algorithm *will not* automatically increase the size of the target container when copying elements to it. The algorithm simply assumes that the target container is large enough.

There is no requirement that *result* point into the same container as *start* and *end*, or even use the same type of container. This means that you can use **copy( )** to copy the contents of one type of container into another. The only restriction is that the element type of the target container must be compatible with the source container.

Another useful aspect of **copy( )** is that it can be used to left-shift elements within the same range as long as the last element in the range does not overlap the destination range.

Example

The following example shows how to use **copy( )** to copy elements from a **list** to a **vector**.

```
// Use copy() to copy elements from a list to a vector.

#include <iostream>
#include <vector>
#include <list>
#include <algorithm>

using namespace std;

template<class T> void show(const char *msg, T cont);

int main()
{
  list<char> lst;

  // Add elements to lst.
  char str[] = "Algorithms act on containers";
  for(int i = 0; str[i]; i++) lst.push_back(str[i]);

  // Create a vector that initially contains 40 periods.
  vector<char> v(40, '.');

  show("Contents of lst:\n", lst);
  show("Contents of v:\n", v);

  // Copy lst into v.
  copy(lst.begin(), lst.end(), v.begin()+5);

  // Display result.
  show("Contents of v after copy:\n", v);
  return 0;
}

template<class T> void show(const char *msg, T cont) {
  cout << msg;
  T::iterator itr;
  for(itr=cont.begin(); itr != cont.end(); ++itr)
    cout << *itr;

  cout << "\n\n";
}
```

The output is shown here:

```
Contents of lst:
Algorithms act on containers

Contents of v:
.......................................

Contents of v after copy:
.....Algorithms act on containers.......
```

Options and Alternatives

The STL provides two useful variations on **copy( )**. The first is **copy_backward( )**, shown here:

> template <class BiIter1, class BiIter2>
>   BiIter2 copy_backward(BiIter1 *start*, BiIter1 *end*, BiIter2 *result*)

This algorithm works like **copy( )**, except that it moves elements from the end of the specified range first, and *result* must initially point to one past the beginning of the destination range. Thus, it can be used to right-shift elements within the same range as long as the first element in the range does not overlap the destination range.

The second copy option is **swap_ranges( )**. It exchanges the contents of one range with another. Thus, it provides a bidirectional copy. It is shown here:

> template <class ForIter1, class ForIter2>
>   ForIter2 swap_ranges(ForIter1 *start1*, ForIter1 *end1*, ForIter2 *start2*)

The **swap_ranges( )** algorithm exchanges elements in the range *start1* through *end1*–1 with elements in the sequence beginning at *start2*. It returns a pointer to the end of the sequence specified by *start2*. The ranges being exchanged must not overlap.

Replace and Remove Elements in a Container

Key Ingredients		
Headers	**Classes**	**Functions**

<algorithm>		template <class ForIter, class T>
		   ForIter remove(ForIter *start*, ForIter *end*,
		         const T &*val*)

		template <class ForIter, class T>
		   void replace(ForIter *start*, ForIter *end*,
		         const T &*old*, const T &*new*)

The STL provides functions that let you replace or remove elements. At the core of this functionality is **replace( )** and **remove( )**. Although both of these operations can be accomplished through the use of container-defined functions, in many cases, these algorithms streamline the task. This recipe demonstrates them.

Step-by-Step

To remove or replace one or more elements in a sequence involves these steps:

1. To remove all elements that match a specified value, call **remove( )**, specifying the range to be modified and the value to remove.
2. To replace all occurrences of elements that match a specified value, call **replace( )**, specifying the range to be modified, the value to replace, and the value to substitute.

Discussion

The **remove( )** algorithm removes all occurrences of a specified element from a specified range. It is shown here:

```
template <class ForIter, class T>
    ForIter remove(ForIter start, ForIter end, const T &val)
```

This algorithm removes all elements in the range *start* through *end*–1 that are equal to *val*. It returns an iterator to the end of the remaining elements. The order of the remaining elements is unchanged.

Within a specified range, the **replace( )** algorithm replaces all occurrences of a specified element with another. It is shown here:

```
template <class ForIter, class T>
    void replace(ForIter start, ForIter end, const T &old, const T &new)
```

Within the specified range *start* through *end*–1, **replace( )** replaces elements that match the value *old* with elements that have the value *new*.

NOTE   *The* **list** *container class provides its own implementation of* **remove( )** *that is optimized for lists. Therefore, when removing elements in a* **list***, you should use that function rather than the* **remove( )** *algorithm.*

Example

The following example shows **remove( )** and **replace( )** in action:

```cpp
// Demonstrate remove() and replace().

#include <iostream>
#include <vector>
#include <algorithm>
using namespace std;

template<class InIter>
    void show_range(const char *msg, InIter start, InIter end);
```

```
int main()
{
  vector<char> v;
  vector<char>::iterator itr, itr_end;

  // Create a vector that contains A B C D E A B C D E.
  for(int i=0; i<5; i++) {
    v.push_back('A'+i);
  }
  for(int i=0; i<5; i++) {
    v.push_back('A'+i);
  }

  show_range("Original contents of v:\n", v.begin(), v.end());
  cout << endl;

  // Remove all A's.
  itr_end = remove(v.begin(), v.end(), 'A');

  show_range("v after removing all A's:\n", v.begin(), itr_end);
  cout << endl;

  // Replace B's with X's
  replace(v.begin(), v.end(), 'B', 'X');

  show_range("v after replacing B with X:\n", v.begin(), itr_end);
  cout << endl;

  return 0;
}

// Show a range of elements from a vector<char>.
template<class InIter>
    void show_range(const char *msg, InIter start, InIter end) {
  InIter itr;

  cout << msg;
  for(itr = start; itr != end; ++itr)
    cout << *itr << " ";
  cout << endl;
}
```

The output is shown here:

```
Original contents of v:
A B C D E A B C D E

v after removing all A's:
B C D E B C D E

v after replacing B with X:
X C D E X C D E
```

Options and Alternatives

The STL provides several alternatives for removing and replacing elements. Two that you will find especially useful are **remove_copy( )** and **replace_copy( )**. Both generate a new sequence that contains the result of the operation. Thus, the original sequence is unaltered.

The prototype for **remove_copy( )** is shown here:

```
template <class InIter, class OutIter, class T>
    OutIter remove_copy(InIter start, InIter end, OutIter result, const T &val)
```

It copies elements from the specified range, removing those that are equal to *val*. It puts the result into the sequence pointed to by *result* and returns an iterator to one past the end of the result. The destination range must be large enough to hold the result.

The prototype for **replace_copy( )** is shown next:

```
template <class InIter, class OutIter, class T>
    OutIter replace_copy(InIter start, InIter end,
                         OutIter result, const T &old, const T &new)
```

It copies elements from the specified range, replacing elements equal to *old* with *new*. It puts the result into the sequence pointed to by *result* and returns an iterator to one past the end of the result. The destination range must be large enough to hold the result.

There are variations on **remove( )**, **replace( )**, **remove_copy( )**, and **replace_copy( )** that allow you to specify a unary predicate that determines when an element should be removed or replaced. These are called **remove_if( )**, **replace_if( )**, **remove_copy_if( )**, and **replace_copy_if( )**.

Another algorithm that removes elements from a sequence is **unique( )**. It removes consecutive duplicate elements from a range. It has the two forms shown here:

```
template <class ForIter>
    ForIter unique(ForIter start, ForIter end)
```

```
template <class ForIter, class BinPred>
    ForIter unique(ForIter start, ForIter end, BinPred pfn)
```

Consecutive duplicate elements in the specified range are removed. The second form allows you to specify a binary predicate that determines when one element is equal to another. **unique( )** returns an iterator to the end of the resulting range. For example, assuming the preceding program, if **v** contains the sequence AABCCBDE, then after this statement executes

```
itr_end = unique(v.begin(), v.end());
```

the range **v.begin( )** to **itr_end** will contain ABCBDE. The STL also provides **unique_copy( )**, which works just like **unique( )**, except that the result is put into another sequence.

Merge Two Sorted Sequences

Key Ingredients		
Headers	**Classes**	**Functions**
<algorithm>		template <class InIter1, class InIter2, class OutIter> OutIter merge(InIter1 *start1*, InIter1 *end1*, InIter2 *start2*, InIter2 *end2*, OutIter *result*)
		template <class BIter> void inplace_merge(BIter *start*, BIter *mid*, BIter *end*)

There are two STL algorithms that merge two sorted sequences: **merge( )** and **inplace_merge( )**. For both, the result is a sorted sequence that contains the contents of both of the original sequences. As you may recall, merging is directly supported by the **list** container. However, it is not provided for the other built-in containers. Therefore, if you want to merge sequences of elements from anything other than a **list** container, you will need to use one of the merge algorithms.

There are two ways in which a merge can take place. First, the result can be stored in a third sequence. Second, if the merge involves two sequences from the same container, then the result of the merge can be stored in-place. The first approach is provided by **merge( )**, and the second approach is provided by **inplace_merge( )**. This recipe illustrates both.

Step-by-Step

To merge two sequences, storing the outcome in a third sequence involves these steps:

1. Ensure that the sequences to be merged are sorted.

2. Call **merge( )**, passing in the ranges to be merged and an iterator to the start of the destination range that will hold the result.

To merge two sequences in-place involves these steps:

1. Ensure that the sequences to be merged are sorted.

2. Call **inplace_merge( )**, passing in the ranges to be merged. The result will be stored in-place.

Discussion

The **merge( )** algorithm merges two sorted sequences and stores the result in a third sequence. It has two forms. The one used by this recipe is shown here:

```
template <class InIter1, class InIter2, class OutIter>
    OutIter merge(InIter1 start1, InIter1 end1,
                  InIter2 start2, InIter2 end2,
                  OutIter result)
```

The **merge( )** algorithm merges two ordered sequences, placing the result into a third sequence. The ranges to be merged are defined by *start1*, *end1* and *start2*, *end2*. The result is put into the container pointed to by *result*. The container pointed to by *result* must be large enough to hold the elements that will be stored in it because the merged elements overwrite the existing elements. The **merge( )** algorithm does not insert new elements. An iterator to one past the end of the resulting sequence is returned.

It is important to understand that **merge( )** does not require that the input sequences or the resulting sequence be from the same type of container. For example, you can use **merge( )** to merge a sequence from an instance of **vector** with a sequence from an instance of **deque**, storing the result in a **list** object. Thus, **merge( )** offers a way to combine elements from separate containers.

The **inplace_merge( )** algorithm performs a merge on two sorted consecutive ranges within the same container, with the result replacing the original two ranges. It has two forms. The one used by this recipe is shown here:

```
template <class BiIter>
    void inplace_merge(BiIter start, BiIter mid, BiIter end)
```

Within a single sequence, the **inplace_merge( )** algorithm merges the range *start* through *mid*–1 with the range *mid* through *end*–1. Both ranges must be sorted. After executing, the resulting sequence is sorted and is contained in the range *start* to *end*–1.

NOTE *The **list** container class provides its own implementation of **merge( )** that is optimized for lists. Therefore, when merging lists, you should use that function rather than the **merge( )** algorithm.*

Example

The following example shows **merge( )** and **inplace_merge( )** in action. It uses **merge( )** to merge a **vector** with a **deque**. The result is stored in a **list**. Notice that both the input sequences are sorted and the result is sorted. It then uses **inplace_merge( )** to merge two sequences within the same vector.

```cpp
// Demonstrate merge() and inplace_merge().

#include <iostream>
#include <vector>
#include <deque>
#include <list>
#include <algorithm>

using namespace std;

template<class InIter>
    void show_range(const char *msg, InIter start, InIter end);

int main()
{
  vector<char> v;
  deque<char> dq;
```

```
  list<char> result(26);
  list<char>::iterator res_end;

  // First, demonstrate merge().

  for(int i=0; i < 26; i+=2) v.push_back('A'+i);
  for(int i=0; i < 26; i+=2) dq.push_back('B'+i);

  show_range("Original contents of v:\n", v.begin(), v.end());
  cout << endl;

  show_range("Original contents of dq:\n", dq.begin(), dq.end());
  cout << endl;

  // Merge v with dq.
  res_end = merge(v.begin(), v.end(),
                  dq.begin(), dq.end(),
                  result.begin());

  show_range("Result of merging v with dq:\n", result.begin(), res_end);
  cout << "\n\n";

  // Now, demonstrate inplace_merge().

  vector<char> v2;
  for(int i=0; i < 26; i+=2) v2.push_back('B'+i);
  for(int i=0; i < 26; i+=2) v2.push_back('A'+i);

  show_range("Original contents of v2:\n", v2.begin(), v2.end());
  cout << endl;

  // Merge two ranges within v2.
  inplace_merge(v2.begin(), v2.begin()+13, v2.end());

  show_range("Contents of v2 after in-place merge:\n", v2.begin(),
v2.end());

  return 0;
}

// Show a range of elements.
template<class InIter>
    void show_range(const char *msg, InIter start, InIter end) {

  InIter itr;

  cout << msg;

  for(itr = start; itr != end; ++itr)
    cout << *itr << " ";
  cout << endl;
}
```

The output is shown here:

```
Original contents of v:
A C E G I K M O Q S U W Y

Original contents of dq:
B D F H J L N P R T V X Z

Result of merging v with dq:
A B C D E F G H I J K L M N O P Q R S T U V W X Y Z


Original contents of v2:
B D F H J L N P R T V X Z A C E G I K M O Q S U W Y

Contents of v2 after in-place merge:
A B C D E F G H I J K L M N O P Q R S T U V W X Y Z
```

Options and Alternatives

There is a second form of **merge( )** that lets you specify a comparison function that determines when one element is less than another. It is shown here:

```
template <class InIter1, class InIter2, class OutIter, class Comp>
    OutIter merge(InIter1 start1, InIter1 end1,
                  InIter2 start2, InIter2 end2,
                  OutIter result, Comp cmpfn)
```

It works just like the first form, except that *cmpfn* is used to compare two elements. When using this form, the sequences being merged must also be ordered in accordance with *compfn*.

There is also a second form of **inplace_merge( )** that lets you specify a comparison function. It is shown here:

```
template <class BiIter, class Comp>
    void inplace_merge(BiIter start, BiIter mid, BiIter end, Comp cmpfn)
```

It works like the first version, except that it uses *cmpfn* to determine when one element is less than another. As you would expect, the sequences must also be sorted in accordance with *cmpfn*.

Create and Manage a Heap

Key Ingredients		
Headers	**Classes**	**Functions**

<algorithm>		template <class RandIter>
		  void make_heap(RandIter *start*,
		              RandIter *end*)

		template <class RandIter> void pop_heap(RandIter *start*, RandIter *end*)

		template <class RandIter>
		  void push_heap(RandIter *start*,
		              RandIter *end*)

		template <class RandIter> void sort_heap(RandIter *start*, RandIter *end*)

A heap is a data structure in which the top element (also called the first element) is the largest element in the sequence. Heaps allow fast (logarithmic time) insertion and removal of an element. They are useful in creating priority queues in which the highest priority item must be immediately available but a completely sorted list is not needed. The STL provides four algorithms that support heap operations, and this recipe demonstrates their use.

Step-by-Step

To create and manage a heap involves these steps:

1. To create a heap, call **make_heap( )**, specifying the range of elements to be made into a heap.
2. To add an element into the heap, call **push_heap( )**.
3. To remove an element from the heap, call **pop_heap( )**.
4. To sort the heap, call **sort_heap( )**.

Discussion

A heap is constructed by using the **make_heap( )** algorithm. It has two forms. The one used by this recipe is shown here:

```
template <class RandIter>
  void make_heap(RandIter start, RandIter end)
```

It constructs a heap from the sequence defined by *start* and *end*. Any container that supports random-access iterators can be used to hold a heap. Building a heap takes linear time.

You can push a new element onto the heap using **push_heap( )**. It has two forms. The one used by this recipe is shown here:

```
template <class RandIter>
  void push_heap(RandIter start, RandIter end)
```

It puts the element at *end*–1 onto the heap defined by *start* through *end*–2. In other words, the current heap ends at *end*–2 and **push_heap( )** adds the element at *end*–1. The result is a heap that ends at *end*–1. Pushing an element onto a heap consumes logarithmic time.

You can remove an element using **pop_heap( )**. It has two forms. The one used by this recipe is shown here:

```
template <class RandIter>
    void pop_heap(RandIter start, RandIter end)
```

The **pop_heap( )** exchanges the *start* and *end*–1 elements and then rebuilds the heap. The resulting heap ends at *end*–2. Popping an element from a heap consumes logarithmic time.

You can sort a heap into ascending order using **sort_heap( )**. Its prototype is shown here:

```
template <class RandIter>
    void sort_heap(RandIter start, RandIter end)
```

The **sort_heap( )** algorithm sorts a heap within the range specified by *start* and *end*. Sorting a heap requires time proportional to N log N.

Example

Here is program that builds a heap, then adds and removes elements. It ends by sorting the heap.

```cpp
// Demonstrate the heap algorithms.

#include <iostream>
#include <vector>
#include <algorithm>

using namespace std;

void show(const char *msg, vector<char> vect);

int main()
{
  vector<char> v;
  int i;

  for(i=0; i<20; i+=2) v.push_back('A'+i);

  show("v before building heap:\n", v);
  cout << endl;

  // Construct a heap.
  make_heap(v.begin(), v.end());

  show("v after building heap:\n", v);
  cout << endl;
```

```
  // Push H onto heap.
  v.push_back('H'); // first put H into vector
  push_heap(v.begin(), v.end()); // now, push H onto heap

  show("v after pushing H onto heap:\n", v);
  cout << endl;

  // Pop value from heap.
  pop_heap(v.begin(), v.end());

  show("v after popping from heap:\n", v);
  cout << endl;

  // Sort the heap
  sort_heap(v.begin(), v.end()-1);
  show("v after sorting the heap:\n", v);

  return 0;
}

// Display the contents of a vector<char>.
void show(const char *msg, vector<char> vect) {
  cout << msg;
  for(unsigned i=0; i < vect.size(); ++i)
    cout << vect[i] << " ";
  cout << "\n";
}
```

Here is the output from the program.

```
v before building heap:
A C E G I K M O Q S

v after building heap:
S Q M O I K E A G C

v after pushing H onto heap:
S Q M O I K E A G C H

v after popping from heap:
Q O M H I K E A G C S

v after sorting the heap:
A C E G H I K M O Q S
```

Notice the contents of **v** after calling **pop_heap( )**. The S is still present, but it is now at the end. As described, popping from a heap causes the first element to be moved to the end and then a new heap is constructed on the remaining (N–1) elements. Therefore, although the popped element (S, in this case) remains in the container, it is not part of the heap. Also notice that the call to **sort_heap( )** specifies **v.end( )–1** as the endpoint of the sort. This is because the S is no longer part of the heap, having been removed by the previous step.

Options and Alternatives

All of the heap functions have a second form that lets you specify a comparison function that determines when one element is less than another. These versions are shown here:

    template <class RandIter, class Comp>
        void make_heap(RandIter *start*, RandIter *end*, Comp *cmpfn*)

    template <class RandIter, class Comp>
        void push_heap(RandIter *start*, RandIter *end*, Comp *cmpfn*)

    template <class RandIter, class Comp>
        void pop_heap(RandIter *start*, RandIter *end*, Comp *cmpfn*)

    template <class RandIter, class Comp>
        void sort_heap(RandIter *start*, RandIter *end*, Comp *cmpfn*)

In all cases, *cmpfn* specifies the comparison function used to determine the ordering of the elements.

Although the heap algorithms are certainly useful, they require that you manually manage the heap. Fortunately, there is an easier approach that is applicable to many situations: the **priority_queue** container adaptor. It automatically maintains the elements in the container in order of priority.

Create an Algorithm

Key Ingredients		
Headers	**Classes**	**Functions**
		template<*iter-types, other-types*> *ret-type name*(*iter-args, other-args*)
		template<*iter-types, other-types, pred_type*> *ret-type name*(*iter-args, other-args, predicate*)

Although the STL provides a rich set of built-in algorithms, you can also create your own. This is possible because the STL was designed to easily accommodate extensions. As long as you follow a few simple rules, your algorithms will be fully compatible with the STL's containers and other elements. Therefore, by creating your own algorithms, you expand the STL framework to meet your needs. This recipe shows the process.

Step-by-Step

To create your own algorithm involves these steps:

1. Create a template function that takes one or more iterators as arguments.
2. Perform all operations through the iterators passed to the function.
3. If a predicate is needed, include it in the parameter list for the function, and then define the predicate.

Discussion

In general, the process of creating an algorithm is simple. Just create a template function that operates through iterators that are passed as arguments. (Technically, an algorithm can also operate through references, but the vast majority of the time, iterators should be used.) The iterator type is specified by a template parameter. Thus, a custom algorithm's prototype will look like the prototypes for the built-in algorithms. Keep in mind one important point: The generic type name that you give an iterator has no effect on the types of iterators that you can actually use when calling the algorithm. The generic iterator type names are simply conventions that document the types of iterators required by the algorithm. Thus, using the name **BiIter** in a template does not enforce that only iterators with bidirectional capabilities can be used. Rather, it is the operators applied to the iterator within the algorithm that determine what capabilities are required. For example, if you apply + or – to the iterator, then only random-access iterators can be used as arguments.

In principle, a custom algorithm can return any type of value. For example, consider the wide variety of return types found in the built-in algorithms. **find( )** returns an iterator, **count( )** returns an integer value, and **equal( )** returns a Boolean result. The preceding notwithstanding, here is a good rule to follow: When it makes sense for your algorithm to return an iterator, it should. Doing so often makes your algorithm more versatile because it enables the result of one algorithm to be used as input for another. Of course, the specific nature of your algorithm will dictate its return type.

If your algorithm needs to use a predicate, include a template parameter for the predicate. Then, supply the predicate when the algorithm is called.

Putting it all together, here are the principal general forms of an algorithm:

```
template<iter-types, other-types >
  ret-type name(iter-args, other-args)

template<iter-types, other-types, pred_type>
  ret-type name(iter-args, other-args, predicate)
```

Of course, your specific application will dictate type-specific return type, argument types, and predicate type.

As a point of interest, several of the examples in this chapter use a function called **show_range( )**. It takes a pointer to a null-terminated string and two iterators as arguments. It then displays the string followed by the elements within the specified range. Because **show_range( )** accesses the elements through iterators, it works much like an algorithm. In my opinion, however, it is not an algorithm in the purest sense because it produces output that is hard-coded to be displayed on **cout**. Nevertheless, it does show how iterators streamline the creation of functions that can be applied to containers. (It is possible to output information to a stream through an iterator. See *Use the Stream Iterators* for details.)

Example

The following example shows a custom algorithm called **disjoint( )**, which compares the elements in two ranges. If the two ranges contain no common elements, then **disjoint( )** returns true. Otherwise, it returns false.

```
// This function is an algorithm that determines if the contents of
// two ranges are disjoint. That is, if they contain no elements
// in common.
template<class InIter>
  bool disjoint(InIter start, InIter end,
                InIter start2, InIter end2) {

  InIter itr;

  for( ; start != end; ++start)
    for(itr = start2; itr != end2; ++itr)
      if(*start == *itr) return false;

  return true;
}
```

As you can see, all operations occur through iterators. Because the iterators move only in the forward direction and because they retrieve but do not store values, **disjoint( )** can be called with any type of iterator that supports input operations.

The following program puts **disjoint( )** into action. Notice that the program also makes use of the **show_range( )** function, which displays the elements within a range. As mentioned, this function is used by several of the examples in this chapter and works in a fashion very similar to an algorithm because it operates through iterators.

```
// This program demonstrates the disjoint() algorithm.

#include <iostream>
#include <list>
#include <algorithm>

using namespace std;

template<class InIter>
  void show_range(const char *msg, InIter start, InIter end);

template<class InIter>
  bool disjoint(InIter start, InIter end,
                InIter start2, InIter end2);

int main()
{
  list<char> lst1, lst2, lst3;

  for(int i=0; i < 5; i++) lst1.push_back('A'+i);
  for(int i=6; i < 10; i++) lst2.push_back('A'+i);
  for(int i=8; i < 12; i++) lst3.push_back('A'+i);

  show_range("Contents of lst1: ", lst1.begin(), lst1.end());
```

```
    show_range("Contents of lst2: ", lst2.begin(), lst2.end());
    show_range("Contents of lst3: ", lst3.begin(), lst3.end());

    cout << endl;

    // Test lst1 and lst2.
    if(disjoint(lst1.begin(), lst1.end(), lst2.begin(), lst2.end()))
      cout << "lst1 and lst2 are disjoint\n";
    else cout << "lst1 and lst2 are not disjoint.\n";

    // Test lst2 and lst3.
    if(disjoint(lst2.begin(), lst2.end(), lst3.begin(), lst3.end()))
      cout << "lst2 and lst3 are disjoint\n";
    else cout << "lst2 and lst3 are not disjoint.\n";

    return 0;
}

// Show a range of elements.
template<class InIter>
    void show_range(const char *msg, InIter start, InIter end) {

  InIter itr;

  cout << msg;

  for(itr = start; itr != end; ++itr)
    cout << *itr << " ";
  cout << endl;
}

// This function is an algorithm that determines if the contents of
// two ranges are disjoint. That is, if they contain no elements
// in common.
template<class InIter>
  bool disjoint(InIter start, InIter end,
                InIter start2, InIter end2) {

  InIter itr;

  for( ; start != end; ++start)
    for(itr = start2; itr != end2; ++itr)
      if(*start == *itr) return false;

  return true;
}
```

The output is shown here:

```
Contents of lst1: A B C D E
Contents of lst2: G H I J
Contents of lst3: I J K L

lst1 and lst2 are disjoint
lst2 and lst3 are not disjoint.
```

Bonus Example: Use a Predicate with a Custom Algorithm

It's an easy matter to add a predicate, such as a comparison function, to an algorithm. Simply specify a generic type for the function and then include a parameter of that type in the argument list. Inside the algorithm, call the function when it is needed through its parameter. For example, here is an overload of **disjoint( )** that lets you specify a predicate that determines when one element is equal to another:

```
// This version of disjoint() lets you specify a comparison function
// that determines when two elements are equal.
template<class InIter, class Comp>
  bool disjoint(InIter start, InIter end,
               InIter start2, InIter end2, Comp cmpfn) {

  InIter itr;

  for( ; start != end; ++start)
    for(itr = start2; itr != end2; ++itr)
      if(cmpfn(*start, *itr)) return false;

  return true;
}
```

Pay special attention to the **cmpfn** parameter. It can receive either a function pointer or a function object. It then uses this function to determine when two elements are equal. The following program demonstrates this version of **disjoint( )** to ignore case differences when determining if two ranges of characters are disjoint. It uses the binary predicate function **equals_ignorecase( )** to determine when two characters are equal independently of case differences.

```
// Demonstrate a version of disjoint() that takes a comparison function.

#include <iostream>
#include <list>
#include <algorithm>
#include <cctype>

using namespace std;

template<class InIter>
  void show_range(const char *msg, InIter start, InIter end);

template<class InIter>
  bool disjoint(InIter start, InIter end,
               InIter start2, InIter end2);

// Overload disjoint() to take a comparison function.
template<class InIter, class Comp>
  bool disjoint(InIter start, InIter end,
               InIter start2, InIter end2, Comp cmpfn);

bool equals_ignorecase(char ch1, char ch2);
```

```cpp
int main()
{
  list<char> lst1, lst2;

  for(int i=0; i < 5; i++) lst1.push_back('A'+i);
  for(int i=2; i < 7; i++) lst2.push_back('a'+i);

  show_range("Contents of lst1: ", lst1.begin(), lst1.end());
  show_range("Contents of lst2: ", lst2.begin(), lst2.end());

  cout << endl;

  // Test lst1 and lst2.
  cout << "Testing lst1 and lst2 in a case-sensitive manner.\n";
  if(disjoint(lst1.begin(), lst1.end(), lst2.begin(), lst2.end()))
     cout << "lst1 and lst2 are disjoint\n";
  else cout << "lst1 and lst2 are not disjoint.\n";

  cout << endl;

  // Test lst1 and lst2, but ignore case differences.
  cout << "Testing lst1 and lst2 while ignoring case differences.\n";
  if(disjoint(lst1.begin(), lst1.end(), lst2.begin(), lst2.end(),
              equals_ignorecase))
     cout << "lst1 and lst2 are disjoint\n";
  else cout << "lst1 and lst2 are not disjoint.\n";

  return 0;
}

// Show a range of elements.
template<class InIter>
    void show_range(const char *msg, InIter start, InIter end) {

  InIter itr;

  cout << msg;

  for(itr = start; itr != end; ++itr)
    cout << *itr << " ";
  cout << endl;
}

// This function is an algorithm that determines if the contents of
// two ranges are disjoint. That is, if they contain no elements
// in common.
template<class InIter>
  bool disjoint(InIter start, InIter end,
                InIter start2, InIter end2) {

  InIter itr;
```

```
    for( ; start != end; ++start)
      for(itr = start2; itr != end2; ++itr)
        if(*start == *itr) return false;

    return true;
}

// This overload of disjoint() lets you specify a comparison function
// that determines when two elements are equal.
template<class InIter, class Comp>
  bool disjoint(InIter start, InIter end,
                InIter start2, InIter end2, Comp cmpfn) {

    InIter itr;

    for( ; start != end; ++start)
      for(itr = start2; itr != end2; ++itr)
        if(cmpfn(*start, *itr)) return false;

    return true;
}

// This function returns true if ch1 and ch2 represent the
// same letter despite case differences.
bool equals_ignorecase(char ch1, char ch2) {
  if(tolower(ch1) == tolower(ch2)) return true;
  return false;
}
```

The output is shown here:

```
Contents of lst1: A B C D E
Contents of lst2: c d e f g

Testing lst1 and lst2 in a case-sensitive manner.
lst1 and lst2 are disjoint.

Testing lst1 and lst2 while ignoring case differences.
lst1 and lst2 are not disjoint.
```

Options and Alternatives

Although creating your algorithm is quite easy, as the preceding examples show, often you won't need to. In many cases, you can achieve the desired result by using **for_each( )** or **transform( )** and specifying a function that performs the desired operation. In other cases, you may be able to use the predicate forms of one of the other standard STL algorithms. Of course, when neither of these approaches works, it is a simple matter to create your own algorithm.

Use a Built-In Function Object

Key Ingredients		
Headers	**Classes**	**Functions**
<functional>	divides	ret-type operator(*arg-list*)
	equal_to	
	greater	
	greater_equal	
	less	
	less_equal	
	logical_and	
	logical_not	
	logical_or	
	minus	
	modulus	
	multiplies	
	negate	
	not_equal_to	
	plus	

This recipe shows how to use the built-in function objects defined by the STL. An overview of function objects is presented near the start of this chapter, but it will be helpful to begin by summarizing the key points:

- Function objects are instances of classes that define **operator( )**.

- A function object can be used in place of a function pointer, such as when passing a predicate to an algorithm.

- There are two types of function objects: unary and binary. A unary function object requires one argument; a binary function object requires two.

- Function objects offer more flexibility, and in some cases, may be more efficient than function pointers.

The STL provides several built-in function objects, which are the subject of this recipe. It is also possible to create your own function objects. This is described by the following recipe.

Step-by-Step

To use a built-in function object involves these steps:

1. Create an instance of the desired function object. Specify the type of data upon which it will operate in its type argument.

2. Pass the object created in Step 1 as an argument to any algorithm that requires a function argument.

Discussion

All of the built-in function objects are template classes, which means that they can work on any type of data for which their associated operation is defined. The built-in function objects use the header **<functional>**.

The STL defines several binary function objects and two unary function objects. The unary function objects are **logical_not** and **negate**. The built-in binary function objects are shown here.

plus	minus	multiplies	divides	modulus
equal_to	not_equal_to	greater	greater_equal	less
less_equal	logical_and	logical_or		

Each function object performs the action implied by its name. For example, **negate** returns the negation of a value, **less** returns true if one value is less than another, and **divides** returns the result of dividing one value by another.

The two function objects used by the example are **negate** and **multiplies**. Here is how they are declared:

```
template <class T> struct negate : unary_function<T, T> {
    T operator( ) (const T & a) const;
};

template <class T> struct multiples : binary_function<T, T, T> {
    T operator( ) (const T & a, const T & b) const;
};
```

Notice that these are declared using the keyword **struct**. Recall that in C++, **struct** creates a class type. The other function objects are declared in a similar fashion.

To use a function object, you must first construct one. For example,

```
negate<int>()
```

constructs a **negate** object for use on operands of type **int**, and

```
multiplies<double, double>()
```

constructs a **multiplies** object for use on **double** operands.

Often, an instance of a function object is not constructed until it is actually passed to an algorithm. For example, this statement:

```
transform(start1, end1, start2, negate<double>());
```

constructs a **negate** function object and passes it to **transform( )** in one step. Frequently, there is no need to construct a stand-alone instance.

Example

The following example demonstrates the unary function object **negate** and the binary function object **multiplies**. The same techniques apply to any built-in function object.

NOTE *Another example that uses a built-in function object is found in* Sort a Container. *It uses the **greater** function object to sort a container in reverse order.*

```cpp
// Demonstrate negate and multiplies function objects.

#include <iostream>
#include <vector>
#include <algorithm>
#include <functional>

using namespace std;

template<class T> void show(const char *msg, T cont);

int main()
{
  vector<int> v, v2, result(10);

  for(unsigned i=0; i < 10; ++i) v.push_back(i);
  for(unsigned i=0; i < 10; ++i) v2.push_back(i);

  show("Contents of v:\n", v);
  show("Contents of v2:\n", v2);
  cout << endl;

  // Multiply v and v2 together.
  transform(v.begin(), v.end(), v2.begin(), result.begin(),
            multiplies<int>());

  show("Result of multiplying the elements in v with those in v2:\n",
       result);
  cout << endl;

  // Next, negate the contents of result.
  transform(v.begin(), v.end(), v.begin(), negate<int>());

  show("After negating v:\n", v);

  return 0;
}

// Display the contents of a container.
template<class T> void show(const char *msg, T cont) {
  cout << msg;

  T::iterator itr;
  for(itr=cont.begin(); itr != cont.end(); ++itr)
    cout << *itr << " ";

  cout << "\n";
}
```

The output is shown here:

```
Contents of v:
0 1 2 3 4 5 6 7 8 9
Contents of v2:
0 1 2 3 4 5 6 7 8 9

Result of multiplying the elements in v with those in v2:
0 1 4 9 16 25 36 49 64 81

After negating v:
0 -1 -2 -3 -4 -5 -6 -7 -8 -9
```

Options and Alternatives

As a general rule, if a built-in function object will handle the situation, you should use it. In cases in which it won't, you can create your own function object, as described in the next recipe. Another alternative is to pass a pointer to a standard function. For example, given a container that contains a character sequence, you can pass the **islower( )** function to **remove_if( )** to remove all lowercase letters.

A function object can have a value bound to it through the use of a binder. See *Use a Binder* for details.

Create a Custom Function Object

Key Ingredients		
Headers	**Structures**	**Functions and Typedefs**
<functional>	binary_function	argument_type result_type
<functional>	unary_function	first_argument_type second_argument_type result_type

		result_type operator(argument_type *arg*)
		result_type
		   operator(first_argument_type *arg1*,
		        second_argument_type *arg2*)

One of the key components of the STL is the function object. As explained in *Function Object Overview*, a function object is an instance of a class that implements **operator( )**. Thus, when the function call operator, which is ( ), is executed on the object, **operator( )** is executed. A function object can be passed to any algorithm that requires a function pointer. Thus, a function object can be used as a predicate. There are several built-in function objects, such as **less**, and their use is described by the preceding recipe. You can also create your own function objects. This recipe shows the process.

Before we begin, a few words about why you might want to create your own function objects. At first glance, it may seem that function objects require a bit more work than simply using function pointers but offer no advantages. This is not the case. Function objects expand the scope and power of the STL in three ways.

First, a function object can provide a more efficient mechanism by which functions are passed to algorithms. For example, it is possible for the compiler to in-line a function object. Second, using a function object can simplify and better structure the implementation of complicated operations, because the class that defines a function object can hold values and provide additional capabilities. Third, a function object defines a type name. A function does not. This enables function objects to be specified as template type arguments. Therefore, while there is nothing wrong with using function pointers where applicable, function objects offer a powerful alternative.

Step-by-Step

To create a function object involves these steps:

1. Create a class that implements **operator( )**.

2. For the greatest flexibility, have the class from Step 1 inherit either the **unary_function** or **binary_function** structure, depending on whether you are creating a unary or binary function object. These define standard type names for the function's argument(s) and return type.

3. When implementing the class, avoid creating side effects.

Discussion

To create a function object, define a class that overloads the **operator( )** function and then create an instance of that class. This instance can be passed to an algorithm, which can then call the **operator( )** function through the instance.

There are two types of function objects: unary and binary. A unary function object implements **operator( )** such that it takes one argument. For a binary function object, **operator( )** takes two arguments. As they are used with STL algorithms, each argument receives an element from the range(s) on which the algorithm is operating. Thus, the type of argument must be compatible with the type of element passed to it.

All of the built-in STL function objects are template classes. Your function objects can also be defined as template classes, but there is no requirement for this. Sometimes, a custom function object serves a specific purpose and a template version is not useful.

To gain the greatest flexibility for your function object, your class should also inherit one of these structures defined by the STL:

```
template <class Argument, class Result> struct unary_function {
  typedef Argument argument_type;
  typedef Result result_type;
};
```

```
template <class Argument1, class Argument2, class Result>
struct binary_function {
  typedef Argument1 first_argument_type;
  typedef Argument2 second_argument_type;
  typedef Result result_type;
};
```

A class that creates a unary function object inherits **unary_function**. A class that creates a binary function object inherits **binary_function**. Both **unary_function** and **binary_function** are declared in the **<functional>** header. In general, they must be inherited as public, which is the default for structures.

The **unary_function** and **binary_function** structures provide typedefs for the argument type(s) and the return type of the function object. These names are used by some adaptors and may be helpful in other cases. Therefore, you should use these names in your function object. In other words, you should use **result_type** as the return type for **operator( )**. You should use **argument_type** as the type of the argument to **operator( )** for a unary function object and use **first_argument_type** and **second_argument_type** as the types of the arguments for a binary function object. Therefore, the general forms of **operator( )** look like these:

result_type operator(argument_type *arg*)

result_type operator(first_argument_type *arg1*, second_argument_type *arg2*)

A function object should not create side effects. In other words, it should not perform actions unrelated to its intended purpose. For example, a function object whose purpose is to compare two elements for equality should not modify one of the elements in the process.

Example

The following example shows examples both unary and binary function objects. It reworks the example program for the recipe *Use transform( ) to Change a Sequence*. In that version, function pointers are passed to the **transform( )** algorithm. The functions compute the reciprocal of a value and the midpoint between two values. This version of the program uses function objects instead of function pointers. It creates a unary function object class called **reciprocal** that computes the reciprocal of a value. It creates a binary function object class called **midpoint** that computes the midpoint between two values.

```
// Demonstrate both unary and binary function objects.
//
// This program reworks the example shown in the recipe
// "Use transform() to Change a Sequence."  That program
// used function pointers in calls to transform().
// This version uses function objects.

#include <iostream>
#include <vector>
#include <algorithm>
#include <functional>
```

```
using namespace std;

// A function object that computes a reciprocal.
class reciprocal : unary_function<double, double> {
public:
  result_type sum;

result_type operator()(argument_type val) {
   if(val == 0.0) return 0.0;
   return 1.0 / val; // return reciprocal
  }
};

// A function object that finds the midpoint between
// two values.
class midpoint : binary_function<int, int, double> {
public:
  result_type operator()(first_argument_type a, second_argument_type b) {
    return((a-b) / 2) + b;
  }
};

template<class T> void show(const char *msg, vector<T> vect);

int main()
{
  int i;

  vector<double> v;

  // Put values into v.
  for(i=1; i < 10; ++i) v.push_back((double)i);

  show("Initial contents of v:\n", v);
  cout << endl;

  // First, demonstrate a unary function object.

  // Transform v by applying the reciprocal function object.
  // Put the result back into v.
  cout << "Use a unary function object in calls to transform() to\n";
  cout << "compute reciprocals for v and store the results back in v.\n";
  transform(v.begin(), v.end(), v.begin(), reciprocal());

  show("Transformed contents of v:\n", v);
  cout << endl;

  // Transform v a second time, putting the result into a new sequence.
  cout << "Use a unary function object to transform v again.\n";
  cout << "This time, store the results in v2.\n";
  vector<double> v2(10);
  transform(v.begin(), v.end(), v2.begin(), reciprocal());
```

```
    show("Here is v2:\n", v2);
    cout << endl;

    vector<int> v3, v4, v5(10);
    for(i = 0; i < 10; ++i) v3.push_back(i);
    for(i = 10; i < 20; ++i) if(i%2) v4.push_back(i); else v4.push_back(-i);

    show("Contents of v3:\n", v3);
    show("Contents of v4:\n", v4);
    cout << endl;

    // Now, demonstrate a binary function object.
    cout << "Now, use a binary function object to find the midpoints\n";
    cout << "between elements in v3 and v4 and store the results in v5.\n";
    transform(v3.begin(), v3.end(), v4.begin(), v5.begin(), midpoint());

    show("Contents of v5:\n", v5);

    return 0;
}

// Display the contents of a vector<int>.
template<class T> void show(const char *msg, vector<T> vect) {
    cout << msg;
    for(unsigned i=0; i < vect.size(); ++i)
        cout << vect[i] << " ";
    cout << "\n";
}
```

The output is shown here:

```
Initial contents of v:
1 2 3 4 5 6 7 8 9

Use a unary function object in calls to transform() to
compute reciprocals for v and store the results back in v.
Transformed contents of v:
1 0.5 0.333333 0.25 0.2 0.166667 0.142857 0.125 0.111111

Use a unary function object to transform v again.
This time, store the results in v2.
Here is v2:
1 2 3 4 5 6 7 8 9 0

Contents of v3:
0 1 2 3 4 5 6 7 8 9
Contents of v4:
-10 11 -12 13 -14 15 -16 17 -18 19

Now, use a binary function object to find the midpoints
between elements in v3 and v4 and store the results in v5.
Contents of v5:
-5 6 -5 8 -5 10 -5 12 -5 14
```

Bonus Example: Use a Function Object to Maintain State Information

Although the preceding example demonstrates how to create two different function objects, neither shows the real power of function objects. For example, function objects can be used with binders and negators, and this is described in *Use a Binder* and *Use a Negator*. Another important feature of function objects is their ability to maintain state information. It is possible for the class that defines a function object to include instance variables that store information about the use of the function object, such as the outcome of some computation. This can be useful in a variety of contexts. For example, a variable could hold the success or failure of an operation. The ability to maintain state information greatly expands the types of problems to which a function object can be applied.

The following example demonstrates the ability of a function object to store state information by reworking the summation function used in the **for_each( )** example shown in *Cycle Through a Container with for_each( )*. In that example, a pointer to a function called **summation( )** was passed to **for_each( )**. This function constructed a running total of the values in the range over which **for_each( )** operated. The **summation( )** function used a static variable to hold the current sum. Each time the function was called, the value passed to the function was added to the running total and the running total (i.e., the current summation) was returned. While this approach worked, it is hardly elegant. A far better approach is to convert **summation( )** into a function object in which the running total is held in an instance variable. Not only does this allow the summation to be obtained without a function call, it also enables the total to be reset.

Here is one way to create a summation function object class:

```
// A function object that computes an integer summation.
class summation : unary_function<int, void> {
public:
  argument_type sum;

  summation() { sum = 0; }

  // Add to the running total and return a
  // reference to the invoking object.
  result_type operator()(argument_type i) {
    sum += i;
  }
};
```

Notice that the running total is held in a field called **sum** inside the **summation** class. This allows the summation to be obtained from the object, rather than having to invoke a function. To reset the object, simply assign zero to **sum**.

The following program reworks the **for_each( )** example so that it uses the **summation** function object:

```
// Use a function object with for_each().

#include <iostream>
#include <vector>
#include <algorithm>
#include <functional>
```

```
using namespace std;

// A function object that computes an integer summation.
class summation : unary_function<int, void> {
public:
  argument_type sum;

  summation() { sum = 0; }

  // Add to the running total and return a
  // reference to the invoking object.
  result_type operator()(argument_type i) {
    sum += i;
  }
};

int main()
{
  vector<int> v;

  for(int i=1; i < 11; i++) v.push_back(i);

  cout << "Contents of v: ";
  for(unsigned i=0; i < v.size(); ++i)
    cout << v[i] << " ";
  cout << "\n";

  // Declare a function object that receives the object
  // returned by for_each().
  summation s;

  // This calls for_each() with a function object, rather than
  // a function pointer.  The function object returned by
  // for_each() can be used to obtain the summation total.
  s = for_each(v.begin(), v.end(), summation());
  cout << "Summation of v: " << s.sum << endl;

  // Change the value of v[4] and recompute the summation.
  // Because a new function object is created, the
  // summation once again begins at zero.
  cout << "Setting v[4] to 99\n";
  v[4]= 99;
  s = for_each(v.begin(), v.end(), summation());
  cout << "Summation of v is now: " << s.sum;

  return 0;
}
```

Notice how **for_each( )** is called:

```
s = for_each(v.begin(), v.end(), summation());
```

It is passed a new instance of **summation**. This function object is used by this invocation of **for_each( )**. Recall that the **for_each( )** algorithm returns the function object that it is passed. In this case, this object is assigned to **s**, which is a **summation** object. This means that **s** will contain the summation. This value can be obtained from **s.sum**.

Options and Alternatives

When using a function object, you have the option of binding a value to it. This procedure is described in *Use a Binder* and *Use a Negator*.

In some cases, you can use a built-in function object, rather than a custom one. For example, if you want to determine if one value is greater than another, you can use the **greater** function object. See *Use a Built-In Function Object* for details.

Although function objects are more powerful than function pointers, there is nothing wrong with using a function pointer in situations for which it is appropriate. For example, if a vector holds characters, then it is fine to pass a pointer to the standard **tolower( )** function to **transform( )** to convert letters to lowercase. In this case, there would be little, if any, benefit in creating an entire class to handle this operation.

Use a Binder

Key Ingredients		
Headers	**Classes**	**Functions**

<functional>		template <class Op, class T>
		    binder1st<Op>
		        bind1st(const Op &*bin_func_obj*,
		            const T &*value*)
		template <class Op, class T>
		    binder2nd<Op>
		        bind2nd(const Op &*bin_func_obj*,
		            const T &*value*)

The recipe shows how to bind a value to a function object. Recall that a binary function object takes two parameters. Normally, these parameters receive values from the range or ranges upon which the object is operating. For example, when sorting, the binary comparison function receives pairs of elements from the range being ordered. While the default behavior of binary function objects is quite useful, there are times when you will want to alter it. To understand why, consider the following.

Suppose that you want to remove all elements from a sequence that are greater than some value, such as 10. Your first thought, quite naturally, is to use the **greater** function object. However, by default, **greater** receives both values from the range on which it is operating. Thus, by itself, there is no way to have it compare elements from one sequence with the value 10. To use **greater** for this purpose, you need some way to *bind* the value 10 to its right-hand operand. That is, you need some way to make **greater** perform the following comparison:

> *val* > 10

where *val* is an element from the sequence. Fortunately, the STL provides a mechanism, called *binders*, that accomplishes this. A binder links a value to one of the arguments of a binary function object. The outcome of a binder is a unary function object, which can be used anywhere that any other unary function object can.

There are two binders defined by the STL: **bind1st( )** and **bind2nd( )**. This recipe demonstrates their use.

Step-by-Step

To use a binder to bind a value to a function object involves these steps:

1. To bind a value to the first argument of a binary function object, call **bind1st( )**.

2. To bind a value to the second argument of a binary function object, call **bind2nd( )**.

3. Use the result of the binder anywhere that a unary predicate is required.

Discussion

The prototypes for **bind1st( )** and **bind2nd( )** are shown here:

> template <class Op, class T>
>   binder1st<Op> bind1st(const Op &*bin_func_obj*, const T &*value*)

> template <class Op, class T>
>   binder2nd<Op> bind2nd(const Op &*bin_func_obj*, const T &*value*)

Here, *bin_func_obj* specifies the binary function object to which *value* will be bound. **bind1st( )** returns a unary function object (encapsulated as a **binder1st** object) that has *bin_func_obj*'s left-hand operand bound to *value*. **bind2nd( )** returns a unary function object (encapsulated in a **binder2nd** object) that has *bin_func_obj*'s right-hand operand bound to *value*. For example,

```
bind1st(less<double>, 0.01)
```

binds the value 0.01 to the first (left) argument of the **less** function object, and

```
bind2nd(less<double>, 0.01)
```

binds the value to the second (right) argument. Of the two, **bind2nd( )** is the more commonly used.

The **binder1st** and **binder2nd** classes represent the unary function objects returned by the binders. They are also declared in **<functional>**. Normally, you won't use the **binder1st** or **binder2nd** class directly. Instead, you will usually pass the outcome of a binder directly to an algorithm. Therefore, **binder1st** and **binder2nd** are not described further here.

Because a binder converts a binary function object into a unary function object, the result of a binder can be passed to any algorithm that requires a unary predicate. For example, this passes a unary function object to **find_if( )**:

```
find_if(v.begin(), v.end(), bind2nd(less<int>, 19))
```

This causes **find_if( )** to return an iterator to the first value in **v** that is less than 19.

Example

The following program demonstrates **bind2nd( )**. It uses the **remove_if( )** algorithm to remove elements from a sequence based upon the outcome of a predicate. Recall that it has this prototype:

```
template <class ForIter, class UnPred>
     ForIter remove_if(ForIter start, ForIter end, UnPred pfn)
```

The algorithm removes elements from the sequence defined by *start* and *end* for which the unary predicate defined by *pfn* is true. The algorithm returns a pointer to the new end of the sequence, which reflects the deletion of the elements.

The following program removes all values from a sequence that are greater than the value 10. Since the predicate required by **remove_if** is unary, we cannot simply use the **greater** function object as-is because **greater** is a binary function object. Instead, we must bind the value 10 to the second argument of **greater** using the **bind2nd( )** binder.

```
// Demonstrate bind2nd().

#include <iostream>
#include <list>
#include <functional>
#include <algorithm>

using namespace std;

template<class InIter>
  void show_range(const char *msg, InIter start, InIter end);

int main()
{
  list<int> lst;
  list<int>::iterator res_itr;

  for(unsigned i=1; i < 20; ++i) lst.push_back(i);

  show_range("Original sequence:\n", lst.begin(), lst.end());
  cout << endl;

  // Use bind2nd() to create a unary function object
  // that will return true when a value is greater than 10.
  // This is used by remove_if() to remove all elements from
  // lst that are greater than 10.
  res_itr = remove_if(lst.begin(), lst.end(),
                  bind2nd(greater<int>(), 10));
```

```
  show_range("Resulting sequence:\n", lst.begin(), res_itr);

  return 0;
}

// Show a range of elements.
template<class InIter>
    void show_range(const char *msg, InIter start, InIter end) {

  InIter itr;

  cout << msg;

  for(itr = start; itr != end; ++itr)
    cout << *itr << " ";
  cout << endl;
}
```

The output produced by the program is shown here.

```
Original sequence:
1 2 3 4 5 6 7 8 9 10 11 12 13 14 15 16 17 18 19

Resulting sequence:
1 2 3 4 5 6 7 8 9 10
```

As the output shows, the resulting sequence contains the elements 1 through 10. Those elements greater than 10 have been removed. Here is how it works. When **remove_if( )** executes, the binary function object **greater** receives an element from **lst** in its first parameter and the value 10 in its second, since the second parameter is bound to 10 using **bind2nd( )**. Thus, for each element in the sequence, the comparison

element > 10

is evaluated. When it is true, the element is removed.

Options and Alternatives

Although **bind2nd( )** is typically the more commonly used of the two binders, **bind1st( )** is available as an alternative. As explained, the **bind1st( )** binder binds a value to the first parameter. To see the effects of this, try substituting this line into the preceding program:

```
endp = remove_if(lst.begin(), lst.end(), bind1st(greater<int>(), 10));
```

This causes elements from the sequence to be passed to the second parameter of **greater**, with the value 10 bound to the first parameter. Thus, for each element in the sequence, the following comparison is performed:

10 > element

This causes **greater** to return true for elements that are less than 10. The output produced after you have substituted **bind1st( )** is shown here.

```
Original sequence:
1 2 3 4 5 6 7 8 9 10 11 12 13 14 15 16 17 18 19

Resulting sequence:
10 11 12 13 14 15 16 17 18 19
```

As you can see, those elements that are less than 10 have been removed.

Although valid, I dislike using **bind1st( )** as just shown because it seems counterintuitive. If you want to remove elements that are less than 10, it would be better to use this statement:

```
endp = remove_if(lst.begin(), lst.end(), bind2nd(less<int>(), 10));
```

Here, the **less** function object is used and the results reflect what one would normally expect to occur when **less** is employed. Using **bind1st( )** and reversing the comparison achieves the same results, but adds a bit of confusion for no reason.

Use a Negator

Key Ingredients		
Headers	**Classes**	**Functions**
<functional>		template <class Pred> unary_negate<Pred> not1(const Pred &*unary_pred*)
		template <class Pred> binary_negate<Pred> not2(const Pred &*binary_pred*)

There is an object related to a binder, called a *negator*. The negators are **not1( )** and **not2( )**. They return the negation of (i.e., the complement of) whatever predicate they modify. The negators streamline the STL because they enable you to efficiently adapt a predicate to produce the opposite result, thus avoiding the need to create a second predicate. This recipe demonstrates their use.

Step-by-Step

To use a negator involves these steps:

1. To negate a unary predicate, use **not1( )**.
2. To negate a binary predicate, use **not2( )**.

Discussion

The negators are **not1( )** and **not2( )**. They have these prototypes:

> template <class Pred> unary_negate<Pred>
>   not1(const Pred &*unary_pred*)

> template <class Pred> binary_negate<Pred>
>   not2(const Pred &*binary_pred*)

The **not1( )** negator is for use with unary predicates, with the predicate to negate passed in *unary_pred*. To negate binary predicates, use **not2( )**, passing the binary predicate in *binary_pred*. The result of both negators is a predicate that returns the negation of the original predicate represented as either a **unary_negate** or **binary_negate** object.

Typically, you will not interact with the **unary_negate** or **binary_negate** class directly, and they are not further described here. Instead, the outcome of **not1( )** or **not2( )** is typically passed directly to an algorithm. For example, this statement removes elements from a container if they are not equal to 'A':

```
remove_if(v.begin(), v.end(),  not1(bind2nd(equal_to<char>(), 'A')));
```

Although **equal_to** is a binary function object, the binder **bind2nd( )** converts it into a unary object. This is why **not1( )** rather than **not2( )** is used.

Example

The following example demonstrates both **not1( )** and **not2( )**. First, it shows one way to sort a sequence into descending order using the negation of the **less** function object to determine sorting order. It then uses **not1( )** to remove all elements not equal to H.

```
// Demonstrate not1() and not2().

#include <iostream>
#include <vector>
#include <algorithm>
#include <functional>

using namespace std;

template<class InIter>
  void show_range(const char *msg, InIter start, InIter end);

int main()
{
  vector<char> v;

  for(int i=0; i < 26; i++) v.push_back('A'+i);

  show_range("Original ordering of v:\n", v.begin(), v.end());
  cout << endl;

  // Use not2() to reverse sort v.
  sort(v.begin(), v.end(), not2(less<char>()));
```

```
  show_range("After sorting v using not2(less<char>()):\n",
             v.begin(), v.end());
  cout << endl;

  // Use not1() to remove all characters that are not equal to H.
  vector<char>::iterator res_end;
  res_end = remove_if(v.begin(), v.end(),
                      not1(bind2nd(equal_to<char>(), 'H')));

  show_range("v after removing elements not equal to H:\n",
             v.begin(), res_end);

  return 0;
}

// Show a range of elements.
template<class InIter>
    void show_range(const char *msg, InIter start, InIter end) {
  InIter itr;

  cout << msg;
  for(itr = start; itr != end; ++itr)
    cout << *itr << " ";
  cout << endl;
}
```

It produces the following output:

```
Original ordering of v:
A B C D E F G H I J K L M N O P Q R S T U V W X Y Z

After sorting v using not2(less<char>()):
Z Y X W V U T S R Q P O N M L K J I H G F E D C B A

v after removing elements not equal to H:
H
```

Options and Alternatives

Although negating the outcome of a predicate can be very useful and can streamline the handling of many situations, it may not always be the best choice. Sometimes, you will want to create a separate predicate that performs the negation. For example, consider a case in which the negation of some operation can be performed more efficiently by computing the negative result directly, rather than reversing the outcome of the affirmative result. In this situation, creating a separate predicate is more efficient than first computing the result and then negating it. In essence, you may encounter a case in which the negation is faster to compute than the affirmative result. In this situation, it does not make sense to first compute the affirmative and then negate it.

Use the Pointer-to-Function Adaptor

Key Ingredients		
Headers	**Classes**	**Functions**
<functional>	pointer_to_unary_function	Result operator( )(Arg *arg*) const;
<functional>	pointer_to_binary_function	Result operator( )(Arg *arg1*, Arg2 *arg2*) const;
<functional>		template <class Arg, class Result> pointer_to_unary_function< Arg, Result> ptr_fun(Result (*func*)(Arg)) template <class Arg1, class Arg2, class Result> pointer_to_binary_function< Arg1, Arg2, Result> ptr_fun(Result (*func*)(Arg1, Arg2))

The header **<functional>** defines several classes, called *function adaptors,* that allow you to adapt a function pointer to a form that can be used by various STL components. Several of these adaptors are designed for situations beyond the scope of this book, but one is of special interest because it solves a very common problem: allowing a function pointer to be used with a binder or negator.

As preceding recipes have shown, it is possible to pass a pointer to a function (rather than passing a function object) as a predicate to an algorithm. As long as the function performs the desired operation, there is no trouble in doing this. However, if you want to bind a value or use a negator with that function, then trouble will occur, because it is not possible to apply these modifiers directly to function pointers. To allow functions to be used with binders and negators, you will need to use the pointer-to-function adaptors.

Step-by-Step

To adapt a function pointer into a function object involves these steps:

1. To create a function object from a unary function, call **ptr_fun( )**, passing in a pointer to the unary function. The result is a unary function object.

2. To create a function object from a binary function, call **ptr_fun( )**, passing in the pointer to the binary function. The result is a binary function object.

Discussion

The pointer-to-function adaptor is **ptr_fun( )**. Both of its forms are shown here:

```
template <class Arg, class Result>
  pointer_to_unary_function<Arg, Result>
    ptr_fun(Result (*func)(Arg))
```

```
template <class Arg1, class Arg2, class Result>
  pointer_to_binary_function<Arg1, Arg2, Result>
    ptr_fun(Result (*func)(Arg1, Arg2))
```

It returns either an object of type **pointer_to_unary_function** or an object of type **pointer_to_binary_function**. These classes are shown here:

```
template <class Arg, class Result>
class pointer_to_unary_function:
  public unary_function<Arg, Result>
{
public:
  explicit pointer_to_unary_function(Result (*func)(Arg));
  Result operator()(Arg arg) const;
};
```

```
template <class Arg1, class Arg2, class Result>
class pointer_to_binary_function:
  public binary_function<Arg1, Arg2, Result>
{
public:
  explicit pointer_to_binary_function(
            Result (*func)(Arg1, Arg2));
  Result operator()(Arg1 arg1, Arg2 arg2) const;
};
```

You won't normally interact with these classes directly. Their main purpose is to construct a function object that encapsulates *func*. For **pointer_to_unary_function**, **operator( )** returns

   func(arg)

And for **pointer_to_binary_function**, **operator( )** returns

   func(arg1, arg2)

The result type of **operator( )** is specified by the **Result** generic type. Therefore, an object of these classes can be passed as an argument to a binder or negator.

Example

Here is an example that uses **ptr_fun( )**. It creates a vector of character pointers that point to character strings. It then uses the standard library function **strcmp( )** to find the pointer that points to "Three". Since **strcmp( )** is not a function object, the adaptor **ptr_fun( )** is used to allow the value "Three" to be bound to **strcmp( )**'s second parameter using **bind2nd( )**. Since **strcmp( )** returns false on success, the negator **not1( )** is applied to reverse this condition.

Without the use of **ptr_fun( )**, it would not be possible to apply **bind2nd( )** to **strcmp( )**. That is, since **strcmp( )** is a function, it is not possible for it to be used with **bind2nd( )** directly.

```cpp
// Use a pointer-to-function adaptor.

#include <iostream>
#include <vector>
#include <algorithm>
#include <functional>
#include <cstring>

using namespace std;

template<class InIter>
  void show_range(const char *msg, InIter start, InIter end);

int main()
{
  vector<char *> v;
  vector<char *>::iterator itr;

  v.push_back("One");
  v.push_back("Two");
  v.push_back("Three");
  v.push_back("Four");
  v.push_back("Five");

  show_range("Sequence contains: ", v.begin(), v.end());
  cout << endl;

  cout << "Searching sequence for Three.\n\n";

  // Use a pointer-to-function adaptor.
  itr = find_if(v.begin(), v.end(),
        not1(bind2nd(ptr_fun(strcmp), "Three")));

  if(itr != v.end()) {
    cout << "Found!\n";
    show_range("Sequence from that point is: ", itr, v.end());
  }

  return 0;
}

// Show a range of elements.
template<class InIter>
    void show_range(const char *msg, InIter start, InIter end) {

  InIter itr;
  cout << msg;
  for(itr = start; itr != end; ++itr)
    cout << *itr << " ";
  cout << endl;
}
```

The program's output is shown here.

```
Sequence contains: One Two Three Four Five

Searching sequence for Three.

Found!
Sequence from that point is: Three Four Five
```

Options and Alternatives

Another approach to adapting a function is to create your own function object class. Have its **operator( )** call the function and return the result. While far less elegant than using a pointer-to-function adaptor, this technique may be useful in situations in which the result of the function is processed a bit before use.

The **ptr_fun( )** adaptor works only on non-member functions. The STL defines adaptors for member functions, which are called **mem_fun( )** and **mem_fun_ref( )**. These are collectively called the *pointer-to-member* function adaptors.

Use the Stream Iterators

Key Ingredients		
Headers	**Classes**	**Functions and Operators**
<iterator>	istream_iterator	* ++
<iterator>	ostream_iterator	* ++
<iterator>	istreambuf_iterator	* ++ bool equal(istreambuf_iterator<CharType, Attr> &*ob*)
<iterator>	ostreambuf_iterator	* ++ bool failed const throw( )

The STL defines four classes that enable you to obtain iterators to I/O streams. These are commonly referred to as the *stream iterators,* and they are among some of the STL's most interesting objects because they allow an I/O stream to be operated on in much the same way as you operate on containers. The benefits of the stream iterators are most apparent when used with algorithms, where a stream can provide input to or receive output from some action. Although most I/O operations will still use the standard I/O operators and functions, the ability to apply algorithms to streams offers a new way to think about I/O programming. The stream iterators can also simplify certain difficult or tedious I/O situations. Although an in-depth discussion of the stream iterators is quite lengthy and is beyond the scope of this book, this recipe describes the basic approach needed to use them.

Step-by-Step

To use the stream iterators to input data involves these steps:

1. To create an iterator to a formatted input stream, construct an object of type **istream_iterator**, specifying the input stream.

2. To create an iterator to a character-based input stream, construct an object of type **istreambuf_iterator**, specifying the input stream.

3. To input data from the stream, dereference the iterator. Then, increment the iterator. This causes it to read the next item from the stream. Repeat this process until all data is read or the end of the stream is reached.

4. An iterator that indicates end-of-stream is constructed by the default constructor.

To use the stream iterators to output data involves these steps:

1. To create an iterator to a formatted output stream, construct an object of type **ostream_iterator**, specifying the output stream.

2. To create an iterator to a character-based output stream, construct an object of type **ostreambuf_iterator**, specifying the output stream.

3. To output data to the stream, assign the value through the dereferenced iterator. There is no need to increment the iterator. Each assignment automatically advances the output.

4. If an output error occurs, the **failed( )** function will return true.

Discussion

The STL defines four stream iterator classes. They are declared in **<iterator>** and are shown here.

Class	Description
istream_iterator	An input stream iterator.
istreambuf_iterator	An input streambuf iterator.
ostream_iterator	An output stream iterator.
ostreambuf_iterator	An output streambuf iterator.

One important difference between the iterators is that **istream_iterator** and **ostream_iterator** can directly operate on various types of data, such as **int** or **double**. The **istreambuf_iterator** and **ostreambuf_iterator** iterators can operate only on characters. However, the advantage that **istreambuf_iterator** and **ostreambuf_iterator** offer is that they enable you to perform low-level file I/O. An overview of each class is given here.

The Formatted Stream Iterators

The **istream_iterator** and **ostream_iterator** iterators are capable of reading or writing formatted data, which means that they can read or write character, integer, floating point, Boolean, and string values. This makes them especially useful when operating on streams that contain human-readable information. For example, you could use **ostream_iterator** to write an integer to **cout**, or **istream_iterator** to read a string from **cin**.

The **istream_iterator** class supports input iterator operations on a stream. Its template definition is shown here:

```
template <class T, class CharType=char, class Attr = char_traits<CharType>,
        class Diff = ptrdiff_t> class istream_iterator:
    public iterator<input_iterator_tag, T, Diff, const T *, const T &>
```

Here, **T** is the type of data being transferred, **CharType** is the character type (**char** or **wchar_t**) that the stream is operating upon, and **Diff** is a type capable of holding the difference between two addresses. Notice that **T** is the only generic type parameter that does not default. Therefore, it must be specified when an **istream_iterator** is created. **istream_iterator** has the following constructors:

```
istream_iterator( )

istream_iterator(istream_type &stream)

istream_iterator(const istream_iterator<T, CharType, Attr, Diff> &ob)
```

The first constructor creates an iterator that indicates end-of-stream. This object can be used to check for the end of input. (That is, it will compare equal to end-of-stream.) The second creates an iterator to the stream specified by *stream*. It then reads the first object from the stream. The type **istream_type** is a **typedef** that specifies the type of the input stream. The third form is **istream_iterator**'s copy constructor.

The **istream_iterator** class defines the following operators: –>, *, ++. The –> and the * act as expected. The ++ operator requires a bit of explanation. When used in its prefix form, the ++ causes the next value to be read from the input stream. When used in its postfix form, the current value of the stream is stored and then the next value of the stream is read. In either case, to retrieve the value, use the * operator on the iterator. The operators == and != are also defined for objects of type **istream_iterator**.

The **ostream_iterator** class supports output iterator operations on a stream. Its template definition is shown here:

```
template <class T, class CharType=char, class Attr = char_traits<CharType> >
class ostream_iterator:
    public iterator<output_iterator_tag, void, void, void, void>
```

Here, **T** is the type of data being transferred and **CharType** is the character type (**char** or **wchar_t**) that the stream is operating upon. Notice that **T** is the only generic type parameter that does not default. Thus, it must be specified when an **ostream_iterator** is created. **ostream_iterator** has the following constructors:

ostream_iterator(ostream_type &*stream*)

ostream_iterator(ostream_type &*stream*, const CharType **delim*)

ostream_iterator(const ostream_iterator<T, CharType, Attr> &*ob*)

The first creates an iterator to the stream specified by *stream*. The type **ostream_type** is a **typedef** that specifies the type of the output stream. The second form creates an iterator to the stream specified by *stream* and uses the delimiters specified by *delim*. The delimiters are written to the stream after every output operation. The third form is **ostream_iterator**'s copy constructor.

The **ostream_iterator** class defines the following operators: =, *, ++. For **ostream_iterator**, the ++ operator has no effect. To write to the output stream, simply assign a value through the * operator.

The Low-Level Stream Iterators

The low-level stream iterators are **istreambuf_iterator** and **ostreambuf_iterator**. These iterators read and write characters, not formatted data. The principal advantage of the low-level stream iterators is that they give your program access to a raw I/O stream on a byte-by-byte basis, avoiding character translations that are possible with the formatted stream iterators. When using these iterators, there is a one-to-one correspondence between what is in the stream and what is written or read via the iterator.

The **istreambuf_iterator** class supports low-level character-input iterator operations on a stream. Its template definition is shown here:

```
template <class CharType, class Attr = char_traits<CharType> >
class istreambuf_iterator:
    public iterator<input_iterator_tag, CharType, typename Attr::off_type,
              CharType *, CharType &>
```

Here, **CharType** is the character type (**char** or **wchar_t**) that the stream is operating upon. **istreambuf_iterator** has the following constructors:

istreambuf_iterator( ) throw( )

istreambuf_iterator(istream_type &*stream*) throw( )

istreambuf_iterator(streambuf_type **streambuf*) throw( )

The first constructor creates an iterator that indicates end-of-stream. The second creates an iterator to the stream specified by *stream*. The type **istream_type** is a **typedef** that specifies the type of the input stream. The third form creates an iterator to the stream specified by *streambuf*. The type **streambuf_type** is a **typedef** that specifies the type of the stream buffer.

The **istreambuf_iterator** class defines the following operators: *, ++. The ++ operator works as described for **istream_iterator**. To read a character from the string, apply * to the iterator. To move to the next character, increment the iterator. The operators == and != are also defined for objects of type **istreambuf_iterator**.

istreambuf_iterator defines the member function **equal( )**, which is shown here:

bool equal(istreambuf_iterator<CharType, Attr> &*ob*)

Its operation is a bit counterintuitive. It returns true if the invoking iterator and *ob* both point to the end of the stream. It also returns true if both iterators do not point to the end of the stream. There is no requirement that what they point to be the same. It returns false otherwise. The == and != operators work in the same fashion.

The **ostreambuf_iterator** class supports low-level character-output iterator operations on a stream. Its template definition is shown here:

template <class CharType, class Attr = char_traits<CharType> >
class ostreambuf_iterator:
    public iterator<output_iterator_tag, void, void, void, void>

Here, **CharType** is the character type (**char** or **wchar_t**) that the stream is operating upon. **ostreambuf_iterator** has the following constructors:

ostreambuf_iterator(ostream_type &*stream*) throw( )

ostreambuf_iterator(streambuf_type **streambuf) throw( )

The first creates an iterator to the stream specified by *stream.* The type **ostream_type** is a **typedef** that specifies the type of the input stream. The second form creates an iterator using the stream buffer specified by *streambuf.* The type **streambuf_type** is a **typedef** that specifies the type of the stream buffer.

The **ostreambuf_iterator** class defines the following operators: =, *, ++. The ++ operator has no effect. To write a character to the stream, simply assign a value through the * operator.

The **ostreambuf_iterator** class also defines the function **failed( )**, as shown here:

bool failed( ) const throw( )

It returns false if no failure has occurred and true otherwise.

Example

The following program demonstrates the how **istream_iterator** and **ostream_iterator** can be used to read from **cin** and write to **cout**. Although you will not normally use the stream iterators for this purpose, the program clearly illustrates how they work. Of course, the real power of the stream iterators is found when they are used with algorithms, which is demonstrated by the bonus example that follows.

```
// Use istream_iterator and ostream_iterator to read from cin and write to
// cout.

#include <iostream>
#include <iterator>
#include <string>
#include <vector>
```

```
using namespace std;

int main()
{
  unsigned i;
  double d;
  string str;
  vector<int> vi;
  vector<double> vd;
  vector<string> vs;

  // Use istream_iterator to read from cin.

  // Create an input stream iterator for int.
  cout << "Enter some integers, enter 0 to stop.\n";
  istream_iterator<int> int_itr(cin);
  do {
    i = *int_itr; // read next int
    if(i != 0) {
      vi.push_back(i); // store it
      ++int_itr; // input next int
    }
  } while (i != 0);

  // Create an input stream iterator for doubles
  cout << "Enter some doubles, enter 0 to stop.\n";
  istream_iterator<double> double_itr(cin);
  do {
    d = *double_itr; // read next double
    if(d != 0.0) {
      vd.push_back(d); // store it
      ++double_itr; // input next double
    }
  } while (d != 0.0);

  // Create an input stream iterator for string.
  cout << "Enter some strings, enter 'quit' to stop.\n";
  istream_iterator<string> string_itr(cin);
  do {
    str = *string_itr; // read next string
    if(str != "quit") {
      vs.push_back(str); // store it
      ++string_itr;
    }
  } while (str != "quit"); // input next string

  cout << endl;

  cout << "Here is what you entered:\n";
  for(i=0; i < vi.size(); i++) cout << vi[i] << " ";
  cout << endl;

  for(i=0; i < vd.size(); i++) cout << vd[i] << " ";
```

```
  cout << endl;

  for(i=0; i < vs.size(); i++) cout << vs[i] << " ";


  // Now, use ostream_iterator to write to cout.

  // Create an output iterator for string.
  ostream_iterator<string> out_string_itr(cout);
  *out_string_itr = "\n";
  *out_string_itr = string("\nThis is a string\n");
  *out_string_itr = "This is too.\n";

  // Create an output iterator for int.
  ostream_iterator<int> out_int_itr(cout);
  *out_int_itr = 10;
  *out_string_itr = " ";
  *out_int_itr = 15;
  *out_string_itr = " ";
  *out_int_itr = 20;

  *out_string_itr = "\n";

  // Create an output iterator for bool.
  ostream_iterator<bool> out_bool_itr(cout);
  *out_bool_itr = true;
  *out_string_itr = " ";
  *out_bool_itr = false;

  return 0;
}
```

A sample run is shown here:

```
Enter some integers, enter 0 to stop.
1 2 3 0
Enter some doubles, enter 0 to stop.
1.1 2.2 3.3 0.0
Enter some strings, enter 'quit' to stop.
This is a test
quit

Here is what you entered:
1 2 3
1.1 2.2 3.3
This is a test

This is a string
This is too.
10 15 20
1 0
```

Bonus Example: Create an STL-Based File Filter

Although using stream iterators to write to or read from the console, as is done in the previous example, is an intriguing use, it does not show their real power. It is not until you combine the stream iterators with algorithms does their real potential emerge. The following program shows an example of how they can streamline an otherwise tedious programming project.

As explained, the low-level stream iterators operate on characters, bypassing the buffering and possible character translations that might occur with the high-level stream iterators. This makes them perfect for manipulating the contents of a file through an algorithm. Being able to operate on the contents of a file through one or more STL algorithms is a powerful concept. It is often possible to implement a sophisticated file operation that would normally require several lines of code in just a single call to an algorithm. The example shown here demonstrates this. It implements a relatively simple file filter.

A *file filter* is a utility program that removes or replaces specific information when it copies a file. The following program is a simple example of such a filter. It copies a file and in the process replaces one character with another. The name of the file, the character to replace, and the replacement character are specified on the command line. To handle the replacement, it uses the character stream iterators and the **replace_copy( )** algorithm.

```
// Use istreambuf_iterator, ostreambuf_iterator, and replace_copy()
// to filter a file.

#include <iostream>
#include <fstream>
#include <iterator>
#include <algorithm>

using namespace std;

int main(int argc, char *argv[])
{
  if(argc != 5) {
    cout << "Usage: replace in out oldchar newchar\n";
    return 1;
  }

  ifstream in(argv[1]);
  ofstream out(argv[2]);

  // Make sure files opened successfully.
  if(!in.is_open()) {
    cout << "Cannot open input file.\n";
    return 1;
  }
  if(!out.is_open()) {
    cout << "Cannot open output file.\n";
    return 1;
  }

  // Create stream iterators.
```

```
istreambuf_iterator<char> in_itr(in);
ostreambuf_iterator<char> out_itr(out);

// Copy the file, replacing characters in the process.
replace_copy(in_itr, istreambuf_iterator<char>(),
             out_itr, *argv[3], *argv[4]);

// The destructors for both ofstream and ifstream call close(),
// so the following calls are not necessary in this case.
// However, to avoid confusion, this book explicitly closes
// all files.
in.close();
out.close();

return 0;
}
```

To understand the effects of the program, assume a file called **Test.dat** that contains the following:

```
This is a test that uses the stream iterator with an algorithm.
```

Next, assuming that the program is called Replace, after this command line executes:

```
C:>Replace Test.dat Test2.dat t X
```

All occurrences of 't' will be replaced by 'X' when **Test.dat** is copied into **Test2.dat**. Therefore, the contents of **Test2.dat** will be:

```
This is a XesX XhaX uses Xhe sXream iXeraXor wiXh an algoriXhm.
```

Notice that once the files are open, it takes only one statement, the call to **replace_copy( )**, to copy the file, replacing all occurrences of one character with another in the process. To do this without the use of **replace_copy( )** would require several lines of code. If you think about it, it becomes clear that the STL algorithms offer an elegant solution to many types of file-handling tasks. This is one of the more important, yet under-utilized capabilities of the STL.

Options and Alternatives

The stream iterators are really a "one-of-a-kind" feature. There isn't a directly parallel alternative. If you want to operate on streams through iterators, you will do so through the stream iterators as just described. Of course, you could always create your own custom implementations, but there would seldom (if ever) be a reason to do so. The stream iterators offer a powerful alternative to the "normal" approach to I/O, such as the I/O operators and manipulators.

For recipes that focus on the C++ I/O system, see Chapter 5.

Use the Insert Iterator Adaptors

Key Ingredients		
Headers	**Classes**	**Functions**

<iterator>		template <class Cont>
		  front_insert_iterator<Cont>
		    front_inserter(Cont &cnt)
		
		template <class Cont>
		  back_insert_iterator<Cont>
		    back_inserter(Cont &cnt)
		
		template <class Cont, class OutIter>
		  insert_iterator<Cont>
		    inserter(Cont &cnt, OutIter itr)

The STL defines three iterator adaptors that are used to obtain an iterator that inserts, rather than overwrites, elements in a container. These adaptors are called **back_inserter( )**, **front_inserter( )**, and **inserter( )**. They are declared in **<iterator>**. This recipe shows how to use them.

The insert iterator adaptors are quite useful tools. To understand why, consider the following two behaviors associated with iterators. First, when using normal iterators to copy an element into a container, the current contents of the target range are overwritten. That is, the element being copied is not inserted into the container, but replaces (that is, overwrites) the previous element. Thus, the previous contents of the target container are not preserved. Second, when elements are copied into a container through a normal iterator, it is possible to overrun the end of the container. Recall that a container will not automatically increase its size when it is used as the target of an algorithm; it must be large enough to accommodate the number of elements that it will receive before a copy operation takes place. An insert iterator allows you to alter these two behaviors.

When an element is added to a container through an insert iterator, the element is inserted at the location pointed to by the iterator, with any remaining elements moving over to make room for the new element. Thus, the original contents of the container are preserved. If necessary, the size of the container is increased to accommodate the inserted element. It is not possible to overrun the end of the target container.

Step-by-Step

To adapt an iterator for insertion operations involves these steps:

1. To obtain an iterator that can insert at any point in a container, call **inserter( )**, specifying the container and an iterator to the point at which you want the insertion to occur.

2. To obtain an iterator that can insert at the end of a container, call **back_inserter( )**, specifying the container.

3. To obtain an iterator that can insert at the front of a container, call **front_inserter( )**, specifying the container.

Discussion

To obtain an iterator that can insert elements at any point in a container, use the **inserter( )** function, shown here:

```
template <class Cont, class OutIter> insert_iterator<Cont>
    inserter(Cont &cnt, OutIter itr)
```

Here, *cnt* is the container being operated upon and *itr* points to the location at which the insertions will occur. It returns an iterator of type **insert_iterator**. The **insert_iterator** class encapsulates an output iterator that inserts objects into a container.

To obtain an iterator that can insert elements onto the end of a container, call **back_inserter( )**. It is shown here:

```
template <class Cont> back_insert_iterator<Cont> back_inserter(Cont &cnt)
```

The container receiving the insertions is passed via *cnt*. It returns an iterator of type **back_insert_iterator**. The **back_insert_iterator** class encapsulates an output iterator that inserts objects onto the end of a container. The receiving container must support the **push_back( )** function.

To obtain an iterator that can insert elements onto the front of a container, call **front_inserter( )**. It is shown here:

```
template <class Cont> front_insert_iterator<Cont> front_inserter(Cont &cnt)
```

The container receiving the insertions is passed via *cnt*. It returns an iterator of type **front_insert_iterator**. The **front_insert_iterator** class encapsulates an output iterator that inserts objects onto the front of a container. The receiving container must support the **push_front( )** function. This means that a **vector**, for example, cannot be the target of a **front_insert_iterator**.

Example

Each of the insert iterators insert into, rather than overwrite, the contents of a container. The following example demonstrates each type of insert iterator by copying the contents of one **deque** into another. Because insert iterators are used, the original **deque** is not overwritten. Rather, the new elements are inserted into it.

```
// Use insert iterator adaptors to insert one deque
// into another by way of the copy() algorithm.

#include <iostream>
#include <iterator>
#include <deque>
#include <string>

using namespace std;

void show(const char *msg, deque<string> dq);

int main()
{
```

```
    deque<string> dq, dq2, dq3, dq4;

    dq.push_back("Iterators");
    dq.push_back("are");
    dq.push_back("the");
    dq.push_back("the");
    dq.push_back("STL");
    dq.push_back("together.");

    dq2.push_back("glue");
    dq2.push_back("that");
    dq2.push_back("holds");

    dq3.push_back("At");
    dq3.push_back("the");
    dq3.push_back("end.");

    dq4.push_back("front.");
    dq4.push_back("the");
    dq4.push_back("At");

    cout << "Original size of dq: " << dq.size() << endl;
    show("Original contents of dq:\n", dq);
    cout << endl;

    // Use an insert_iterator to insert dq2 into dq.
    copy(dq2.begin(), dq2.end(), inserter(dq, dq.begin()+3));

    cout << "Size of dq after inserting dq2: ";
    cout << dq.size() << endl;
    show("Contents of dq after inserting dq2:\n", dq);
    cout << endl;

    // Use a back_insert_iterator to insert dq3 into dq.
    copy(dq3.begin(), dq3.end(), back_inserter(dq));

    cout << "Size of dq after inserting dq3: ";
    cout << dq.size() << endl;
    show("Contents of dq after inserting dq3:\n", dq);
    cout << endl;

    // Use a front_insert_iterator to insert dq4 into dq.
    copy(dq4.begin(), dq4.end(), front_inserter(dq));

    cout << "Size of dq after inserting dq4: ";
    cout << dq.size() << endl;
    show("Contents of dq after inserting dq4:\n", dq);

    return 0;
}

// Display the contents of a deque<string>.
void show(const char *msg, deque<string> dq) {
```

```
    cout << msg;
    for(unsigned i=0; i < dq.size(); ++i)
      cout << dq[i] << " ";
    cout << "\n";
}
```

Here is the output from the program.

```
Original size of dq: 6
Original contents of dq:
Iterators are the the STL together.

Size of dq after inserting dq2: 9
Contents of dq after inserting dq2:
Iterators are the glue that holds the STL together.

Size of dq after inserting dq3: 12
Contents of dq after inserting dq3:
Iterators are the glue that holds the STL together. At the end.

Size of dq after inserting dq4: 15
Contents of dq after inserting dq4:
At the front. Iterators are the glue that holds the STL together. At the
end.
```

As you can see, the **dq2** was inserted into the middle, **dq3** was inserted on the end, and **dq4** was inserted at the front of **dq**. In the process, **dq** was automatically increased in size to hold the additional elements. If an insert iterator had not been used, the original contents of **dq** would have been overwritten.

Options and Alternatives

The insert iterator adaptors are often used when an algorithm copies the result of an operation to another container. This situation occurs with algorithms such as **replace_copy( )**, **reverse_copy( )**, **remove_copy( )**, and so on. It also occurs with most of the set algorithms. By using an insert iterator adaptor, you can enable those algorithms to insert the result into the target container, rather than overwriting the existing elements. This capability greatly expands the types of problems to which these algorithms can be applied.

CHAPTER

Working with I/O

This chapter presents recipes that use the C++ I/O system. As all readers know, I/O is an integral part of nearly all programming projects. As a result, most computer languages have significant subsystems devoted to it, and C++ is no exception. The C++ I/O library is rich in its capabilities, yet flexible and easy to use. It is also extensible. Based on a sophisticated class hierarchy, the I/O system offers the programmer a well-organized framework that can be applied to nearly any situation.

Because of the importance of I/O, it is a topic that generates many "How-To" questions, both from newcomers and experienced pros. Of course, given the size and scope of the I/O library, it is not possible to present recipes that cover all aspects and nuances of this powerful subsystem. To do so would require a complete book of its own. Instead, this chapter answers several of the most common questions. As you might expect, its main focus is on handling files, including recipes that show how to read and write data, perform random access, and detect errors. Other recipes describe how to create custom I/O manipulators, overload the I/O operators, and use a string-based stream.

As an added bonus, a recipe is included that describes the core of the I/O system inherited from the C language. Because C++ was built on C, C++ also includes the entire C file system. Although not recommended for C++ programs, the C file system is still in widespread use in legacy C code. The C-based recipe will be of interest to anyone who needs to maintain C code or port C code to C++.

One other point: Although formatting data for input and operations is also handled by the I/O system, this topic is explored on its own in Chapter 6. The focus of this chapter is on the foundation of C++ I/O.

Here are the recipes contained in this chapter:

- Write Formatted Data to a Text File
- Read Formatted Data from a Text File
- Write Unformatted Binary Data to a File
- Read Unformatted Binary Data from a File
- Use **get( )** and **getline( )** to Read from a File
- Read from and Write to a File
- Detecting EOF
- Use Exceptions to Detect and Handle I/O Errors

279

- Use Random-Access File I/O
- Look Ahead in a File
- Use the String Streams
- Create Custom Inserters and Extractors
- Create a Parameterless Manipulator
- Create a Parameterized Manipulator
- Obtain or Set a Stream's Locale
- Use the C-Based File System
- Rename and Remove a File

NOTE *As explained in* Use the Stream Iterators *in Chapter 4, it is possible to use STL algorithms in conjunction with stream iterators to perform a wide variety of I/O and file handling tasks. In some cases, the use of stream iterators and algorithms simplifies some otherwise complicated tasks. However, the focus of this chapter is the C++ I/O system. As such, the recipes do not use the STL algorithms. Just remember that the stream iterators and STL algorithms offer an interesting alternative that may be useful in some cases.*

I/O Overview

The C++ I/O system is based on a cohesive, interrelated collection of classes that provide the functionality necessary to perform efficient input and output operations on a variety of different devices, including the console and disk files. Although no part of the I/O system is difficult to master, it is quite large, relying on several classes and many functions. Therefore, a brief overview of the C++ I/O system is given here. This discussion is sufficient for the purposes of the recipes in this chapter, but readers who will be doing advanced I/O programming, such as deriving classes to handle specialized devices, will need to study the I/O system in significantly greater detail.

C++ Streams

At the foundation of the C++ I/O system is the *stream*. A stream is an abstraction that either produces or consumes information. All streams behave in the same manner, even if the actual physical devices to which they are linked differ. This means that the way that you operate on one type of stream is the same for all streams. For example, the **put( )** function can be used to write to the screen, to a disk file, or to the printer.

In its most common form, a stream is a logical interface to a file. As C++ defines the term *file*, it can refer to a disk file, the screen, the keyboard, a port, a file on tape, and so on. Although files differ in form and capabilities, all streams are the same. The advantage to this approach is that to you, the programmer, one hardware device will look much like any other. The stream provides a consistent interface.

A stream is linked to a file through an *open* operation. A stream is disassociated from a file through a *close* operation.

There are two types of streams: *text* and *binary*. A text stream is used for human-readable information. In a text stream, some character translations may take place. For example, when the newline character is output, it may be converted into a carriage-return/linefeed sequence.

For this reason, there might not be a one-to-one correspondence between what is sent to the stream and what is written to the file. A binary stream can be used with any type of data. No character translations will occur, and there is a one-to-one correspondence between what is sent to the stream and what is actually contained in the file.

One more concept to understand is that of the *current location*. The current location (also referred to as the *current position*) is the location in a stream where the next I/O operation will occur. For example, consider a situation in which a stream is linked to a file. If a file is 100 bytes long and half the file has been read, the next read operation will occur at byte 50, which is the current location.

To summarize: In C++, I/O is performed through a logical interface called a stream. All streams have similar properties, and every stream is operated upon by the same I/O functions, no matter what type of file it is associated with. A file is the actual physical entity that contains the data. Even though files differ, streams do not. (Of course, some devices may not support all operations, such as random-access operations, so their associated streams will not support these operations either.)

The C++ Stream Classes

The standard C++ I/O system is constructed from a rather complex system of template classes. These classes are shown here.

Class	Purpose
basic_ios	Provides general-purpose I/O operations.
basic_streambuf	Low-level support for I/O.
basic_istream	Support for input operations. Inherits **basic_ios**.
basic_ostream	Support for output operations. Inherits **basic_ios**.
basic_iostream	Support for input/output operations. Inherits **basic_istream** and **basic_ostream**.
basic_filebuf	Low-level support for file I/O. Inherits **basic_streambuf**.
basic_ifstream	Support for file input. Inherits **basic_istream**.
basic_ofstream	Support for file output. Inherits **basic_ostream**.
basic_fstream	Support for file input/output. Inherits **basic_iostream**.
basic_stringbuf	Low-level support for string-based I/O. Inherits **basic_streambuf**.
basic_istringstream	Support for string-based input. Inherits **basic_istream**.
basic_ostringstream	Support for string-based output. Inherits **basic_ostream**.
basic_stringstream	Support for string-based input/output. Inherits **basic_iostream**.

Also part of the I/O class hierarchy is the non-template class **ios_base**. It provides definitions for various elements of the I/O system that are not dependent upon template parameters.

The C++ I/O system utilizes two related but different template class hierarchies. The first is derived from the low-level I/O class called **basic_streambuf**, which requires the **<streambuf>** header. This class supplies the basic, low-level input and output operations of a stream buffer, which provides the underlying support for the entire C++ I/O system. Each stream contains a **basic_streambuf** object, although you don't typically need to access it directly. The classes **basic_filebuf** and **basic_stringbuf** are derived from **basic_streambuf**. Unless you are doing advanced I/O programming, you will not need to use **basic_streambuf** or its subclasses directly. Rather, you will use its features through functions defined by the stream classes.

The class hierarchy that you will most commonly be working with is derived from **basic_ios**. It is declared in the **<ios>** header. This is a high-level I/O class that defines features common to all streams, such as error checking and status information. A base class for **basic_ios** is **ios_base**. As explained, it defines several non-template traits used by **basic_ios**, such as formatting The **basic_ios** class is used as a base for several derived classes, including **basic_istream**, **basic_ostream**, and **basic_iostream**. These classes provide the core functionality required by streams capable of input, output, and input/output, respectively.

The I/O classes are parameterized for the types of characters that they act upon and for the traits associated with those characters. For example, here is the template specification for **basic_ios**:

```
template <class CharType, class CharTraits = char_traits<CharType> >
    class basic_ios: public ios_base
```

Here, **CharType** specifies the type of character (such as **char** or **wchar_t**) and **CharTraits** specifies a type that describes the attributes of **CharType**. Notice that **CharTraits** defaults to **char_traits<CharType>**. The generic type **char_traits** is a utility class that defines the attributes associated with a character.

To perform file I/O, you must include the header **<fstream>** in your program. It defines several classes, including **basic_ifstream**, **basic_ofstream**, and **basic_fstream**. These classes are derived from **basic_istream**, **basic_ostream**, and **basic_iostream**, respectively. Remember, **basic_istream**, **basic_ostream**, and **basic_iostream** are derived from **basic_ios**, so the file streams also have access to all operations defined by **basic_ios**.

The I/O system also supports using a **string** as a source or destination for I/O operations. To do so, you will use the string stream classes. Low-level support is provided by **basic_stringbuf**, which is derived from **basic_streambuf**. The string stream classes are **basic_istringstream**, **basic_ostringstream**, and **basic_stringstream**. These classes are derived from **basic_istream**, **basic_ostream**, and **basic_iostream**, respectively. They create string streams capable of input, output, and input/output.

As mentioned, each stream has an object derived from **basic_streambuf** associated with it, but most of time you won't need to interact with the **basic_streambuf** object directly. Instead, in most cases (including all of the recipes in this chapter), you will use the features provided by the stream classes, which are derived from **basic_ios**. The following sections give a brief overview of each. The individual recipes describe in depth the features that they use. We will begin with **ios_base**.

ios_base

The **ios_base** class encapsulates those aspects of I/O that are common to all streams and that do not depend on template parameters. It requires the **<ios>** header. The **ios_base** class defines several types and functions. Here are the types used in this book:

fmtflags	A bitmask that determines the format of information that is output.
iostate	A bitmask that indicates the status of a stream.
openmode	The bitmask that indicates how a file is opened.
seekdir	An enumeration that controls how random-access I/O is handled.

Here is a sampling of its methods:

flags( )	Gets or sets all of the format flags.
setf( )	Gets or sets specific format flags.
unsetf( )	Clears one or more format flags.
precision( )	Gets or sets the precision.
width( )	Gets or sets the field width.
imbue( )	Sets the locale.
getloc( )	Gets the locale.

basic_ios

The **basic_ios** class inherits **ios_base** and then defines those template-related features that are common to all streams. It uses the **<ios>** header. It defines the following **typedefs** that indicate type (and, therefore, the size) of several types used by the I/O system. They are shown here:

char_type	The character type.
int_type	The integer type.
pos_type	A type that can represent a position within a file.
off_type	A type that can represent an offset within a file.
traits_type	A type that describes the character traits.

The **basic_ios** class also defines several functions. The ones used in this chapter are shown here:

clear( )	Clears the I/O error flags.
exceptions( )	Sets or obtains the errors that can cause an exception to be thrown.
eof( )	Returns true if the end of the file has been reached.
bad( )	Returns true if an unrecoverable error has occurred.
fail( )	Returns true if an error has occurred.
fill( )	Gets or sets the fill character used to pad a stream.
good( )	Returns true if no error has occurred.
rdstate( )	Obtains a bitmask that contains the I/O status flags.
setstate( )	Sets one or more I/O flags.

Notice that many of these have to do with the flags that represent the state of an I/O stream. These are used to detect and handle errors and the end-of-file condition. (Error handling techniques are described later in this overview.)

The **basic_ios** class also defines the ***** and the **!** operators that can be applied to a stream. The ***** operator returns a null pointer if the stream is bad and non-null pointer otherwise. The **!** returns the result of **fail( )**. Therefore, if no errors have occurred, **!** returns false. Otherwise, it returns true.

basic_istream

The **basic_istream** class inherits **basic_ios** and defines the functionality common to all input streams. Thus, **basic_istream** is at the core of all input streams. It requires the **<istream>** header.

The **basic_istream** class defines the **>>** extractor, which reads formatted data from the input stream. This operator is overloaded for all of the built-in types. Several functions are defined by **basic_istream**. The ones used in this chapter are shown here:

gcount( )	Returns the number of characters read by the last input operation.
get( )	Reads and removes one or more characters from the input stream.
getline( )	Reads and removes a line of text from the input stream.
ignore( )	Reads and discards characters from the input stream.
peek( )	Reads, but does not remove, a character from the input stream.
putback( )	Returns a character to the input stream.
read( )	Reads and removes characters from the input stream.
seekg( )	Sets the file position for input.
tellg( )	Returns the current position in the input stream.
unget( )	Returns to the input stream the last character read from that stream.

basic_ostream

The **basic_ostream** class inherits **basic_ios** and defines the functionality common to all output streams. Thus, **basic_ostream** is a base class for **basic_ofstream**, for example. It requires the **<ostream>** header.

The **basic_ostream** class defines the **<<** inserter, which writes formatted data to the output stream. This operator is overloaded for all of the built-in types. Several functions are defined by **basic_ostream**. The ones used in this chapter are shown here:

flush( )	Writes buffered data to the output stream.
put( )	Writes a character to the output stream.
seekp( )	Sets the current file position for output.
tellp( )	Returns the current position in the output stream.
write( )	Writes characters to the output stream.

basic_iostream

The **basic_iostream** class inherits both **basic_istream** and **basic_ostream**. Therefore, it encapsulates the features of a stream that is capable of both input and output.

basic_ifstream

The **basic_ifstream** class inherits **basic_istream** and adds the functionality required for file input. It requires the **<fstream>** header. It defines four functions, of which the following three are used by this chapter:

close( )	Closes a file, releasing any system resources used by that file.
is_open( )	Returns true if a file is open.
open( )	Opens a file for input. It is also possible to use a **basic_ifstream** constructor to open a file.

basic_ofstream

The **basic_ofstream** class inherits **basic_ostream** and adds the functionality required for file output. It requires the **<fstream>** header. It defines four functions, of which the following three are used by this chapter:

close( )	Closes a file, releasing any system resources used by that file.
is_open( )	Returns true if a file is open.
open( )	Opens a file for output. It is also possible to use a **basic_ofstream** constructor to open a file.

basic_fstream

The **basic_fstream** class inherits **basic_iostream**. Thus, it contains the functionality required for file input and output. It requires the **<fstream>** header. It defines four functions, of which the following three are used by this chapter:

close( )	Closes a file, releasing any system resources used by that file.
is_open( )	Returns true if a file is open.
open( )	Opens a file for input and output. It is also possible to use a **basic_fstream** constructor to open a file.

The Stream Class Specializations

As explained, the C++ stream classes are templates that take the type of character and its traits as type parameters. This means that the I/O system can operate on streams based on 8-bit characters and streams based on wide characters. As a convenience, the I/O library creates two specializations of the template class hierarchies just described: one for **char** and one for **wchar_t**. By using these specializations, you don't have to continually supply the type parameters when declaring and using stream objects.

Here is a list of the mapping of template class names to their **char** and **wchar_t** versions:

Template Class	Specialization for char	Specialization for wchar_t
basic_ios	ios	wios
basic_istream	istream	wistream
basic_ostream	ostream	wostream
basic_iostream	iostream	wiostream
basic_fstream	fstream	wfstream
basic_ifstream	ifstream	wifstream
basic_ofstream	ofstream	wofstream
basic_istringstream	istringstream	wistringstream
basic_ostringstream	ostringstream	wostringstream
basic_stringstream	stringstream	wstringstream
basic_streambuf	streambuf	wstreambuf
basic_filebuf	filebuf	wfilebuf
basic_stringbuf	stringbuf	wstringbuf

Notice that the names used for **char**-based streams are simply the template class name with the **basic_** removed. For example, the **char**-based version of **basic_ifstream** is **ifstream**. The **char**-based version of **basic_ios** is **ios**. The wide-character streams use the same approach, but add the **w**.

The specializations are the names that are typically used when programming, because they automatically create the desired stream type, rather than having to specify a type argument. For example, you will normally use **ifstream** to open a file, not **basic_ifstream<char>**, and you will normally specify **ios**, not **basic_ios<char>**. Not only is using the specialization shorter, it also ensures that the proper stream objects are created in all cases, thus avoiding errors.

Of the two stream types, **char**-based streams are by far the most widely used. One reason for this is that in C++, a **char** corresponds to a byte, and at the lowest level, all I/O is byte-based. Therefore, unless you are explicitly operating on wide characters, the **char**-based streams are the proper ones to use.

Because most streams are based on **char**, the **char**-based names will be used in the examples and discussions throughout the remainder of this chapter and elsewhere in this book.

*REMEMBER In this chapter and throughout this book, the **char**-based stream names, such as **ios** and **ofstream**, are used in the examples and discussions.*

C++'s Predefined Streams

When a C++ program begins execution, four built-in streams are automatically opened. They are:

Stream	Meaning	Default Device
cin	Standard input	Keyboard
cout	Standard output	Screen
cerr	Standard error output	Screen
clog	Buffered version of cerr	Screen

The streams **cout**, **clog**, and **cerr** are instances of **ostream**. The **cin** stream is an instance of **istream**. Thus, all are **char**-based and use the header **<iostream>**.

By default, the standard streams are used to communicate with the console. However, in environments that support I/O redirection, the standard streams can be redirected to other devices or files. For the sake of simplicity, the examples in this chapter assume that no I/O redirection has occurred.

Standard C++ also defines these four additional streams: **win**, **wout**, **werr**, and **wlog**. These are wide-character versions of the standard streams, and are based on characters of type **wchar_t**. Wide characters are used to hold the large character sets associated with some human languages.

The Format Flags

Each stream has associated with it a set of format flags that control the way information is formatted. These flags are contained in a bitmask enumeration called **fmtflags** that is defined by **ios_base**. Because formatting is such a large topic, it is covered on its own in Chapter 6. Therefore, a discussion of the format flags and recipes that use them is deferred until then.

The I/O Manipulators

The C++ I/O system provides a number of *manipulators,* which are functions that can be included in a formatted I/O expression. They are used to set or clear the format flags mentioned in the preceding section. They can also be used for other purposes, such as outputting a null or skipping white space on input. Some manipulators, such as **endl** (which inserts a newline into an output stream) are familiar to all C++ programmers. Others are less well known. It is also possible to create your own manipulators.

The built-in manipulators are described in detail in Chapter 6, which presents recipes related to formatting data. This chapter does, however, show how to create your own manipulators. Custom manipulators can be used for whatever purpose you desire. One common use is to provide a convenient means of controlling a non-standard device, such as a plotter, that requires special format or positioning codes.

Checking for Errors

File I/O poses a special challenge when it comes to error handling because I/O failures are a very real possibility when reading or writing files. Despite the fact that computer hardware (and the Internet) is much more reliable than in the past, it still fails at a fairly high rate, and any such failure must be handled in a manner consistent with the needs of your application. In general, your code must monitor all file operations for errors and take appropriate action if one occurs.

The C++ I/O system provides extensive abilities for detecting errors. As mentioned earlier, **ios_base** defines a type called **iostate** that represents the various types of errors that can occur, encoded into a bitmask. These error flags are defined by the following values:

badbit	Set if a catastrophic error has occurred.
failbit	Set if a possibly recoverable error has occurred.
eofbit	Set if the end of the file has been reached. (This is not necessarily an error condition.)
goodbit	A value that indicates that none of the other bits are set.

Notice that **eofbit** is included in the list of flags. An end-of-file condition does not always represent an error. Such a determination is context-based. (For example, if you are purposely looking for the end of a file, it is not an "error" when you find it!) Recall that **ios_base** is inherited by **basic_ios**, so these format flags are members of all stream classes. For **char**-based streams, you will typically refer to these values through the **ios** specialization—for example, **ios::failbit**.

In the **basic_ios** class are defined several functions that can obtain the state of the **iostate** flags. They are shown here:

bool bad( ) const	Returns true if **badbit** is set.
bool eof( ) const	Returns true if **eofbit** is set.
bool fail( ) const	Returns true if **failbit** is set.
bool good( ) const	Returns true if no bits are set.
iostate rdstate( ) const	Returns the current bitmask value associated with the stream.

You can use these functions to watch for errors. For example, one way to confirm that no errors have occurred is to call **good( )** on the stream, as shown here:

```
if(mystream.good()) cout << "No errors.\n";
```

Another way to check for errors is to use the **rdstate( )** function, shown here:

iostate rdstate( ) const

It returns a value in which the status bits are encoded. For example, this sequence reports the success or failure of an I/O operation:

```
if(!(mystream.rdstate() & (ios::badbit | ios::failbit))) {
  cout << "File successfully written.\n";
} else {
  cout << "A file error occurred.";
}
```

Of course, it's usually easier to simply call **good( )**.

Once an error bit has been set, it stays set until it is cleared. To clear an error, call **clear( )**. It is defined by **ios** and is shown here:

void clear(iostate *flag* = ios::goodbit)

It clears (i.e., resets) all flags. It then sets the flags to *flag*. You can set more than one flag by OR-ing them together. By default, it sets no flags. Thus, by default, it simply clears all error conditions.

You can also test the status of a stream by use of the **!** operator. As explained earlier, the **!** returns the outcome of **fail( )**. Therefore, if a stream has experienced an error, then **!** will return true. For example:

```
if(!mystream()) {
  // ... error occurred
}
```

Another way to handle errors is to use exception handling. This technique is described in detail in the recipe *Use Exceptions to Detect and Handle I/O Errors.*

In the examples in this chapter, any I/O errors that do occur are handled by simply displaying a message. While acceptable for the example programs, real applications will usually need to provide a more sophisticated response to an I/O error. For example, you might want to give the user the ability to retry the operation, specify an alternative operation, or otherwise gracefully handle the problem. Preventing the loss or corruption of data is a primary goal. Part of being a great programmer is knowing how to effectively manage the things that might go wrong when an I/O operation fails.

One final point: A common mistake that occurs when handling files is forgetting to close a file when you are done with it. Open files use system resources. Thus, there are limits to the number of files that can be open at any one time. Closing a file also ensures that any data written to the file is actually written to the physical device. Therefore, the rule is very simple: If you open a file, close the file. Although files are closed automatically when a file stream's destructor executes (such as at the end of an application), it's best not to rely on this because it can lead to sloppy programming and bad habits. It is better to explicitly close each file when it is no longer needed, properly handling any errors that might occur. For this reason, all files are explicitly closed by the examples in this chapter, even when the program is ending.

Opening and Closing a File

Before any I/O operations can take place on a file, the file must be opened. Although the specifics will differ, based on the type of file being opened, the general procedure is the same for all types of files. For this reason, it makes sense to describe the basic file-opening techniques in one place, rather than in each recipe. For convenience, the following discussion uses the names defined by the **char** specializations, but the same basic techniques would also apply to wide-character files.

In C++, you open a file by linking it to a stream. Therefore, before you can open a file, you must first obtain a stream instance. There are three types of streams: input, output, and input/output. To create a file input stream, use **ifstream**. To create a file output stream, use **ofstream**. File streams that will be performing both input and output operations are declared as objects of the **fstream** class. For example, this fragment creates one input stream, one output stream, and one stream capable of both input and output:

```
ifstream in;   // input
ofstream out;  // output
fstream io;    // input and output
```

Once you have created a stream, you can associate it with a file by using **open( )**. This function is a member of each of the three stream classes. The prototype for each is shown here:

void ifstream::open(const char *fname, ios::openmode *mode* = ios::in)

void ofstream::open(const char *fname, ios::openmode *mode* = ios::out)

void fstream::open(const char *fname, ios::openmode *mode* = ios::in | ios::out)

Here, *fname* is the name of the file; it can include a path specifier. The value of *mode* determines how the file is opened. It must be one or more of the values defined by **openmode**, which is an enumeration defined by **ios** (through its base class **ios_base**). Here are the values defined by **openmode**:

app	Output is appended to the end of the file.
ate	An initial seek is made to the end of the file.
binary	The file is opened in binary mode rather than text mode. (Text mode is the default.)
in	The file is opened for input. (Cannot be used with **ofstream**.)
out	The file is opened for output. (Cannot be used with **ifstream**.)
trunc	The file is truncated.

More than one mode value can be included by OR-ing them together using the | operator. Following is a detailed description of their effect.

The **in** value specifies that the file is capable of input. The **out** value specifies that the file is capable of output. In all cases, at least one of these values must be used when opening a file.

Including **app** causes all output to a file to be appended to the end. This value can be used only with files capable of output. Including **ate** causes a seek to the end of the file to occur when the file is opened. Although **ate** causes an initial seek to end-of-file, I/O operations can still occur anywhere within the file.

The **binary** value causes a file to be opened in binary mode. By default, all files are opened in text mode. In text mode, various character translations may take place, such as carriage return, linefeed sequences being converted into newlines. However, when a file is opened in binary mode, no such character translations will occur. Understand that any file, whether it contains formatted text or raw data, can be opened in either binary or text mode. The only difference is whether character translations take place.

The **trunc** value causes the contents of a preexisting file by the same name to be destroyed, and the file is truncated to zero length.

Because **ios** inherits **ios_base**, you will often see these mode values qualified with **ios::** rather than **ios_base::**. For example, you will often see **ios::out** rather than **ios_base::out**. This book uses the **ios::** form because it is shorter. (Actually, you could also use such constructs as **ofstream::out** or **ifstream::in**, but traditionally, **ios::** has been used.)

Putting together the pieces, the following fragment creates an output stream called **fout** and uses **open( )** to link it to a file called **test.dat**. Although it uses **ofstream** (which creates an output file stream), the general approach applies to all file streams.

```
// Create an ofstream object.
ofstream fout;

// Open a file on fout.
fout.open("test.dat");
```

This sequence first creates an **ofstream** object called **fout**, which is not yet linked to a file. Therefore, although **fout** is an instance of **ofstream**, it cannot be used to write output because it is not yet associated with a specific file. The call to **open( )** links **fout** with the file called **test.dat** and opens the file for output operations. After **open( )** returns, it is possible to write to the file via **fout**. Because the mode parameter of **open( )** automatically defaults to **ios::out**, there is no need to specify it explicitly in this case.

While there is nothing whatsoever wrong with the preceding "two-step" approach, all of the file stream classes (**fstream**, **ofstream**, and **ifstream**) let you open a file at the same time that the stream object is being created by passing the name of the file to the constructor. Here are the file stream constructors that let you specify a file:

ofstream(const char *fname, ios::openmode mode = ios::out)

ifstream(const char *fname, ios::openmode mode = ios::in)

fstream(const char *fname, ios::openmode mode = ios::in | ios::out)

As you can see, the mode parameter defaults to a value appropriate for the stream. For example, here is a much more compact way to create **fout** and link it to **test.dat**:

```
ofstream fout("test.dat");
```

When this statement executes, it constructs an **ofstream** object that is linked to a file called **test.dat**, and it then opens that file for output. As before, although **ofstream** is used by this example, the same general approach applies to all file streams.

It is important to understand that both **open( )** and the file stream constructors *attempt* to open a file. However, this attempt can fail for a variety of reasons, such as when the caller does not have the proper security permissions to open the file, or if the open-file limit supported by the environment has been reached. Therefore, before using a file, you must confirm that it has been successfully opened. There are several ways to do this. One way is to call **is_open( )** on the file stream instance. It is shown here:

```
bool is_open( )
```

It returns true if the file is open and false otherwise. For example, the following sequence verifies that **fout** is actually open:

```
ofstream fout("test.dat");
// Verify that the file has been successfully opened.
if(!fout.is_open()) {
  cout << "fout could not be opened.\n";
  // handle the error
}
```

This works because if the attempt to open the file fails, then **is_open( )** will return false, because **fout** is not open. It is important to understand that you can use **is_open( )** any time you need to know if a file is open. Its use is not limited to verifying that the open operation succeeded.

Although using **is_open( )** is valid, and is used occasionally in this book for the sake of illustration, there are other ways to verify that the file has been successfully opened. These other ways are based on the fact that failure-to-open creates an error condition in the stream. Specifically, if a file cannot be opened (either through an explicit call to **open( )** or by the file stream constructor), then the failure flag **failbit** will be set on the stream to indicate an I/O failure. Therefore, if the file cannot be opened, a call to **fail( )** on that stream will return true. This means that you can detect a failure by calling **fail( )** on the stream. Therefore, here is another way to detect a failure to open:

```
ofstream fout("test.dat");
if(fout.fail()) {
  cout << "fout could not be opened.\n";
  // handle the error
}
```

In this case, if the attempt to open the file fails, **fail( )** will return true. However, there is a simpler way.

As explained earlier, when the ! operator is applied to a file stream, it returns the result of **fail( )** called on the same stream. Therefore, to test for a failure to open, you can use this sequence:

```
ofstream fout("test.dat");
if(!fout) {
  cout << "fout could not be opened.\n";
  // handle the error
}
```

This is the form that you will usually see used in professionally written code.

When you are done with a file, you must ensure that it is closed. In general, a file is automatically closed by the file stream's destructor when the file stream instance goes out of scope, such as when the program ends. You can also explicitly close a file by calling **close( )**, which is supported by all file stream classes. It is shown here:

```
void close( )
```

Closing a file causes the contents of any buffers to be flushed and the system resources linked to the file to be released.

Although files are closed automatically when the file stream is destroyed, many programmers believe that it is better practice to explicitly close a file when it is no longer needed. One reason for this is that open files consume system resources. Closing the file releases those resources. Therefore, all examples in this chapter explicitly close all files, even at the end of a program, simply to explicitly illustrate the use of **close( )** and to emphasize that files must be closed.

Write Formatted Data to a Text File

Key Ingredients		
Headers	**Classes**	**Functions and Operators**
<fstream>	ofstream	void close( )
		bool good( ) const
		void open(const char *fname,
		ios::openmode mode = ios::out)
<ostream>		<<

C++ gives you two ways to write data to a file. First, you can write unformatted data in its raw, binary form. Second, you can write formatted data. This is data in its textual, human-readable form. In this approach, the format of the data written to the file will be the same as you would see on the screen. A file that contains formatted data is commonly referred to as a *text file*. The writing of formatted data to a text file is the subject of this recipe.

Step-by-Step

To write formatted data to a file involves these steps:

1. Create an instance of **ofstream**.
2. Open the file by calling **open( )** on the **ofstream** instance created in Step 1. Alternatively, you can open the file at the same time you create the **ofstream** object. (See the *Discussion* section for this recipe.)
3. Confirm that the file has been successfully opened.
4. Write data to the file by using the **<<** insertion operator.
5. Close the file by calling **close( )**.
6. Confirm that the write operations have been successful. This can be done by calling **good( )** on the output stream.

Discussion

A general overview of opening and closing a file is found in *Opening and Closing a File* near the start of this chapter. The specifics relating to **ofstream** are presented here.

To create an output stream linked to a file, create an object of type **ofstream**. It has these two constructors:

ofstream( )

explicit ofstream(const char *fname, ios::openmode *mode* = ios::out)

The first creates an **ofstream** instance that is not yet linked to a file. The second creates an **ofstream** instance and then opens the file specified by *fname* with the mode specified by *mode*. Notice that *mode* defaults to **ios::out**. This causes the file to be created, and any preexisting file with the same name is destroyed. Also, the file is automatically opened for text output. (By default, all files are opened in text mode. For binary output, you must explicitly request binary mode.) The **ofstream** class requires the **<fstream>** header.

If you use the default constructor, then you will need to link a file to the **ofstream** instance after it is constructed. To do this, call **open( )**. The version defined by **ofstream** is shown here:

void open(const char *fname, ios::openmode *mode* = ios::out)

It opens the file specified by *fname* with the mode specified by *mode*. Notice that, like the **ofstream** constructor, *mode* defaults to **ios::out**.

Before attempting to write to the file, you must confirm that the file has been opened. You can do this in various ways. The approach used by this recipe is to apply the **!** operator to the **ofstream** instance. Recall that the **!** operator returns the outcome of a call to **fail( )** on the stream. Therefore, if it returns true, the open operation has failed.

Once an output file has been successfully opened, you can write formatted output to it through the **<<** inserter operator. It is defined for all objects of type **ostream**, which includes **ofstream** because it inherits **ostream**. It uses the header **<ostream>**, which is typically included when you include **<fstream>**, so you don't need to include it explicitly. The **<<** operator is used to write formatted output to a file in the same way that it is used to write output to the console via **cout**. For example, assuming that **fout** represents an open output file, the following writes an integer, a string, and a floating-point to it:

```
fout << 10 << " This is a test " << 1.109;
```

Because the file has been open for text-based output, this information is written in its human-readable form. Therefore, the file will contain the following:

```
10 This is a test 1.109
```

When you are done writing to a file, you must close it. This is done by calling **close( )**, shown here:

void close( )

The file is automatically closed when the **ofstream** destructor is called. However, for the reasons stated in *Opening and Closing a File*, this book will explicitly call **close( )** in all cases.

This recipe verifies that no I/O errors have occurred by calling **good( )** on the stream. It is shown here:

    bool good( ) const

It returns true if no error flags are set.

Example

The following example writes formatted data to a text file called **test.dat**. Notice that the *mode* parameter of the **ofstream** constructor is not specified. This means that it defaults to **ios::out**. For the sake of illustration, the program uses the **good( )** function to report the success or failure of the file operations. As explained, other approaches are possible.

```
// Write formatted output to a text file.

#include <iostream>
#include <fstream>

using namespace std;

int main()
{
  // Create an ofstream object and attempt to
  // open the file test.dat.
  ofstream fout("test.dat");

  // Verify that the file has been successfully opened.
  if(!fout) {
    cout << "Cannot open file.\n";
    return 1;
  }

  // Write output to the file.
  fout << 10 << " " << -20 << " " << 30.2 << "\n";
  fout << "This is a test.";

  // Explicitly close the file.
  fout.close();

  if(!fout.good()) {
    cout << "A file error occurred.";
    return 1;
  }
}
```

The contents of **test.dat** are shown here:

```
10 -20 30.2
This is a test.
```

As you can see, the data is stored in its human-readable, text format.

Options and Alternatives

When using **ofstream**, the *mode* parameter of **open( )** or the **ofstream** constructor must include **ios::out** (as it does by default), but you can also include other values. One of the most helpful is **ios::app** because it causes all output to take place at the end of the file. This means that the contents of a preexisting file by the same name are not lost. Instead, output is added to the end of the previous contents. For example, if you use this call to **ofstream( )** to open **test.dat** in the example program:

```
ofstream fout("test.dat", ios::out | ios::app);
```

then the output will be written to the end of the file. Therefore, each time you run the program, the file will get larger.

To cause an initial seek to the end of the file, include **ios::ate**. After the initial seek to the end, output can occur anywhere.

Although using **good( )** is a convenient way to confirm the success of a formatted output operation, it is not the only way. For example, you can use the **bad( )** or **fail( )** functions. You can also use **rdstate( )**. See *Checking for Errors* in the overview for details.

Another way to watch for possible I/O errors is through the use of exceptions. To do this, you must specify the errors that will throw exceptions by calling **exceptions( )** on the **ofstream** object. Then, you must catch exceptions of type **ios_base::failure**. (See *Use Exceptions to Detect and Handle I/O Errors* for details.)

If you want to write binary data, open the output stream in binary mode. (See *Write Unformatted Binary Data to a File* for details.) To read formatted data from a file, use **ifstream**. (See *Read Formatted Data from a Text File*.) To open a file for both input and output, create an **fstream** object. (See *Read from and Write to a File*.)

Read Formatted Data from a Text File

Key Ingredients		
Headers	**Classes**	**Functions and Operators**
<fstream>	ifstream	void close( ) bool good( ) const void open(const char *fname, ios::openmode mode = ios::in)
<istream>		>>

You can read formatted data from a text file by using the formatted input capabilities of the C++ I/O system. Here, *formatted data* means the human-readable, text-based form of the data rather than its raw binary representation. For example, given a file that contains the following:

10 Hello 123.23

you can use the formatted input features of C++ to read the integer 10, the string Hello, and the floating-point value 123.23, storing the result in an **int**, **string**, and **double** value, respectively. In general, you can read strings, integers, booleans, and floating-point values that are stored in their human-readable form. This recipe shows the process.

Step-by-Step

To read formatted data from a file involves these steps:

1. Create an instance of **ifstream**.

2. Open the file by calling **open( )** on the **ifstream** instance created in Step 1. Alternatively, you can open the file at the same time you create the **ifstream** object. (See the *Discussion* section for this recipe.)

3. Confirm that the file has been successfully opened.

4. Read data from the file by using the **>>** extraction operator.

5. Close the file by calling **close( )**.

6. Confirm that the read operations have been successful. This can be done by calling **good( )** on the input stream.

Discussion

A general overview of opening and closing a file is found in *Opening and Closing a File* near the start of this chapter. The specifics relating to **ifstream** are presented here.

To create an input stream linked to a file, create an object of type **ifstream**. It has these two constructors:

ifstream( )

explicit ifstream(const char *fname*, ios::openmode *mode* = ios::in)

The first creates an **ifstream** instance that is not yet linked to a file. The second creates an **ifstream** instance and then opens the file specified by *fname* with the mode specified by *mode*. Notice that *mode* defaults to **ios::in**. This causes the file to be automatically opened for text input. (By default, all files are opened in text mode. For binary input, you must explicitly request binary mode.) The file specified by *fname* must exist. If it doesn't, an error will result. The **ifstream** class requires the **<fstream>** header.

If you use the default constructor, then you will need to link a file to the **ifstream** instance after it is constructed. To do this, call **open( )**. The version defined by **ifstream** is shown here:

void open(const char *fname*, ios::openmode *mode* = ios::in)

It opens the file specified by *fname* with the mode specified by *mode*. Notice that, like the **ifstream** constructor, *mode* defaults to **ios::in**.

Before attempting to read from the file, you must confirm that the file has been opened. You can do this in various ways. The approach used by this recipe is to apply the **!** operator to the **ifstream** instance. Recall that the **!** operator returns the outcome of a call to **fail( )** on the stream. Therefore, if it returns true, the open operation has failed.

Once an input file has been successfully opened, you can read formatted data from it by using the **>>** extractor operator. It is defined for all objects of type **istream**, which includes **ifstream** because it inherits **istream**. It uses the header **<istream>**, which is typically included when you include **<fstream>**, so you don't need to include it explicitly. The **>>** operator is used to read formatted input from a file in the same way that it is used to read input from the console via **cin**. For example, assuming that **fin** represents a valid open input file, the following reads an **int**, a **string**, and a **double** from it:

```
int x;
string str;
double val;

fin >> x;
fin >> str;
fin >> val;
```

Assuming that the file referred to by **fin** contains the following:

10 Hello 123.23

then, after reading the data, **x** will have the value 10, **str** will contain the string Hello, and **val** will have the value 123.23.

When you are done reading from a file, you must close it. This is done by calling **close( )**, shown here:

void close( )

The file is automatically closed when the **ifstream** destructor is called. However, for the reasons stated in *Opening and Closing a File*, this book will explicitly call **close( )** in all cases.

This recipe verifies that no I/O errors have occurred by calling **good( )** on the stream. It is shown here:

bool good( ) const

It returns true if no error flags are set.

Example

The following example shows how to read formatted input from a text file. It reads the file produced by the example program in *Write Formatted Data to a Text File*.

```
// Read formatted data from a file.
//
//    Note: This program reads the test.dat file
//    produced by the example program shown in
//
//        Write Formatted Data to a Text File
//
//    The test.dat file created by that program
//    contains the following data:
//
//      10 -20 30.2
//      This is a test.
```

```
#include <iostream>
#include <fstream>
#include <string>

using namespace std;

int main()
{
  int i, n;
  double d;
  string str;

  // Create an ifstream object and attempt to open the file test.dat.
  ifstream fin("test.dat");

  // Verify that the file has been successfully opened.
  if(!fin) {
    cout << "Cannot open file.\n";
    return 1;
  }

  // Read the formatted data.
  fin >> i;
  fin >> n;
  fin >> d;
  fin >> str;

  // Close the input file.
  fin.close();

  // Confirm that no input errors occurred.
  if(!fin.good()) {
    cout << "A file error occurred.";
    return 1;
  }

  // Display the data.
  cout << i << " " << n << " " <<
          d << " " << str << "\n";

  return 0;
}
```

The output is shown here:

```
10 -20 30.2 This
```

Notice that only the word "This" rather than the entire sentence "This is a test." is displayed. This is because the **>>** operator uses whitespace as a field separator. Thus, the line

```
fin >> str;
```

stops reading characters when the first space is encountered, which is the space that follows "This" in the sentence. Additional input operations are required to read the rest of the sentence.

Options and Alternatives

As was pointed out, when reading a string, the **>>** operator reads characters until a whitespace character is encountered. If you want to read an entire line of text, then you will want to use one of the unformatted input functions, such as **getline( )**. See *Use get( ) and getline( ) to Read from a File.*

In some input situations, you will want to read data until you reach the end of the file. You can determine when the end of a file has been encountered by calling **eof( )** on the stream. See *Detecting EOF.*

Although using **good( )** is a convenient way to confirm the success of a formatted input operation, it is not the only way. For example, you can use the **bad( )** or **fail( )** functions. You can also use **rdstate( )** or use the **!** operator on the stream. See *Checking for Errors* in the overview for details. You can also watch for possible I/O errors through the use of exceptions. To do this, you must specify the errors that will throw exceptions by calling **exceptions( )** on the **ifstream** object. Then, you must catch exceptions of type **ios_base::failure**. (See *Use Exceptions to Detect and Handle I/O Errors* for details.)

When reading a string via the **>>** extraction operator, you should avoid using a character array to receive the input. Use a **string** instead. If you use a character array, then it is possible that the end of the array could be overrun by an unexpectedly long input sequence. This is one source of the infamous "buffer-overrun" security flaw. Since **string** is a dynamic data structure, it can better deal with unexpectedly long input. In some cases, it might be even better to completely avoid using **>>** to read strings, relying on the unformatted input functions instead. See *Read Unformatted Binary Data from a File.*

If you want to read binary data, open the input stream in binary mode. (See *Read Unformatted Binary Data from a File* for details.) To write formatted data to a file, use **ofstream**. (See *Write Formatted Data to a Text File.*) To open a file for both input and output, create an **fstream** object. (See *Read from and Write to a File.*)

Write Unformatted Binary Data to a File

Key Ingredients		
Headers	**Classes**	**Functions**
<fstream>	ofstream	void close( )
		bool good( ) const
		void open(const char *fname, ios::openmode mode = ios::out)
		ostream &write(const char *str, streamsize num)

The recipe *Write Formatted Data to a Text File* described how to write formatted (i.e., text-based) data to a text file. Although this type of output is useful in many situations, often, you will want to write unformatted data. Here, "unformatted" means output that is written on a byte-by-byte basis in its raw binary form, without being translated or formatted into a human-readable representation. Unformatted output is typically used to create data files, in which the data is stored in its binary form. Of course, you can also use unformatted output to create a text file by writing values of type **char**. Whatever the purpose, this recipe shows the basic procedure used to write unformatted output to a file.

Step-by-Step

One way to write unformatted output to a file involves these steps:

1. Create an instance of **ofstream**.
2. Open the file by calling **open( )** on the **ofstream** instance created in Step 1. Alternatively, you can open the file at the same time you create the **ofstream** object. (See the *Discussion* section for this recipe.)
3. Confirm that the file has been successfully opened.
4. One way to write unformatted data to the file is to call **write( )**.
5. Close the file by calling **close( )**.
6. Confirm that the write operations have been successful. This can be done by calling **good( )** on the input stream.

Discussion

A general overview of opening and closing a file is found in *Opening and Closing a File* near the start of this chapter. The specifics relating to using **ofstream** to write unformatted, binary data are presented here.

To perform unformatted binary output, you must have an object of type **ofstream** that supports binary operations. The **ofstream** class uses the header **<fstream>** and it defines these two constructors:

ofstream( )

explicit ofstream(const char *fname, ios::openmode *mode* = ios::out)

The first creates an **ofstream** instance that is not yet linked to a file. The second creates an **ofstream** instance and then opens the file specified by *fname* with the mode specified by *mode*. Notice that *mode* defaults to **ios::out**, but does not include the **ios::binary** flag. By default, a file is opened in text mode. To open a file for unformatted output, the mode argument must specify both **ios::out** and **ios::binary**. For example, the following opens a file called **test.dat** for binary output:

```
ofstream fout("test.dat", ios::out | ios::binary);
```

This causes any preexisting file with the name **test.dat** to be destroyed and a new file to be created.

When the **binary** mode flag is specified, data is written in its raw, binary form, thus preventing possible character translations (such as a newline being converted into a carriage-return/linefeed sequence) that might occur when the file is opened in text mode. (Remember, if **ios::binary** is not specified, the file is automatically opened in text mode.) Failure to use binary mode can result in the bit pattern contained in the file being different from the bit pattern of the original block of memory that was written. Therefore, you must always specify **ios::binary** when opening a file for binary output.

   If you use the default constructor, then you will need to link a file to the **ofstream** instance after it is constructed by calling **open( )**. The version defined by **ofstream** is shown here:

   void open(const char *fname, ios::openmode mode = ios::out)

It opens the file specified by fname with the mode specified by mode. Notice that, like the **ofstream** constructor, mode defaults to **ios::out**. Therefore, you must explicitly specify **ios::out** and **ios::binary** to write unformatted binary data.

   Before attempting to write to the file, you must confirm that the file has been opened. You can do this in various ways. The approach used by this recipe is to apply the ! operator to the **ofstream** instance. Recall that the ! operator returns the outcome of a call to **fail( )** on the stream. Therefore, if it returns true, the open operation has failed.

   One way to write unformatted output to a file is to use the **write( )** function. It writes a block of data to a stream. It is shown here:

   ostream &write(const char *buf, streamsize num)

Here, buf is a pointer to the block of memory to write and num specifies the number of bytes to write. The **streamsize** type is defined as some form of integer that is capable of holding the largest number of bytes that can be transferred in any one I/O operation. The function returns a reference to the stream. Although buf is specified as **char ***, you can use **write( )** to write any type of binary data. Simply cast a pointer to that data to **char *** and specify the length of the block in bytes. (Recall that in C++, a **char** is always exactly one byte long.) For example, this sequence writes the **double** value in **val** to **fout**:

```
double val = 10.34;
fout.write((char *) &val, sizeof(double);
```

Understand that the data is written in its internal, floating-point format. Therefore, the file contains the bit-pattern image of **val**, not its human-readable form.

   When you are done writing to a file, you must close it. This is done by calling **close( )**, shown here:

   void close( )

The file is automatically closed when the **ofstream** destructor is called. However, for the reasons stated in *Opening and Closing a File*, this book will explicitly call **close( )** in all cases.

   This recipe verifies that no I/O errors have occurred by calling **good( )** on the stream. It is shown here:

   bool good( ) const

It returns true if no error flags are set.

Example

The following example demonstrates the writing of binary data to a file. It creates a structure called **inventory** that stores the name, quantity, and cost of an item in inventory. Next, it creates a three-element array of **inventory** structures called **inv** and stores inventory information in that array. It then writes that array to a file called **InvDat.dat**. After the program ends, this file will contain a bit-by-bit copy of the information contained in **inv**.

```cpp
// Use write() to output a block of binary data.

#include <iostream>
#include <fstream>
#include <cstring>

using namespace std;

// A simple inventory structure.
struct inventory {
  char item[20];
  int quantity;
  double cost;
};

int main()
{
  // Create and open a file for binary output.
  ofstream fout("InvDat.dat", ios::out | ios::binary);

  // Confirm that the file opened without error.
  if(!fout) {
    cout << "Cannot open file.\n";
    return 1;
  }

  // Create some inventory data.
  inventory inv[3];

  strcpy(inv[0].item,"Hammers");
  inv[0].quantity = 3;
  inv[0].cost = 9.99;

  strcpy(inv[1].item, "Pliers");
  inv[1].quantity = 12;
  inv[1].cost = 7.85;

  strcpy(inv[2].item, "Wrenches");
  inv[2].quantity = 19;
  inv[2].cost = 2.75;

  // Write inventory data to the file.
  for(int i=0; i<3; i++)
    fout.write((const char *) &inv[i], sizeof(inventory));

  // Close the file.
  fout.close();

  // Confirm that there were no file errors.
```

```
  if(!fout.good()) {
    cout << "A file error occurred.";
    return 1;
  }

  return 0;
}
```

Options and Alternatives

Another way to write unformatted data to a stream is called **put( )**. It is shown here:

ostream &put(char *ch*)

This function writes the byte value passed in *ch* to the associated stream. (Remember in C++, a **char** is one byte long. Thus, each call to **put( )** writes one byte of data.) The function returns a reference to the stream. Here is an example of how it can be used. Assuming that **fout** is an open output stream, the following writes the characters in the string pointed to by **str**:

```
const char *str = "Hello";
while(*str) fout.put(*str++);
```

After this sequence executes, the file will contain the characters "Hello".

Both **put( )** and **write( )** can be used on a text-based output stream (that is, a stream not specified as binary). However, if you do so, then some character translations may occur. For example, a newline will be converted into a carriage-return, linefeed sequence. In general, if you are using either **put( )** or **write( )**, you will normally open the file for binary operations.

By default, when a file is opened for output, the contents of any preexisting file by the same name are destroyed. You can prevent this by including the flag **ios::app** in the *mode* parameter of **open( )** or the **ofstream** constructor. It causes all output to occur at the end of the file, thus preserving its contents. To cause an initial seek to the end of the file, include **ios::ate**. After the initial seek to the end, output can occur anywhere.

Although using **good( )** is a convenient way to confirm the success of an unformatted output operation, it is not the only way. For example, you can use the **bad( )** or **fail( )** functions. You can also use **rdstate( )**. See *Checking for Errors* in the overview for details. You can also watch for possible I/O errors through the use of exceptions. To do this, you must specify the errors that will throw exceptions by calling **exceptions( )** on the **ofstream** object. Then, you must catch exceptions of type **ios_base::failure**. (See *Use Exceptions to Detect and Handle I/O Errors* for details.)

Another way to watch for errors when using **write( )** or **put( )** is to check the status of the stream. Because both **write( )** and **put( )** return a reference to the stream upon which they are operating, you can apply the **!** operator to the returned object. Recall that when **!** is applied to a stream, it returns the result of **fail( )** applied to the same stream. Therefore, you can test for a successful call to **write( )** like this:

```
if(!write(...)) { // ... handle the write error
```

For example, in the preceding program, you could use the following sequence to write the inventory records, confirming the success of each output operation in the process:

```
if(!fout.write((const char *) &inv[i], sizeof(inventory))) {
    cout << "Error writing file.";
    // handle the error ...
}
```

Taking this approach to checking for errors streamlines your source code. However, because each call to **write( )** also results in an **if** statement being evaluated (which takes time), it *does not* streamline your program's performance. As a general rule, exceptions offer a better alternative in this type of situation.

To read unformatted, binary information from a file, see *Read Unformatted Binary Data from a File*. To read formatted data from a file, use **ifstream**. (See *Read Formatted Data from a Text File*.)

Read Unformatted Binary Data from a File

Key Ingredients		
Headers	**Classes**	**Functions**
<fstream>	ifstream	void close( )
		bool good( ) const
		void open(const char *fname, ios::openmode mode = ios::in)
		ostream &read(char *str, streamsize num)

The recipe *Read Formatted Data from a Text File* described how to read formatted (i.e., text-based) data from a text file. Although formatted input is useful in many contexts, often, you will want to read unformatted data in its raw binary format, without any character translations (which are possible with formatted input). For example, if you were creating a file-comparison utility, you would want to operate on the binary data within the files on a byte-by-byte basis. Whatever the need, this recipe shows the basic procedure used to read unformatted input from a file.

Step-by-Step

One way to read unformatted, binary input from a file involves these steps:

1. Create an instance of **ifstream**.
2. Open the file by calling **open( )** on the **ifstream** instance created in Step 1. Alternatively, you can open the file at the same time you create the **ifstream** object. (See the *Discussion* section for this recipe.)

3. Confirm that the file has been successfully opened.

4. One way to read unformatted data from the file is to call **read( )**.

5. Close the file by calling **close( )**.

6. Confirm that the read operations have been successful. This can be done by calling **good( )** on the input stream.

Discussion

A general overview of opening and closing a file is found in *Opening and Closing a File* near the start of this chapter. The specifics relating to using **ifstream** to read unformatted, binary data are presented here.

To perform unformatted binary input, you must have an object of type **ifstream** that supports binary operations. The **ifstream** class uses the header **<fstream>** and it defines these two constructors:

ifstream( )

explicit ifstream(const char *fname*, ios::openmode *mode* = ios::in)

The first creates an **ifstream** instance that is not yet linked to a file. The second creates an **ifstream** instance and then opens the file specified by *fname* with the mode specified by *mode*. Notice that *mode* defaults to **ios::in**, but does not include the **ios::binary** flag. By default, files are opened in text mode. To open a file for binary input, the *mode* argument must specify both **ios::in** and **ios::binary**. For example, the following opens a file called **test.dat** for binary input:

```
ifstream fout("test.dat", ios::in | ios::binary);
```

When the **binary** mode flag is specified, data is read on a byte-by-byte basis in its raw, binary form. This prevents the possible character translations (such as a newline being converted into a carriage-return/linefeed sequence) that might occur when the file is opened in text mode. (If **ios::binary** is not specified, the file is automatically opened in text mode.) Failure to use binary mode can result in information that is read being different from that which is in the file. Therefore, you must always specify **ios::binary** when opening a file for binary output.

If you use the default constructor, then you will need to link a file to the **ifstream** instance after it is constructed. To do this, call **open( )**. The version defined by **ifstream** is shown here:

void open(const char *fname*, ios::openmode *mode* = ios:in)

It opens the file specified by *fname* with the mode specified by *mode*. Notice that, like the **ifstream** constructor, *mode* defaults to **ios::in**. Therefore, you must explicitly specify **ios::in** and **ios::binary** to read unformatted binary data.

Before attempting to read from the file, you must confirm that the file has been opened. You can do this in various ways. The approach used by this recipe is to apply the **!** operator to the **ifstream** instance. Recall that the **!** operator returns the outcome of a call to **fail( )** on the stream. Therefore, if it returns true, the open operation has failed.

One way to read unformatted output to a file is to use the **read( )** function. It reads a block of data from a stream. It is shown here:

istream &read(char *buf, streamsize num)

Here, buf is a pointer to the block of memory (such as an array) into which the input will be stored. The number of bytes to read is specified by num. The **streamsize** type is defined as some form of integer that is capable of holding the largest number of bytes that can be transferred in any one I/O operation. The function returns a reference to the stream. If less than the specified number of bytes are available (which will happen if you attempt to read at the end of the file), **read( )** will read less than num bytes and **failbit** will be set in the invoking stream (which indicates an error). Although buf is specified as **char ***, you can use **read( )** to read any type of binary data. Simply cast a pointer to that data to **char *** and specify the length of the block in bytes. (Recall that in C++, a **char** is always exactly one byte long.) The example program shows the process.

When you are done reading from a file, you must close it. This is done by calling **close( )**, shown here:

void close( )

The file is automatically closed when the **ifstream** destructor is called. However, for the sake of illustration, this book will explicitly call **close( )** in all cases.

This recipe verifies that no I/O errors have occurred by calling **good( )** on the stream. It is shown here:

bool good( ) const

It returns true if no error flags are set.

Example

The following example illustrates how to read unformatted binary data. It does so by reading the **InvDat.dat** file created by the example program in *Write Unformatted Binary Data to a File*. This file contains three **inventory** structures. After the call to **read( )**, the **inv** array will contain the same bit pattern as that stored in the file.

```
// Use read() to input blocks of binary data.
//
//    This program reads the InvDat.dat file
//    that was created by the example program
//    from
//
//    Write Unformatted Binary Data to a File

#include <iostream>
#include <fstream>

using namespace std;

// A simple inventory structure.
struct inventory {
```

```
    char item[20];
    int quantity;
    double cost;
};

int main()
{
  // Open the file for binary input.
  ifstream fin("InvDat.dat", ios::in | ios::binary);

  // Confirm that the file opened without error.
  if(!fin) {
    cout << "Cannot open file.\n";
    return 1;
  }

  inventory inv[3];

  // Read blocks of binary data.
  for(int i=0; i<3; i++)
    fin.read((char *) &inv[i], sizeof(inventory));

  // Close the file.
  fin.close();

  // Confirm that there were no file errors.
  if(!fin.good()) {
    cout << "A file error occurred.\n";
    return 1;
  }

  // Display the inventory data read from the file.
  for(int i=0; i < 3; i++) {
    cout << inv[i].item << "\n";
    cout << " Quantity on hand: " << inv[i].quantity;
    cout << "\n Cost: " << inv[i].cost << "\n\n";
  }

  return 0;
}
```

The output is shown here:

```
Hammers
 Quantity on hand: 3
 Cost: 9.99

Pliers
 Quantity on hand: 12
 Cost: 7.85

Wrenches
 Quantity on hand: 19
 Cost: 2.75
```

Options and Alternatives

As explained, **read( )** reads a specified number of bytes from a file. However, if you request more bytes than are available in the file (such as when reading near or at the end of the file), **read( )** will obtain fewer than the requested number of bytes. You can determine how many bytes were actually read by calling **gcount( )**. It is shown here:

   streamsize gcount( ) const

It returns the number of characters read by a previous call to **read( )**, or to any other unformatted input function. You can see the **gcount( )** function in action in the Bonus Example for the recipe *Detecting EOF.*

   The preceding example used **good( )** to check for errors, but there are several alternatives. See *Checking for Errors* in the overview and the recipe *Use Exceptions to Detect and Handle I/O Errors* for details. You can also check for input errors by monitoring the status of the stream. Because **read( )** returns a reference to the stream upon which it is operating, you can apply the **!** operator to the returned object. Recall that when **!** is applied to a stream, it returns the result of **fail( )** applied to the same stream. Therefore, you can test for a successful call to **read( )** like this:

```
if(!read(...)) { // ... handle the read error
```

For example, in the preceding program, you could use the following sequence to read the inventory records, confirming the success of each read operation in the process:

```
// Read blocks of binary data.
for(int i=0; i<3; i++)
  if(!fin.read((char *) &inv[i], sizeof(inventory))) {
    cout << "Error reading file.";
    // handle the error ...
  }
```

Taking this approach to checking for errors streamlines your source code. However, because each call to **read( )** also results in an **if** statement being evaluated (which takes time), it *does not* streamline your program's performance. As a general rule, exceptions offer a better alternative in this type of situation.

   Another way to read character-based unformatted input is to use either the **get( )** or **getline( )** function. They are described in *Use get( ) and getline( ) to Read from a File.*

   In some input situations, you will want to read data until you reach the end of the file. You can determine when the end of a file has been encountered by calling **eof( )** on the stream. See *Detecting EOF.*

   To read formatted data, open the output stream in text mode. See *Read Formatted Data from a Text File* for details. To write formatted data to a file, use **ofstream**. See *Write Formatted Data to a Text File*. To open a file for both input and output, create an **fstream** object. See *Read from and Write to a File.*

Use get( ) and getline( ) to Read from a File

Key Ingredients		
Headers	**Classes**	**Functions**
<ifstream>	ifstream	istream &get(char &ch)
		istream &get(char *buf, streamsize num)
		istream &getline(char *buf, streamsize num)

The previous recipe described how to read unformatted binary data by using the **read( )** function. This function is especially useful when reading blocks of data, as the example program in the previous recipe illustrated. However, when reading **char**-based data, such as individual characters or lines of text, the **get( )** and **getline( )** functions may prove more convenient. This recipe shows how to use them.

Step-by-Step

To read characters from a file by using **get( )** involves these steps:

1. Open the file for input. It can be opened in either text or binary mode. Be aware, however, that if the file is opened in text mode, some character translations may take place, such as converting newline characters into carriage-return, linefeed sequences.

2. One way to read a single character is to use **get(char &ch)**.

3. One way to read a sequence of characters is to use **get(char *buf, streamsize num)**.

4. Confirm that the read operations have been successful.

To read a complete line of text by use of **getline( )** involves these steps:

1. Open the file for input. It can be opened in either text or binary mode. Be aware, however, that if the file is opened in text mode, some character translations may take place, such as converting newline characters into carriage-return, linefeed sequences.

2. One way to read a line that is terminated by a newline character is to call **getline(char *buf, streamsize num)**.

3. Confirm that the read operations have been successful.

Discussion

Earlier recipes describe the steps needed to open a file for input or output in either text or binary mode. See those recipes for details on opening a file.

There are several versions of **get( )**. The two used by this recipe are shown here:

istream &get(char &*ch*)

istream &get(char *buf*, streamsize *num*)

The first form reads a single character from the invoking stream and puts that value in *ch*. The second form reads characters into the array pointed to by *buf* until *num–1* characters have been read, a newline character is found, or the end of the file has been encountered. The array pointed to by *buf* will be null-terminated by **get( )**. If the newline character is encountered in the input stream, it is *not* extracted. Instead, it remains in the stream until the next input operation. Both return a reference to the stream.

The **getline( )** function has the two forms. The one used by this recipe is shown here:

istream &getline(char *buf*, streamsize *num*)

It reads characters into the array pointed to by *buf* until *num–1* characters have been read, a newline character has been found, or the end of the file has been encountered. The array pointed to by *buf* will be null-terminated by **getline( )**. If the newline character is encountered in the input stream, it is extracted but is not put into *buf*. The function returns a reference to the stream.

As you can see, **getline( )** is virtually identical to the **get(*buf*, *num*)** version of **get( )**. Both read characters from input and put them into the array pointed to by *buf* until either *num–1* characters have been read or the newline character is encountered. The difference is that **getline( )** reads and removes the newline from the input stream; **get( )** does not.

It is important to understand that **get( )** and **getline( )** can be used on files opened in either text or binary mode. The only difference is that if the file is opened in text mode, some character translations, such as converting newlines to carriage-return, linefeed sequences, may occur.

When using either **get( )** or **getline( )**, you must ensure that the array that will be receiving input is large enough to hold the input that it will receive. Therefore, it must be at least as large as the character count passed in *num*. Failure to follow this rule can result in a buffer overrun, which can (and probably will) cause a program crash. It is also a potential threat to security because it leaves your application open to the infamous "buffer overrun attack." In general, extreme care must be exercised when inputting data into an array.

You can confirm the success of **get( )** or **getline( )** in the same way as you do a call to **read( )**. See the previous recipe and *Checking for Errors* in the overview near the start of this chapter for details.

Example

The following example shows **get( )** and **getline( )** in action.

```
// Use get() and getline() to read characters.

#include <iostream>
#include <fstream>

using namespace std;

int main()
{
  char ch;
  char str[256];

  // First, write some data to a file.
```

```
ofstream fout("test.dat");
if(!fout) {
  cout << "Cannot open file for output.\n";
  return 1;
}

// Write to the file.
fout << "This is a line of text.\n";
fout << "This is another line of text.\n";
fout << "This is the last line of text.\n";

fout.close();
if(!fout.good()) {
  cout << "An error occurred when writing to the file.\n";
  return 1;
}

// Now, open the file for input.
ifstream fin("test.dat", ios::in);
if(!fin) {
  cout << "Cannot open file for input.\n";
  return 1;
}

cout << "Use get():\n";

// Get the first three characters from the file.
cout << "Here are the first three characters: ";
for(int i=0; i < 3; ++i) {
  fin.get(ch);
  cout << ch;
}
cout << endl;

// Now, use get() to read to the end of the line.
fin.get(str, 255);
cout << "Here is the rest of the first line: ";
cout << str << endl;

// Because the previous call to get() did not remove
// the newline character from the input stream, it must
// be removed by another call to get(ch):
fin.get(ch);

cout << "\nNow use getline():\n";

// Finally, use getline() to read the next two lines.
fin.getline(str, 255);
cout << str << endl;
fin.getline(str, 255);
cout << str;

fin.close();
```

```
  if(!fin.good()) {
    cout << "Error occurred while reading or closing the file.\n";
    return 1;
  }

  return 0;
}
```

The output is shown here:

```
Use get():
Here are the first three characters: Thi
Here is the rest of the first line: s is a line of text.

Now use getline():
This is another line of text.
This is the last line of text.
```

In the program, notice this sequence:

```
// Now, use get() to read to the end of the line.
fin.get(str, 255);
cout << "Here is the rest of the first line: ";
cout << str << endl;

// Because the previous call to get() did not remove
// the newline character from the input stream, it must
// be removed by another call to get(ch):
fin.get(ch);
```

As explained, the **get(*buf, num*)** version of **get( )** does not remove a newline character from the input stream. Therefore, the newline will be read by the next input operation. Often, as is the case with the example program, it is necessary to remove and discard the newline character. This is handled by the call to the **get(*ch*)** version.

Options and Alternatives

There is another form of **get( )** that provides an alternative when reading just one character. It is shown here:

   int get( )

This form of **get( )** returns the next character from the stream. It returns a value that represents end-of-file if the end of the file is reached. For **char**-based streams, such as **ifstream**, the EOF value is **char_traits<char>::eof( )**.

When reading a sequence of characters via **get( )**, you can specify the delimiter by using this form:

   istream &get(char *buf*, streamsize *num*, char *delim*)

It works just like **get(*buf, num*)** described in the recipe, except that it stops reading when the character passed in *delim* is encountered (or *num*–1 characters have been read, or the end of the file has been reached).

When reading a line of text via **getline( )**, you can specify the delimiter by using this form:

istream &getline(char *buf*, streamsize *num*, char *delim*)

It works just like **getline(*buf*, *num*)** described in the recipe, except that it stops reading when the character passed in *delim* is encountered (or *num*–1 characters have been read, or the end of the file has been reached).

Read from and Write to a File

Key Ingredients		
Headers	**Classes**	**Functions**
<fstream>	fstream	void close( )
		ostream &flush( )
		istream &get(char &*ch*)
		bool good( ) const
		void open(const char *fname*,
		ios::openmode *mode* = ios::in I ios::out)
		ostream &put(char *ch*)

It is possible to open a file so that it can be used for both input and output. This is commonly done when a data file needs to be updated. Instead of rewriting the entire file, you can write just a small portion of it. This is especially valuable in files that use fixed-length records, because it offers a convenient way to update one record without rewriting the entire file. Of course, opening a file for both input and output is useful in other situations, such as when you want to read the contents of a file, modify it, and then write the modified contents back to the same file. By using a file opened for input and output, you only need to open and close the file once, thus streamlining your code. Whatever your purpose, this recipe shows the basic procedures necessary to read from and write to a file.

Step-by-Step

To perform both input and output operations on a file involves the following steps:

1. Open the file for both reading and writing by creating an object of type **fstream**. The **fstream** class inherits both **ifstream** and **ofstream**. This means that it is capable of both input and output operations.

2. Use the output functions defined by **ofstream** to write to the file. The one used by this recipe is **put( )**.

3. Use the input functions defined by **ifstream** to read from the file. The one used by this recipe is **get( )**.

4. For many compiler implementations, when switching between input and output, you will need to call **seekg( )**, **seekp( )**, or **flush( )**. This recipe uses **flush( )**.

5. Close the file.

6. Confirm that the I/O operations have been successful. This can be done by calling **good( )** on the input stream or in a number of other ways.

Discussion

A general overview of opening and closing a file is found in *Opening and Closing a File* near the start of this chapter. Information relating specifically to **fstream** is presented here.

The **fstream** class inherits the **iostream** class, which inherits both **istream** and **ostream**. This makes it able to support both input and output operations. Furthermore, all of the techniques described by the preceding recipes, such as reading from and writing to an **ifstream** or **ofstream**, apply to **fstream**. The only difference is that **fstream** supports both read and write.

To perform input/output operations, you must have an object of type **fstream** that supports both input and output operations. The **fstream** class uses the header **<fstream>** and it defines these two constructors:

fstream( )

explicit fstream(const char *fname, ios::openmode *mode* = ios::in | ios::out)

The first creates an **fstream** instance that is not yet linked to a file. The second creates an **fstream** instance and then opens the file specified by *fname* with the mode specified by *mode*. Notice that *mode* defaults to both **ios::in** and **ios::out**. Also, notice that it does not include the **ios::binary** flag. Therefore, by default, the file is opened in text mode. To open a file for binary I/O, include the **ios::binary** flag. When a file is opened in text mode, some character translations may occur, such as a newline being replaced by a carriage-return, linefeed sequence. Opening a file in binary mode prevents such translations.

If you use the default constructor, then you will need to link a file to the **fstream** instance after it is constructed by calling **open( )**. The version defined by **fstream** is shown here:

void open(const char *fname, ios::openmode *mode* = ios::in | ios::out)

It opens the file specified by *fname* with the mode specified by *mode*. Notice that, like the **fstream** constructor, *mode* defaults to **ios::in | ios::out**. Therefore, the file is automatically opened for read/write operations when *mode* defaults.

Before attempting to write to the file, you must confirm that the file has been opened. You can do this in various ways. The approach used by this recipe is to apply the **!** operator to the **fstream** instance. Recall that the **!** operator returns the outcome of a call to **fail( )** on the stream. Therefore, if it returns true, the open operation has failed.

Once open, you can read from and write to the file using any of the methods provided by **istream** and **ostream**, such as **get( )**, **put( )**, **read( )**, and **write( )**. These methods have been described by the preceding recipes.

For some compilers, you will need to flush output by calling **flush( )** or perform a seek operation by calling **seekg( )** or **seekp( )** when switching between read and write operations.

This recipe uses **flush( )**. (For details on **seekg( )** and **seekp( )**, see *Use Random-Access File I/O*.) The **flush( )** method is defined by **ostream** and is shown here:

    ostream &flush( )

It flushes the output buffer. This ensures that the contents of the buffer are written to the file. The C++ I/O system uses buffers to improve the efficiency of file operations. For input, data is read from the file a buffer at a time. When the end of the input buffer is reached, the next buffer's worth is read. For output, when you write data, it is actually written to an output buffer. It is not until that buffer is full that the data is physically written to the file. The **flush( )** function alters this behavior and causes the current contents of the buffer to be written to the file, whether the buffer is full or not. This ensures that the contents of the file immediately reflect any write operations that may have taken place. As it relates to read/write files, calling **flush( )** after you have written to the file ensures that read operations reflect the actual state of the file.

Example

The following example shows how to open a text file called **test.dat** for reading and writing. The **test.dat** file must exist. After it opens the file, it writes three X's to the start of the file. Next, it flushes the output buffer and then reads the next ten characters from the file.

```
// Use fstream to read and write a file.

#include <iostream>
#include <fstream>

using namespace std;

int main()
{
  char ch;

  // Open a file for input and output operations.
  fstream finout("test.dat");

  if(!finout) {
    cout << "Cannot open file for output.\n";
    return 1;
  }

  // Write three X's.
  for(int i=0; i < 3; ++i) finout.put('X');

  if(!finout.good()) {
    cout << "Error occurred while writing to the file.\n";
    return 1;
  }

  // Flush the output buffer.
  finout.flush();
```

```
// Get the next ten characters from the file.
cout << "Here are the next ten characters: ";
for(int i=0; i < 10; ++i) {
  finout.get(ch);
  cout << ch;
}
cout << endl;

if(!finout.good()) {
  cout << "Error occurred while reading from the file.\n";
  return 1;
}

finout.close();

if(!finout.good()) {
  cout << "Error occurred while closing the file.\n";
  return 1;
}

  return 0;
}
```

Assuming that **test.dat** contains the following:

```
abcdefghijklmnop
```

the program will produce this output:

```
Here are the next ten characters: defghijklm
```

and the contents of **test.dat** will be changed to:

```
XXXdefghijklmnop
```

Options and Alternatives

For performing read/write operations on a file, there really is no good alternative to using **fstream**.

Detecting EOF

Key Ingredients		
Headers	**Classes**	**Functions**
<fstream>	ifstream	bool eof( ) const

In some cases, you will want to know when the end of the file has been reached. For example, if you are reading a list of values from a file, then you might want to continue reading until there are no more values to obtain. This implies that you have some way to know when the end of the file has been reached. Fortunately, the C++ I/O system supplies such a function to do this: **eof( )**. This recipe shows how to use it.

Step-by-Step

To detect EOF involves these steps:

1. Open the file being read for input.
2. Begin reading data from the file.
3. After each input operation, determine if the end of the file has been reached by calling **eof( )**.

Discussion

The **eof( )** function determines if the end of a file has been reached. It is declared by **istream**, which is inherited by **ifstream**. It is shown here:

    bool eof( ) const

It returns true if the end of the stream has been encountered and false otherwise.

There is an important aspect of the C++ I/O system that relates to end-of-file. When an attempt is made to read at the end of the file, both **ios::eofbit** and **ios::failbit** are set. Therefore, encountering the end of the file is also considered an error condition, even if you intended it to happen. Furthermore, if you want to detect an input failure that is caused by something other than the encounter with end-of-file, then you will need to explicitly test for this by excluding the end-of-file condition from the check. For example, this if statement succeeds if either **badbit** or **failbit** is set, but not **eofbit**:

```
if(!fin.eof() && (fin.fail() || fin.bad())) { // ...
```

Remember, an input operation can fail for many reasons. Encountering end-of-file is just one.

Because the I/O status flags stay set until cleared, encountering end-of-file will cause **good( )** to return false, even though you purposely caused the condition. You need to take this into account when watching for and handling errors. For example, after the end of the file has been encountered, you can use the **clear( )** function to reset the I/O flags. See *Checking for Errors* in the overview for details, including the **clear( )**, **good( )**, **bad( )**, and **fail( )** functions.

Example

The following example demonstrates **eof( )**. It creates a program that reads and displays the contents of a text file. It uses **eof( )** to know when all of the file has been read. Notice that it uses the **get( )** function defined by **istream**. It is described in *Use get( ) and getline( ) to Read from a File*.

```
// Use eof() to read and display a text file.
//
// The name of the file is specified on the command
```

```cpp
// line. For example, assuming that you call this program
// Show, the following command line will display the
// file called test.txt:
//
//    Show test.txt
//

#include <iostream>
#include <fstream>

using namespace std;

int main(int argc, char *argv[])
{
  char ch;

  if(argc != 2) {
    cout << "Usage: Show <filename>\n";
    return 1;
  }

  // Create an ifstream object and attempt to open the file.
  ifstream fin(argv[1]);

  // Verify that the file has been successfully opened.
  if(!fin) {
    cout << "Cannot open file.\n";
    return 1;
  }

  do {
    // Read the next character, if there is one.
    fin.get(ch);

    // Check for an error NOT caused by reaching EOF.
    if(!fin.eof() && (fin.fail() || fin.bad())) {
      cout << "Input Error\n";
      fin.close();
      return 1;
    }

    // If EOF not yet encountered, display the next character.
    if(!fin.eof()) cout << ch;
  } while(!fin.eof());

  // Clear the eof and fail bits.
  fin.clear();

  // Close the input file.
  fin.close();

  // Confirm that the file closed without error.
  if(!fin.good()) {
```

```
      cout << "Error closing file.";
      return 1;
    }

  return 0;
}
```

Notice that the program checks for input errors that are unrelated to an end-of-file condition. This lets the program report if something unexpected happened when reading the file. After end-of-file is encountered, the I/O status bits are cleared and the file is closed. This lets us confirm that the close operation succeeded without error. Of course, your own applications will dictate how you approach checking for errors. The foregoing program shows just one example.

Bonus Example: A Simple File-Comparison Utility

The following program puts **eof( )** to good use. It creates a simple file utility that compares two files. It opens both files for binary input. This means that the program can be used on both text and binary files, such as executable files. It compares the two files by reading a buffer of data from each by use of **read( )** and then comparing the contents of the buffers. It uses **eof( )** to determine when both files have been read to their completion. If the files are differing lengths, or if their contents don't match, the files differ. Otherwise, they are the same. Notice that the program uses the **gcount( )** function to determine how many bytes of data have been obtained by **read( )**. When input is performed at the end of the file, the number of bytes read may be less than requested in the call to **read( )**.

```
// A simple file-comparison utility.

#include <iostream>
#include <fstream>
using namespace std;

int main(int argc, char *argv[])
{
  bool equal = true;
  bool ferr = false;

  unsigned char buf1[1024], buf2[1024];

  if(argc!=3) {
    cout << "Usage: compfiles <file1> <file2>\n";
    return 1;
  }

  // Open both files for binary operations.
  ifstream f1(argv[1], ios::in | ios::binary);
  if(!f1) {
    cout << "Cannot open " << argv[1] << endl;
    return 1;
  }

  ifstream f2(argv[2], ios::in | ios::binary);
```

```
if(!f2) {
  cout << "Cannot open " << argv[2] << endl;
  f1.close();
  if(!f1.good())
    cout << "Error closing " << argv[1] << endl;
  return 1;
}

cout << "Comparing files...\n";

do {

  // Read a buffer full of data from both files.
  f1.read((char *) buf1, sizeof buf1);
  f2.read((char *) buf2, sizeof buf2);

  // Check for read errors.
  if(!f1.eof() && !f1.good()) {
    cout << "Error reading " << argv[1] << endl;
    ferr = true;
    break;
  }
  if(!f2.eof() && !f2.good()) {
    cout << "Error reading " << argv[2] << endl;
    ferr = true;
    break;
  }

  // If the two files differ in length, then at the
  // end of the file, the gcounts will be different.
  if(f1.gcount() != f2.gcount()) {
    cout << "Files are different lengths.\n";
    equal = false;
    break;
  }

  // Compare contents of buffers.
  for(int i=0; i < f1.gcount(); ++i)
    if(buf1[i] != buf2[i]) {
      cout << "Files differ.\n";
      equal = false;
      break;
    }

} while(!f1.eof() && !f2.eof() && equal);

if(!ferr && equal) cout << "Files are the same.\n";

// Clear eofbit, and possibly error bits.
f1.clear();
f2.clear();

f1.close();
```

```
  f2.close();

  if(!f1.good() || !f2.good()) {
    cout << "Error closing files.\n";
    return 1;
  }

  return 0;
}
```

Options and Alternatives

You can detect end-of-file in several other ways. First, you can use the **rdstate( )** function, which returns all of the status flags in the form of a bitmask. You can then test for end-of-file by OR-ing **ios::eofbit** with the value returned by **rdstate( )**. (The **rdstate( )** function is described in *Checking for Errors*.)

If you use this form of **get( )**

int get( )

then the value obtained from **ifstream::traits_type::eof( )** is returned when end-of-file is encountered. The **typedef traits_type** specifies values associated with the type of characters used by the stream, which are **char** in the case of **ifstream**. Therefore, when using this form of **get( )**, the following sequence detects end-of-file:

```
ch = fin.get();
if(ch == ifstream::traits_type::eof()) cout << "EOF found";
```

Of course, using the **eof( )** function defined by **ifstream** is much easier!

Use Exceptions to Detect and Handle I/O Errors

Key Ingredients		
Headers	**Classes**	**Functions**
<ios>	ios	void exceptions(iostate exc)
<ios>	ios_base::failure	const char *what( ) const

The C++ I/O system gives you two ways to watch for errors. First, you can use the functions **good( )**, **bad( )**, **fail( )**, and **rdstate( )** to explicitly interrogate the status flags. This approach is described in *Checking for Errors* in the overview at the start of this chapter. It is also the approach used by most of the recipes in this chapter because it is the way in which errors are detected by default. The second way involves the use of exceptions. In this approach, an I/O error causes an exception to be thrown. Your code can catch this exception and take appropriate action to handle the error. This recipe shows how to use exceptions to detect and handle I/O errors.

Step-by-Step

To detect and handle I/O errors through the use of exceptions involves the following steps:

1. On the stream that you want to monitor for errors, call the **exceptions( )** function, passing in an **iostate** bitmask that contains the flag or flags for the exception or exceptions that you want to generate errors.
2. Perform I/O operations from within a **try** block.
3. The **catch** statement of the **try** block must catch exceptions of type **failure**. This is the type of exception generated by the I/O system.
4. To determine what type of failure occurred, call **what( )** on the exception object.

Discussion

By default, the I/O system does not throw an exception when an error occurs. Therefore, to use exceptions, you must explicitly request the use of exceptions. Furthermore, you must specify what types of errors will throw an exception. To do this, you will use the **exceptions( )** function. This function is defined by **ios_base** and is inherited by all stream classes. It is shown here:

void exceptions(iostate *exc*)

Here, *exc* is a bitmask that contains **iostate** values that represent the conditions that will throw an exception. These values are **ios_base::failbit, ios_base::badbit, ios_base::goodbit,** and **ios_base::eofbit.** As it relates to **char**-based streams, these values are typically referred to as **ios::failbit, ios::badbit, ios::goodbit,** and **ios::eofbit.** Therefore, to cause a **char** stream called **mystream** to generate exceptions whenever an error causes **failbit** to be set, you can use the following:

```
mystream.exceptions(ios::failbit);
```

After this call, any time an I/O error causes **failbit** to be set, an exception is generated. One other point: As explained in *Checking for Errors* in the overview at the start of this chapter, end-of-file is not always considered an error in the strict sense, but you can use exceptions to watch for it.

Once you have turned on exceptions, you must perform I/O operations inside a **try** block that catches exceptions that have a base type of **ios_base::failure**. Notice that this class is a member class of **ios_base**. It is declared as shown here:

```
class ios_base::failure : public exception {
public:
   explicit failure(const string &str);
   virtual ~failure();
   virtual const char *what( ) const throw( );
};
```

Notice that it inherits **exception**, which is a base class for all exceptions. The **what( )** function returns a string that describes the exception. In theory, you might be able to use the string returned by **what( )** to determine what occurred. In practice, it's usually better to rely on your own program logic to perform this function, because the string returned by **what( )** may not be specific to the actual cause of the error. For example, it might just state which error bit was set. Furthermore, this string may (probably will) differ between compilers, or even between different versions of the same compiler. This is why it is often not particularly helpful.

Example

The following example shows how to use exceptions to handle errors when performing I/O. It reworks the example program from *Write Unformatted Binary Data to a File* so that it uses exceptions to detect and handle I/O errors. Notice that each I/O operation—opening the file, reading data, and closing the file—is performed within its own **try** block. This makes it easy to respond to each exception in an individualized manner. Of course, the approach that you use must be suited to your specific application and needs. Notice that the program uses the string returned by **what( )** to display the error. This is included simply for demonstration purposes. Except for debugging, you would not normally display this string.

```
// Use exceptions to watch for and handle I/O errors.
//
//  This program reworks the example program in:
//
//     Write Unformatted Binary Data to a File
//
// so that it uses exceptions to detect and handle I/O errors.

#include <iostream>
#include <fstream>
#include <cstring>

using namespace std;

// A simple inventory structure.
struct inventory {
  char item[20];
  int quantity;
  double cost;
};

int main()
{
  int completion_status = 0;

  // Create an output stream.
  ofstream fout;

  // Turn on exceptions for I/O errors.
  fout.exceptions(ios::failbit | ios::badbit);

  // Attempt to open the file for binary output.
```

```
  try {
    fout.open("InvDat.dat", ios::out | ios::binary);
  } catch(ios_base::failure exc) {
    cout << "Cannot open file.\n";
    cout << "String returned by what(): " << exc.what() << endl;
    return 1;
  }

  // Create some inventory data.
  inventory inv[3];

  strcpy(inv[0].item,"Hammers");
  inv[0].quantity = 3;
  inv[0].cost = 9.99;

  strcpy(inv[1].item, "Pliers");
  inv[1].quantity = 12;
  inv[1].cost = 7.85;

  strcpy(inv[2].item, "Wrenches");
  inv[2].quantity = 19;
  inv[2].cost = 2.75;

  // Write inventory data to the file. If an error occurs,
  // the exception will be handled by the catch statement.
  try {
    for(int i=0; i<3; i++)
      fout.write((const char *) &inv[i], sizeof(inventory));
  } catch(ios_base::failure exc) {
    cout << "An error occurred when writing to the file.\n";
    cout << "String returned by what(): " << exc.what() << endl;
    completion_status = 1;
  }

  // Also handle an error that might occur when closing the file.
  try {
    // Close the file.
    fout.close();
  } catch(ios_base::failure exc) {
    cout << "An error occurred when attempting to close the file.\n";
    cout << "String returned by what(): " << exc.what() << endl;
    completion_status = 1;
  }

  return completion_status;
}
```

There are some important points that need to be made about the preceding example. First, notice that if the file cannot be opened, then the program exits. This is proper, because if the file can't be opened, then it can't be written to and there is no reason to continue. Furthermore, because the file isn't open, it does not need to be closed. Therefore, it is proper to exit the program at this point.

Next, notice that the exception handler for **write( )** does not exit the program. Instead, it sets the **completion_status** variable to 1 and then lets program execution continue. At this point, even though an error has occurred, the file is still open and should be closed. Therefore, execution is allowed to continue on to the call to **close( )**.

It is important to understand that in this example, the file will be automatically closed when the program ends because **ofstream**'s destructor closes the file (as explained in the overview presented earlier in this chapter). However, in most real-world programs, the situation is not so easy. For example, if the user is allowed to retry a file operation, then it is imperative that you ensure that the previous attempt closed the file. Otherwise, problems will result. For example, it may become impossible to open the file again, since it was never closed. Also, the program will consume system resources, such as file handles, which are finite in number. The point is that since an exception causes an abrupt change in the normal flow of execution, it is necessary to ensure in such cases that any file that was opened is closed.

Options and Alternatives

As explained in *Checking for Errors*, you can watch for errors by using the functions **good( )**, **fail( )**, **rdstate( )**, and, in some cases, **eof( )**. Although the use of exceptions can simplify error handling in some cases, for many short programs, such as those in this book, the use of the error-reporting functions is easier. This is especially true when what you care about is that the overall I/O operation—opening, reading or writing, and closing—succeeded. For this reason, most of the programs in this book that perform file I/O will use the error-reporting functions and not exceptions. Of course, which approach you use is dictated by the specific aspects and needs of your application.

Use Random-Access File I/O

Key Ingredients		
Headers	**Classes**	**Functions**
<fstream>	ifstream	istream &seekg(off_type *offset*, ios::seekdir *origin*)
<fstream>	ofstream	ostream &seekp(off_type *offset*, ios::seekdir *origin*)

In general, there are two ways in which a file can be accessed: sequentially or randomly. With sequential access, the file pointer moves through the file in a strictly linear fashion, from start to finish. With random access, it is possible to position the file pointer at any location within the file. Thus, random access lets you read from or write to a specific portion of a file, as needed, on demand. It is important to understand that any file can be accessed in either fashion. Therefore, random access is not dependent upon the file, but rather the functions used to access the file. That said, usually, random access is used on a file that is comprised of fixed-length records. Through random access, it is possible to read or write a specific record. This recipe shows the techniques required to use random access in C++.

Step-by-Step

To use random access involves these steps:

1. Open the desired file for binary I/O.
2. For input files, move the get pointer by calling **seekg( )**.
3. For output files, move the put pointer by calling **seekp( )**.
4. For files capable of both input and output, use **seekg( )** to move the get pointer. Use **seekp( )** to move the put pointer.
5. Once the file location has been set, perform the desired operation.

Discussion

The C++ I/O system manages two pointers associated with a file. One is the *get pointer,* which specifies where in the file the next input operation will occur. The other is the *put pointer,* which specifies where in the file the next output operation will occur. Each time an input or output operation takes place, the appropriate pointer is automatically sequentially advanced. By using the random-access functions, you can position the get or put pointer at will, enabling the file to be accessed in nonsequential fashion.

The **seekg( )** and **seekp( )** functions change the location of the get and set pointers respectively. They each have two forms. The ones used by this recipe are shown here:

istream &seekg(off_type *offset*, ios::seekdir *origin*)

ostream &seekp(off_type *offset*, ios::seekdir *origin*)

Here, **off_type** is an integer type defined by **ios** that is capable of containing the largest valid value that *offset* can have. **seekdir** is an enumeration defined by **ios_base** (which is inherited by **ios**) that determines how the seek will take place.

The **seekg( )** function moves the associated file's get pointer *offset* number of characters from the specified *origin,* which must be one of these three values:

beg	Beginning-of-file
cur	Current location
end	End-of-file

The **seekp( )** function moves the associated file's current put pointer *offset* number of characters from the specified *origin,* which must be one of the values just shown.

The **seekp( )** function is declared by **ostream** and is inherited by **ofstream**. The **seekg( )** function is declared by **istream** and is inherited by **ifstream**. Both **istream** and **ostream** are inherited by **fstream**, which is capable of both input and output operations.

Generally, random-access I/O should be performed only on those files opened for binary operations. The character translations that may occur on text files could cause a position request to be out of sync with the actual contents of the file.

When a file is opened for both read and write operations, such as when using an **fstream** object, then you must usually perform a seek operation when switching between reading and writing. (See *Read from and Write to a File*.)

Example

The following program uses both **seekp( )** and **seekg( )** to reverse characters in a file. The name of the file and the number of characters to reverse, starting from the beginning, is specified on the command line. Because both read and write operations are needed, the file is opened using **fstream**, which is capable of both input and output.

```
// Demonstrate random-access I/O.
//
// This program reverses the first N characters within a
// file. The name of the file and the number of characters
// to reverse are specified on the command line.

#include <iostream>
#include <fstream>
#include <cstdlib>

using namespace std;

int main(int argc, char *argv[])
{
  long n, i, j;
  char ch1, ch2;

  if(argc!=3) {
    cout << "Usage: Reverse <filename> <num>\n";
    return 1;
  }

  // Open the file for binary input and output operations.
  fstream finout(argv[1], ios::in | ios::out | ios::binary);

  if(!finout) {
    cout << "Cannot open input file.\n";
    return 1;
  }

  // Convert the string representation of the number of
  // characters to reverse into a long value.
  n = atol(argv[2]) - 1;

  // Use random access to reverse the characters.
  for(i=0, j=n; i < j; ++i, --j) {

    // First, get the two characters.
```

```
      finout.seekg(i, ios::beg);
      finout.get(ch1);
      finout.seekg(j, ios::beg);
      finout.get(ch2);

      // Now, write them to the opposite locations.
      finout.seekp(i, ios::beg);
      finout.put(ch2);
      finout.seekp(j, ios::beg);
      finout.put(ch1);

      // Confirm the success of each read/write cycle.
      if(!finout.good()) {
        cout << "Error reading or writing characters.";
        finout.clear();
        break;
      }
    }

    // Close the file.
    finout.close();

    // Confirm that no errors occurred when closing the file.
    if(!finout.good()) {
      cout << "A file error occurred.";
      return 1;
    }

    return 0;
}
```

To use the program, specify the name of the file that you want to reverse, followed by the number of characters to reverse. For example, to reverse the first ten characters of a file called TEST, use this command line:

```
reverse test 10
```

If the file had contained:

```
abcdefghijklmnopqrstuvwxyz
```

then the file will contain the following after the program executes:

```
jihgfedcbaklmnopqrstuvwxyz
```

Bonus Example: Use Random-Access I/O to Access Fixed-Size Records

As mentioned, one of the main uses of random-access I/O is on databases that contain fixed-size records. For example, consider a database that contains inventory information. To find a specific entry in that file, you will need to scan it record by record. You may also want to update a specific record or delete a record. These types of operations are made easy through the use of random-access I/O. The following example gives you an idea of the process.

It uses the **InvDat.dat** created by the example program in *Write Unformatted Binary Data to a File*. It displays the entry that you specify by number on the command line.

```
// Use random-access I/O to read specific inventory records
// from a data file. This program reads the file InvDat.dat,
// which is created by the example program in the recipe:
//
//    Write Unformatted Binary Data to a File

#include <iostream>
#include <fstream>
#include <cstdlib>

using namespace std;

// A simple inventory structure.
struct inventory {
  char item[20];
  int quantity;
  double cost;
};

int main(int argc, char *argv[])
{
  inventory entry;
  long record_num;

  if(argc != 2) {
    cout << "Usage: ShowRecord <record-num>\n";
    return 1;
  }

  // Convert the string representation of the entry
  // number into a long value.
  record_num = atol(argv[1]);

  // Confirm that the record number is greater than or
  // equal to zero.
  if(record_num < 0) {
    cout << "Record numbers must be greater than or equal to 0.\n";
    return 1;
  }

  // Open the file for binary input.
  ifstream fInvDB("InvDat.dat", ios::in | ios::binary);

  // Confirm that the file opened without error.
  if(!fInvDB) {
    cout << "Cannot open file.\n";
    return 1;
  }

  // Read and display the entry specified on the command line.
```

```
  // First, seek to the desired record.
  fInvDB.seekg(sizeof(inventory) * record_num, ios::beg);

  // Next, read the record.
  fInvDB.read((char *) &entry, sizeof(inventory));

  // Close the file.
  fInvDB.close();

  // Confirm that there were no file errors.
  if(!fInvDB.good()) {
    cout << "A file error occurred.\n";
    return 1;
  }

  // Display the inventory for the specified entry.
  cout << entry.item << endl;
  cout << "Quantity on hand: " << entry.quantity;
  cout << "\nCost: " << entry.cost << endl;

  return 0;
}
```

Here is a sample run:

```
C:>ShowRecord 1
Pliers
Quantity on hand: 12
Cost: 7.85
```

The key feature of the program is the use of **seekg( )** to move to the specified record through the use of this statement:

```
fInvDB.seekg(sizeof(inventory) * record_num, ios::beg);
```

To find a specific record, it first multiplies the size of the **inventory** structure (which is the length of each record in the database) by the number of the record to obtain. It then seeks to this location in the file. The same basic approach can be applied to any file that contains fixed-length records.

Using random access, it is also possible to update a record in place. For example, in the preceding program, if you open the file for both input and output by using an **fstream** object, as shown here:

```
fstream fInvDB("InvDat.dat",
               ios_base::in | ios_base::binary | ios::out);
```

then the following sequence changes the specified record and then reads the updated information:

```
// Create a new inventory item.
strcpy(entry.item, "Drill");
entry.quantity = 3;
entry.cost = 9.99;
```

```
// Set the put pointer at the start of the record by calling seekp().
fInvDB.seekp(sizeof(inventory) * record_num, ios::beg);

// Change the record.
fInvDB.write((char *) &entry, sizeof(inventory));

// Set the get pointer to the start of the record by calling seekg().
fInvDB.seekg(sizeof(inventory) * record_num, ios::beg);

// Next, read the updated record.
fInvDB.read((char *) &entry, sizeof(inventory));
```

Options and Alternatives

You can determine the current position of each file pointer by using these functions:

pos_type tellg( )

pos_type tellp( )

Here, **pos_type** is a type defined by **basic_ios** that is capable of holding the largest value that either function can return. You can use the values returned by **tellg( )** and **tellp( )** as arguments to the following forms of **seekg( )** and **seekp( )**, respectively:

istream &seekg(pos_type *pos)*

ostream &seekp(pos_type *pos)*

These functions allow you to save the current file location, perform other file operations, and then reset the file location to its previously saved position.

Look Ahead in a File

Key Ingredients		
Headers	**Classes**	**Functions**

<fstream>	ifstream	istream &ignore(streamsize *num*=1,
		                        int_type *delim* =
		                        traits_type::eof( ))

		int_type peek( )
		istream &unget( )

There are some input situations that are made easier by being able to look ahead in a file. For example, if a file contains context-sensitive information, then you might need to process one part of it differently than you do another. C++ provides three functions that aid in this task: **peek( )**, **unget( )**, and **ignore( )**. They enable you to obtain but not remove the next character in the file, return a character to the stream, and skip over one or more characters. This recipe shows how they are used.

Step-by-Step

File look-ahead involves the following steps:

1. To obtain but not remove the next character from the input stream, call **peek( )**.
2. To return a character to the input stream, call **unget( )**.
3. To ignore characters until a specific character is encountered or a specific number of characters is ignored, call **ignore( )**.

Discussion

You can obtain the next character in the input stream without removing it from that stream by using **peek( )**. It has this prototype:

    int_type peek( )

It returns the next character in the stream or the end-of-file indicator if end-of-file is encountered, which is **traits_type::eof( )**. The **int_type** type is a **typedef** for some form of integer.

You can return the last character read from a stream back to that stream by using **unget( )**. This lets the character be read by the next input operation. The **unget( )** function is shown here:

    istream &unget( )

If no characters have yet been read from the stream, an error occurs and **badbit** is set. The function returns a reference to the stream.

The **ignore( )** function reads and discards characters from the input stream. It has this prototype:

    istream &ignore(streamsize *num*=1, int_type *delim*=traits_type::eof( ))

It reads and discards characters until either *num* characters have been ignored (1 by default) or until the character specified by *delim* is encountered. By default, *delim* is **traits_type::eof( )**. If the delimiting character is encountered, it is removed from the input stream. If end-of-file is encountered, then the **eofbit** status flag associated with the stream is set. The **streamsize** type is a **typedef** for some form of integer that is capable of holding the largest number of bytes that can be transferred in any one I/O operation. The type **int_type** is a **typedef** for some form of integer. The function returns a reference to the stream.

Of the three functions, the one that is the most interesting is **ignore( )** because it gives you an easy and efficient way to search a stream for an occurrence of a character. Once this character has been found, you can begin reading (or writing) the stream at that point. This can be very useful in a number of situations. For example, if you have a stream that contains employee ID numbers in the form #dddd (such as #2244), then you can easily search for an ID number by ignoring characters until a # is found.

Example

The following example shows **peek( )**, **unget( )**, and **ignore( )** in action. The program first creates a data file called **test.dat** that contains several employee IDs. However, there are two types of IDs. The first is a four-digit number in the form #dddd, such as #0101. The second ID is a placeholder that uses a word to describe why the ID number is missing. The program then looks for, reads, and displays all IDs in the file. To accomplish this, it makes use of file look-ahead.

```
// Demonstrate peek(), unget(), and ignore().
//
// This program reads a file that contains two types
// of IDs. The first is a four-digit number in this
// form: #dddd. The second is a word that describes
// why the ID number is missing. The program creates
// a data file called test.dat that contains several
// ID numbers. The program then looks for, reads, and
// displays all IDs in the file.

#include <iostream>
#include <fstream>
#include <cctype>

using namespace std;

int main()
{
  char ch;
  char idnum[5];

  // Null-terminate idnum so that it can hold a char * string.
  idnum[4] = 0;

  // Create an ofstream object and attempt to open the file test.dat.
  ofstream fout("test.dat");

  // Verify that the file has been successfully opened.
  if(!fout) {
    cout << "Cannot open test.dat for output.\n";
    return 1;
  }

  // Write some information to the file.
  fout << "Tom Tommy #5345\nRalph Rolof #denied\nTed Terry #6922\n";
  fout << "Harry Holden #pending\n, Skip Jones, #8875\n";

  // Close the output file.
  fout.close();

  if(!fout.good()) {
    cout << "Error creating data file.";
    return 1;
  }
```

```
// Attempt to open the test.dat file.
ifstream fin("test.dat");

if(!fin) {
  cout << "Cannot open test.dat for input.\n";
  return 1;
}

// Use exceptions to watch for errors.
fin.exceptions(ios::badbit | ios::failbit);

try {

  // Find and display all ID numbers:
  do {
    // Find the start of an ID number.
    fin.ignore(40, '#');

    // If the end of the file is encountered, stop reading.
    if(fin.eof()) {
      fin.clear(); // clear eofbit
      break;
    }

    // Obtain but don't extract the next character after the #.
    ch = fin.peek();

    // See if the next character is a digit.
    if(isdigit(ch)) {

      // If the character is a digit, read the ID number. Because
      // idnum has a null in its fifth character, reading four
      // characters into the first four elements creates a
      // null-terminated string.
      fin.read((char *)idnum, 4);

      cout << "ID #: " << idnum << endl;

    } else {

      // Since the next char is not a digit, read the description.
      cout << "ID not available: ";

      ch = fin.get();
      while(isalpha(ch)) {
        cout << ch;
        ch = fin.get();
      };

      // Put back the non-letter char so that it can be found
      // and processed by other get() statements.
      fin.unget();
```

```
        cout << endl;
      }
    } while(fin.good());
  } catch(ios_base::failure exc) {
    cout << "Error reading data file.\n";
  }

  try {
    // Close test.dat for input.
    fin.close();
  } catch (ios_base::failure exc) {
    cout << "Error closing data file.";
    return 1;
  }

  return 0;

}
```

The output is shown here:

```
ID #: 5345
ID not available: denied
ID #: 6922
ID not available: pending
ID #: 8875
```

This program uses look-ahead to read the IDs in the file. First, it uses **ignore( )** to find a # character. This character marks the start of an ID. It then uses **peek( )** to determine if what follows is an actual ID number or a verbal description. If the character obtained from **peek( )** is a digit, a four-digit number is read. Otherwise, the description is read. The description ends as soon as a non-alphabetic character is read. In this case, the last character read is put back into the input stream.

One other point of interest: Notice that the program uses a combination of exceptions and error-detecting functions to watch for errors. This is part of the power of the C++ I/O system: You can use whatever approach works best for the situation at hand.

Options and Alternatives

As explained, **unget( )** returns the most recently read character to the invoking stream. You can "return" a character other than the one most recently read by calling **putback( )**. It is shown here:

   istream &putback(char *ch*)

It puts *ch* into the stream so that it will be the first character read by the next input operation. If an error occurs, **badbit** is set on the invoking stream.

Another function that is sometimes useful in look-ahead situations is **readsome( )**. Essentially, it reads characters from the input buffer. If there are not enough characters in the buffer to fulfill the request, then **eofbit** is set on the invoking stream. The function is shown here:

   streamsize readsome(char **buf*, streamsize *num*)

It attempts to read *num* characters from the input buffer, storing them in *buf*. It returns the number of characters actually read.

Another function that can be useful when looking ahead in a file (and for many other purposes) is **gcount( )**. It is shown here:

    streamsize gcount( ) const

It returns the number of characters read by a previous call to an unformatted input function.

Use the String Streams

Key Ingredients		
Headers	**Classes**	**Functions**
<sstream>	istringstream ostringstream stringstream	string str( ) const

As explained in *I/O Overview*, C++ supports the use of a string as a source or destination for I/O operations. To enable this, it defines three string stream template classes called **basic_istringstream**, **basic_ostringstream**, and **basic_stringstream**. Their **char**-based forms are shown here:

istringstream	Uses a **string** for input.
ostringstream	Uses a **string** for output.
stringstream	Uses a **string** for input and output.

In general, the string stream classes work like the other stream classes, the only difference being that the source or destination for data is a **string** rather than some external device. This recipe demonstrates their use.

Step-by-Step
Using a string stream involves these steps:

1. Create a string stream by using one of the string stream constructors.
2. Perform I/O on the stream in the same way as you would using any other type of stream, such as a file stream.
3. To obtain the contents of a string buffer, call **str( )**.

Discussion

To create a string stream, you will use one of the string stream constructors. Each string stream defines two constructors: one that initializes the string stream with a string and another that doesn't. When performing input, you will usually initialize the string. For output, you will often not need to initialize the string. For input/output situations, whether you initialize the string depends on your application.

The **istringstream** constructor used by this recipe is shown here:

explicit istringstream(const string &*buf*, ios::openmode *mode* = ios::in)

It creates a **char**-based input stream based on a string. It initializes that string with the contents of *buf*. Therefore, read operations will obtain the characters passed via *buf*.

The **ostringstream** constructor used by this recipe is shown here:

explicit ostringstream(ios::openmode *mode* = ios::out)

It creates a **char**-based output stream based on a string. All write operations will put characters into a string maintained by **ostringstream**.

The **stringstream** constructor used by this recipe is shown here:

explicit stringstream(ios::openmode *mode* = ios::in | ios::out)

It creates a **char**-based string stream capable of input and output. The buffer is not initialized. When switching between reading and writing, you must usually perform a seek or flush operation. (See *Read from and Write to a File*.)

You can obtain the current contents of the string by calling this version of **str( )**:

string str( ) const

It returns a copy of the contents of the current string buffer.

One other point: It is not necessary to close a string stream. In fact, the string stream classes do not define either an **open( )** or **close( )** function. This is because the string stream classes do not operate on external devices. They simply treat a string as the source of input or the destination of output for the stream. This is also why it is not necessary to confirm that a string stream was successfully created before using it.

Example

The following example shows the string stream classes in action.

```
// Use a string stream.

#include <iostream>
#include <sstream>

using namespace std;

int main()
{
  char ch;
```

```
// Create an output string stream.
ostringstream strout;

cout << "Use an output string stream called strout.\n";

// Write output to the string stream..
strout << 10 << " " << -20 << " " << 30.2 << "\n";
strout << "This is a test.";

// Now, obtain a copy of the current contents of the stream buffer
// and use it to display the contents of the buffer.
cout << "The current contents of strout as obtained from str():\n"
     << strout.str() << endl;

// Write some more to strout.
strout << "\nThis is some more output.\n";

cout << endl;

cout << "Use an input string stream called strin.\n";

// Now, use the contents of strout to create strin:
istringstream strin(strout.str());

// Display the contents of strin via calls to get().
cout << "Here are the current contents of strin via get():\n";
do {
  ch = strin.get();
  if(!strin.eof()) cout << ch;
} while(!strin.eof());

cout << endl;


// Now create string stream for input/output.
cout << "Now, use an input/output string stream called strinout.\n";

stringstream strinout;

// Write some output to strinout.
strinout << 10 << " + " << 12 << " is " << 10+12 << endl;

// Now, display the contents of strinout via get().
cout << "Here are the current contents of strinout via get():\n";
do {
  ch = strinout.get();
  if(!strinout.eof()) cout << ch;
} while(!strinout.eof());
cout << endl;

// Clear eofbit on strinout.
strinout.clear();
```

```
    strinout << "More output to strinout.\n";

    // The following will continue reading from the point
    // at which the previous reads stopped.
    cout << "Here are the characters just added to strinout:\n";
    do {
      ch = strinout.get();
      if(!strinout.eof()) cout << ch;
    } while(!strinout.eof());
}
```

The output is shown here:

```
Use an output string stream called strout.
The current contents of strout as obtained from str():
10 -20 30.2
This is a test.

Use an input string stream called strin.
Here are the current contents of strin via get():
10 -20 30.2
This is a test.
This is some more output.

Now, use an input/output string stream called strinout.
Here are the current contents of strinout via get():
10 + 12 is 22

Here are the characters just added to strinout:
More output to strinout.
```

Options and Alternatives

When creating an **ostringstream** instance, it is possible to initialize the buffer with a character sequence by using this version of its constructor:

> explicit ostringstream(const string &*buf*, ios::openmode *mode* = ios::out)

Here, the contents of *buf* will be copied into the output buffer.

When creating an **istringstream** instance, it is not necessary to initialize the input buffer with a character sequence. (You can set the contents of the string stream buffer after the fact by calling a second form of **str( )**, shown shortly.) Here is the version of the **istringstream** that does not initialize the input buffer:

> explicit istringstream(ios::openmode *mode* = ios::in)

Notice that only the *mode* is specified, and it defaults to input.

For **stringstream**, you can initialize the buffer with a known character sequence by using this form of its constructor:

> explicit stringstream(const string *buf*, ios::openmode *mode* = ios::in | ios::out)

The contents of *buf* are copied into the buffer associated with the **stringstream** object.

For all three string stream classes, you can set the contents of the buffer by calling this form of **str( )**:

void str(const string &*buf*)

It reinitializes the buffer with the contents of *buf.*

Create Custom Inserters and Extractors

Key Ingredients		
Headers	**Classes**	**Functions**
<ostream>	ostream	ostream &operator<<(ostream &stream, const *class_type* &*obj*)
<istream>	istream	istream &operator>>(istream &stream, *class_type* &*obj*)

In the language of C++, the **<<** output operator is referred to as the *insertion operator* because it inserts characters into a stream. Likewise, the **>>** input operator is called the *extraction operator* because it extracts characters from a stream. The operator functions that overload the insertion and extraction operators are generally called *inserters* and *extractors*, respectively. The C++ I/O classes overload the inserter and extractor operators for all of the built-in types. However, it is also possible to create your own overloaded versions of these operators for class types that you create. This recipe shows the procedure.

Step-by-Step

To overload an inserter for class objects involves these steps:

1. Overload the **<<** operator so that it takes a reference to an **ostream** in its first parameter and a **const** reference to the object to output in the second parameter.

2. Implement the inserter so that it outputs the object in the manner that you desire.

3. Have the inserter return the stream reference.

4. Typically, you will make the inserter a friend of the class on which it is operating so that it has access to the private members of the class.

To overload an extractor for class objects involves these steps:

1. Overload the **>>** operator so that it takes a reference to an **istream** in its first parameter and a reference to the object receiving input in the second parameter.

2. Implement the extractor so that it reads the input stream and stores the data in an object of the class.

3. Have the extractor return the stream reference.

4. Typically, you will make the extractor a friend of the class on which it is operating so that it has access to the private members of the class.

Discussion

It is quite simple to create an inserter for a class that you create. Here is a typical general form for an inserter:

```
ostream &operator<<(ostream &stream, const class_type &obj)
{
    // body of inserter
    return stream;
}
```

Notice that the function returns a reference to a stream of type **ostream**. Further, the first parameter to the function is a reference to the output stream. The second parameter is a **const** reference to the object being inserted. Technically, the second parameter can receive a copy of the object (that is, it can be a value parameter), and it need not be **const**. However, most often when an object is output, it is not altered, and passing by reference is usually faster than passing by value. Therefore, usually, the second parameter is a **const** reference to the object. Of course, this is governed by the specific situation. In all cases, the inserter must return *stream*. This allows the inserter to be used in a larger I/O expression.

Within an inserter function, you may put any type of procedures or operations that you want. That is, precisely how the inserter outputs the object is completely up to you. In all cases, though, for the inserter to be in keeping with good programming practices, it should not produce side effects. Therefore, it should not modify the object. It should also not perform operations that are unrelated to insertion. For example, having an inserter recycle unused memory as a side effect to an insertion operation is probably not a very good idea!

Extractors are the complement of inserters. They store input in an object. The general form of an extractor function is:

```
istream &operator>>(istream &stream, class_type &obj)
{
    // body of extractor
    return stream;
}
```

Extractors return a reference to a stream of type **istream**, which is an input stream. The first parameter must also be a reference to a stream of type **istream**. Notice that the second parameter must be a reference to an object of the class for which the extractor is overloaded. This is so the object can be modified by the input (extraction) operation.

Like inserters, an extractor should confine its operation to reading data from the input stream and storing it in the specified object. It should not generate side effects. Nor should it read more input than that needed by the object. For example, an extractor should not normally read a trailing space.

In many cases, you will want to make the inserter or extractor a friend of the class for which it is overloaded. Doing so grants it access to the private members of the class. This might be required to obtain data for output or to store data from input. Of course, this may not be possible if you are creating an inserter or extractor for a class to which you do not have the source code, such as a third-party class.

Example

The following shows examples of a custom inserter and extractor. It creates a class called **ThreeD**, which stores three-dimensional coordinates. It uses a custom inserter to output the coordinates. It uses a custom extractor to read the coordinates.

```
// Demonstrate a custom inserter and extractor for objects
// of type ThreeD.

#include <iostream>

using namespace std;

class ThreeD {
  int x, y, z; // 3-D coordinates
public:
  ThreeD(int a, int b, int c) { x = a; y = b; z = c; }

  // Make the inserter and extractor friends of ThreeD.
  friend ostream &operator<<(ostream &stream, const ThreeD &obj);
  friend istream &operator>>(istream &stream, ThreeD &obj);

  // ...
};

// ThreeD inserter. Display the X, Y, Z coordinates.
ostream &operator<<(ostream &stream, const ThreeD &obj)
{
  stream << obj.x << ", ";
  stream << obj.y << ", ";
  stream << obj.z << "\n";
  return stream;  // return the stream
}

// ThreeD extractor. Get three-dimensional values.
istream &operator>>(istream &stream, ThreeD &obj)
{
  stream >> obj.x >> obj.y >> obj.z;
  return stream;
}

int main()
{
  ThreeD td(1, 2, 3);

  cout << "The coordinates in td: " << td << endl;

  cout << "Enter new three-d coordinates: ";
  cin >> td;
```

```
    cout << "The coordinates in td are now: " << td << endl;

    return 0;
}
```

A sample run is shown here:

```
The coordinates in td: 1, 2, 3

Enter new three-d coordinates: 9 8 7
The coordinates in td are now: 9, 8, 7
```

Options and Alternatives

As mentioned, when creating an inserter, it's not technically necessary to pass the object being output by reference. In some cases, you might want to use a value parameter instead. This might make sense when operating on very small objects in which the amount of time it takes to push the object on the stack (which is what happens when an argument is passed by value) is less than the amount of time it takes to push the address of the object (which is what happens when an object is passed by reference).

Create a Parameterless Manipulator

Key Ingredients		
Headers	**Classes**	**Functions**
<istream>	istream	istream &*manip-name*(istream &*strm*)
<ostream>	ostream	ostream &*manip-name*(ostream &*strm*)

I/O manipulators are functions that are embedded within an I/O expression. They either affect the underlying stream, such as by changing its format flags, or they insert characters into or extract characters from the stream. Because they operate within an I/O expression, manipulators streamline the coding of many tasks. C++ supplies many built-in manipulators, and they are described in Chapter 6, where recipes related to formatting data are presented. It is, however, also possible to create your own custom manipulators.

Typically, a custom manipulator is used to consolidate a sequence of separate I/O operations into a single step. For example, it is not uncommon to have situations in which the same sequence of I/O operations occurs frequently within a program. In these cases, you can use a custom manipulator to perform these actions, thus simplifying your source code and preventing errors. Here is another example: You may need to perform I/O operations on a nonstandard device. For example, you might use a manipulator to send control codes to a special type of printer or to an optical recognition system. A custom manipulator can simplify this process by allowing you to send the codes by name. Whatever the purposes, custom manipulators are popular extensions to the C++ I/O system.

There are two basic types of manipulators: those that operate on input streams and those that operate on output streams. In addition to these two broad categories, there is a secondary division: those manipulators that take an argument and those that don't. The techniques used to create parameterless manipulators differ from those used to create parameterized manipulators. This recipe shows how to create parameterless custom manipulators. The following recipe shows one way to create parameterized manipulators.

Step-by-Step

To create your own parameterless output manipulator involves these steps:

1. Create a function that takes a reference to an **ostream** object as a parameter and returns a reference to an **ostream**.
2. Inside that function, perform actions on the **ostream** passed as an argument.
3. Return a reference to the **ostream** argument.

To create your own parameterless input manipulator involves these steps:

1. Create a function that takes a reference to an **istream** object as a parameter and returns a reference to an **istream**.
2. Inside that function, perform actions on the **istream** passed as an argument.
3. Return a reference to the **istream** argument.

Discussion

All parameterless output manipulator functions have this skeleton:

```
ostream &manip-name(ostream &stream)
{
  // your code here
  return stream;
}
```

Here, *manip-name* is the name of the manipulator and *stream* is a reference to the output stream on which the manipulator will operate. Notice that *stream* is also returned. This is necessary to allow the manipulator to be used as part of a larger I/O expression. It is important to note that even though the manipulator has as its single argument a reference to the stream upon which it is operating, no argument is used when the manipulator is inserted in an output operation.

All parameterless input manipulators have this skeleton:

```
istream &manip-name(istream &stream)
{
  // your code here
  return stream;
}
```

An input manipulator receives a reference to the stream for which it was invoked. This stream must be returned by the manipulator. Even though the manipulator takes an **istream** argument, no arguments are passed when the manipulator is invoked.

Once you have defined a manipulator, you can use it by simply specifying its name in an insertion or extraction expression. The reason this works is that the >> and << operators are overloaded to accept a function pointer that has a stream reference as its only parameter. The overloaded << and >> operators are implemented such that they call the function, through the pointer, passing in a reference to the stream. This process lets your custom manipulator receive a reference to the stream that it will be affecting.

It is important to understand that (except in highly unusual cases) your manipulator must operate on the stream passed to it. A common mistake that beginners make is to hardcode a reference to a stream, such as **cout**, rather than use the stream passed to the parameter. The trouble is that your manipulator will work correctly in some cases and fail in others. Although such an error is usually easy to find and correct, it can occasionally be daunting, depending on what stream you hardcoded. The rule is easy: A manipulator must operate on the stream that it is passed.

Example

The following example shows both an input and an output custom manipulator. The output manipulator is called **star_fill( )**. It specifies the asterisk (*) as the fill character and sets the field width to 10. Therefore, after a call to **star_fill( )**, the number 1234 is displayed as ******1234. (For information on formatting data, see Chapter 6.) The input manipulator is called **skip_digits( )**. It skips leading digits in the input stream. Therefore, if the input stream contains 9786ABC0101, then **skip_digits( )** reads and discards the leading 9786, leaving ABC0101 in the input stream.

```
// Demonstrate a custom output manipulator called star_fill() and
// a custom input manipulator called skip_digits().

#include <iostream>
#include <iomanip>
#include <string>
#include <cctype>

using namespace std;

// A simple output manipulator that sets the fill character
// to * and sets the field width to 10.
ostream &star_fill(ostream &stream) {

  stream << setfill('*') << setw(10);

  return stream;
}

// A simple input manipulator that skips leading digits.
istream &skip_digits(istream &stream) {
  char ch;

  do {
    ch = stream.get();
```

```
  } while(!stream.eof() && isdigit(ch));
  if(!stream.eof()) stream.unget();

  return stream;
}

int main()
{
  string str;

  // Demonstrate the custom output manipulator.
  cout << 512 << endl;
  cout << star_fill << 512 << endl;

  // Demonstrate the custom input manipulator.
  cout << "Enter some characters: ";
  cin >> skip_digits >> str;
  cout << "Contents of str: " << str;

  return 0;
}
```

Here is a sample run:

```
512
*******512
Enter some characters: 123ABC
Contents of str: ABC
```

Options and Alternatives

If you have correctly coded your custom manipulator so that it operates on the stream that
it was passed, then it can be used on any type of stream. For example, in the preceding
program, you can use **star_fill( )** on a file stream or a string stream. To confirm this, add the
following sequence to the program. It uses **star_fill( )** on an **ostringstream** and an **ofstream**.

```
  // Use star_fill() on a stringstream.
  ostringstream ostrstrm;
  ostrstrm << star_fill << 29;
  cout << ostrstrm.str();

  // Use star_fill on an ofstream.
  ofstream fout("test.dat");
  if(!fout) {
    cout << "Error opening file.\n";
    return 1;
  }
  fout << star_fill << 19;
```

After recompiling, you will see that **star_fill( )** works correctly on both **ostrstrm** and **fout**.

You can also create parameterized manipulators. The process is the subject of the
next recipe.

Create a Parameterized Manipulator

Key Ingredients		
Headers	**Classes**	**Functions and Fields**
<istream>	istream	istream &operator>>(istream &*stream*, *manip-class mc*)
<ostream>	ostream	ostream &operator<<(ostream &*stream*, *manip-class mc*)
	manip-class	user-defined

As the previous recipe shows, it is very easy to create a parameterless manipulator. The reason is that **<<** or **>>** are overloaded for (among many other things) a function pointer. As explained in the preceding recipe, when a parameterless manipulator is used, a pointer to it is passed to the overloaded inserter or extractor and the function is called, with the stream being passed as an argument. Unfortunately, this simple mechanism will not work for a manipulator that requires an argument because there is no way to pass the argument via the function pointer. As a result, the creation of a parameterized manipulator relies on a fundamentally different mechanism, which is a bit more complicated. Furthermore, there are various ways to implement a parameterized manipulator. This recipe shows one relatively easy, straightforward way.

Step-by-Step

To create a parameterized output manipulator involves these steps:

1. Create a class whose name is the name of the manipulator. For example, if the name of the manipulator is **mymanip**, then the name of the class is **mymanip**.

2. Create a private field in the class that will hold the argument passed to the manipulator. The type of the field must be the same as the type of data that will be passed to the manipulator.

3. Create a constructor for the class that has one parameter, which is the same type as the type of the data that will be passed to the manipulator. Have the constructor initialize the value of the field from Step 2 with the value passed to the constructor.

4. Create an overloaded inserter that takes an **ostream** reference as its first argument and an object of the class from Step 1 as its second argument. Inside this function, perform the manipulator's actions. Return a reference to the stream.

5. Make the overloaded inserter a friend of the class from Step 1.

6. To use the manipulator, use the class' constructor in the output expression, passing in the desired argument. This will cause an object to be constructed, and then the overloaded inserter will be called, using that object as the right-hand operand.

To create a parameterized input manipulator involves these steps:

1. Create a class whose name is the name of the manipulator. For example, if the name of the manipulator is **mymanip**, then the name of the class is **mymanip**.

2. Create a private field in the class that will hold the argument passed to the manipulator. The type of the field must be the same as the type of data that will be passed to the manipulator.

3. Create a constructor for the class that has one parameter, which is the same type as the type of the data that will be passed to the manipulator. Have the constructor initialize the value of the field from Step 2 with the value passed to the constructor.

4. Create an overloaded extractor that takes an **istream** reference as its first argument and an object of the class from Step 1 as its second argument. Inside this function, perform the manipulator's actions. Return a reference to the stream.

5. Make the overloaded extractor a friend of the class from Step 1.

6. To use the manipulator, use the class' constructor in the input expression, passing in the desired argument. This will cause an object to be constructed, and then the overloaded extractor will be called, using that object as the right-hand operand.

Discussion

In general, creating a parameterized manipulator involves two items. The first is a class that stores the argument passed to the manipulator. The second is an inserter or extractor that is overloaded to take an object of that class as the right-hand operand. When the manipulator is included in an I/O expression, an object of the class is constructed, with the argument being saved. The inserter or extractor then operates on that object and is able to access the argument.

Let's work through this step by step, creating a simple parameterized inserter called **indent**, which indents output by a specified number of spaces. For example, the expression

```
cout << indent(10) << "Hi";
```

will cause ten spaces to be output, followed by the string "Hi". As explained, all parameterized manipulators need two items. The first is a class that stores the argument passed to the manipulator. Therefore, to create the **indent** manipulator, begin by creating a class called **indent** that stores the argument passed to its constructor and specifies an overloaded inserter as a friend, as shown here:

```
// A class that supports the indent output manipulator.
class indent {
  int len;
public:
  indent(int i) { len = i; }
  friend ostream &operator<<(ostream &stream, indent ndt);
};
```

As you can see, the constructor takes one argument, which it stores in the private field **len**. This is the only functionality that **indent** provides. It simply stores the argument. It does, however, declare **operator<<( )** to be a friend. This gives the operator function access to the private **len** field.

The second item you need to create is an overloaded inserter that takes an **indent** instance as a right-hand operand. (See *Create Custom Inserters and Extractors* for details on creating an inserter or extractor.) Have this operator output the number of spaces specified by the **len** field of the object on which it is operating. Here is one way to implement this function:

```
// Create an inserter for objects of type indent.
ostream &operator<<(ostream &stream, indent ndt) {

  for(int i=0; i <  ndt.len; ++i) stream << " ";

  return stream;
}
```

As you can see, this operator takes an **ostream** reference as its left-hand operand and an **indent** object as its right-hand operand. It outputs the number of spaces specified by the **indent** object and then returns the stream. Because **operator<<( )** is a friend of **indent**, it can access the **len** field, even though it is private.

When **indent** is used within an output expression, it causes an object of type **indent** to be created with the specified argument. Then, the overloaded **operator<<( )** function is invoked, passing in the stream and the newly created **indent** object.

Example

The following example shows both a parameterized input and a parameterized output manipulator. The input manipulator is called **skipchar**, and on input, it skips leading characters that match the one passed to **skipchar**. For example, **skipchar('X')** skips leading X's. The output manipulator is **indent**, described in the *Discussion* section for this recipe.

```
// Create simple parameterized input and output manipulators.
//
// The indent manipulator outputs a specified number of spaces.
// The skipchar manipulator skips a specified character on input.

#include <iostream>
#include <string>
#include <sstream>

using namespace std;

// Together, the following class and overloaded operator create
// the indent manipulator.

// A class that supports the indent output manipulator.
class indent {
  int len;
public:
  indent(int i) { len = i; }
  friend ostream &operator<<(ostream &stream, indent ndt);
};
```

```
// Create an inserter for objects of type indent.
ostream &operator<<(ostream &stream, indent ndt) {

  for(int i=0; i <  ndt.len; ++i) stream << " ";

  return stream;
}

// Together, the following class and overloaded operator create
// the skipchar manipulator.

// A class that supports the skipchar input manipulator.
class skipchar {
  char ch;
public:
  skipchar(char c) { ch = c; }
  friend istream &operator>>(istream &stream, skipchar sc);
};

// Create an extractor for objects of type skipchar.
istream &operator>>(istream &stream, skipchar sc) {
  char ch;

  do {
    ch = stream.get();
  } while(!stream.eof() && ch == sc.ch);
  if(!stream.eof()) stream.unget();

  return stream;
}

// Demonstrate indent and skipchar.
int main() {
  string str;

  // Use indent to indent output.
  cout << indent(9) << "This is indented 9 places.\n"
       << indent(9) << "So is this.\n" << indent(18)
       << "But this is indented 18 places.\n\n";

  // Use skipchar to ignore leading zeros.
  cout << "Enter some characters: ";
  cin >> skipchar('0') >> str;
  cout << "Leading zeros are skipped. Contents of str: "
       << str << "\n\n";

  // Use indent on an ostringstream.
  cout << "Use indent with a string stream.\n";
  ostringstream ostrstrm;
  ostrstrm << indent(5) << 128;
  cout << "Contents of ostrstrm:\n" << ostrstrm.str() << endl;

  return 0;
}
```

A sample run is shown here:

```
        This is indented 9 places.
        So is this.
                    But this is indented 18 places.

Enter some characters: 000abc
Leading zeros are skipped. Contents of str: abc

Use indent with a string stream.
Contents of ostrstrm:
    128
```

Options and Alternatives

This recipe shows an easy way to create parameterized manipulators, but it is not the only way. In the header **<iomanip>** are defined the parameterized manipulators specified by Standard C++. If you examine this header, you will probably see a more sophisticated approach, which utilizes templates and possibly complex macros. You could use the approach shown in that header to create your own parameterized manipulators that integrate with the class types defined by that header. However, because the classes in **<iomanip>** are implementation-specific, they may (probably will) differ between compilers. The approach used by the recipe is portable. Also, typically, the mechanism used by **<iomanip>** is fairly complicated and can be difficult to understand without significant study. Often, it is simply easier to use the technique shown in this recipe. Frankly, it is the approach that I like.

Obtain or Set a Stream's Locale

Key Ingredients		
Headers	**Classes**	**Functions**
<ios>	ios_base	locale getloc( ) const
<ios>	ios	locale imbue(const locale &*newloc*)
<locale>	locale	string name( ) const

You can obtain or set the **locale** object associated with a stream. In C++, locale-specific information is encapsulated within a **locale** object. This object defines various locale-related items, such as the currency symbol, the thousands separator, and so on. Each stream has a locale associated with it. To aid in internationalization, you may want to obtain a stream's **locale** object or set it to a new one. This recipe shows the process.

Step-by-Step

To obtain the current **locale** object associated with a stream involves these steps:

1. Create a **locale** instance that will receive a copy of the current locale.
2. Call **getloc( )** on the stream to obtain a copy of the current locale.

To set the locale associated with a stream involves these steps:

1. Create a **locale** instance that encapsulates the desired locale.
2. Call **imbue( )** on the stream, passing in the **locale** object from Step 1.

Discussion

The **locale** class encapsulates geopolitical information about a program's execution environment. For example, a program's locale determines the currency symbol, the time format, and the date format, among many others. The **locale** class requires the header **<locale>**. Each stream has a **locale** object associated with it.

To obtain a stream's current locale, call **getloc( )** on the stream. It is shown here:

locale getloc( ) const

It returns the **locale** object associated with the stream.

To set a stream's locale, call **imbue( )** on the stream. It is shown here:

locale imbue(const locale &*newloc*)

The invoking stream's locale is set to *newloc,* and the old locale is returned.

An easy way to construct a **locale** instance is to use this locale constructor:

explicit locale(const char **name*)

Here, *name* specifies the name of the locale, such as german, spanish_spain, or US. If *name* does not represent a valid locale, then a **runtime_error** exception is thrown.

Given a **locale** instance, you can obtain its name by calling **name( )**. It is shown here:

string name( ) const

The human-readable name of the locale is returned.

Example

The following example shows how to obtain and set a stream's locale. It first displays the stream's current locale, which is typically the C locale (which is usually the default locale for a C++ program). It then sets the locale to German_Germany. Finally, it obtains and displays the money symbol and the character used for the thousands separator.

```
// Demonstrate getloc() and imbue() on a stream.

#include <iostream>
#include <fstream>
#include <locale>
```

```
using namespace std;

int main()
{
  ofstream fout("test.dat");

  if(!fout) {
    cout << "Cannot open file.\n";
    return 1;
  }

  // Display the name of the current locale.
  cout << "The original locale is " << fout.getloc().name();
  cout << "\n\n";

  cout << "Setting the locale to German_Germany.\n";

  // Create a locale object for Germany.
  locale loc("German_Germany");

  // Set fout's locale to loc.
  fout.imbue(loc);

  // Display the name of the new locale.
  cout << "The current locale is now " << fout.getloc().name();
  cout << endl;

  // First, confirm that moneypunct facet is available.
  if(has_facet<moneypunct<char, true> >(fout.getloc())) {
    // Obtain the moneypunct facet.
    const moneypunct<char, true> &mp =
      use_facet<moneypunct<char, true> >(fout.getloc());

    // Display the currency symbol and thousands separator.
    cout << "Money symbol: " << mp.curr_symbol() << endl;
    cout << "Thousands separator: " << mp.thousands_sep() << endl;
  }

  fout.close();

  if(!fout.good()) {
    cout << "Error closing file.\n";
    return 1;
  }

  return 0;
}
```

The output is shown here:

```
The original locale is C

Setting the locale to German_Germany.
```

```
The current locale is now German_Germany.1252
Money symbol: EUR
Thousands separator: .
```

Options and Alternatives

As mentioned, at the core of internationalization is the **locale** class. It encapsulates a set of *facets* that describe the geopolitical aspects of the execution environment. The facets are represented by classes declared within **<locale>**, such as **moneypunct** used in the example. Others include **numpunct**, **num_get**, **num_put**, **time_get**, and **time_put**. You can use these classes to read and write information that is formatted relative to a specific locale. See Chapter 6 for recipes related to formatting data.

Use the C-Based File System

Key Ingredients		
Headers	**Classes**	**Functions**
<cstdio>		int fclose(FILE *fp)
		int feof(FILE *fp)
		int ferror(FILE*fp)
		FILE *fopen(const char *fname, const char *mode)
		int fgetc(FILE *fp)
		int fputc(int ch, FILE *fp)

The preceding recipes have described how to perform a wide variety of file-handling tasks by using the C++ I/O system, which is based on the hierarchy of classes described in the overview at the start of this chapter. This is the I/O system that you will normally use when writing C++ code. That said, no C++ cookbook would be complete without at least one recipe that describes the basics of using C++'s "other I/O system," which is the one inherited from C.

As nearly all C++ programmers know, C++ was built on the C language. As a result, C++ includes the entire C language. This is why the **for** loop in C, for example, works just like it does in C++. It is also why C-based functions, such as **tolower( )**, are readily available for use in a C++ program. This is important because C defines a complete I/O system of its own, which is separate from the one defined by C++. You have probably already seen C-based I/O in action in third-party code. For example, the main console output function is **printf( )** and a commonly used input function is **scanf( )**. In fact, variants of these functions are used in some of the recipes in Chapter 6, where formatting data is described.

Because the C file system is fully supported by C++, you will occasionally see it used in C++ programs. Perhaps more importantly, much legacy C code is still in widespread use.

If you will be maintaining such code, or possibly upgrading it to the C++ I/O system, then a basic working knowledge of the C file system is a necessity. Finally, in my opinion, no one can really call themselves a C++ programmer without having at least passing knowledge of the C language subset, including its approach to I/O.

This recipe demonstrates the basic mechanism required to open, close, read, and write a file. It also shows how to detect errors. Although there is much more to C-based file I/O than can be presented in one recipe, it will give you a general understanding of the key elements.

Step-by-Step

To use the C I/O system to read or write a file involves these steps:

1. Open a file by calling **fopen( )**.
2. Confirm that the file is open by testing the value returned by **fopen( )**. If it is **NULL**, the file is not open.
3. If the file is opened for input, read characters by calling **fgetc( )**.
4. If the file is opened for output, write characters by calling **fputc( )**.
5. Close the file by calling **fclose( )**.
6. Check for errors by calling **ferror( )**.
7. Check for end-of-file by calling **feof( )**.

Discussion

Although the C file system utilizes the same high-level concept of the stream, the way it works differs substantially from the C++ file system. A key difference is that the C I/O functions operate through *file pointers,* rather than on objects of classes that encapsulate a file. (As will be explained, the file pointer represents a file.) Therefore, the C file system centers not on a class hierarchy, but around the file pointer.

A file pointer is obtained by opening a file. Once you have a file pointer, you can operate on it through one or more of the C I/O functions. The ones used by this recipe are shown here: All require the header **<cstdio>**. This is the C++ version of the original **stdio.h** header file used by C.

Name	Function
fopen( )	Opens a file.
fclose( )	Closes a file.
fputc( )	Writes a character to a file.
fgetc( )	Reads a character from the file.
feof( )	Returns true if end-of-file is reached.
ferror( )	Returns true if an error has occurred.

The **<cstdio>** header provides the prototypes for the I/O functions and defines these three types: **size_t**, **fpos_t**, and **FILE**. The **size_t** type is some variety of unsigned integer, as is **fpos_t**. The **FILE** type describes a file. It merits closer examination.

The file pointer is the common thread that unites the C I/O system. It is a pointer to a structure of type **FILE**. This structure contains information that defines various things about the file, including its name, status, and the current position of the file. In essence, the file pointer identifies a specific file and is used by the associated stream to direct the operation of the I/O functions. In order to read or write files, your program needs to use file pointers. To obtain a file pointer variable, use a statement like this:

```
FILE *fp;
```

Also defined in **<cstdio>** are several macros. The ones relevant to this recipe are **NULL** and **EOF**. The **NULL** macro defines a null pointer. The **EOF** macro is usually defined as –1 and is the value returned when an input function tries to read past the end of the file.

An overview of each C I/O function used by this recipe follows.

fopen( )

The **fopen( )** function opens a stream for use and links a file with that stream. Then it returns the file pointer associated with that file. Most often (and for the rest of this discussion) the file is a disk file. The **fopen( )** function has this prototype:

FILE *fopen(const char *fname, const char *mode)

where fname is a pointer to a string of characters that make up a valid file name and may include a path specification. The string pointed to by mode determines how the file will be opened. The following table shows the legal values for mode. (Strings like "r+b" may also be represented as "rb+.")

Mode	Meaning
r	Open a text file for reading.
w	Create a text file for writing.
a	Append to a text file.
rb	Open a binary file for reading.
wb	Create a binary file for writing.
ab	Append to a binary file.
r+	Open a text file for read/write.
w+	Create a text file for read/write.
a+	Append or create a text file for read/write.
r+b	Open a binary file for read/write.
w+b	Create a binary file for read/write.
a+b	Append or create a binary file for read/write.

Notice that a file can be opened in either text or binary mode. In most implementations, in text mode, carriage return/linefeed sequences are translated to newline characters on input. On output, the reverse occurs: Newlines are translated to carriage return/linefeeds. No such translations occur on binary files.

As stated, **fopen( )** function returns a file pointer. Your program should never alter the value of this pointer. If an error occurs when it is trying to open the file, **fopen( )** returns a null pointer. You must confirm that the file was successfully opened by testing the value returned by **fopen( )**. Here is an example of how to open a file when using **fopen( )**. It attempts to open a file called **test.dat** for output.

```
FILE *fp;

if ((fp = fopen("test.dat","w"))==NULL) {
  cout << "Cannot open test.dat for output.\n";
  exit(1);
}
```

If the file cannot be opened for any reason, such as if it is read-only, then the call to **fopen( )** will fail and a null pointer will be returned. Of course, the test for an open failure can be written a bit more compactly, like this:

```
if (!(fp = fopen("test.dat","w"))) { // ...
```

The explicit test against **NULL** is not needed because a null pointer is a false value.

fclose( )
The **fclose( )** function closes a stream that was opened by a call to **fopen( )**. It writes any data still remaining in the disk buffer to the file and does a formal operating-system–level close on the file. Failure to close a stream invites trouble, including lost data, destroyed files, and possible intermittent errors in your program. Therefore, you should always close a file when you are done with it. Closing a file also frees any system resources used by the file, making them available for reuse.

The **fclose( )** function has this prototype:

int fclose(FILE *fp)

where fp is the file pointer returned by the call to **fopen( )**. A return value of zero signifies a successful close operation. The function returns **EOF** if an error occurs. A call to **fclose( )** will fail when a disk has been prematurely removed from the drive or there is no more space on the disk, for example.

fputc( )
The **fputc( )** function writes characters to a file. It is shown here:

int fputc(int ch, FILE *fp)

The fp parameter specifies the file to write to, and ch is the character to write. Although ch is defined as an **int**, only the low-order byte is written. If **fputc( )** is successful, it returns ch. Otherwise, it returns **EOF**.

fgetc( )

The **fgetc( )** function reads characters from a file. It is shown here:

   int fgetc(FILE *fp)

The *fp* parameter specifies the file to read from. It returns the next character in the file, returned as an **int** value. It returns an **EOF** when the end of the file has been reached. Therefore, to read to the end of a text file, you could use the following code:

```
do {
  ch = fgetc(fp);
} while(ch != EOF);
```

However, **fgetc( )** also returns **EOF** if an error occurs. You can use **ferror( )** to determine precisely what has occurred.

feof( )

As just described, **fgetc( )** returns **EOF** when the end of the file has been encountered. However, testing the value returned by **fgetc( )** may not be the best way to determine when you have arrived at the end of a file. First, the C file system can operate on both text and binary files. When a file is opened for binary input, an integer value that will test equal to **EOF** may be read. This would cause the input routine to indicate an end-of-file condition even though the physical end of the file had not been reached. Second, **fgetc( )** returns **EOF** when it fails *and* when it reaches the end of the file. Using only the return value of **fgetc( )**, it is impossible to know which occurred. To solve these problems, C includes the function **feof( )**, which determines when the end of the file has been encountered. The **feof( )** function is shown here:

   int feof(FILE *fp)

It returns true if the end of the file has been reached; otherwise, it returns false. Therefore, the following statement reads a binary file until the end of the file is encountered:

```
while(!feof(fp)) ch = fgetc(fp);
```

Of course, you can apply this method to text files as well as binary files.

ferror( )

The **ferror( )** function determines whether a file operation has produced an error. The **ferror( )** function is shown here:

   int ferror(FILE *fp)

The *fp* parameter specifies the file in question. The function returns true if an error has occurred during the last file operation; otherwise, it returns false.

Example

The following program illustrates the C-based file I/O. It copies a text file. In the process, it removes tabs and substitutes the appropriate number of spaces. To use the program, specify the name of the input file, the name of the output file, and the tab size on the command line.

```cpp
// Demonstrate C-based file I/O.
//
// This program copies a file, substituting spaces for
// tabs in the process. It uses the C I/O system to
// handle the file I/O.

#include <iostream>
#include <cstdio>
#include <cstdlib>

using namespace std;

int main(int argc, char *argv[])
{
  FILE *in, *out;
  int tabsize;
  int tabcount;
  char ch;
  int completion_status = 0;

  if(argc != 4) {
    cout << "usage: detab <in> <out> <tab size>\n";
    return 1;
  }

  if((in = fopen(argv[1], "rb"))==NULL) {
    cout << "Cannot open input file.\n";
    return 1;
  }

  if((out = fopen(argv[2], "wb"))==NULL) {
    cout << "Cannot open output file.\n";
    fclose(in);
    return 1;
  }

  // Get the tab size.
  tabsize = atoi(argv[3]);

  tabcount = 0;

  do {
    // Read a character from the input file.
    ch = fgetc(in);

    if(ferror(in)) {
      cout << "Error reading input file.\n";
      completion_status = 1;
      break;
    }

    // If tab found, output appropriate number of spaces.
    if(ch == '\t') {
      for(int i=tabcount; i < tabsize; ++i) {
        // Write spaces to the output file.
```

```
      fputc(' ', out);
    }
    tabcount = 0;
  }
  else {
    // Write the character to the output file.
    fputc(ch, out);

    ++tabcount;
    if(tabcount == tabsize) tabcount = 0;
    if(ch == '\n' || ch == '\r') tabcount = 0;
  }

  if(ferror(out)) {
    cout << "Error writing to output file.\n";
    completion_status = 1;
    break;
  }
} while(!feof(in));

fclose(in);
fclose(out);

if(ferror(in) || ferror(out)) {
  cout << "Error closing a file.\n";
  completion_status = 1;
}

return completion_status;
}
```

Options and Alternatives

You can read and write blocks of data using the C I/O system by using the functions **fread( )** and **fwrite( )**. They are shown here:

> size_t fread(void *buf, size_t *num_bytes*, size_t *count*, FILE *fp*)
> size_t fwrite(const void *buf, size_t *num_bytes*, size_t *count*, FILE *fp*)

For **fread( )**, *buf* is a pointer to a region of memory that will receive the data from the file. For **fwrite( )**, *buf* is a pointer to the information that will be written to the file. The value of *count* determines how many items are read or written, with each item being *num_bytes* bytes in length. The file acted upon is specified by *fp*. The **fread( )** function returns the number of items read. This value may be less than *count* if the end of the file is reached or an error occurs. The **fwrite( )** function returns the number of items written. This value will equal *count* unless an error occurs.

There are alternative versions of **fgetc( )** and **fputc( )** called **getc( )** and **putc( )**. They work just like **fgetc( )** and **fputc( )**, except that they can be implemented as macros.

You can perform random-access operations using the C I/O system with **fseek( )**. It is shown here:

> int fseek(FILE *fp*, long *offset*, int *origin*)

The file acted upon is specified by *fp*. The number of bytes from *origin* that will become the new current position is passed in *offset*. The value of *origin* must be one of the following values (defined in **<cstdio>**):

Origin	Macro Name
Beginning of file	SEEK_SET
Current position	SEEK_CUR
End of file	SEEK_END

Therefore, to seek from the start of the file, *origin* should be **SEEK_SET**. To seek from the current position, use **SEEK_CUR**, and to seek from the end of the file, use **SEEK_END**. The **fseek( )** function returns zero when successful and a non-zero value if an error occurs.

The C I/O system supports several functions that support formatted I/O. You have probably seen some of them before. The two most commonly encountered are **printf( )**, which outputs formatted data to the console, and **scanf( )**, which reads formatted data from the console. There are also variations of these, called **fprintf( )** and **fscanf( )**, which operate on a file, and **sprintf( )** and **sscanf( )**, which use a string for input or output. Chapter 6, which presents recipes for formatting data, gives a brief overview of these functions.

You can reset the current file position to the start of the file by calling **rewind( )**. It is shown here:

   void rewind(FILE *fp)

The file to rewind is specified by *fp*.

To flush a stream using the C I/O system, call **fflush( )**, shown here:

   int fflush(FILE *fp)

It writes the contents of any buffered data to the file associated with *fp*. If you call **fflush( )** with *fp* being null, all files opened for output are flushed. The **fflush( )** function returns zero if successful; otherwise, it returns **EOF**.

You can rename a file by calling **rename( )**. You can erase a file by calling **remove( )**. These functions are described by the next recipe.

One last point: Although C++ supports both the C and the C++ I/O systems, there are some guidelines that you should follow to avoid problems. First, once a stream has been opened using one of the systems, it should be acted on by only the functions defined by that system. In other words, you should not mix both C and C++ I/O *on the same file*. Second, in general, it is better to use the C++ class-based I/O system. C++ supports the C I/O system for backward compatibility with existing C programs. The C I/O system is not intended for new C++ programs.

Rename and Remove a File

Key Ingredients		
Headers	**Classes**	**Functions**
<cstdio>		int remove(const char *fname)
		int rename(const char *oldname, const char *newname)

The previous recipe presented a brief overview of C-based file I/O. As mentioned there, C++ fully supports the entire C I/O system, so it is usually better to use the I/O system for C++. However, there are two functions defined by the C I/O system that offer simple solutions to two common tasks: renaming a file and erasing a file. The functions are **rename( )** and **remove( )**. They are declared in **<cstdio>**, and this recipe shows how to use them.

Step-by-Step

To rename a file involves one step:

1. Call **rename( )**, specifying both the current name of the file and its new name.

To erase a file involves one step:

1. Call **remove( )**, specifying the name of the file to remove.

Discussion

The **rename( )** function renames a file. It is shown here:

int rename(const char *oldname, const char *newname)

The current name of the file is passed in *oldname*. The new name of the file is passed in *newname*. It returns zero if successful and non-zero otherwise. In general, the file must be closed before an attempt is made to rename it. Also, as a general rule, it is not possible to rename a read-only file. Furthermore, it is not possible to give a file a name that is already used by another file. In other words, you can't create a situation in which duplicate file names exist in the same directory.

The **remove( )** function erases a file. It is shown here:

int remove(const char *fname)

It removes from the file system the file whose name is specified by *fname*. It returns zero if successful and non-zero otherwise. The file must be closed before an attempt is made to erase it. As a general rule, the file must also not be read-only or otherwise prevented from being removed.

Example

The following example shows both **rename( )** and **remove( )** in action. It creates a file called **test.dat**. Then, if the command-line argument is "rename," it renames **test.dat** to **test2.dat**. If the command-line argument is "erase," it removes **test2.dat**.

```
// Demonstrate rename() and remove().

#include <iostream>
#include <cstdio>
#include <cstring>
#include <fstream>

using namespace std;

int main(int argc, char *argv[])
{
  int result;

  if(argc != 2) {
    printf("usage: EraseRenname <erase/rename>\n");
    exit(1);
  }

  ofstream fout("test.dat");

  if(!fout) {
    cout << "Cannot open test.dat file.\n";
    return 1;
  }

  fout << "Write some data to the file.";

  fout.close();

  if(!fout.good()) {
    cout << "Error writing to or closing file.\n";
    return 0;
  }

  if(!strcmp("erase", argv[1])) {
    result = remove("test2.dat");
    if(result) {
      cout << "Cannot remove file.\n";
      return 1;
    }
  } else if(!strcmp("rename", argv[1])) {
    result = rename("test.dat", "test2.dat");
    if(result) {
      cout << "Cannot rename file.\n";
      return 1;
    }
  }
```

```
  } else
    cout << "Invalid command-line argument.\n";

  return 0;
}
```

Options and Alternatives

All operating systems provide low-level API functions that erase and rename files. They may offer more finely grained control over these operations. For example, they may let you specify a security descriptor. For detailed control, you might want to use the operating system primitives rather than **remove( )** or **rename( )**.

In some environments, you can use **rename( )** to rename a directory. It may also be possible to move a file from one directory to another by using **rename( )**. Check your compiler's documentation for details.

Formatting Data

W hether you are displaying the time and date, working with monetary values, or simply wanting to limit the number of decimal digits, formatting data is an important part of many programs. It's also an aspect of programming that raises many questions. One reason for this is the size and complexity of the problem: There are many different types of data, formats, and options. Another reason is the richness of the C++ formatting capabilities. Often, there is more than one way to produce a desired format. For example, you can set various formatting attributes by using functions such as **setf( )**, **width( )**, or **precision( )**, or with I/O manipulators, such as **setw**, **fixed**, or **showpos**. Here is another example: You can format time and date by using either the C++ localization library or the **strftime( )** function inherited from C. Frankly, choosing an approach is sometimes a difficult decision, especially when legacy code is involved. Of course, the benefit of such extensive and flexible support for formatting is that you can use the best technique for the job at hand.

This chapter examines the topic of formatting and presents recipes that demonstrate various ways to solve several common formatting tasks. In the process, it describes aspects of localization, including the use of facets. Although the main emphasis is on the formatting features defined by C++, the original C-based approach is also included.

Here are the recipes contained in this chapter:

- Access the Format Flags via Stream Member Functions
- Display Numeric Values in Various Formats
- Set the Precision
- Set the Field Width and Fill Character
- Justify Output
- Use I/O Manipulators to Format Data
- Format Numeric Values for a Locale
- Format Monetary Values Using the **money_put** Facet
- Use the **moneypunct** and **numpunct** Facets
- Format Time and Date Using the **time_put** Facet
- Format Data into a String

- Format Time and Date Using **strftime( )**
- Use **printf( )** to Format Data

One important note before we begin. As explained in Chapter 5, the C++ I/O system is built on generic classes that can operate on different types of characters. Furthermore, it declares specializations of those classes for **char** and **wchar_t**. For convenience, this chapter uses the **char** specializations exclusively. Thus, the **char**-specialization names, such as **ios**, **ostream**, and **istream**, are used (rather than **basic_ios**, **basic_ostream**, **basic_istream**, and so on). However, the information also applies to streams defined on other character types.

Formatting Overview

There are several ways in which the format of data can be specified or affected. You can:

- Use stream member functions to set or clear one or more format flags.
- Use stream member functions to set the field width, precision, and fill character.
- Use an I/O manipulator within a formatted output expression to set format flags or other attributes.
- Use the functionality defined by the C++ localization library to format numeric values, monetary values, and time and date.
- Use the **printf( )** family of functions, which are inherited from the C language, to format data (except for time and date).
- Use **strftime( )**, also inherited from C, to format time and date.

All of these are demonstrated by recipes in this chapter, but the primary focus is on the first four because they represent the modern C++ approach to formatting. The **printf( )** and **strftime( )** functions, which are inherited from C, are covered for completeness, but most new code should use the C++ features.

Although the specifics of each formatting approach are described by the recipes, a general overview is presented here.

The Format Flags

Each stream has associated with it a set of format flags that control the way information is formatted. These flags are contained in a bitmask enumeration called **fmtflags** that is defined by **ios_base**. (See Chapter 5 for details on streams and the C++ I/O system in general.) The format flags are shown here:

boolalpha	dec	fixed	hex
internal	left	oct	right
scientific	showbase	showpoint	showpos
skipws	unitbuf	uppercase	

Following is a brief description of each flag. Several are explored in detail in the recipes.

The **left**, **right**, and **internal** flags determine how data is justified within a field. They form a group in which only one should be set at any given time. When the **left** flag is set, output is left-justified. When **right** is set, output is right-justified. When the **internal** flag is set, a numeric value is padded to fill a field by inserting the fill character (which is a space by default) between any sign or base character. In many locales, the default is right justification.

By default, numeric values are output in decimal, but it is possible to select the number base by using the **oct**, **hex**, and **dec** flags. These flags form a group in which only one should be set at any given time. When the **oct** flag is set, output is displayed in octal. Setting the **hex** flag causes output to be displayed in hexadecimal. To return output to decimal, set the **dec** flag.

Setting **showbase** causes the base of numeric values to be shown. For hexadecimal, a value will be preceded by a 0x. For example, 1F will be displayed as 0x1F. For octal, the value will be preceded by a 0, as in 076. Decimal values are unaffected.

By default, when scientific notation is displayed, the **e** is in lowercase. Also, when a hexadecimal value is displayed, the **x** is in lowercase. When **uppercase** is set, these characters are displayed in uppercase.

Setting **showpos** causes a leading plus sign to be displayed before positive values.

Setting **showpoint** causes a decimal point and trailing zeros to be displayed for all floating-point output—whether needed or not.

Setting the **scientific** flag causes floating-point numeric values to be displayed using scientific notation. When **fixed** is set, floating-point values are displayed using fixed-point notation. These flags form a group in which only one should be set at any given time. When neither flag is set, the compiler chooses an appropriate method.

When **unitbuf** is set, the buffer is flushed after each insertion operation.

When **boolalpha** is set, booleans can be input or output using the keywords **true** and **false**. Otherwise, the digits 1 and 0 are used.

The **skipws** flag applies to input streams. When it is set, leading whitespace characters (spaces, tabs, and newlines) are discarded when performing input on a stream. When **skipws** is cleared, whitespace characters are not discarded.

Also defined are the values **basefield**, **adjustfield**, and **floatfield**. The **basefield** is defined as **oct | dec | hex**. Thus, **basefield** lets you refer to the fields **oct**, **dec**, and **hex** collectively. Similarly, the **left**, **right**, and **internal** fields are combined in **adjustfield**. Finally, the **scientific** and **fixed** fields can be referenced as **floatfield**. As the recipes will demonstrate, these values simplify setting a specific flag within a group of flags.

The format flags are defined by **ios_base**, which is a base class for **basic_ios**. As explained in Chapter 5, the C++ I/O system creates specializations for streams of type **char** and **wchar_t**. The **char** specialization of **basic_ios** is **ios**. Therefore, it is common to see the format flags referred to through **ios**, as in **ios::oct**. This is the approach that this chapter will use. (Although it is perfectly fine to use **ios_base::oct** if you prefer.)

The Field Width, Precision, and Fill Character

In addition to the format flags just described, each C++ stream has associated with it three attributes that affect formatting. These are the field width, the precision, and the fill character. The field width specifies the minimum number of characters that a formatted item will occupy. By default, the field width is equal to the number of characters in the item being displayed, but you can change this so that an item is contained within a larger space.

By default, the character used to pad output is the space, but you can change this. Finally, the default precision of floating-point values is 6, but this, too, is under your control.

Format-Related Stream Member Functions

Each C++ stream contains its own set of format flags and the field width, precision, and fill character attributes. For any given stream, the format flags can be set, cleared, or interrogated by using the **setf( )**, **unsetf( )**, and **flags( )** functions. These are members of **ios_base**. The field width is set by **width( )**, and the precision is set by **precision( )**. Both are also members of **ios_base**. The fill character is set by **fill( )**, which is a member of **ios**. They are described in detail in the recipes.

The I/O Manipulators

Another way to set the format flags and attributes is through the use of a manipulator. A *manipulator* is a function (or in some cases, an object) that is included in a formatted I/O expression. It can be used to set or clear the format flags or otherwise affect the stream. C++ defines several standard manipulators. They are shown here:

boolalpha	dec	endl
ends	fixed	flush
hex	internal	left
nobooalpha	noshowbase	noshowpoint
noshowpos	noskipws	nounitbuf
nouppercase	oct	resetiosflags(fmtflags *f*)
right	scientific	setbase(int *base)*
setfill(int *ch)*	setiosflags(fmtflags *f*)	setprecision(int *p*)
setw(int *w)*	showbase	showpoint
showpos	skipws	unitbuf
uppercase	ws	

The manipulators fall into two general categories: parameterized and parameterless. A parameterized manipulator requires an argument when it is used. An example of a parameterized manipulator is **setw**. It sets the field width to the size passed to it. A parameterless manipulator does not take an argument. For example, the **endl** manipulator does not have an argument. Most of the standard manipulators do not take arguments.

The majority of parameterless manipulators are defined by the header **<ios>**, which is automatically included by other headers, such as **<iostream>**. Three are defined by the **<ostream>** header: **endl**, **ends**, and **flush**. The parameterized manipulators are defined in **<iomanip>**. The manipulators are described in detail in *Use I/O Manipulators to Format Data*.

Format Data Using the Localization Library

To format data beyond the basic capabilities provided by the format flags and attributes requires the use of one or more library functions and classes. For some types of formatting, you can use functions inherited from C (the language on which C++ was built). These are mostly useful for maintaining legacy code and are described by the following sections. For new code, you will usually use the formatting features defined by the *localization library*. This library is defined in the **<locale>** header, and it provides support for formatting data, such as monetary values and time and date, whose representation is sensitive to culture and language.

The localization library is based on the **locale** class, which defines a locale. A locale encapsulates the geopolitical information associated with a stream. It is important to understand that each stream has its own **locale** object. Thus, setting a stream's locale affects only that stream. This differs from the C language, in which a global locale is available. (C++ still supports the global locale to provide backward compatibility with C, but the stream-based locales are much more flexible.)

The key to using a **locale** instance to handle formatting is the *facet*. A facet is an instance of a class that inherits **locale::facet**. Each facet describes some aspect of the locale. For example, the facet that handles monetary formatting is **money_put**. The facet that formats time and date is **time_put**. By using a facet, data can be formatted as you desire and also automatically tailored to a specific locale. This makes the C++ localization subsystem very powerful. A general overview of facets is presented shortly, and specific information about the facets that handle numeric values, monetary values, and time and date is given in the recipes.

The printf( ) **Family of Functions**

Because C++ was built on C, it includes all of the function libraries defined by C. This means that C++ supports the **printf( )** family of functions. These functions are part of C's I/O system and provide the mechanism by which a C program formats data. Although the use of **printf( )** is not recommended for new C++ code, it is the function that you will use when writing C programs. It is also frequently encountered in legacy code. Therefore, no C++ cookbook would be complete without a discussion of its features.

There are several variations on **printf( )**. The ones used in this chapter are:

printf( )	Displays formatted output on the standard output device, which is the console by default.
fprintf( )	Writes formatted output to a file.
sprintf( )	Writes formatted output to string.

All require the header **<cstdio>**, and all work in the same basic way. It is simply the target of the output that changes. The operation of these functions is described in *Use printf( ) to Format Data*.

NOTE   *Wide-character versions of the **printf( )** family of functions are also available. For example, the wide-character version of **printf( )** is **wprintf( )**. The wide-character versions use the header* **<cwchar>**.

The strftime( ) **Function**

Another formatting function inherited from C is **strftime( )**. It formats time and date information. Although the C++ facets, such as **time_put**, provide more flexibility, the **strftime( )** function can be easier to use in some cases. It is also commonly encountered in legacy C code. It is described in *Format Time and Date Using **strftime( )***.

Facet Overview

Facets are the means by which data is formatted in C++. They are part of the localization library, which requires the header **<locale>**. Perhaps the single most important thing to understand about facets is that they are easier to use than they first appear. Don't be intimidated by the rather complex template syntax. Once you understand the general process, it is easy to create any type of localized format you desire. Because several recipes make use of facets, it makes sense to describe the general procedure in one place, with the individual recipes describing specifics.

All facets are classes that are derived from **locale::facet**. There are several built-in facets, such as **money_put**, **time_get**, and **num_put**, which are also declared in **<locale>**. These classes are used to format data for output or read formatted data from input. This chapter is concerned only with formatting data for output, so the input facets are not used here. Furthermore, this chapter uses only the facets that format numeric values, monetary values, or the time and date. The localization library defines other facets that handle other locale-sensitive needs.

Conceptually, using a facet is easy: Obtain a facet by calling **use_facet( )**, and then call functions on that facet to format data or obtain localization information. However, in practice, the process is usually a bit more involved. Here is a general outline of the steps:

1. Construct a **locale** object.
2. Set the desired locale by calling **imbue( )** on the stream that will be receiving the formatted output. Pass **imbue( )** the **locale** object from Step 1.
3. Obtain a facet by calling **use_facet( )**, specifying the name of the facet. This is a global function defined by **<locale>**.
4. To format numeric values, monetary values, or the time and date, or to obtain information about a format, use the functions defined by the facet obtained in Step 3.

Let's look more closely at these steps.

The **locale** class defines several constructors. The one used by this chapter is shown here:

explicit locale(const char *loc_name)

The name of the locale is passed via *loc_name*. This must be a valid locale name. If *loc_name* is invalid, a **runtime_error** is thrown. What constitutes a valid name is implementation-dependent. This book uses locale strings that are compatible with Microsoft's Visual C++. You will need to check your compiler's documentation for the locale strings that it supports.

To set a stream's locale, call **imbue( )**. It is defined by **ios_base** and is available in all stream objects. The process of a setting a locale is described in detail in *Obtain or Set a Stream's Locale* in Chapter 5. For convenience, **imbue( )** is shown again here:

locale imbue(const locale &*newloc*)

The invoking stream's locale is set to *newloc*, and the old locale is returned.

To obtain a facet, call **use_facet( )**. It is a global function and is shown here:

template <class Facet> const Facet &use_facet(const locale &*loc*)

Here, **Facet** must be a valid facet. It specifies the facet that will be obtained, which will normally be one defined by **<locale>**. (It is possible to create custom facets, but you seldom need to do so.) The locale for which the facet will be obtained is passed in *loc*. The **use_facet( )** function returns a reference to the facet specified by **Facet**. If the facet does not exist, **bad_cast** is thrown. (If necessary, you can determine if a facet exists by calling **has_facet( )**, which is also a global function defined by **<locale>**.)

There are several predefined facets. The ones used by this book are:

num_put	Formats numeric values.
money_put	Formats monetary values.
time_put	Formats time and date.
numpunct	Obtains punctuation and rules related to numeric formats.
moneypunct	Obtains punctuation and rules related to monetary formats.

The recipes show their declarations, but all are template classes that take the character type as a type argument. (Some also take other type arguments.) The **num_put**, **money_put**, and **time_put** facets format numbers, money, and time and date, respectively. They define the **put( )** function, which formats the value that it is passed according to the rules encapsulated by the facet. (Each of the **put( )** functions is described in its own recipe.) The **numpunct** facet encapsulates information about the punctuation and rules governing the format of numeric data. The **moneypunct** facet encapsulates the punctuation and rules governing the format of monetary values.

To obtain a facet, you will call **use_facet( )**, specifying the facet's name as the type parameter. For example, this obtains a **money_put** facet associated with the locale currently used by **cout**:

```
const money_put<char> &mp = use_facet<money_put<char> >(cout.getloc());
```

Notice that the **char** version of **money_put** is requested because **cout** is a **char** stream. Once you have a facet, you can use it for formatting by calling functions on it. The recipes describe the process in detail.

Here is a very important point: When using a C++ stream, numbers are automatically output by use of the **num_put** facet. Therefore, you don't need to manually obtain this facet to display numeric values in a locale-specific way. Simply set the locale of the stream by use of **imbue( )**, and the value will automatically be formatted for that locale.

NOTE *You can also set the locale globally, using the **setlocale( )** C legacy function. However, this approach is not recommended for new code. The facet-based locale system used by C++ offers a better and more flexible approach.*

Access the Format Flags via Stream Member Functions

Key Ingredients		
Headers	**Classes**	**Functions**
<ios>	ios_base	fmtflags setf(fmtflags *flags*)
		void unsetf(fmtflags *flags*)
		fmtflags flags( )

For any given stream, you can change the way data is formatted by changing one or more format flags. For example, if you set the **showpos** flag, then positive numeric values are displayed with a leading + sign. There are two ways in which the format flags can be set. First, you can use functions that are defined by all stream classes, such as **setf( )**. Second, you can use an I/O manipulator. This recipe shows how to use the stream member functions. Manipulators are described by a later recipe.

Step-by-Step

To use stream member functions to set, clear, or obtain the format flags involves these steps:

1. To set one or more flags on a stream, call **setf( )**.
2. To clear one or more flags on a stream, call **unsetf( )**.
3. To obtain the current format flag settings, call **flags( )**.

Discussion

For any given stream, you can set a format flag by calling the **setf( )** function, which is declared by **ios_base**. Therefore, **setf( )** is a member of all stream classes. It is shown here:

fmtflags setf(fmtflags *flags*)

This function returns the previous settings of the format flags and turns on those flags specified by *flags*. For example,

```
mystream.setf(ios::showpos);
```

turns on the **showpos** flag for the stream called **mystream**.

The complement of **setf( )** is **unsetf( )**. It is also declared by **ios_base**. It clears one or more format flags. Its general form is:

void unsetf(fmtflags *flags*)

The flags specified by *flags* are cleared. All other flags are unaffected. Therefore, to turn off the **boolalpha** flag for **mystream**, you would use this statement:

```
mystream.unsetf(ios::boolalpha);
```

You can set or clear more than one flag in a single call to **setf( )** or **unsetf( )** by OR-ing two or more flags together. For example, this turns on both the **showpos** and **boolalpha** flags:

```
mystream.setf(ios::showpos | ios::boolalpha);
```

The following turns off the **uppercase** and **boolalpha** flags:

```
mystream.unsetf(ios::uppercase | ios::boolalpha);
```

You can obtain the current format flag settings by using **flags( )**. It is shown here:

fmtflags flags( ) const

It returns the current format flag bitmask. It, too, is declared by **ios_base**.

It is important to understand that each stream instance has its own set of format flags. Therefore, changing the flag settings for a stream affects only that stream. The format flags of any other stream are unchanged.

Example

The following example shows how to set and clear format flags. It first sets the **boolalpha** flag on **cout** and then displays a **bool** value. It then clears the **boolalpha** flag and redisplays the value. Notice the difference in the output.

```
// Demonstrate the setf() and unsetf() functions.

#include <iostream>

using namespace std;

int main()
{
  // Set the boolalpha flag on cout.
  cout.setf(ios::boolalpha);

  cout << "The value true when the boolapha flag is set: "
       << true << endl;;

  // Now, clear the boolalpha flag.
  cout.unsetf(ios::boolalpha);

  cout << "The value true when the boolapha flag is cleared: "
       << true << endl;;

  return 0;
}
```

The output is shown here:

```
The value true when the boolapha flag is set: true
The value true when the boolapha flag is cleared: 1
```

Bonus Example: Display the Format Flag Settings

When debugging format problems, it is sometimes helpful to see how all of the format flags are set. It has been my experience that some compilers behave in unexpected ways due to the interaction of seemingly unrelated flags. Also, there can be differences between compilers when two flags conflict. For example, if both the **oct** and **dec** flags are set, which format is used? Different compilers might resolve this situation differently. (Of course, good programming practice dictates that only one of the flags **oct**, **dec**, or **hex** is set at any one time.) Being able to see the actual flag settings can help explain otherwise unusual results. Towards this end, the following program creates a function called **showflags( )**, which takes a stream as an argument and displays the current settings of that stream's format flags:

```
// This program creates a function called showflags()
// that displays the format flag settings associated
// with a given stream.

#include <iostream>

using namespace std;

void showflags(ios &strm) ;

int main()
{
  // Show default condition of format flags.
  cout << "Default settings for cout:\n";
  showflags(cout);

  // Set the right, showpoint, and fixed flags.
  cout.setf(ios::right | ios::showpoint | ios::fixed);

  // Show flags after call to setf().
  cout << "Flags after setting right, showpoint, and fixed:\n";
  showflags(cout);

  return 0;
}

// This function displays the status of the format flags
// for the specified stream.
void showflags(ios &strm)
{
  ios::fmtflags f;

  // Get the current flag settings.
  f = strm.flags();

  if(f & ios::boolalpha) cout << "boolalpha:\ton\n";
  else cout << "boolalpha:\toff\n";

  if(f & ios::dec) cout << "dec:\t\ton\n";
  else cout << "dec:\t\toff\n";
```

```
    if(f & ios::hex) cout << "hex:\t\ton\n";
    else cout << "hex:\t\toff\n";

    if(f & ios::oct) cout << "oct:\t\ton\n";
    else cout << "oct:\t\toff\n";

    if(f & ios::fixed) cout << "fixed:\t\ton\n";
    else cout << "fixed:\t\toff\n";

    if(f & ios::scientific) cout << "scientific:\ton\n";
    else cout << "scientific:\toff\n";

    if(f & ios::right) cout << "right:\t\ton\n";
    else cout << "right:\t\toff\n";

    if(f & ios::left) cout << "left:\t\ton\n";
    else cout << "left:\t\toff\n";

    if(f & ios::internal) cout << "internal:\ton\n";
    else cout << "internal:\toff\n";

    if(f & ios::showbase) cout << "showbase:\ton\n";
    else cout << "showbase:\toff\n";

    if(f & ios::showpoint) cout << "showpoint:\ton\n";
    else cout << "showpoint:\toff\n";

    if(f & ios::showpos) cout << "showpos:\ton\n";
    else cout << "showpos:\toff\n";

    if(f & ios::uppercase) cout << "uppercase:\ton\n";
    else cout << "uppercase:\toff\n";

    if(f & ios::unitbuf) cout << "unitbuf:\ton\n";
    else cout << "unitbuf:\toff\n";

    if(f & ios::skipws) cout << "skipws:\t\ton\n";
    else cout << "skipws:\t\toff\n";

    cout << " \n";
}
```

The output is shown here. (This output was generated by Visual C++. Your compiler may show different default settings.)

```
Default settings for cout:
boolalpha:      off
dec:            on
hex:            off
oct:            off
fixed:          off
scientific:     off
right:          off
```

```
left:              off
internal:          off
showbase:          off
showpoint:         off
showpos:           off
uppercase:         off
unitbuf:           off
skipws:            on

Flags after setting right, showpoint, and fixed:
boolalpha:         off
dec:               on
hex:               off
oct:               off
fixed:             on
scientific:        off
right:             on
left:              off
internal:          off
showbase:          off
showpoint:         on
showpos:           off
uppercase:         off
unitbuf:           off
skipws:            on
```

Options and Alternatives

There is an overloaded form of **setf( )** that takes this general form:

fmtflags setf(fmtflags *flags1*, fmtflags *flags2*)

In this version, only the flags specified by *flags2* are affected. They are first cleared and then set according to the flags specified by *flags1*. Note that even if *flags1* contains other flags, only those specified by *flags2* will be affected. The previous flag settings are returned. Perhaps the most common use of the two-parameter form of **setf( )** is when setting the number base, justification, and floating-point format flags. See the following recipes for details.

You can set all of the format flags by using this overloaded version of **flags( )**:

fmtflags flags(fmtflags *flags*)

This version sets the entire format flags bitmask to the value passed in *flags*. The previous bitmask is returned.

The format flags can be set by various manipulators. For example, the **noboolalpha** manipulator clears the **boolalpha** flag. You can also set or clear one or more flags using the **setiosflags** and **resetiosflags** manipulators. See *Use I/O Manipulators to Format Data*.

Display Numeric Values in Various Formats

Key Ingredients		
Headers	**Classes**	**Functions and Flags**
<ios>	ios_base	fmtflags setf(fmtflags *flags*)
		void unsetf(fmtflags *flags*)
		oct
		hex
		dec
		showbase
		showpos
		fixed
		scientific
		basefield
		floatfield

Through the use of the format flags, you can control several aspects of the numeric format. For example, you can output integers in decimal, hexadecimal, or octal, or display floating-point values in either fixed or scientific notation. This recipe demonstrates those flags that affect the format of numbers.

Step-by-Step

Using the format flags to change the format of numeric data involves these steps:

1. To format an integer in decimal, clear the flags specified by **basefield** and then set the **dec** flag. Normally, decimal format is the default for an output stream.

2. To format an integer in hexadecimal, clear the flags specified by **basefield** and then set the **hex** flag.

3. To format an integer in octal, clear the flags specified by **basefield** and then set the **oct** flag.

4. To show the base of an octal or hexadecimal value, set the **showbase** flag.

5. To format a floating-point value in fixed notation, clear the flags specified by **floatfield** and then set the **fixed** flag.

6. To format a floating-point value in scientific notation, clear the flags specified by **floatfield** and then set the **scientific** flag.

7. To cause a + sign to be displayed before positive values, set the **showpos** flag.

8. To ensure that the decimal point is always included in a floating-point value, set the **showpoint** flag.

9. To cause letters in numeric values (hexadecimal digits greater than 0, the **e** in scientific notation, and the **x** in the hexadecimal base indicator) to be displayed in uppercase, set the **uppercase** flag.

Discussion

The format flags are set or cleared by the **setf( )** and **unsetf( )** functions, which are described in detail by the preceding recipe.

In general, you can display integer values in decimal (the default), hexadecimal, or octal. This is controlled by the settings of the **dec**, **hex**, and **oct** flags, respectively. To set the number base, you must turn on the desired flag and turn off the other two flags. For example, to output integers in octal, you must turn on **oct** and turn off **dec** and **hex**. Collectively, the flags **oct**, **hex**, and **dec** can be referred to as **basefield**.

The easiest way to turn on one flag and ensure that the other two are off is to use the two-argument form of **setf( )**. As explained in the previous recipe, it has this general form:

fmtflags setf(fmtflags *flags1*, fmtflags *flags2*)

In this version, only the flags specified by *flags2* are affected. They are first cleared and then set according to the flags specified by *flags1*. Therefore, to set a number base, you will pass **basefield** to *flags2* (which causes the **oct**, **hex**, and **dec** flags to be cleared) and pass the desired number base flag to *flags1*. For example, the following sets the number base of **cout** to hexadecimal:

```
cout.setf(ios::hex, ios::basefield);
```

After this call, the **hex** flag will be set and the **dec** and **oct** flags will be cleared. This means that all integer output to **cout** will be displayed in hexadecimal.

When displaying integers, you can cause the base to be shown by setting the **showbase** flag. When set, values displayed in octal begin with a leading 0. Values displayed in hexadecimal begin with a leading 0x. Decimal values are unaffected.

Be default, floating-point values are formatted in either fixed-point format or in scientific notation, whichever is shorter. You can specify fixed-point representation by setting the **fixed** flag. You can specify scientific notation by setting the **scientific** flag. In either case, the other flag must be turned off. The easiest way to do this is to use the two-argument form of **setf( )**, specifying **floatfield** as the flags to turn off. Recall that **floatfield** combines both the **fixed** and **scientific** flags.

To cause a leading + sign to precede positive values, set the **showpos** flag. In general, **showpos** only affects floating-point values and integers displayed in decimal. Integers displayed in octal or hexadecimal will not be affected.

To cause a decimal point to be displayed, even when there are no fractional digits, set the **showpoint** flag.

By default, letters in numeric values, which include the hexadecimal digits a-f, the **e** in scientific notation, and the **x** in the hexadecimal base indicator, are displayed in lowercase. To change this to uppercase, specify the **uppercase** flag.

Example

The following example shows the numeric formatting flags in action:

```cpp
// Demonstrate the numeric format flags.
//
// This example uses cout, but any output stream
// could be substituted.

#include <iostream>

using namespace std;

int main()
{
  int x = 100;
  double f = 98.6;
  double f2 = 123456.0;
  double f3 = 1234567.0;

  cout.setf(ios::hex, ios::basefield);
  cout << "x in hexadecimal: " << x << endl;

  cout.setf(ios::oct, ios::basefield);
  cout << "x in octal: " << x << endl;

  cout.setf(ios::dec, ios::basefield);
  cout << "x in decimal: " << x << "\n\n";

  cout << "f, f2, and f3 in default floating-point format:\n";
  cout << "f: " << f << "  f2: " << f2 << "  f3: " << f3 << endl;

  cout.setf(ios::scientific, ios::floatfield);
  cout << "After setting scientific flag:\n";
  cout << "f: " << f << "  f2: " << f2 << "  f3: " << f3 << endl;

  cout.setf(ios::fixed, ios::floatfield);
  cout << "After setting fixed flag:\n";
  cout << "f: " << f << "  f2: " << f2 << "  f3: " << f3 << "\n\n";

  // Return to default floating-point format.
  cout << "Returning to default floating-point format.\n";
  cout.unsetf(ios::fixed);

  cout << "f2 in default format: " << f2 << "\n\n";

  // Set the showpoint flag.
  cout << "Setting showpoint flag.\n";
  cout.setf(ios::showpoint);
  cout << "f2 with showpoint set: " << f2 << "\n\n";

  cout << "Clearing the showpoint flag.\n\n";
  cout.unsetf(ios::showpoint);

  // Set the showpos flag.
  cout.setf(ios::showpos);
  cout << "Setting showpos flag.\n";
```

```
    cout << "x in decimal after setting showpos: " << x << endl;
    cout << "f in default notation after setting showpos: " << f << "\n\n";

    // Set the uppercase flag.
    cout << "Setting uppercase flag.\n";
    cout.setf(ios::uppercase);
    cout << "f3 with uppercase flag set: " << f3 << endl;

    return 0;
}
```

The output is shown here:

```
x in hexadecimal: 64
x in octal: 144
x in decimal: 100

f, f2, and f3 in default floating-point format:
f: 98.6   f2: 123456   f3: 1.23457e+006
After setting scientific flag:
f: 9.860000e+001   f2: 1.234560e+005   f3: 1.234567e+006
After setting fixed flag:
f: 98.600000   f2: 123456.000000   f3: 1234567.000000

Returning to default floating-point format.
f2 in default format: 123456

Setting showpoint flag.
f2 with showpoint set: 123456.

Clearing the showpoint flag.

Setting showpos flag.
x in decimal after setting showpos: +100
f in default notation after setting showpos: +98.6

Setting uppercase flag.
f3 with uppercase flag set: +1.23457E+006
```

Options and Alternatives

The numeric format flags can be set using manipulators. For example, the **showpoint** flag can be set by the **showpoint** manipulator and cleared by the **noshowpoint** manipulator. See *Use I/O Manipulators to Format Data* for details.

For any given stream, the default precision is 6 digits, but you can change this by calling the **precision( )** function. See *Set the Precision* for details You can also specify a field width in which the value is displayed by calling **width( )** and the fill character used to pad fields that are larger than the output by calling **fill( )**. These are described in *Set the Field Width and Fill Character*.

Set the Precision

Key Ingredients		
Headers	**Classes**	**Functions**
<ios>	ios_base	streamsize precision(streamsize *prec*)

Each stream has a precision setting associated with it that determines how many digits are displayed when a floating-point value is formatted. The default precision is 6. You can change this by calling **precision( )**. As explained in the discussion that follows, the exact meaning of the precision differs based on what floating-point format is used.

Step-by-Step

To set the precision involves the following steps:

1. Set the precision by calling **precision( )** on the stream.
2. In some cases, you may need to adjust the floating-point format by setting either the **fixed** or **scientific** flag to achieve the desired results.

Discussion

Each stream has its own precision attribute. The precision is set by calling **precision( )** on the stream. This function is a member of **ios_base** and is inherited by all stream classes. One of its forms is shown here:

    streamsize precision(streamsize *prec*)

The precision of the invoking stream is set to *prec*. The previous precision is returned. The default precision of a stream is 6. The **streamsize** type is defined as some form of integer that is capable of holding the largest number of bytes that can be transferred in any one I/O operation.

The precise effect of the precision is based on the floating-point format being used. For the default format, the precision determines the number of significant digits displayed. For fixed-point or scientific notation, the precision determines the number of digits displayed to the right of the decimal point. (Scientific notation is used when the **scientific** flag is set and the **fixed** flag is cleared. Fixed-point notation is used when the **scientific** flag is cleared and the **fixed** flag is set.)

Setting the precision answers one of the most common "How-To" questions: "How do I display two decimal places?" This is easily accomplished by setting the **fixed** flag and then setting the precision to 2. After doing this, two decimal places will be displayed in all cases, even when there are no significant decimal digits. More generally, if you need to specify a fixed number of decimal digits, then set the **fixed** flag and specify the number of digits in a call to **precision( )**.

Example

The following example shows the effects of setting the precision:

```
// Demonstrate setting the precision.

#include <iostream>

using namespace std;

int main()
{
  double f = 123456.123456789;

  cout << "Using default numeric format.\n";
  cout << "f with default precision: " << f << "\n\n";

  cout << "Setting the precision to 9.\n";
  cout.precision(9);
  cout << "f with precision of 9: " << f << "\n\n";

  cout << "Switching to fixed-point format.\n";
  cout.setf(ios::fixed, ios::floatfield);

  cout << "f with precision of 9 in fixed-point: " << f << "\n\n";

  // Now, display two decimal places.
  cout << "Display two decimal places in all cases: ";
  cout.precision(2);
  cout << 12.456 << " " << 10.0 << " " << 19.1 << endl;

  return 0;
}
```

The output is shown here:

```
Using default numeric format.
f with default precision: 123456

Setting the precision to 9.
f with precision of 9: 123456.123

Switching to fixed-point format.
f with precision of 9 in fixed-point: 123456.123456789

Display two decimal places in all cases: 12.46 10.00 19.10
```

Options and Alternatives

There is a second form of **precision( )**, shown here:

```
streamsize precision( ) const
```

This form returns the current precision, but does not change it.

Another way to set a stream's precision is to use the I/O manipulator **setprecision**. It is described in *Use the I/O Manipulators to Format Data.*

Set the Field Width and Fill Character

Key Ingredients		
Headers	**Classes**	**Functions**
<ios>	ios_base	streamsize width(streamsize *w*)
<ios>	ios	char fill(char *ch*)

This recipe shows how to specify a field width and a fill character. By default, when a value is output, it occupies only as much space as the number of characters that it takes to display it. This is often exactly what you want. However, sometimes, you will want the value to fill a certain field width, such as when you want columns of data to line up. Although there are various ways to achieve that outcome, by far, the easiest is to specify a field width. Once done, each item will be automatically padded so that it fills the field width. The default fill character is a space, and this is often what you want, but you can change it.

Step-by-Step

To specify the field width and the fill character involves these steps:

1. To specify a field width, call **width( )** on the stream.
2. To change the fill character, call **fill( )** on the stream.

Discussion

You can specify a minimum field width by using the **width( )** function. It has two forms. The one used in this recipe is shown here:

    streamsize width(streamsize *w*)

Here, *w* becomes the field width and the previous field width is returned. As a general rule, the field width must be set immediately before outputting the item for which you want the field width to apply. After that item is output, the field width returns to its default. (I have seen implementations in which setting the field width once applied to all subsequent output, but this is nonstandard behavior.) The **streamsize** type is a **typedef** for some form of integer.

After you set a minimum field width, when a value uses less than the specified width, the field will be padded with the current fill character (space, by default) to reach the desired width. If the size of the value exceeds the minimum field width, then the field will be overrun. No values are truncated.

In the default locale, output is right-justified. This means that if a field needs to be padded to achieve a specified width, then padding characters will be added to the left of the data. When output is left-justified, padding will be added to the right of the data. When the **internal** flag is set, padding is added within the interior of some types of numeric formats. For example, if the **showpos** flag is set, then padding takes place between the leading + sign and the digits. See *Justify Output* for details.

When a field needs to be filled, it is filled with the fill character, which is a space by default. You can specify a different character by using the **fill( )** function. It has two forms. The one used here is:

    char fill(char *ch*)

After a call to **fill( )**, *ch* becomes the new fill character and the old one is returned.

Example

The following example demonstrates setting the field width and the fill character. There are two important things to notice in this program. First, that a call to **width( )** affects only the next item output. Second, that fill characters are added between the + sign and the digits when numeric data is displayed when the **internal** and **showpos** flags are set.

```
// Demonstrate width() and fill().

#include <iostream>

using namespace std;

int main()
{
  // Use default width.
  cout << "Hello" << endl;

  // Set width to 10.
  cout.width(10);
  cout << "Hello" << endl;

  // Notice how width returns to default after an item is output.
  cout << "Hello" << endl;

  // Now set the width and the fill character.
  cout.width(10);
  cout.fill('*');
  cout << "Hello" << endl;

  // Notice that fill character stays set.
  cout.width(12);
  cout << 123.45 << endl;

  // Now, pad the field width with spaces and
  // set the internal and showpos flags.
  cout.width(12);
  cout.fill(' ');
```

```
   cout.setf(ios::showpos | ios::internal);
   cout << 765.34 << endl;

   return 0;
}
```

The output is shown here:

```
Hello
      Hello
Hello
*****Hello
******123.45
+      765.34
```

Bonus Example: Line Up Columns of Numbers

One of the most common uses of a minimum field width is to create tables in which columns of numbers line up one over another. To do this, simply specify a field width that is at least as large as the maximum number of digits that you will display, plus the decimal point and + sign, if present. The following program demonstrates the process by creating a table of the powers of 2 and 3. Notice that the columns line up.

```
// Line up columns of data.

#include <iostream>

using namespace std;

int main()
{

  cout << "Root | Square |    Cube\n";
  for(int i = 1; i < 11; ++i) {
    cout.width(4);
    cout << i << " |";
    cout.width(7);
    cout << i * i << " |";
    cout.width(8);
    cout << i * i * i;
    cout << endl;
  }

  return 0;
}
```

Here is the output:

```
Root | Square |    Cube
   1 |      1 |       1
   2 |      4 |       8
   3 |      9 |      27
   4 |     16 |      64
   5 |     25 |     125
```

```
 6  |    36  |    216
 7  |    49  |    343
 8  |    64  |    512
 9  |    81  |    729
10  |   100  |   1000
```

Options and Alternatives

There are overloaded forms of **width( )** and **fill( )**, which are shown here:

char fill( ) const

streamsize width( ) const

These forms obtain, but do not change, the current settings.

Another way to set a stream's field width and fill character is to use the I/O manipulators **setw** and **setfill**. They are described in *Use I/O Manipulators to Format Data.*

Justify Output

Key Ingredients		
Headers	**Classes**	**Functions and Flags**
<ios>	ios_base	fmtflags setf(fmtflags *flags*)
		fmtflags setf(fmtflags *flags1*, *flags2*)
		adjustfield
		internal
		left
		right

Typically, output is right-justified by default. This means that when a field width exceeds the size of the data, padding is added to the beginning of the field to achieve the desired width. (See the preceding recipe for details on field widths and the fill character.) You can change this behavior by setting either the **left** or **internal** format flag. You can return to right justifcation by setting the **right** flag. This recipe shows the process.

Step-by-Step

To set the justification involves these steps:

1. To left-justify output, clear the flags specified by **adjustfield** and then set the **left** flag.

2. To right-justify output, clear the flags specified by **adjustfield** and then set the **right** flag.

3. To use internal padding to justify numeric values, clear the flags specified by **adjustfield** and then set the **internal** flag.

Discussion

There are three format flags that affect justification: **right**, **left**, and **internal**. Collectively, these flags can be referred to by the value **adjustfield**. In general, only one of these flags should be set at any time. Therefore, when changing the justification method, you must turn on the flag you want and ensure that the other two flags are cleared. This is easily accomplished by use of the two-argument form of **setf( )** and the **adjustfield** value. You will see an example of this shortly. (See *Access the Format Flags via Stream Member Functions* for a description of setting the format flags with **setf( )**.)

As a general rule, output is right-justified by default. This means that if the field width is larger than the data, padding will occur to the left of the data. For example, consider this sequence:

```
cout << 12345678 << endl;
cout.width(8);
cout << "test" << endl;
```

It produces the following output:

```
12345678
    test
```

When the string "test" is output in a field that is 8 characters wide, it is padded by 4 characters on the left, as the output shows.

To specify left justification, set the **left** format flag, as shown in this sequence:

```
cout.setf(ios::left, ios::adjustfield);
cout << 12345678 << endl;
cout.width(8);
cout << "test" << "|" << endl;
```

It produces this output:

```
12345678
test    |
```

As you can see, the padding is added to the right of the data, rather than the left. This makes the data line up on the left. Notice how the **left** flag is set by use of the two-argument form of **setf( )**. It first clears all of the flags referred to by **adjustfield** and then sets the **left** flag. This ensures that only the left **flag** is set.

When outputting numeric data, you can cause padding to be inserted within portions of the format by turning on the **internal** flag. For example, if you turn on the **showpos** flag (which causes a + sign to be shown for positive values), then any padding will take place between the + sign and the digits.

Example

The following program shows the justification format flags in action.

```
// Demonstrate the left, right, and internal format flags.

#include <iostream>
```

```
using namespace std;

int main()
{

  // Use default width.
  cout << "Default format.\n";
  cout << "|";
  cout << 123.45 << "|" << "\n\n";

  // Use default right justification
  cout << "Right-justify in a field width of 12.\n";
  cout << "|";
  cout.width(12);
  cout << 123.45 << "|" << "\n\n";

  // Switch to left justification.
  cout << "Left-justify in a field width of 12.\n";
  cout.setf(ios::left, ios::adjustfield);
  cout << "|";
  cout.width(12);
  cout << 123.45 << "|" << "\n\n";

  // Turn on showpos, use left-justification.
  cout << "Turning on showpos flag.\n";
  cout.setf(ios::showpos);
  cout << "Left-justify set in a field width of 12 again.\n";
  cout << "|";
  cout.width(12);
  cout << 123.45 << "|" << "\n\n";

  // Now, use internal.
  cout << "Turning on internal justification.\n";
  cout.setf(ios::internal, ios::adjustfield);
  cout << "Internal justification in a field width of 12.\n";
  cout << "|";
  cout.width(12);
  cout << 123.45 << "|" << endl;

  return 0;
}
```

The output is shown here:

```
Default format.
|123.45|

Right-justify in a field width of 12.
|      123.45|

Left-justify in a field width of 12.
|123.45      |
```

```
Turning on showpos flag.
Left-justify set in a field width of 12 again.
|+123.45      |

Turning on internal justification.
Internal justification in a field width of 12.
|+      123.45|
```

Options and Alternatives

You can set the justification mode by use of the I/O manipulators **left**, **right**, and **internal**. They are described in *Use I/O Manipulators to Format Data.*

Use I/O Manipulators to Format Data

Key Ingredients		
Headers	**Classes**	**Functions**
<ios>		endl
		fixed
		left
		right
		scientific
		showpoint
		showpos
<iomanip>		resetiosflags(ios_base::fmtflags *flags*)
		setprecision(int *prec*)
		setw(int *w*)

C++ contains an extensive set of I/O manipulators that let you embed formatting directives into an I/O expression. The manipulators are used to set or clear the format flags associated with a stream. They also let you specify the field width, precision, and fill character. Thus, they duplicate the functionality supplied by the stream member functions, providing a convenient alternative that enables more compact code to be written.

There are several different manipulators defined by C++. This recipe shows how to use a representative sample. Because all manipulators work in the same basic way, the techniques presented here apply to all manipulators.

Step-by-Step

To use an I/O manipulator involves these steps:

1. To use a parameterized manipulator, include the **<iomanip>** header. Most of the parameterless manipulators are defined by **<ios>**, which is normally included by another I/O header, such as **<iostream>**.

2. To invoke a manipulator, embed its name within an output expression. If the manipulator takes an argument, then specify that argument within parentheses. Otherwise, simply use the name of the manipulator without any parentheses.

Discussion

There are two basic types of I/O manipulators: parameterless and parameterized. We will begin with the parameterless manipulators. The parameterless manipulators that operate on output streams are shown here:

Manipulator	Purpose
boolalpha	Turns on **boolalpha** flag.
endl	Outputs a newline.
ends	Outputs a null.
dec	Turns on **dec** flag. Turns off the **hex** and **oct** flags.
fixed	Turns on **fixed** flag. Turns off the **scientific** flag.
flush	Flushes the stream.
hex	Turns on **hex** flag. Turns off the **dec** and **oct** flags.
internal	Turns on **internal** flag. Turns off the **left** and **right** flags.
left	Turns on **left** flag. Turns off the **right** and **internal** flags.
noboolalpha	Turns off **boolalpha** flag.
noshowbase	Turns off **showbase** flag.
noshowpoint	Turns off **showpoint** flag.
noshowpos	Turns off **showpos** flag.
nounitbuf	Turns off **unitbuf** flag.
nouppercase	Turns off **uppercase** flag.
oct	Turns on **oct** flag. Turns off the **dec** and **hex** flags.
right	Turns on **right** flag. Turns off the **left** and **internal** flags.
scientific	Turns on **scientific** flag. Turns off the **fixed** flag.
showbase	Turns on **showbase** flag.
showpoint	Turns on **showpoint** flag.
showpos	Turns on **showpos** flag.
unitbuf	Turns on **unitbuf** flag.
uppercase	Turns on **uppercase** flag.

Most of these manipulators are declared in the **<ios>** header (which is automatically included by other headers, such as **<iostream>**). However, **endl**, **ends**, and **flush** are declared in **<ostream>**.

The parameterless output manipulators control the setting of the various format flags. For example, to turn on the **showpoint** flag, use the **showpoint** manipulator. To turn off the **showpoint** flag, use the **noshowpoint** manipulator. Notice that the manipulators that control the number base, justification, and floating-point format automatically select the specified format, turning off the other flags in the group. For example, the **hex** manipulator automatically turns on the **hex** flag and turns off the **dec** and **oct** flags. Therefore, to select hexadecimal output, you simply include the **hex** manipulator. The **dec** and **oct** flags are automatically cleared.

To use a parameterized manipulator, you must include **<iomanip>**. It defines the following manipulators:

resetiosflags (ios_base::fmtflags *f)*	Turn off the flags specified in *f*.
setbase(int *base)*	Set the number base to *base*.
setfill(int *ch)*	Set the fill character to *ch*.
setiosflags(ios_base::fmtflags *f)*	Turn on the flags specified in *f*.
setprecision (int *p)*	Set the number of digits of precision.
setw(int *w)*	Set the field width to *w*.

For example, to set the field width to 20, embed **setw(20)** in an output expression. As is the case with the **width( )** function, **setw** affects only the width of the next item to be output. You can use the **setiosflags( )** and **resetiosflags( )** to set or clear any arbitrary combination of flags.

I/O manipulators are embedded in an I/O expression. For example:

```
cout << setprecision(8) << left << 123.23;
```

This sets the precision to 8, turns on the left-justification flag, and then outputs the number 123.23.

Although the manipulators provide the same functionality as the **setf( )**, **unsetf( )**, **width( )**, **precision( )**, and **fill( )** member functions described in the preceding recipes, they do so in a more streamlined fashion. For example, consider this expression:

```
cout << setw(12) << fixed << showpos << 98.6 << setw(10) << avg;
```

In a single line, it sets the field width to 12, turns on the **fixed** and **showpos** flags, and then outputs the number 98.6. It then sets the field width to 10 and outputs the value of **avg**. The same result can be obtained by use of stream member functions, but in a less compact form:

```
cout.width(12);
cout.setf(ios::fixed, ios::floatfield);
cout.setf(showpos);
cout << 98.6;
cout.width(10);
cout << avg;
```

Example

The following example shows several of the I/O manipulators in action.

```cpp
// Demonstrate several I/O manipulators.

#include <iostream>
#include <iomanip>

using namespace std;

int main()
{
  cout << "Default format: " << 123.123456789 << endl;

  cout << "Fixed format with precision of 7: ";
  cout << setprecision(7) << fixed << 123.123456789 << endl;

  cout << "Scientific format with precision of 7: ";
  cout << scientific << 123.123456789 << endl;

  cout << "Return to default format: ";
  cout << resetiosflags(ios::floatfield) << setprecision(6)
       << 123.123456789 << "\n\n";

  cout << "Use a field width of 20:\n";
  cout << "|" << setw(20) << "Testing" << "|\n\n";
  cout << "Use a field width of 20 with left justification:\n";
  cout << "|" << setw(20) << left << "Testing" << "|\n\n";

  cout << "Returning to right justification.\n\n" << right;

  cout << "Booleans in both formats: ";
  cout << true << " " << false << " " << boolalpha
       << true << " " << false << "\n\n";

  cout << "Default: " << 10.0 << endl;
  cout << "After setting the showpos and showpoint flags: ";
  cout << showpos << showpoint  << 10.0 << "\n\n";

  cout << "The setw manipulator is very useful when repeated field\n"
       << "widths must be specified. For example:\n";
  cout << setw(8) << "this" << endl <<  setw(8) << "is" << endl
       << setw(8) << "a" << endl << setw(8) << "column" << endl
       << setw(8) << "of" << endl << setw(8) << "words";

  return 0;
}
```

The output is shown here:

```
Default format: 123.123
Fixed format with precision of 7: 123.1234568
Scientific format with precision of 7: 1.2312346e+002
```

```
Return to default format: 123.123

Use a field width of 20:
|             Testing|

Use a field width of 20 with left justification:
|Testing             |

Returning to right justification.

Booleans in both formats: 1 0 true false

Default: 10
After setting the showpos and showpoint flags: +10.0000

The setw manipulator is very useful when repeated field
widths must be specified. For example:
    this
      is
       a
  column
      of
   words
```

Options and Alternatives

You can set the format flags by making explicit calls to **setf( )** on the stream. You can set the width, precision, and fill character by calling **width( )**, **precision( )**, and **fill( )** on the stream. This approach is described by the preceding recipes.

You can create your own manipulators. The techniques required to do so are described in Chapter 5.

Format Numeric Values for a Locale

Key Ingredients		
Headers	**Classes**	**Functions**
<ios>	ios_base	locale imbue(const &locale *newloc*)
<locale>	locale	

When numeric values are output to a stream, they are automatically formatted by the **num_put** facet defined by that stream's current locale. Therefore, to format a numeric value for a specific locale is easy: Simply change the stream's locale to the one desired. The **num_put** facet for the new locale will automatically be used. This recipe shows the process.

Step-by-Step

To format numbers relative to a specific locale involves these steps:

1. Create a **locale** object that represents the desired locale.
2. Set the stream's locale to the one created in Step 1 by calling **imbue( )**.

Discussion

Instructions for setting a stream's locale are presented in *Obtain or Set a Stream's Locale* in Chapter 5. They are summarized here.

The current locale defines several aspects of a numeric format, including the characters used for the decimal point and thousands separator. As a general rule, the default locale is the "C" locale. This locale defines a standard C/C++ environment, which uses the period as the decimal point and provides little other formatting. For many applications, the default locale is fine. However, in cases in which you want numeric values to be displayed in a format compatible with the user's locale, you will need to specify that locale explicitly.

One way to construct a **locale** instance is to use this locale constructor:

explicit locale(const char *name)

Here, *name* specifies the name of the locale, such as German, Spanish_Spain, or US. If *name* does not represent a valid locale, then a **runtime_error** exception is thrown. What constitutes a valid locale name may (probably will) vary from compiler to compiler. The examples shown in this book work with Microsoft's Visual C++, and might work for other compilers, but you should consult your compiler's documentation for details.

To set a stream's locale, call **imbue( )** on the stream. It is shown here:

locale imbue(const locale &*newloc*)

The invoking stream's locale is set to *newloc,* and the old locale is returned.

Example

The following example shows the way different locales affect the format of numbers. The program begins by displaying a value in the default format (which is typically determined by the C locale). It then specifies the English locale and displays the same value. Finally, it uses the German locale. Notice that in English, the thousands separator is a comma and the decimal point is a period. In German, this is reversed, with the thousands separator being the period and the decimal point being the comma. Also notice that the **fixed** flag and the precision are set, but these are not affected by the locale setting.

```
// Format numeric values relative to a locale.

#include <iostream>
#include <locale>
#include <iomanip>

using namespace std;

int main()
```

```
{
  // Use a fixed format with 2 decimal places.
  cout << fixed << setprecision(2);

  cout << "Default format: " << 12345678.12 << "\n\n";

  // Set the locale to English.
  locale eloc("English");
  cout.imbue(eloc);

  cout << "English format: " << 12345678.12 << "\n\n";

  locale gloc("German");
  cout.imbue(gloc);

  cout << "German format: " << 12345678.12 << "\n\n";
  return 0;
}
```

The output is shown here:

```
Default format: 12345678.12

English format: 12,345,678.12

German format: 12.345.678,12
```

Options and Alternatives

You can format numeric values in a monetary format by using the **money_put** facet. It automatically uses the current locale. See *Format Monetary Values Using the **money_put** Facet* for details.

Although the preceding example, and many of the examples in this chapter, use **cout** as the target stream, the same basic approach works with all output streams. For example, the following sequence creates an **ofstream** called **fout** and connects it to a file called **test.dat**. It then turns on the **fixed** flag and sets the precision to 2. Next, it sets the locale to German. Finally, it outputs 12345678.12 to **fout**.

```
ofstream fout("test.dat");
fout.imbue(locale("German"));
fout << fixed << setprecision(2);
fout << 12345678.12;
```

After this sequence executes, **test.dat** will contain the following:

```
12.345.678,12
```

As you can see, it is formatted for German.

Although using the formatted I/O operator **<<** is the easiest (and most often the best) way to format numeric output, you can use the **num_put** facet directly. This is done by first obtaining a reference to a **num_put** facet for the current locale by calling **use_facet( )**, which is described in *Facet Overview* near the start of this chapter. Then, using this reference, call **put( )** to format a value and output it to a stream.

The **num_put** facet is declared like this:

template <class CharT, class OutItr = ostreambuf_iterator<CharT> >
    class num_put : public locale::facet { // ...

CharT specifies the type of characters being operated upon. **OutItr** specifies the iterator type that is used to write formatted data. Notice that it defaults to **ostreambuf_iterator**.
    The **put( )** function defined by **num_put** has several versions. Here is one. It formats a **double** value.

iter_type put(iter_type *strm_itr*, ios_base &*strm*,
            char_type *fillchar*, double *val*) const

An iterator to the output stream is passed in *strm_itr*. The type **iter_type** is a **typedef** for the iterator type. By default, this type is **ostreambuf_iterator**. There is an automatic conversion to this type from any **basic_ostream** object, so typically, you will simply pass the stream being acted upon. Pass a reference to the output stream in *strm*. Its flag settings, precision, and width are used to govern the format. The fill character is passed in *fillchar*. The value to be formatted is passed in *val*.
    Putting together the pieces, the following sequence uses **num_put** to display the number 1024.256 in fixed format, with a precision of 2 and a width of 20, in the current locale.

```
cout << fixed << setprecision(2) << setw(20);
const num_put<char> &np = use_facet<num_put<char> >(cout.getloc());
np.put(cout, cout, ' ', 1024.256);
```

As you can see, this involves much more effort than does the << operator and gains nothing for the effort.
    You can read a number in a locale-sensitive manner by using the **num_get** facet. It defines the **get( )** function that reads a number in its stream form.

Format Monetary Values Using the money_put Facet

Key Ingredients		
Headers	**Classes**	**Functions**
<ios>	ios_base	locale getloc( ) const
<ios>	ios	locale imbue(const &locale *newloc*)
<locale>	locale	template <class Facet> const Facet &use_facet(const locale &*loc*)

<locale>	money_put	iter_type put(iter_type *strm_itr*,
		        bool *int_cur_sym*,
		        ios_base &*strm*,
		        char_type *fillchar*,
		        long double *val*) const

As it relates to formatting, perhaps the single most frequently asked "How-To" question is "How do I display monetary values?" Because the default numeric format is not designed for this purpose, the proper approach is a source of much confusion. Fortunately, the solution is quite easy: Simply use the **money_put** facet defined by the C++ localization library. Doing so automatically produces the correct format for the current locale. This recipe shows the process.

Step-by-Step

To display a monetary value via the **money_put** facet involves these steps:

1. Construct a **locale** object that represents the locale for which the monetary value will be formatted.

2. Set the locale by calling **imbue( )** on the stream that will be receiving the formatted output. Pass **imbue( )** the **locale** object from Step 1.

3. Obtain the **money_put** facet by calling **use_facet( )**, specifying the locale from which to obtain the facet. In general, this will be the current locale used by the output stream. You can obtain this locale by calling **getloc( )** on the stream.

4. Format the data by calling **put( )** on the object returned by **use_facet( )**, specifying the stream to which the output will be written.

Discussion

A general overview of the C++ localization subsystem was presented near the start of this chapter. The **imbue( )** and **getloc( )** functions are described in *Obtain or Set a Stream's Locale* in Chapter 5. The **imbue( )** method is also summarized by the preceding recipe. Recall that **imbue( )** sets a stream's locale.

The **money_put** facet is declared as shown here:

```
template <class CharT, class OutItr = ostreambuf_iterator<CharT> >
   class money_put : public locale::facet { // ...
```

CharT specifies the type of characters being operated upon. **OutItr** specifies the iterator type that is used to write formatted data. Notice that it defaults to **ostreambuf_iterator**.

To obtain the **money_put** facet, you must call **use_facet( )**. This function is described in *Facet Overview* near the start of this chapter. Recall that it is a global generic function defined by **<locale>**, with the following prototype:

```
template <class Facet> const Facet &use_facet(const locale &loc)
```

The template parameter **Facet** specifies the facet, which will be **money_put** in this case. The locale is passed via *loc*. A reference to the facet is returned. Thus, **use_facet( )** obtains a specific version of the facet tailored to the locale. A **bad_cast** exception is thrown if the desired facet is not available. In general, the predefined facets, including **money_put**, will be available.

Usually, the **locale** instance passed to **use_facet( )** will be the one used by the output stream to which the facet will be applied. You can obtain a stream's current locale by calling **getloc( )** on the stream. It is shown here:

```
locale getloc( ) const
```

It returns the **locale** object associated with the stream.

Using the facet returned by **use_facet( )**, you can format a monetary value by calling **put( )**. It has two forms. The one used by this recipe is shown here:

iter_type put(iter_type *strm_itr*, bool *int_cur_sym*, ios_base &*strm*,
            char_type *fillchar*, long double *val*) const

An iterator to the output stream is passed in *strm_itr*. The type **iter_type** is a **typedef** for the iterator type. By default, this type is **ostreambuf_iterator**. There is an automatic conversion to this type from any **basic_ostream** object, so typically, you will simply pass the stream being acted upon. If the currency symbol is to be shown in its international form, pass true to *int_cur_sym*. Pass false to use the local symbol. Pass a reference to the output stream in *strm*. If its **showbase** flag is set, then the currency symbol will be shown. The fill character is passed in *fillchar*. The value to be formatted is passed in *val*. The **put( )** function returns an iterator that points one position past the last character output.

The one peculiarity associated with **money_put** is that it operates on data that does not contain a decimal point. For example, the value 1724.89 is passed to **put( )** as 172489. The money formatter automatically adds the comma and decimal point. For US dollars, it is transformed into 1,724.89. If you have enabled the domestic currency symbol, then the result is $1,724.89.

Example

The following example shows how to use **money_put**.

```
// Use money_put to output monetary values.

#include <iostream>
#include <locale>

using namespace std;

int main()
{
  double balance = 5467.87;

  locale usloc("English_US");
  locale gloc("German_Germany");

  // Set showbase flag so that currency symbol is displayed.
  cout << showbase;

  cout << "Money format for US dollars:\n";
  cout.imbue(usloc);
  const money_put<char> &us_mon =
        use_facet<money_put<char> >(cout.getloc());

  us_mon.put(cout, false, cout, ' ', "123456");
  cout << endl;
  us_mon.put(cout, true, cout, ' ', -299);
  cout << endl;
```

```
us_mon.put(cout, false, cout, ' ', balance * 100);
cout << "\n\n";

cout << "Now show money in international German format:\n";
cout.imbue(gloc);
const money_put<char> &g_mon =
        use_facet<money_put<char> >(cout.getloc());

g_mon.put(cout, true, cout, ' ', 123456);
cout << endl;
g_mon.put(cout, true, cout, ' ', -299);
cout << endl;
g_mon.put(cout, true, cout, ' ', balance * 100);

return 0;
}
```

The output is shown here:

```
Money format for US dollars:
$1,234.56
USD-2.99
$5,467.87

Now show money in international German format:
EUR1.234,56
EUR-2,99
EUR5.467,87
```

Options and Alternatives

There is a second form of **put( )** that formats a string version of the value. It is shown here:

> iter_type put(iter_type *strm_itr*, bool *int_cur_sym*, ios_base &*strmflags*,
>   char_type *fillchar*, string &*strval*) const

It works just like the first version, except that the value to be formatted is passed as a string in *strval*.

As explained, if you request a facet that is not available, then a **bad_cast** exception is thrown. To avoid this possibility, you can determine if a facet is available for a given locale by calling **has_facet( )**. This is a global template function defined by **<locale>**. It is shown here:

> template <class Facet> bool has_facet(const locale &*loc*) throw( )

It returns true if the specified facet is available and false otherwise. In general, the standard facets will always be available, but custom facets may not be. In either case, you may want to use **has_facet( )** to confirm that a facet can be used. Doing so can avoid an exception.

You can read formatted monetary values by using the **money_get** facet. It defines the function **get( )**, which reads a currency value in its string form.

Use the moneypunct and numpunct Facets

Key Ingredients		
Headers	**Classes**	**Functions**
<locale>	moneypunct	string_type cur_symbol( ) const
		char_type decimal_point( ) const
		int frac_digits( ) const
		char_type thousands_sep( ) const
		string grouping( ) const
<locale>	numpunct	char_type decimal_point( ) const
		char_type thousands_sep( ) const
		string grouping( ) const

Although formatting numeric values via **num_put** and monetary values via **money_put** is usually the best option, you can take control of the process if you like. The key is to obtain the punctuation and rules used to format monetary and numeric values relative to a locale. This punctuation includes the currency symbol, the thousands separator, and the decimal point. The rules include the number of fractional digits displayed and the number of digits in a group. Both are available through the **moneypunct** and **numpunct** facets. This recipe shows how to obtain them.

Step-by-Step

To use the **numpunct** facet involves these steps:

1. Obtain the **numpunct** facet for a specified locale by calling **use_facet( )**. Use this facet to obtain the numeric punctuation and rules for the locale as described in the following steps.
2. Obtain the decimal point character by calling **decimal_point( )**.
3. Obtain the thousands separator by calling **thousands_sep( )**.
4. Obtain the rule that governs digit groupings by calling **grouping( )**.

To use the **moneypunct** facet involves these steps:

1. Obtain the **moneypunct** facet for a specified locale by calling **use_facet( )**. Use this facet to obtain the numeric punctuation and rules for the locale as described in the following steps.
2. Obtain the currency symbol by calling **cur_symbol( )**.
3. Obtain the decimal point character by calling **decimal_point( )**.
4. Obtain the thousands separator by calling **thousands_sep( )**.

5. Obtain the number of fractional digits used to represent monetary values by calling **frac_digits( )**.

6. Obtain the rule that governs digit groupings by calling **grouping( )**.

Discussion

The punctuation and rules for numeric values are encapsulated within the **numpunct** facet. It is declared as shown here:

```
template <class CharT> class numpunct : public locale::facet { // ...
```

The **CharT** specifies the type of characters being operated upon. Like all facets, it inherits **locale::facet**.

You can obtain a reference to a **numpunct** facet by calling **use_facet( )**, specifying **numpunct** as the facet to obtain. The **use_facet( )** function is defined globally by **<locale>**, as described in the *Facet Overview*. The following sequence shows how to use it to obtain a **numpunct** facet for the locale currently used by **cout**:

```
const numpunct<char> &numpunct = use_facet<numpunct<char> >(cout.getloc());
```

Given a reference to the **numpunct** facet, you can obtain the various punctuation and rules that relate to numeric values. Each value is tailored to the facet's locale. These items are available through functions. The ones used by this recipe are shown here:

Function	Description
char_type decimal_point( ) const	Returns the character used as the decimal point.
char_type thousands_sep( ) const	Returns the character used to separate (i.e., group) thousands.
string grouping( ) const	Returns rules that define the digit groupings.

Here, **char_type** is a **typedef** for the type of character, which will be **char** for **char**-based streams.

The punctuation and rules for monetary values are encapsulated within the **moneypunct** facet. It is declared as shown here:

```
template <class CharT, bool Intl = false>
    class moneypunct : public locale::facet, public money_base { // ...
```

The **CharT** specifies the type of characters being operated upon. The **Intl** type indicates whether international or local formats are used. The default is local. Like all facets, it inherits **locale::facet**. The **money_base** class defines aspects of monetary formats that are dependent upon type parameters. It is described more fully in the *Options and Alternatives* section for this recipe.

As is the case with **numpunct**, a reference to **moneypunct** is obtained by calling **use_facet( )**. Here is an example:

```
const moneypunct<char> &us_moneypunct = use_facet<moneypunct<char>
                                     >(cout.getloc());
```

This statement obtains the **moneypunct** facet for the locale used by **cout**.

Given a reference to the **moneypunct** facet, you can obtain the various punctuation and rules that relate to numeric values by calling functions through the reference. Each value is tailored to the facet's locale. The ones used by this recipe are shown here:

Function	Description
string_type cur_symbol( ) const	Returns the character(s) used as the currency symbol.
char_type decimal_point( ) const	Returns the character used as the decimal point.
int frac_digits( ) const	Returns the number of fraction digits normally displayed for monetary values.
char_type thousands_sep( ) const	Returns the character used to separate (i.e., group) thousands.
string grouping( ) const	Returns rules that define the digit groupings.

Here, **char_type** is a **typedef** for the type of character, which will be **char** for **char**-based streams, and **string_type** is a **typedef** for the type of **string**, which will be **string** for **char**-based streams.

The value returned by **grouping( )** is the same for both **numpunct** and **moneypunct**. It is a string value in which the unicode value of each character in the string represents the number of digits in a group, moving from right to left, and beginning with the first group to the left of the decimal point. If the size of the specific group is not specified, the previous group size is used. Therefore, if the group sizes are all the same, then only one value is specified. Remember, it is the unicode value of the character that is used, not its human-readable digit. Therefore, the character '\003' (not '3') represents 3 digits.

Example

The following example shows how to use **moneypunct** and **numpunct** to obtain the punctuation and grouping rules for the United States:

```
// Demonstrate monetary and numeric punctuation and grouping.

#include <iostream>
#include <locale>

using namespace std;

int main()
{
  // Create a locale for US English.
  locale usloc("English_US");

  // Set the locale of cout to US English.
  cout.imbue(usloc);

  // Get a moneypunct facet for cout.
  const moneypunct<char> &us_monpunct =
        use_facet<moneypunct<char> >(cout.getloc());

  cout << "Monetary punctuation for US:\n";
  cout << "  Currency symbol: " << us_monpunct.curr_symbol() << endl;
```

```
cout << "  Decimal point: " << us_monpunct.decimal_point() << endl;
cout << "  Thousands separator: " << us_monpunct.thousands_sep() << endl;
cout << "  Fraction digits: " << us_monpunct.frac_digits() << endl;

cout << "  Number of grouping rules: "
     << us_monpunct.grouping().size() << endl;

for(unsigned i=0; i < us_monpunct.grouping().size(); ++i)
  cout << "  Size of group " << i << ": "
       << (int)us_monpunct.grouping()[0] << endl;

cout << endl;

// Get a numpunct facet for cout.
const numpunct<char> &us_numpunct =
      use_facet<numpunct<char> >(cout.getloc());

cout << "Numeric punctuation for US:\n";
cout << "  Decimal point: " << us_monpunct.decimal_point() << endl;
cout << "  Thousands separator: " << us_monpunct.thousands_sep() << endl;

cout << "  Number of grouping rules: "
     << us_monpunct.grouping().size() << endl;

for(unsigned i=0; i < us_monpunct.grouping().size(); ++i)
  cout << "  Size of group " << i << ": "
       << (int)us_monpunct.grouping()[0] << endl;

return 0;
}
```

The output is shown here:

```
Monetary punctuation for US:
  Currency symbol: $
  Decimal point: .
  Thousands separator: ,
  Fraction digits: 2
  Number of grouping rules: 1
  Size of group 0: 3

Numeric punctuation for US:
  Decimal point: .
  Thousands separator: ,
  Number of grouping rules: 1
  Size of group 0: 3
```

Options and Alternatives

The **numpunct** facet defines the functions **truename( )** and **falsename( )**, shown here:

string_type truename( ) const

string_type falsename( ) const

They return the names for **true** and **false** relative to the specified locale.

The **moneypunct** facet lets you obtain the signs used to indicate positive and negative monetary values by calling the functions **positive_sign( )** and **negative_sign( )**, shown here:

string_type positive_sign( ) const

string_type negative_sign( ) const

Notice that a string is returned, rather than a single character. This allows for multi-character signs.

Using **moneypunct**, you can also obtain patterns that represent the positive and negative formats by calling **pos_format( )** and **neg_format( )**, respectively. They are shown here:

pattern pos_format( ) const

pattern neg_format( ) const

Each returns a **pattern** object that describes the indicated format.

The **pattern** type is a **struct** defined within the **money_base** class. The **money_base** class is a base class for **moneypunct**. The **money_base** class is shown here:

```
class money_base {
public:
  enum part { none, space, symbol, sign, value };
  struct pattern {
    char field[4];
  };
};
```

Each element in **field** contains a **part** value. (The C++ Standard states that an array of **char**, rather than an array of **part**, is used for **field** "purely for efficiency.") Each element of **pattern** indicates what part of the money format must appear at that point, with the first part being in **field[0]**, the second part in **field[1]**, and so on. Here is what each enumeration constant means:

none	No corresponding output
space	A space
symbol	The currency symbol
sign	The positive or negative sign
value	The value

For example, assuming the previous program, the following sequence displays the negative pattern:

```
// Show the negative numeric pattern.
for(int i=0; i < 4; ++i)
  switch(us_monpunct.neg_format().field[i]) {
    case money_base::none: cout << "none ";
      break;
```

```
  case money_base::value: cout << "value ";
    break;
  case money_base::space: cout << "space ";
    break;
  case money_base::symbol: cout << "symbol ";
    break;
  case money_base::sign: cout << "sign ";
    break;
}
```

It produces the following output:

```
sign symbol value none
```

This indicates that a negative monetary value starts with a sign, followed by the currency symbol, and finally the value.

Format Time and Date Using the time_put Facet

Key Ingredients		
Headers	**Classes**	**Functions**
<ctime>		struct tm &localtime(const time_t *time)
		time_t time(time_t *t_ptr)
<ios>	ios_base	locale getloc( ) const
<ios>	ios	locale imbue(const &locale newloc)
<locale>	locale	template <class Facet>
		const Facet &use_facet(const locale &loc)
<locale>	time_put	iter_type put(iter_type strm_itr,
		ios_base &not_used,
		char_type fillchar,
		const tm *t,
		const char_type *pattern_start,
		const char_type *pattern_end) const

If "How do I display monetary values?" is the most commonly asked formatting question, the second most common is "How do I display the time and date?" Although conceptually easy, formatting the time and date involves more work than you might first think. The trouble is twofold. First, the time and date formats are sensitive to the locale. Therefore, there is no universal format that will work in all cases. Second, there are many ways in which the time and date can be displayed. As a result, there are many options to choose from.

In general, there are two ways to format the date and time using C++. The first is to call the C-based **strftime( )** function. It formats the date and time based on the global locale. (See *Format Time and Date Using strftime( )* for details.) The second approach is defined by C++ and uses the **time_put** facet defined by the localization subsystem. Using **time_put** offers one major advantage: It lets you format the time and date relative to the locale of a specific stream, rather than the global locale used by **strftime( )**. It is also integrated with C++'s other formatting facets, such as **money_put**. For these reasons, formatting date and time by use of **time_put** is the recommended approach for most applications. This recipe shows how to put it into action.

Step-by-Step

To format the time and date using the **time_put** facet involves these steps:

1. Construct a **locale** object that represents the locale for which the time and date will be formatted.
2. Set the locale by calling **imbue( )** on the stream that will be receiving the formatted output. Pass **imbue( )** the **locale** object from Step 1.
3. Obtain the **time_put** facet by calling **use_facet( )**, specifying the locale from which to obtain the facet. In general, this will be the current locale used by the output stream. You can obtain this locale by calling **getloc( )** on the stream.
4. Obtain a **tm** pointer that points to the time to be formatted. One way to obtain this pointer is to call **localtime( )**. It returns the local time as supplied by the computer.
5. Format the time and date by calling **put( )** on the object returned by **use_facet( )**, specifying the stream to which the output will be written.

Discussion

A general overview of the C++ localization subsystem is given near the start of this chapter. The **imbue( )** and **getloc( )** functions are described in *Obtain or Set a Stream's Locale* in Chapter 5. The **imbue( )** and **getloc( )** methods are also summarized by the preceding two recipes.

To format the time and date, you will use the **time_put** facet. It is declared like this:

```
template <class CharT, class OutItr = ostreambuf_iterator<CharT> >
    class time_put : public locale::facet { // ...
```

CharT specifies the type of characters being operated upon. **OutItr** specifies the iterator type that is used to write formatted data. Notice that it defaults to **ostreambuf_iterator**.

To obtain the **time_put** facet, you must call **use_facet( )**. This function is described in *Facet Overview* near the start of this chapter. Recall that it is a global generic function defined by **<locale>**, with the following prototype:

```
template <class Facet> const Facet &use_facet(const locale &loc)
```

The template parameter **Facet** specifies the facet, which will be **time_put** in this case. The locale is passed via *loc*. A reference to the facet is returned. A **bad_cast** exception is thrown if the desired facet is not available. In general, the predefined facets, including **time_put**, will be available.

Using the **time_put** facet obtained from **use_facet( )**, you can format a time value by calling **put( )**. It has two forms. The one used by this recipe is shown here:

iter_type put(iter_type *strm_itr*, ios_base &*not_used*, char_type *fillchar*,
const tm **t*, const char_type **pattern_start*,
const char_type **pattern_end*) const

An iterator to the output stream is passed in *strm_itr*. The type **iter_type** is a **typedef** for the iterator type. By default, this type is **ostreambuf_iterator**. There is an automatic conversion to this type from any **basic_ostream** object, so typically, you will simply pass the stream being acted upon. The *not_used* parameter is not used. (You can pass a reference to the output stream as a placeholder.) The fill character is passed in *fillchar*. A pointer to a **tm** structure that contains the time and date is passed in *t*. A pointer to the start of a string that defines a pattern that will be used to format the time and date is passed in *pattern_start*. A pointer to the end of the pattern string is passed in *pattern_end*. The type **char_type** is a **typedef** for the character type. For **char**-based strings, which are used by this book, this **char_type** is **char**.

The **tm** structure is defined in **<ctime>** and is inherited from C. It stores what is called the "broken-down" form of the time and date. It is shown here:

```
struct tm {
  int tm_sec;   // seconds, 0-61
  int tm_min;   // minutes, 0-59
  int tm_hour;  // hours, 0-23
  int tm_mday;  // day of the month, 1-31
  int tm_mon;   // months since Jan, 0-11
  int tm_year;  // years from 1900
  int tm_wday;  // days since Sunday, 0-6
  int tm_yday;  // days since Jan 1, 0-365
  int tm_isdst  // Daylight Saving Time indicator
}
```

You can construct a **tm** object by manually setting its members, but usually you won't. Most often, you will simply obtain a **tm** object that contains the current time and date by using a function defined by **<ctime>**. The one used by this recipe is **localtime( )** and it is shown here:

struct tm *localtime(const time_t **time*)

It takes the time encoded as a **time_t** value and returns a pointer to a **tm** structure that contains the time broken down into its individual components. The time is represented in local time. The **tm** structure that is pointed to by the pointer returned by **localtime( )** is statically allocated and is overwritten each time the function is called. If you want to save the contents of the structure, you must copy it elsewhere.

You can obtain a **time_t** value in several ways. The approach used by this recipe is to call **time( )**. It is another function defined by **<ctime>** and it obtains the current system time. It is shown here:

time_t time(time_t **t_ptr*)

It returns the current system time. This is typically represented as the number of seconds since January 1, 1970. If the system has no time, –1 is returned. The function can be called either with a null pointer or with a pointer to a variable of type **time_t**. If the latter is used, the variable pointed to by *t_tpr* will also be assigned the time.

In the **put( )** function, the pattern string pointed to by *pattern_start* contains two types of items. The first are normal characters, which are simply displayed as-is. The second are time and date format specifiers, which determine what time and date components are displayed. These format specifiers are the same as those used by the C legacy function **strftime( )**. They are listed in Table 6-1. (See *Format Time and Date Using* **strftime( )**.) The format specifiers begin with a percent sign (%) and are followed by a format command. For example, **%H** causes the hour to be displayed using a 24-hour clock. **%Y** causes the year to be displayed. You can combine both regular characters and time/date specifiers in the same pattern. For example,

```
char *custom_pat = "Today's date is %x";
```

Assuming that the date is January 1, 2008, then this causes the following output:

```
Today's date is 1/1/2008
```

Example

The following example shows **time_put** in action. It displays the time and date in both English and German.

```
// Output time and date using the time_put facets

#include <iostream>
#include <locale>
#include <cstring>
#include <ctime>

using namespace std;

int main()
{
  // Obtain the current system time.
  time_t t = time(NULL);
  tm *cur_time = localtime(&t);

  // Create US and German locales.
  locale usloc("English_US");
  locale gloc("German_Germany");

  // Set the locale to US and get the time_put facet for US.
  cout.imbue(usloc);
  const time_put<char> &us_time =
        use_facet<time_put<char> >(cout.getloc());

  // %c specifies the standard time and date pattern.
  char *std_pat = "%c";
  char *std_pat_end = std_pat + strlen(std_pat);
```

```
// The following custom pattern displays hours and minutes
// followed by the date.
char *custom_pat = "%A %B %d, %Y %H:%M";
char *custom_pat_end = custom_pat + strlen(custom_pat);

cout << "Standard US time and date format: ";
us_time.put(cout, cout, ' ', cur_time, std_pat, std_pat_end);
cout << endl;

cout << "Custom US time and date format: ";
us_time.put(cout, cout, ' ', cur_time, custom_pat, custom_pat_end);
cout << "\n\n";

// Set the locale to Germany and get the time_put facet for Germany.
cout.imbue(gloc);
const time_put<char> &g_time =
        use_facet<time_put<char> >(cout.getloc());

cout << "Standard German time and date format: ";
g_time.put(cout, cout, ' ', cur_time, std_pat, std_pat_end);
cout << endl;

cout << "Custom German time and date format: ";
g_time.put(cout, cout, ' ', cur_time, custom_pat, custom_pat_end);
cout << endl;

  return 0;
}
```

The output is shown here:

```
Standard US time and date format: 10/31/2007 9:27:45 AM
Custom US time and date format: Wednesday October 31, 2007 09:27

Standard German time and date format: 31.10.2007 09:27:45
Custom German time and date format: Mittwoch Oktober 31, 2007 09:27
```

Options and Alternatives

Another way to format the time and date is by using the **strftime( )** function inherited from the C language. If you are using the global locale, then **strftime( )** is a bit easier to use than the **time_put** facet. See *Format Time and Date Using strftime( )* for details.

There is a second form of **put( )** that lets you specify a single time/date format specifier. It is shown here:

iter_type put(iter_type *strm*, ios_base &*not_used*, char_type *fillchar*,
        const tm *t, char *fmt*, char *mod* = 0) const

The first four parameters are the same as the first version. The format specifier is passed in *fmt*, and an optional format modifier is passed in *mod*. Not all environments support modifiers. If they are supported, they are implementation-defined. The function returns an iterator to one past the last character written.

Format Data into a String

Key Ingredients		
Headers	**Classes**	**Functions**
<sstream>	ostringstream	string str( ) const

Sometimes it is useful to construct in advance a string that contains formatted output. This string can then be output when needed. This technique is especially useful when working in a windowed environment, such as Windows, in which data is displayed by a control. In this case, you often need to format the data before it is displayed. This is most easily accomplished in C++ by using a string stream, such as **ostringstream**. Because all streams work the same, the techniques described by the preceding recipes that write the formatted data to a stream such as **cout** also work with string-based streams. Once you have constructed the formatted string, you can display it using any mechanism that you choose. This recipe shows the process.

Step-by-Step

One way to format data to a string involves the following steps:

1. Create an **ostringstream**.
2. Set the format flags, precision, width, and fill character as needed.
3. Output data to the string stream.
4. To obtain the formatted string, call **str( )**.

Discussion

The string streams, including **ostringstream**, are described in Chapter 5. See *Use the String Streams* for details on creating and using a string stream.

The format flags, precision, width, and fill character are set in a string stream in the same way as they are set in any other C++ stream. For example, you can use the **setf( )** function to set the format flags. Use **width( )**, **precision( )**, and **fill( )** to set the width, precision, and fill character. Alternatively, you can use the I/O manipulators to set these items.

To create a formatted string, simply output to the string stream. When you want to use the formatted string, call **str( )** on the string stream to obtain the string. This string can then be displayed, stored, or used however you like.

Example

The following example shows how to create a formatted string by use of a string stream. Once the formatted string has been constructed, it is output in its entirety.

```
// Use a string stream to store formatted output in a string.

#include <iostream>
#include <sstream>
#include <locale>
```

```
#include <iomanip>

using namespace std;

int main()
{
  locale usloc("English_US");

  ostringstream ostr;

  // Set showbase flag so that currency symbol is displayed.
  ostr << showbase;

  // Set the locale of ostr to US English.
  ostr.imbue(usloc);

  // Get a money_put facet for ostr.
  const money_put<char> &us_mon =
          use_facet<money_put<char> >(ostr.getloc());

  // Format a value in US dollars.
  us_mon.put(ostr, false, ostr, ' ', "5498499");

  cout << "Money formatted for US: ";
  cout << ostr.str() << "\n\n";

  // Give a new, empty string to ostr.
  ostr.str(string());

   // Now, construct a table of circular areas.
  ostr << setprecision(4) << showpoint << fixed << left;
  ostr << "Diameter    Area\n";

  cout << "A table of circular areas.\n";
  for(int i=1; i < 10; ++i)
    ostr << left << "    " << setw(6) << i << setw(8)
         << right << i*3.1416 << endl;

  // Display the formatted string.
  cout << ostr.str();

  return 0;
}
```

The output is shown here:

```
Money formatted for US: $54,984.99

A table of circular areas.
Diameter    Area
    1       3.1416
    2       6.2832
    3       9.4248
```

```
4        12.5664
5        15.7080
6        18.8496
7        21.9912
8        25.1328
9        28.2744
```

Options and Alternatives

The C legacy function **sprintf( )** offers another way to write formatted output to a string. It is described in the *Options and Alternatives* section for the recipe *Use printf( ) to Format Data*. Because of its potential for buffer overruns, and because the string streams offer a more flexible alternative, **sprintf( )** is not recommend for new code. It is included in this book only because of its extensive use in legacy C code.

Format Time and Date Using strftime( )

Key Ingredients		
Headers	**Classes**	**Functions**
<ctime>		struct tm &localtime(const time_t *time)
		size_t strftime(char *str, size_t maxsize, const char *fmt, const struct tm *t_ptr)

Although I recommend the use of the **time_put** facet for most time and date formatting, there is an alternative that can be useful in some cases: the **strftime( )** function. This function is defined by C and is still supported by C++. Although it lacks some of the flexibility of the **time_put** facet (described in an earlier recipe), it can be useful when you are displaying the time and date for the global locale. This recipe shows the process.

Step-by-Step

Using **strftime( )** to format the date and time involves these steps:

1. Obtain a **tm** pointer that points to the time to be formatted. For local time, this pointer can be obtained by calling **localtime( )**.

2. Create a **char** array large enough to hold the formatted output. Remember to include room for the null terminator.

3. To format the date and time, call **strftime( )**, specifying the desired formats. You will also pass in a pointer to the **char** array from Step 2 and the **tm** pointer from Step 1.

Discussion

The **strftime( )** function formats the time and date, putting the result into a null-terminated string. It requires the header **<ctime>** and has the prototype shown here:

size_t strftime(char *str, size_t *maxsize*, const char *fmt*,
                const struct tm *t_ptr*)

The time to be formatted is in a **tm** structure pointed to by *t_ptr*. The format of the time and date is specified by the string pointed to by *fmt*. The formatted output is put into the string pointed to by *str*. The result is null-terminated. A maximum of *maxsize* characters will be placed into *str*. It returns the number of characters put into *str* (excluding the null terminator). You must ensure that *str* points to an array large enough to hold the maximum output. Thus, it must be at least *maxsize* elements long. Zero is returned if more than *maxsize* characters are needed to hold the formatted result.

The **strftime( )** function formats the time and date based on *format specifiers*. Each format specifier begins with the percent sign (%) and is followed by a format command. The format commands are used to specify the exact way various time and date information is represented. Any other characters found in *fmt* (the format string) are copied into *str* unchanged. The time and date are formatted according to the global locale, which is the "C" locale by default. The format commands are shown in Table 6-1. Notice that many of the commands are case-sensitive.

To understand how the time and date formats work, let's work through a few examples. Perhaps the most commonly used format is **%c**, which displays the time and date using a standard format appropriate to the locale. The standard time and date formats can be used separately by specifying **%x** (date) and **%X** (time). For example, this format string "%x %X" causes the standard date and time to be displayed.

Although the standard formats are useful, you can take full control, using whatever pieces of the time and/or date you want and in various forms. For example, "%H:%M" displays the time, using only hours and minutes, in a 24-hour format. Notice that the hours are separated from the minutes by a colon. As explained, any character in the format string that is not part of a format specifier will be output as-is. Here is a popular date format: "%A, %B %d %Y". It displays the day, month, and year using the long-name format, as in Thursday, November 01 2007.

In **strftime( )**, the *t_ptr* parameter points to an object of type **tm** that contains what is referred to as the "broken-down" form of the time. The **tm** structure is also defined in **<ctime>**. One way to obtain a **tm** object is to call the **localtime( )** function. It returns a pointer to a **tm** structure that contains the time represented as local time. You can obtain the current time by calling **time( )**. See *Format Time and Date Using the time_put Facet* for additional information on **tm**, **localtime( )**, and **time( )**.

Example

The following example shows the **strftime( )** function in action:

```
#include <iostream>
#include <ctime>

using namespace std;

int main() {
  char str[64];
```

Command	Replaced By
%a	Abbreviated weekday name
%A	Full weekday name
%b	Abbreviated month name
%B	Full month name
%c	Standard date and time string
%d	Day of month as a decimal (1-31)
%H	Hour (0-23)
%I	Hour (1-12)
%j	Day of year as a decimal (1-366)
%m	Month as decimal (1-12)
%M	Minute as decimal (0-59)
%p	Locale's equivalent of AM or PM
%S	Second as decimal (0-61)
%U	Week of year, Sunday being first day (0-53)
%w	Weekday as a decimal (0-6, Sunday being 0)
%W	Week of year, Monday being first day (0-53)
%x	Standard date string
%X	Standard time string
%y	Year in decimal without century (0-99)
%Y	Year including century as decimal
%Z	Time zone name
%%	The percent sign

TABLE 6-1   The **strftime( )** Format Specifiers

```cpp
  // Get the current system time.
  time_t t = time(NULL);

  // Show standard time and date string.
  strftime(str, 64, "%c", localtime(&t));
  cout << "Standard format: " << str << endl;

  // Show a custom time and date string.
  strftime(str, 64, "%A, %B %d %Y %I:%M %p", localtime(&t));
  cout << "Custom format: " << str << endl;

  return 0;
}
```

The sample output is shown here:

```
Standard format: 11/07/07 14:34:17
Custom format: Wednesday, November 07 2007 02:34 PM
```

Options and Alternatives

Some compilers support modifiers for the time and date format commands, but these are implementation-dependent. For example, Microsoft's Visual C++ allows you to modify a command with the **#**. The precise effect varies by command. For example, **%#c** causes the standard time and date string to be displayed in its long form, with the names of the days of the week and month spelled out. You will need to check your compiler's documentation for modifiers that apply to your development environment.

The **strftime( )** function uses the global locale defined by C to determine time and date formats. You can change this locale by calling the C function **setlocale( )**, shown here:

char *setlocale(int *what*, const char *loc*)

The **setlocale( )** function attempts to use the string specified by *loc* to set the locale parameters as specified by *what*. The locale strings are implementation-dependent. Refer to your compiler's documentation for the localization strings that it supports. If *loc* is null, **setlocale( )** returns a pointer to the current localization string. At the time of the call, *what* must be one of the following macros:

LC_ALL	LC_COLLATE	LC_CTYPE
LC_MONETARY	LC_NUMERIC	LC_TIME

LC_ALL refers to all localization categories. **LC_COLLATE** affects the collating functions, such as **strcoll( )**. **LC_CTYPE** alters the way the character functions work. **LC_MONETARY** determines the monetary format. **LC_NUMERIC** determines the numeric format. Finally, **LC_TIME** determines the behavior of the **strftime( )** function. The **setlocale( )** function returns a pointer to a string associated with the *what* parameter. To use **setlocale( )**, you must include **<clocale>**.

The following program reworks the example so that the time and date are displayed in a form compatible with Germany. (The locale string is compatible with Visual C++. Your compiler may require a different string.)

```
#include <iostream>
#include <ctime>
#include <clocale>

using namespace std;

int main() {
  char str[64];

  // Set the locale to Germany.
  setlocale(LC_ALL, "German_Germany");
```

```
  // Get the current system time.
  time_t t = time(NULL);

  // Show standard time and date string.
  strftime(str, 64, "%c", localtime(&t));
  cout << "Standard format: " << str << endl;

  // Show a custom time and date string.
  strftime(str, 64, "%A, %B %Y %I:%M %p", localtime(&t));
  cout << "Custom format: " << str << endl;

  return 0;
}
```

The sample output is shown here:

```
Standard format: 01.11.2007 10:42:20
Custom format: Donnerstag, November 2007 10:42
```

Notice that the time and date now use German language and style.

Although **strftime( )** occasionally offers a convenient alternative, in most cases, you will want to use **time_put** for new code. The reason is that the C++ localization system is fully integrated with C++ streams. Furthermore, each stream can have its own locale. The **strftime( )** function uses the global locale, which is a feature inherited from the C language. The modern approach is for each stream to have its own locale.

Use printf( ) to Format Data

Key Ingredients

Headers	Classes	Functions
<cstdio>		int printf(const char *fmt, ...)

Although the use of facets such as **num_put** and **money_put** is the modern way to format data, facets are probably not the first thing that springs to mind for most C++ programmers. Instead, it is probably the **printf( )** function. Incorporated into C++ as part of its C legacy, **printf( )** is arguably the most widely used, widely understood, and widely copied formatted output function in existence. Even programmers with little knowledge of C or C++ have heard of it. It has also been added to the Java language. Although the formatting flags, functions, and facets defined for C++ streams essentially duplicate its functionality, **printf( )**-style formatting is still widely employed because it offers a compact way to create nearly any type of numeric or string format. It is also used extensively in legacy C code. Frankly, no programmer can be considered a master of C++ without knowing how to handle **printf( )**.

Before we begin, one important point needs to be made: **printf( )** is just one of a family of functions that all work in essentially the same way. The others described in this recipe are

sprintf( ) and **fprintf( )**. All three format data through the use of format specifiers. The difference between these functions is the destination for the formatted output. In the case of **printf( )**, the target is standard out, which is normally the console. For **sprintf( )**, the target is a string, and for **fprintf( )**, it is a file (as specified by a C-style file pointer, not a C++ stream). Except for where formatted data is sent, the information presented in this recipe applies to all three.

NOTE *Most new code should use C++ features for formatting, not* **printf( )**. *C++ formatting is integrated with C++ streams and offers better support for internationalization. Also,* **printf( )** *formats data relative to the global locale, not a stream-based locale. Therefore, the C++ approach is more flexible. Finally, it is usually better to not mix output to* **cout** *with output from* **printf( )**. *As a general rule, for any given stream, you should use either C++ I/O or C I/O. Therefore, if you want to use* **printf( )** *in a program, that program should not also use* **cout**.

Step-by-Step

Formatting data via **printf( )** involves the following steps:

1. Create a format string that contains the desired format specifiers.
2. Pass the format string as the first argument to **printf( )**.
3. Beginning with the second argument to **printf( )**, pass the data you want to format. There must be the same number of arguments as there are format specifiers, and they must be in the same order.

Discussion

The **printf( )** function writes formatted output to the standard output device, which is the console by default. It is shown here:

    int printf(const char *fmt, arg-list)

It formats the data passed in *arg-list* according to the format specifiers contained in *fmt*. It returns the number of characters actually printed. A negative return value indicates that an error has taken place.

The string pointed to by *fmt* consists of two types of items. The first type is made up of characters that will be displayed as-is. The second type contains *format specifiers* that define the way the arguments are formatted. The format specifiers are shown in Table 6-2. Notice that each *format specifier* begins with a percent sign and is followed by a format code. There must be exactly the same number of arguments as there are format specifiers, and the format specifiers and the arguments are matched in order. For example, the following call to **printf( )**:

```
printf("Hi %c %d %s", 'c', 10, "there!");
```

displays

```
Hi c 10 there!
```

If there are insufficient arguments to match the format specifiers, the output is undefined. If there are more arguments than format specifiers, the remaining arguments are discarded. The following sections describe the format specifiers in detail.

Code	Format
%c	Character.
%d	Signed decimal integers.
%i	Signed decimal integers.
%e	Scientific notation (lowercase e).
%E	Scientific notation (uppercase E).
%f	Decimal floating point.
%g	Uses %e or %f, whichever is shorter (if %e, uses lowercase e).
%G	Uses %E or %f, whichever is shorter (if %E, uses uppercase E).
%o	Unsigned octal.
%s	Null-terminated string.
%u	Unsigned decimal integers.
%x	Unsigned hexadecimal (lowercase letters).
%X	Unsigned hexadecimal (uppercase letters).
%p	Displays an address.
%n	The associated argument shall be a pointer to an integer, into which is placed the number of characters written so far.
%%	Prints a % sign.

TABLE 6-2   The Format Specifiers Used by the **printf( )** Family of Functions

Format Characters and Strings

To display an individual character, use **%c**. To print a null-terminated string, use **%s**. You cannot use **printf( )** to display a **string** object.

Format Integers

You can use either **%d** or **%i** to format an **int** value. These format specifiers are equivalent; both are supported for historical reasons. To output an **unsigned int**, use **%u**.

You can display an **unsigned int** in octal or hexadecimal format using **%o** and **%x**, respectively. Since the hexadecimal number system uses the letters A through F to represent the numbers 10 through 15, you can display these letters in either upper- or lowercase. For uppercase, use the **%X** format specifier; for lowercase, use the **%x**.

Format Floating-Point Values

The **%f** format specifier displays a **double** argument in floating-point format. The **%e** and **%E** specifiers tell **printf( )** to display a **double** argument in scientific notation. Numbers represented in scientific notation take this general form:

x.dddddE+/-yy

If you want to display the letter "E" in uppercase, use the **%E** format; otherwise, use **%e**. You can use either **%f** or **%e** by using the **%g** or **%G** format specifiers. This causes **printf( )** to select the format specifier that produces the shortest output. Where applicable, use **%G** if you want "E" shown in uppercase; otherwise, use **%g**.

The Type Prefixes

To allow **printf( )** to display **short** and **long** integers, you will need to add a prefix to the type specifier. These prefixes can be applied to the **d, i, o, u,** and **x** type specifiers. The **l** modifier indicates that a long data type follows. For example, **%ld** means that a **long int** is to be formatted. The **h** modifier indicates a **short int**. Therefore, **%hu** indicates that the data is of type **short unsigned int**.

An **L** modifier can prefix the floating-point specifiers **e, f,** and **g,** and indicates that a **long double** follows.

If you are using a modern compiler that supports the wide-character features, then you can use the **l** modifier with the **c** specifier to indicate a wide character of type **whcar_t**. You can also use the **l** modifier with the **s** specifier to indicate a wide-character string.

Display an Address

To display an address, use the **%p** specifier. The address will be formatted in a way compatible with the type of addressing used by the execution environment.

The %n Specifier

The **%n** specifier is unique because it does not actually format data. Instead, it causes the number of characters that have been written at the time the **%n** is encountered to be stored in an integer variable whose pointer is specified in the argument list. For example, this code fragment displays the number 14 after the line "This is a test":

```
int i;

printf("This is a test%n", &i);
printf("%d", i);
```

Set the Field Width and Precision

The format specifiers can include modifiers that specify the field width and precision. An integer placed between the % sign and the format code acts as a *minimum field-width specifier*. This pads the output to ensure that it is at least a certain minimum length. If the string or number is greater than that minimum, it will be printed in full, even if it overruns the minimum. The default padding is done with spaces. If you want to pad with 0's, place a 0 before the field-width specifier. For example, **%05d** will pad a number of less than 5 digits with 0's so that its total length is 5.

The exact meaning of the *precision modifier* depends on the format specifier being modified. To add a precision modifier, place a decimal point, followed by the precision, after the field-width specifier. For **e, E,** and **f** formats, the precision modifier determines the number of decimal places printed. For example, **%10.4f** will display a number at least ten characters wide with four decimal places. When the precision modifier is applied to the **g** or **G** format code, it determines the maximum number of significant digits displayed. When applied to integers, the precision modifier specifies the minimum number of digits that will be displayed. Leading zeros are added, if necessary.

When the precision modifier is applied to strings, the number following the period specifies the maximum field length. For example, **%5.7s** will display a string that will be at least five characters long and will not exceed seven. If the string is longer than the maximum field width, the characters will be truncated off the end.

The minimum field-width and precision specifiers may be provided by arguments to **printf( )** instead of by constants. To accomplish this, use * as a placeholder. When the format string is scanned, **printf( )** will match each * to an argument in the order in which they occur. For example:

```
printf("|%*.*f|", 8, 3, 98.6);
```

produces the following output:

```
|  98.600|
```

In this example, the first * matches 8, the second * matches 3, and the **f** matches 98.6.

Left-Justify Output

By default, all output is right-justified: If the field width is larger than the data printed, the data will be placed on the right edge of the field. You can force the information to be left-justified by placing a minus sign directly after the %. For example, **%–10.2f** will left-justify a floating-point number with two decimal places in a ten-character field.

The #, +, and Space Flags

In addition to the left-justification flag just described, **printf( )** supports three others. They are **#, +,** and space. Each is described here.

The **#** has a special meaning when used with some **printf( )** format specifiers. Preceding a **g, G, f, e,** or **E** with a **#** ensures that the decimal point will be present, even if there are no decimal digits. If you precede the **x** or **X** format with **#**, the hexadecimal number will be printed with a **0x** prefix. If you precede the **o** format with **#**, the octal value will be printed with a 0 prefix. The **#** cannot be applied to any other format specifiers.

The **+** flag indicates that a signed numeric value will always include a sign, as in +10 or –5.

The space flag causes a space to be added to the start of non-negative values.

Example

The following program shows several examples of **printf( )** in action.

```
// Demonstrate printf().

#include <cstdio>
#include <cmath>

using namespace std;

int main()
{
  int x = 10;
  double val = 568.345;

  // It is not necessary for a call to printf() to include
```

```
// format specifiers or additional arguments.
printf("This is output to the console.\n");

// Display numeric values.
printf("This is x and val: %d %f\n\n", x, val);
printf("This is x in uppercase hex: %X\n", x);

printf("Mix data %d into %f the format string.\n\n", 19, 234.3);

// Specify various precisions, widths, and sign flags.
printf("Here is val in various precisions, widths, and sign flags: \n");
printf("|%10.2f|%+12.4f|% 12.3f|%f|\n", val, val, val, val);
printf("|%10.2f|%+12.4f|% 12.3f|%f|\n", -val, -val, -val, -val);
printf("\n");

// Display column of numbers, right-justified.
printf("Right-justify numbers.\n");
for(int i = 1; i < 11; ++i)
  printf("%2d %8.2f\n", i, sqrt(double(i)));

printf("\n");

// Now, left-justify some strings in a 16-character field.
// Right-justify the quantities.
printf("%-16s Quantity: %3d\n", "Hammers", 12);
printf("%-16s Quantity: %3d\n", "Pliers", 6);
printf("%-16s Quantity: %3d\n", "Screwdrivers", 19);

  return 0;
}
```

The output is shown here:

```
This is output to the console.
This is x and val: 10 568.345000

This is x in uppercase hex: A
Mix data 19 into 234.300000 the format string.

Here is val in various precisions, widths, and sign flags:
|    568.35|    +568.3450|     568.345|568.345000|
|   -568.35|    -568.3450|    -568.345|-568.345000|

Right-justify numbers.
 1     1.00
 2     1.41
 3     1.73
 4     2.00
 5     2.24
 6     2.45
 7     2.65
 8     2.83
 9     3.00
10     3.16
```

```
Hammers          Quantity:   12
Pliers           Quantity:    6
Screwdrivers     Quantity:   19
```

Options and Alternatives

By far, the best way to learn to effectively use **printf( )** is to experiment with it. Although the terseness of its format syntax makes it easy to create some fairly intimidating format specifiers, they all follow the rules described in the discussion. Just break each format down into its parts, and it will become easy to understand what it does.

The **printf( )** function is not used for formatting the time and date. The C function that does this is **strftime( )**, described by the preceding recipe. The C++ approach is to use the **time_put** facet, described by *Format Time and Date Using the **time_put** Facet*.

You can construct in advance a string that contains formatted output by calling **sprintf( )**. Part of the **printf( )** family of functions, **sprintf( )** works just like **printf( )**, except that instead of sending its output to standard out (usually the console), it writes the formatted data to a string. It is shown here:

int sprintf(char *str*, const char **fmt*, ...)

The formatted output is put into the array pointed to by *str*. The result is null-terminated. Thus, on return, the character array pointed to by *str* contains a null-terminated string. It returns the number of characters actually copied into *str*. (The terminating null is not part of the count.) A negative return value indicates an error.

You need to be careful when using **sprintf( )** because of the possibility of system crashes and security risks. It is mentioned here primarily because it is still in widespread use in legacy C code. For new projects, you should use a string stream, such as **ostringstream**, to put formatted data into a string. (See *Format Data into a String*.) When using **sprintf( )**, *you must ensure* that the array pointed to by *str* is large enough to hold the output that it will receive, including the null terminator. Failure to follow this rule will result in a buffer overrun, which could lead to a security breach or a system crash. In no case should you use **sprintf( )** on unchecked data, such as raw data entered by a user. Also, you should not use a user-entered format string because of the same potential for trouble.

NOTE *sprintf( ) has the potential to cause a system crash or a security breach. Its use in new code is not recommended. Many compilers supply nonstandard versions of **sprintf( )**, often called something like **snprintf( )**, that allow you to specify the maximum number of characters that will be copied into the string. If you are maintaining legacy C code, then it is recommended that you use such a function to help avoid problems.*

You can send formatted output to a file by using **fprintf( )**. It is shown here:

int fprintf(FILE **fp*, const char **fmt*, ...)

It works just like **printf( )**, except that the formatted data is written to the file pointed to by *fp*. The return value is the number of characters actually output. If an error occurs, a negative number is returned. Because **fprintf( )** uses the C I/O system, which is based on file pointers rather than stream objects, you will not normally use it in C++ programs. It is, of course, widely used in legacy C code.

Potpourri

One of the problems with writing a programming cookbook is finding an appropriate stopping point. There is a nearly unlimited universe of topics from which to choose, any number of which could merit inclusion. It's difficult to find where to draw the line. Of course, all books must end. Thus, a stopping point, whether easily found or not, is always required. This book is no exception.

In this, the final chapter of the book, I have chosen to conclude with an assortment of recipes that span a variety of topics. These recipes represent techniques that I wanted covered in the book, but for which a complete chapter was, for one reason or another, not appropriate. For example, I wanted to show how to overload C++'s special case operators, such as [ ], –>, **new** and **delete**, and so on. Although several recipes are dedicated to overloading these operators, there are not enough for a chapter of their own. I also wanted to include recipes that address some common but isolated "How-To" questions, such as how to create a copy constructor, implement a conversion function, or use a runtime type ID. All important topics, but none large enough for its own chapter. Despite the wide-ranging nature of the recipes in this chapter, all do have two things in common:

1. They answer a frequently asked question.
2. They are applicable to a wide range of programmers.

Furthermore, all describe key concepts that you can easily adapt and enhance.

Here are the recipes contained in this chapter:

- Operator Overloading Basic Techniques
- Overload the Function Call Operator **( )**
- Overload the Subscripting Operator [ ]
- Overload the –> Operator
- Overload **new** and **delete**
- Overload the Increment and Decrement Operators
- Create a Conversion Function
- Create a Copy Constructor
- Determine an Object's Type at Runtime

- Use Complex Numbers
- Use **auto_ptr**
- Create an Explicit Constructor

Operator Overloading Basic Techniques

Key Ingredients		
Headers	**Classes**	**Functions**
		ret-type operator#(*param-list*)

In C++, operators can be overloaded relative to a class, including classes that you create. This lets you define what a specific operation, such as **+** or **/**, means for an object of the class. It also lets objects of the class be used in expressions, in just the same way that you use the built-in types. Recall that when you define a class, you are creating a new data type. Through operator overloading, you can seamlessly integrate this new data type into your programming environment. This *type extensibility* is one of C++'s most important and powerful features because it lets you expand the C++ type system to fit your needs.

Operator overloading will be familiar territory for most readers because it is a basic C++ skill and most programmers know how to overload the more commonly used operators. For this reason, the operator overloading recipes in this chapter focus on these specialized operators: increment and decrement, **( )**, **[ ]**, **–>**, and **new** and **delete**. Many programmers find these operators confusing when it comes to overloading, and they are the source of many "How-To" questions. However, for completeness, this recipe presents a brief review of the basic techniques used to overload an operator. This overview is sufficient for the purposes of this chapter, but it is not a substitute for an in-depth examination of the topic.

NOTE *For an in-depth look at operator overloading, I recommend my book* C++: The Complete Reference.

Step-by-Step

To overload an operator as a member function of a class involves these steps:

1. Add an **operator** function to the class, specifying the operator that you want to overload.

2. For binary operators, the **operator** function will have one parameter, which will receive the right-hand operand. The left-hand operand will be passed via **this**.

3. For unary operators, the **operator** function will have no parameters. Its single operand is passed via **this**.

4. In the body of the function, perform the operation.

5. Return the result of the operation.

To overload an operator using a non-member function involves these steps:

1. Create a non-member **operator** function that specifies the operator that you want to overload.

2. For binary operators, the **operator** function will have two parameters. The first parameter receives the left-hand operand, and the second parameter receives the right-hand operand. At least one of the operands must be an object of or a reference to the class being acted upon.

3. For unary operators, the **operator** function will have one parameter, which must be an object of or a reference to the class being acted upon. This parameter is the operand.

4. In the body of the function, perform the operation.

5. Return the result of the operation.

Discussion

When you overload an operator, you define the meaning of that operator for a particular class. For example, a class that defines a linked list might use the + operator to add an object to the list. A class that implements a stack might use the + to push an object onto the stack. Another class might use the + operator in an entirely different way. When an operator is overloaded, none of its original meaning is lost. It is simply that a new operation, relative to a specific class, is defined. Overloading the + to handle a linked list, for example, does not cause its meaning relative to integers (i.e., addition) to be changed.

To overload an operator, you must define what the operation means relative to the class to which it is applied. As a general rule, you can use either member functions or non-member functions. (The exceptions to this rule are the operator functions for =, ( ), [ ], and –>, which must be implemented by a non-static member function.) Although similar, there are some differences between the two approaches.

To create an operator function, use the **operator** keyword. The general form of an **operator** function is:

ret-type classname::operator#(*param-list*)
{
  // operations

}

Here, the operator that you are overloading is substituted for the #, and *ret-type* is the type of value returned by the specified operation. Although it can be of any type you choose, the return value is often of the same type as the class for which the operator is being overloaded. This correlation facilitates the use of the overloaded operator in compound expressions. The exceptions are the logical and relational operators, which typically return a **bool** value.

The precise nature of *param-list* depends on what type of operator is being overloaded and whether it is implemented as a member function or a non-member function. For a member unary **operator** function, *param-list* will be empty and the operand is passed through the **this** pointer. For a member binary **operator** function, *param-list* will have one parameter, which receives the right-hand operand. The left-hand operand is passed via **this**. In either case, the object that invokes the operator function is the one passed via the **this** pointer.

For non-member **operator** functions, all arguments are passed explicitly. Therefore, a non-member unary **operator** function will have one parameter, whose type must be a class, class reference, an enumeration, or an enumeration reference. This parameter receives the operand. A non-member binary **operator** function will have two parameters, of which the type of at least one must be a class, class reference, an enumeration, or an enumeration reference. The first parameter receives the left-hand operand, and the second parameter receives the right-hand operand. Notice that a non-member operator function can be overloaded relative to an enumeration type, but this is not common. Typically, operators are overloaded relative to a class type, and that is the focus of this recipe.

Because of the differences between member and non-member operator functions, each is described separately.

Member Operator Functions

When defining an **operator** function that acts on objects of a class that you have created, you will usually use a member function. The reason is simple: Being a member of the class, the function has direct access to all of the class' members. It also has a **this** pointer. This makes it easy for the operator to act on, and possibly alter, an operand.

The best way to understand how to use a member function to overload an operator is to work through some examples. Assume a class called **three_d** that encapsulates three-dimensional coordinates, as shown here:

```
class three_d {
  int x, y, z; // 3-D coordinates
public:
  three_d() { x = y = z = 0; }
  three_d(int i, int j, int k) {x = i; y = j; z = k; }

  // ...
};
```

You can define the **+** operation for **three_d** objects by adding an **operator+( )** function to the class. To do so, first add its prototype to the **three_d** class:

```
three_d operator+(three_d rh_op);
```

Next, implement the function. Here is one way:

```
// Overload + for objects of type three_d.
three_d three_d::operator+(three_d rh_op)
{
  three_d temp;

  temp.x = x + rh_op.x;
  temp.y = y + rh_op.y;
  temp.z = z + rh_op.z;

  return temp;
}
```

This function adds the coordinates of two **three_d** operands together and returns an object that contains the result. Recall that in a member operator function, the left-hand operand invokes the operator function and is passed implicitly via **this**. The right-hand operand is passed explicitly as an argument to the function. Therefore, assuming that **objA** and **objB** are both **three_d** objects, in the following expression

```
objA + objB
```

objA is passed through **this** and **objB** is passed in **rh_op**.

In the implementation of **operator+( )** just shown, notice that neither operand is modified. This is in keeping with the normal semantics of the **+** operator. For example, in the expression 10 + 12, neither the 10 nor 12 is modified. Although there is no rule that enforces it, in general, it is best to have your overloaded operator work in the expected way.

Of course, there are some operators, such as assignment or increment, in which an operand *is* modified by the operation. In this case, you will need to modify an operand in order for your **operator** function to reflect the normal meaning of the operator. For example, again assuming the **three_d** class, here is one way to implement assignment:

```
// Overload assignment for three_d.
three_d three_d::operator=(three_d rh_op)
{
  x = rh_op.x;
  y = rh_op.y;
  z = rh_op.z;

  return *this;
}
```

Here, the coordinate values of the right-hand operand (passed in **rh_op**) are assigned to the left-hand operand (passed via **this**). Thus, the invoking object is changed to reflect the value it is being assigned. Again, this is in line with the expected meaning of =.

Given the two **operator** functions just described and assuming **three_d** objects called **objA**, **objB**, and **objC**, the following statement is valid:

```
objC = objA + objB;
```

First, the addition is performed by **operator+( )**, with **objA** passed through **this** and **objB** passed to **rh_op**. The result becomes the right-hand operand passed to **operator=( )**, with **objC** being passed through **this**. On completion, **objC** will contain the sum of **objA** and **objB**, and **objA** and **objB** will be unchanged.

The preceding version of **operator+( )** added one **three_d** object to another, but you can overload **operator+( )** so that it adds some other type of value. For example, this version of **operator+( )** adds an integer to each coordinate:

```
// Overload + to add an integer to a three_d object.
three_d three_d::operator+(int rh_op)
{
  three_d temp;

  temp.x = x + rh_op;
```

```
  temp.y = y + rh_op;
  temp.z = z + rh_op;

  return temp;
}
```

Once this version of **operator+( )** has been defined, you can use an expression like:

```
objA + 10
```

This causes 10 to be added to each coordinate. Understand that the previous version of **operator+( )**, which adds two **three_d** objects, is still available. It's just that the definition of + relative to **three_d** has been expanded to handle integer addition.

For a unary member operator function, the sole operand is passed through **this**. For example, here is the unary version of **operator–( )**, which negates the coordinate and returns the result:

```
// Overload - for three_d.
three_d three_d::operator-()
{
  three_d temp;

  temp.x = -x;
  temp.y = -y;
  temp.z = -z;

  return temp;
}
```

It is possible to create both a binary and a unary form of some operators, such as + and –. Simply overload the operator function as needed. For member functions, the binary form will have one parameter; the unary form will have none.

The preceding **operator** functions all return an object of type **three_d**, which is the class for which they are defined. This is usually the case, except when overloading the logical or relational operators. Those **operator** functions will usually return a **bool** result, which indicates the success or failure of the operation. For example, here is one way to implement the = = operator for **three_d**:

```
// Overload == for a three_d object.
bool three_d::operator==(three_d rh_op)
{
  if( (x == rh_op.x) && (y == rh_op.y) && (z == rh_op.z) )
    return true;

  return false;
}
```

It compares two **three_d** objects for equality by comparing each pair of values. All of the invoking object's values must be equal to those for the operand on the right for this function to return true.

Non-Member Operator Functions

As mentioned at the start of this discussion, a non-member binary operator function is passed its operands explicitly, through its parameters. (Recall that non-member functions do not have **this** pointers because they are not invoked on an object.) A binary non-member operator function has two parameters, with the left-hand operand being passed to the first parameter and the right-hand operand passed to the second parameter. A unary non-member operator function is passed its operand through its one parameter. Otherwise, non-member operator functions work much like member operator functions.

Although you will often use member functions when overloading operators, there are times when you will need to use non-member operator functions. One case is when you want to be able to use a built-in type (such as **int** or **char** *) on the left side of a binary operator. To understand why, recall that the object that invokes a member operator function is passed in **this**. In the case of a binary operator, it is always the object on the left that invokes the function. This is fine, provided that the object on the left defines the specified operation. For example, assuming a **three_d** object called **objA** and the member function **operator+( )** shown earlier, the following is a perfectly valid expression:

```
objA + 10; // will work
```

Because **objA** is on the left side of the + operator, it invokes the overloaded member function **operator+(int)** function, which adds 10 to **objA**. However, this statement won't work:

```
10 + Ob; // won't work
```

The problem is that the object on the left of the + operator is an integer, a built-in type for which no operation involving an integer and an object of type **three_d** is defined.

The solution to this problem is to overload the + a second time, using a non-member operator function to handle the case in which the integer is on the left. Therefore, the member operator function handles *object + integer,* and the non-member operator function handles *integer + object.* To give the non-member operator function access to the members of the class, declare it as a **friend**. Here is how a non-member version of **operator+( )** can be implemented to handle *integer + object* for the **three_d** class:

```
// Overload operator+() for int + obj. This is a non-member function.
three_d operator+(int lh_op, three_d rh_op) {
  three_d temp;

  temp.x = lh_op + rh_op.x;
  temp.y = lh_op + rh_op.y;
  temp.z = lh_op + rh_op.z;

  return temp;
}
```

Now, the statement

```
10 + Ob; // now OK
```

is legal.

Another time when a non-member operator function is useful is when creating a custom inserter or extractor. As explained in Chapter 5, the << is overloaded so that it outputs (inserts) data into a stream, and the >> is overloaded so that it inputs (extracts) data from a stream. These functions must be non-members because they each take a stream object as the left-hand operand. The right-hand operand is either an object to be output or an object that will receive input. See *Create Custom Inserters and Extractors* in Chapter 5 for details.

One last point: Not all operators can be implemented by non-member functions. For example, the assignment operator must be a member of its class. So must the ( ), [ ], and -> operators.

Example

The following example puts into action the preceding discussion, filling in all of the pieces and demonstrating the operators.

```
// Demonstrate operator overloading basics using the three_d class.
//
// This example uses member functions to overload the binary +,
// -, =, and == operators. It also uses a member function to
// overload the unary -. Notice that the + is overloaded for
// three_d + three_d and for three_d + int.
//
// Non-member functions are used to create custom inserters for
// three_d objects and to overload + for int + three_d.

#include <iostream>

using namespace std;

// A class that encapsulates 3-dimensional coordinates.
class three_d {
  int x, y, z; // 3-D coordinates
public:
  three_d() { x = y = z = 0; }
  three_d(int i, int j, int k) { x = i; y = j; z = k; }

  // Add two three_d objects together.
  three_d operator+(three_d rh_op);

  // Add an integer to a three_d object.
  three_d operator+(int rh_op);

  // Subtract two three_d objects.
  three_d operator-(three_d rh_op);

  // Overload assignment.
  three_d operator=(three_d rh_op);

  // Overload ==.
  bool operator==(three_d rh_op);

  // Overload - for unary operation.
  three_d operator-();
```

```
  // Let the overloaded inserter be a friend.
  friend ostream &operator<<(ostream &strm, three_d op);

  // Let the overloaded + be a friend.
  friend three_d operator+(int lh_op, three_d rh_op);
};

// Overload binary + so that corresponding coordinates are added.
three_d three_d::operator+(three_d rh_op)
{
  three_d temp;

  temp.x = x + rh_op.x;
  temp.y = y + rh_op.y;
  temp.z = z + rh_op.z;

  return temp;
}

// Overload binary + so that an integer can be added to
// a three_d object.
three_d three_d::operator+(int rh_op)
{
  three_d temp;

  temp.x = x + rh_op;
  temp.y = y + rh_op;
  temp.z = z + rh_op;

  return temp;
}

// Overload binary - so that corresponding coordinates are subtracted.
three_d three_d::operator-(three_d rh_op)
{
  three_d temp;

  temp.x = x - rh_op.x;
  temp.y = y - rh_op.y;
  temp.z = z - rh_op.z;

  return temp;
}

// Overload unary - so that it negates the coordinates.
three_d three_d::operator-()
{
  three_d temp;

  temp.x = -x;
  temp.y = -y;
  temp.z = -z;
```

```
  return temp;
}

// Overload assignment for three_d.
three_d three_d::operator=(three_d rh_op)
{
  x = rh_op.x;
  y = rh_op.y;
  z = rh_op.z;

  return *this;
}

// Overload == for a three_d object. It compares each
// coordinate. All of the invoking object's values
// must be equal to those for the operand on the right
// for this function to return true.
bool three_d::operator==(three_d rh_op)
{
  if( (x == rh_op.x) && (y == rh_op.y) && (z == rh_op.z) )
    return true;

  return false;
}

// These are non-member operator functions.
//
// Overload << as a custom inserter for three_d objects.
ostream &operator<<(ostream &strm, three_d op) {
  strm << op.x << ", " << op.y << ", " << op.z << endl;

  return strm;
}

// Overload + for int + obj.
three_d operator+(int lh_op, three_d rh_op) {
  three_d temp;

  temp.x = lh_op + rh_op.x;
  temp.y = lh_op + rh_op.y;
  temp.z = lh_op + rh_op.z;

  return temp;
}

int main()
{
  three_d objA(1, 2, 3), objB(10, 10, 10), objC;

  cout << "This is objA: " << objA;
  cout << "This is objB: " << objB;
```

```
// Obtain the negation of objA.
objC = -objA;
cout << "This is -objA: " << objC;

// Add objA and objB together.
objC = objA + objB;
cout << "objA + objB: " << objC;

// Subtract objB from objA.
objC = objA - objB;
cout << "objA - objB: " << objC;

// Add obj + int.
objC = objA + 10;
cout << "objA + 10: " << objC;

// Add int + obj.
objC = 100 + objA;
cout << "100 + objA: " << objC;

// Compare two objects.
if(objA == objB) cout << "objA is equal to objB.\n";
else cout << "objA is not equal to objB.\n";

  return 0;
}
```

The output is shown here:

```
This is objA: 1, 2, 3
This is objB: 10, 10, 10
This is -objA: -1, -2, -3
objA + objB: 11, 12, 13
objA - objB: -9, -8, -7
objA + 10: 11, 12, 13
100 + objA: 101, 102, 103
objA is not equal to objB.
```

Options and Alternatives

Although the preceding examples have passed **three_d** operands by value, in many cases, you can also pass an operand by reference. For example, here is **operator==( )** changed so that the right-hand operand is passed by reference:

```
bool three_d::operator==(three_d &rh_op)
{
  if( (x == rh_op.x) && (y == rh_op.y) && (z == rh_op.z) )
    return true;

  return false;
}
```

Often, using a reference can increase the performance of your program, because it is usually faster to pass a reference rather than an entire object. Be careful, though. In the case of very small objects, passing by value can be faster.

One place where a reference parameter is valuable is when an operand must be modified by the operator. One such case occurs when a non-member **operator** function is used to implement an increment or decrement operation. See *Overload the Increment and Decrement Operators* for information.

C++ has several special case operators, such as the function call operator **( )** or the subscripting operator **[ ]**. These operators can also be overloaded, but the techniques to do so are individualized for each operator. These special case operators are the subject of the next several recipes.

There are some restrictions that apply to operator overloading:

1. You cannot alter the precedence of any operator.

2. You cannot alter the number of operands required by an operator, although you can choose to ignore an operand.

3. Except for the function call operator **( )**, operator functions cannot have default arguments.

4. The following operators cannot be overloaded:
   . :: .* ?

Technically, you are free to perform any activity inside an operator function and it need not bear any relationship to that operator's normal meaning. However, when you stray significantly from the normal meaning of an operator, you run the risk of dangerously destructuring your program. For example, when someone reading your program sees a statement like **Ob1+Ob2**, he or she expects something resembling, or at least related to, addition. Implementing the **+** so that it acts more like the **| |** operator, for example, is inherently confusing. Therefore, before decoupling an overloaded operator from its normal meaning, be sure that you have sufficient reason to do so.

One good example where decoupling is successful is found in the way C++ overloads the **<<** and **>>** operators for I/O. Although the I/O operations have no relationship to bit-shifting, these operators provide a visual "clue" as to their meaning, and this decoupling works. Here is another good example of decoupling: A stack class might overload the **+** to push an object onto a stack. Although this use differs from addition, it is still intuitively compatible with addition because it "adds" an object to the stack.

Except for the **=** operator, operator functions are inherited by derived classes. However, a derived class is free to overload any operator it chooses (including those overloaded by a base class).

Overload the Function Call Operator ( )

Key Ingredients		
Headers	**Classes**	**Functions**
		ret-type operator( )(*param-list*)

One of the more powerful operators that you can overload is **( )**, the function call operator. It can also be one of the more confusing, especially to newcomers. The function call operator lets you define an operation on an object that cannot be performed by overloading any other operator. For example, you might want to define an operation that takes more than two operands. Or, you might want to define an operation that has no obvious analog with any of the normal operators. In these cases, the function call operator offers an elegant solution. This recipe shows the process.

Step-by-Step

To overload the **( )** function call operator involves these steps:

1. The function call operator must be a non-static member of the class for which it is defined. It cannot be a non-member function. Therefore, add **operator( )** as a member to the class on which it will be operating.

2. Inside **operator( )**, perform the desired actions.

3. On completion, have **operator( )** return the result.

Discussion

When you overload the **( )** function call operator, you are not, per se, creating a new way to call a function. Rather, you are creating an **operator** function that can be passed an arbitrary number of operands by use of the function call syntax. The function call operator must be implemented as a non-static member function of a class. The general form of the function call operator is shown here:

```
ret-type operator( )(param-list) {
   // Perform the desired operation based on the arguments
   // and return the result.
}
```

The function call operator is invoked on an object of its class. The invoking object is passed via **this**, and the arguments are passed to its parameters. If no arguments are needed, then no parameters need be specified. The function returns the result of the operation.

Let's work through an example. Assuming the **three_d** class from the previous recipe, the following function call operator returns a **three_d** object that represents a point whose coordinates are midpoints between the invoking object and its **three_d** argument.

```
// Overload function call. Take a three_d object as a parameter.
// This function returns a three_d object whose coordinates are
// the midpoints between the invoking object and obj.
three_d three_d::operator()(three_d obj)
{
  three_d temp;

  temp.x = (x + obj.x) / 2;
  temp.y = (y + obj.y) / 2;
  temp.z = (z + obj.z) / 2;

  return temp;
}
```

Given three **three_d** objects called **objA**, **objB**, and **objC**, the following calls **operator( )** on **objA**, passing in **objB**:

```
objC = objA(objB);
```

Here, **objA(objB)** translates into this call to the **operator( )** function:

```
objA.operator()(objB)
```

The result is returned and stored in **objC**.

Before moving on, let's review the key points. First, when you overload the **( )** operator, you define the parameters that you want to pass to that function. When you use the **( )** operator in your program, the arguments you specify are copied to those parameters. The object that generates the call (**objA** in the foregoing example) is pointed to by the **this** pointer.

You can overload **operator( )** to allow different types and/or numbers of arguments. For example, here is a version of **operator( )** for **three_d** that takes three **int** arguments. It adds the values of those arguments to the coordinates of the invoking object and returns the result.

```
// Overload function call. Take three ints as parameters.
three_d three_d::operator()(int a, int b, int c)
{
  three_d temp;

  temp.x = x + a;
  temp.y = y + b;
  temp.z = z + c;

  return temp;
}
```

This function allows the following type of statement:

```
objC = objA(1, 2, 3);
```

Here, the values 1, 2, and 3 are added to **objA**'s **x**, **y**, and **z** fields, and the result is returned and stored in **objC**.

One other point: You can also overload **operator( )** so that its parameter list is empty. In this case, no arguments are passed to the function when it is called.

Example

The following example puts together the pieces described in the discussion.

```
// Demonstrate the function call operator.

#include <iostream>

using namespace std;

// A class that encapsulates 3-dimensional coordinates.
class three_d {
  int x, y, z; // 3-D coordinates
public:
  three_d() { x = y = z = 0; }
  three_d(int i, int j, int k) { x = i; y = j; z = k; }

  // Create two function call operator functions.
  three_d operator()(three_d obj);
  three_d operator()(int a, int b, int c);

  // Let the overloaded inserter be a friend.
  friend ostream &operator<<(ostream &strm, three_d op);
};

// Overload function call. Take a three_d object as a parameter.
// This function returns a three_d object whose coordinates are
// the midpoints between the invoking object and obj.
three_d three_d::operator()(three_d obj)
{
  three_d temp;

  temp.x = (x + obj.x) / 2;
  temp.y = (y + obj.y) / 2;
  temp.z = (z + obj.z) / 2;

  return temp;
}

// Overload function call. Take three ints as parameters.
// This version adds the arguments to the coordinates.
three_d three_d::operator()(int a, int b, int c)
{
  three_d temp;

  temp.x = x + a;
  temp.y = y + b;
  temp.z = z + c;

  return temp;
}

// The three_d inserter is a non-member operator function.
ostream &operator<<(ostream &strm, three_d op) {
  strm << op.x << ", " << op.y << ", " << op.z << endl;
```

```
    return strm;
}

int main()
{
  three_d objA(1, 2, 3), objB(10, 10, 10), objC;

  cout << "This is objA: " << objA;
  cout << "This is objB: " << objB;

  objC = objA(objB);
  cout << "objA(objB): " << objC;

  objC = objA(10, 20, 30);
  cout << "objA(10, 20, 30): " << objC;

  // Can use the result of one as an argument to another.
  objC = objA(objB(100, 200, 300));
  cout << "objA(objB(100, 200, 300)): " << objC;

  return 0;
}
```

The output is shown here:

```
This is objA: 1, 2, 3
This is objB: 10, 10, 10
objA(objB): 5, 6, 6
objA(10, 20, 30): 11, 22, 33
objA(objB(100, 200, 300)): 55, 106, 156
```

Options and Alternatives

When the function call operator is implemented for a class, an instance of its class can be used as a *function object*. Function objects are used extensively by the STL. Chapter 4 shows several examples.

The two versions of **operator( )** in the preceding example do not modify the invoking object. Instead, they return the result. Although there is no rule that enforces it, I prefer this approach in most cases. In general, if an object is going to be modified, I prefer it to occur through an overloaded assignment operator, not the function call operator. In other words,

```
objA(objB);
```

should not normally be used as a substitute for

```
objA = objB;
```

In general, **operator( )** should be reserved for operations that do not relate to any of the other operators. I don't like using **operator( )** as a "catch-all" operator that substitutes for an overload of the proper operator. Properly used, **operator( )** is a powerful feature. Poorly used, it can confuse your code.

Overload the Subscripting Operator [ ]

Key Ingredients		
Headers	**Classes**	**Functions**
		ret-type operator[ ](*indx-type idx*)

If I had a favorite operator to overload, it would probably be [ ], the subscripting operator. Why? Because it enables the creation of "safe" arrays, which are arrays in which boundary overruns are prevented. As you know, C++ performs no bounds-checking on normal arrays. However, by wrapping an array inside a class and then allowing access to that array only through the subscripting operator, you can prevent accesses that are outside the array. You can also ensure that only valid values are assigned to the array. This mechanism is employed with great success by the STL, such as in the **vector** and **deque** classes.

The [ ] is, of course, useful in other contexts. For example, a class that encapsulates an IP request might allow access to properties by indexing the object. Basically, any time you have a class that has elements for which indexing makes sense, the subscripting operator offers an elegant approach. This recipe shows the basic techniques needed to implement it.

Step-by-Step

To overload the [ ] subscripting operator involves these steps:

1. The subscripting operator must be a non-static member of the class for which it is defined. It cannot be a non-member function. Therefore, add **operator[ ]( )** as a member to the class on which it will be operating.

2. Inside **operator[ ]( )**, perform the desired action, which usually involves accessing some object through an index.

3. On completion, have **operator[ ]( )** return the object (or a reference to the object) based on the index.

Discussion

The [ ] is a binary operator for the purposes of overloading, and it must be overloaded by a non-static member function. It has this general form:

```
ret-type operator[ ]( indx-type idx)
{
   // Access the item specified by idx.
}
```

The subscript is passed in *idx*, which is often an **int**, but can be any type. For example, in an associative container, *idx* could be a key. The function can return any type, but it will usually be the type of element being obtained.

When the [ ] is evaluated, the object being subscripted must be an instance of the class for which the subscripting operator is defined. This instance is passed via **this**. The object within the [ ] is passed in *idx*. For example, given an object called **obj**, the expression

```
obj[5]
```

translates into this call to the **operator[ ]( )** function:

```
obj.operator[](5)
```

In this case, 5 is passed to the *idx* parameter. A pointer to **obj**, the object that generated the call, is passed via **this**.

You can design the **operator[ ]( )** function in such a way that the [ ] can be used on both the left and right sides of an assignment statement. To do this, simply specify the return value of **operator[ ]( )** as a reference. After doing this, the following expressions are valid:

```
x = obj[4];
obj[5] = 9;
```

Overloading the [ ] operator provides a means of implementing safe array indexing in C++. This is one of its main uses and one of its principal advantages. As you know, in C++, it is possible to overrun (or underrun) an array boundary at runtime. However, if you create a class that contains the array and allow access to that array only through the overloaded [ ] subscripting operator, then you can intercept an out-of-range index. The following example illustrates this.

Example

The following program shows how to overload the subscripting operator by using it to create a "safe array" that prevents boundary errors. It defines a generic class called **safe_array**, which encapsulates an array. The type of the array is specified by a template type parameter called **T**. The length of the array is specified by a non-type template parameter called **len**. The array encapsulated by **safe_array** is called **ar**. The length of the array is stored in a variable called **length**. Both are private members of **safe_array**. The array elements are accessed only through the overloaded **operator[ ]( )**. It first confirms that an array access is within bounds. If it is, **operator[ ]( )** then returns a reference to the element. The length of the array can be obtained by calling the method **getlen( )**.

```
// Overload [] to create a generic safe array type.
//
// The operator[]() function checks for array boundary errors
// so that an overrun or underrun is prevented.
//
// Notice that this example uses a non-type template parameter
// to specify the size of the array.

#include <iostream>
#include <cstdlib>

using namespace std;
```

```
// Here, T specifies the type of the array and the non-type
// parameter len specifies the length of the array.
template <class T, int len> class safe_array {

  // The array ar is declared to be of type T and of length len.
  // The array is private. Access is allowed only through operator[]().
  // In this way, boundary errors can be prevented.
  T ar[len];
  int length;

public:
  // Create a safe_array of type T with a length of len.
  safe_array();

  // Overload the subscripting operator so that it accesses
  // the elements in ar.
  T &operator[](int i);

  // Return the length of the array.
  int getlen() { return length; }
};

// Create a safe_array of type T with a length of len.
// The len variable is a non-type template parameter.
template <class T, int len>  safe_array<T, len>::safe_array() {
  // Initialize the array elements to their default value.
  for(int i=0; i < len; ++i) ar[i] = T();
  length = len;
}

// Return a reference to the element at the specified index.
// Provide range checking to prevent boundary errors.
template <class T, int len> T &safe_array<T, len>::operator[](int i)
{
  if(i < 0 || i > len-1) {
    // Take appropriate action here. This is just
    // a placeholder response.
    cout << "\nIndex value of " << i << " is out-of-bounds.\n";
    exit(1);
  }
  return ar[i];
}

// This is a simple class used to demonstrate an array of objects.
// Notice that the default constructor gives x the value -1.
class myclass {
public:
  int x;
  myclass(int i) { x = i; };
  myclass() { x = -1; }
};

int main()
{
```

```
safe_array<int, 10> i_ar;    // integer array of size 10
safe_array<double, 5> d_ar;  // double array of size 5
int i;

cout << "Initial values for i_ar: ";
for(i=0; i < i_ar.getlen(); ++i) cout << i_ar[i] << "  ";
cout << endl;

// Change the values in i_ar.
for(i=0; i < i_ar.getlen(); ++i) i_ar[i] = i;

cout << "New values for i_ar: ";
for(i=0; i < i_ar.getlen(); ++i) cout << i_ar[i] << "  ";
cout << "\n\n";

cout << "Initial values for d_ar: ";
for(i=0; i < d_ar.getlen(); ++i) cout << d_ar[i] << "  ";
cout << endl;

// Change the values in d_ar.
for(i=0; i < d_ar.getlen(); ++i) d_ar[i] = (double) i/3;

cout << "New values for d_ar: ";
for(i=0; i < d_ar.getlen(); ++i) cout << d_ar[i] << "  ";
cout << "\n\n";;

// safe_array works with objects, too.
safe_array<myclass, 3> mc_ar; // myclass array of size 3

cout << "Initial values in mc_ar: ";
for(i = 0; i < mc_ar.getlen(); ++i) cout << mc_ar[i].x << " ";
cout << endl;

// Give mc_ar some new values.
mc_ar[0].x = 19;
mc_ar[1].x = 99;
mc_ar[2].x = -97;

cout << "New values for mc_ar: ";
for(i = 0; i < mc_ar.getlen(); ++i) cout << mc_ar[i].x << " ";
cout << endl;

// This creates a boundary overrun.
i_ar[12] = 100;

// Comment-out the preceding line and then Uncomment the following
// line to generate a boundary underrun.
//  i_ar[-2] = 100;

return 0;
}
```

The output is shown here:

```
Initial values for i_ar: 0  0  0  0  0  0  0  0  0  0
New values for i_ar: 0  1  2  3  4  5  6  7  8  9

Initial values for d_ar: 0  0  0  0  0
New values for d_ar: 0  0.333333  0.666667  1  1.33333

Initial values in mc_ar: -1 -1 -1
New values for mc_ar: 19 99 -97

Index value of 12 is out-of-bounds.
```

In the program, pay special attention to this statement:

```
i_ar[12] = 100;
```

It attempts to assign 100 to location 12 within **i_ar**. But **i_ar** is only 10 elements long! If this were a normal array, then a boundary overrun would occur. Fortunately, in this case, the attempt is intercepted by **operator[]( )** and the program is terminated before any damage can be done. (In actual practice, some sort of error-handling would be supplied to deal with the out-of-range condition; the program would not have to terminate.)

Options and Alternatives

Although overloading the subscripting operator is usually the best approach in cases in which the concept of a "subscript" applies, you will sometimes see "get" and "put" functions used instead. In this case, the index of the desired item is passed to the "get" or "put" function explicitly as an argument. For example, the following sequence might be used to obtain the third string or to set the fourth string for some set of string values:

```
str = get(3);
put(4, "testing");
```

Of course, subscripting offers a cleaner approach, but the "get" and "put" approach is common in legacy C code. If you find such code, you might want to upgrade it to C++ by overloading [ ].

Overload the -> Operator

Key Ingredients		
Headers	**Classes**	**Functions**
		type *operator->( )

One of the more interesting operators is –>. It is called the *class member access* operator. It is a unary operator that returns a pointer. This pointer is related in some way or another to the object on which –> is invoked. The precise nature of the relationship is defined by the class for which the –> is defined. As it relates to overloading, the –> is the source of many questions—and sometimes confusion. This recipe demonstrates how to overload it. A bonus example is included that shows how an overloaded –> can be used to create a "safe pointer."

Step-by-Step

Overloading the –> operator involves the following steps:

1. The member access operator must be a non-static member of the class for which it is defined. It cannot be a non-member function. Therefore, add **operator–>( )** as a member to the class on which it will be operating.

2. Inside the function, obtain a pointer to, or in some way associated with, the invoking object.

3. Return the pointer.

Discussion

The –> operator is overloaded as a unary operator. Its general usage is shown here:

> *object–>element*

Here, *object* is the object that activates the call. This must be an instance of the class for which the member access operator is defined, and it is passed to **operator–>( )** through **this**. The *element* must be some member accessible within the object. The function must return a pointer to *object* or a pointer to an object managed by *object*. The principal use of the member access operator is to support what are referred to as "safe pointers" or "smart pointers." These are pointers that verify the integrity of a pointer before performing an action through it. Other uses include the creation of pointers that automatically manage memory or that support garbage collection.

The general form of an **operator–>( )** is shown here:

```
type *operator->( ) {
  //  Return a pointer to the invoking object.
}
```

Here, *type* must be the same as the class for which the **operator–>( )** is defined. An **operator–>( )** function must be a non-static member of its class.

Example

The following example demonstrates how to overload –>. It simply returns a pointer to the invoking object. This makes it possible to use –> to access a member of **myclass** through an object, rather than a pointer to an object. Thus, the overload of **operator–>( )** makes the –> and the . operators equivalent. Although this example is useful for illustrating the effect of overloading –> because it is quite short, it does not represent a good use (or recommended

practice). To see how an overloaded –> would normally be employed, refer to the Bonus
Example.

```
// Demonstrate operator->().

#include <iostream>

using namespace std;

class myclass {
public:
  int i;

  // Overload -> to return a pointer to the invoking object.
  myclass *operator->() { return this; }
};

int main()
{
  myclass ob;

  ob->i = 10; // same as ob.i

  cout << ob.i << " " << ob->i;

  return 0;
}
```

The output is shown here:

```
10 10
```

Bonus Example: A Simple Safe Pointer Class

Although the preceding example shows the mechanics of overloading –>, it does not show
its power. Normally, the –> is overloaded to implement a custom pointer type that in one
way or another constrains or monitors actions on the pointer. For example, you might create
a pointer type that provides automatic garbage collection. Perhaps the most common use,
however, is to create a "safe pointer" that prevents invalid actions through the pointer, such
as dereferencing or accessing a member through a null pointer. Such a pointer can be
implemented by overloading the * and –> operators so that they confirm that the pointer is
not null before proceeding with the operation. A simple implementation of this concept is
developed by this example.

The following program creates a simple safe pointer class called **safe_ptr** that prevents
operations on a pointer that is null. It does this by overloading the –> and *. (When used as
the dereferencing operator, the * is overloaded as a unary operator.) These operators are
overloaded to prevent a null pointer from being dereferenced or used to access a member.

The **safe_ptr** class is implemented as a template class in which the type parameter
specifies the base type of the pointer. For example, to create a safe pointer to an **int**, use this
declaration:

```
safe_ptr<int> intptr;
```

Once you have created the safe pointer, you can use it like a normal pointer. For example, you can assign to it the address of an object in memory with the following statement:

```
intptr = new int;
```

You can set or obtain the value of the object through the pointer by using the * operator. For example:

```
*intptr = 23;
```

In the case of pointers to class objects, you can use –> to access a member. For both operators, **safe_ptr** confirms that the pointer is not null before applying the * or –>.

The **safe_ptr** class works by encapsulating a pointer in a field called **ptr**. This is a private member, and access to it is allowed only through overloaded operators, including the overloaded assignment operator. A conversion function is also provided, which provides a conversion from **safe_ptr** to **T ***. This allows a **safe_ptr** to be used as an operand for the **delete** operator, for example.

If an attempt is made to use a null pointer, the overloaded * and –> operators will throw an object of type **bad_ptr**, which is a custom exception class. Code that uses **safe_ptr** will need to watch for that exception.

The following program includes the **safe_ptr** and the **bad_ptr** classes. It also defines a class called **myclass**, which is used to demonstrate –> with a **safe_ptr**. Although quite simple, **safe_ptr** gives you an idea of the power of overloading the –> operator and the power of creating your own pointer types. Custom pointer types can be very useful for preventing errors or for implementing custom memory management schemes. Be aware, of course, that a custom pointer type will always be slower than a raw pointer because of the overhead that your code introduces.

```
// Demonstrate a very simple safe pointer class.

#include <iostream>
#include <string>

using namespace std;

// The exception type thrown by the safe pointer.
class bad_ptr {
public:
  string msg;

  bad_ptr(string str) { msg = str; }
};

// A class used to demonstrate the safe pointer.
class myclass {
public:
  int alpha;
  int beta;
  myclass(int p, int q) { alpha = p; beta = q; }
};

// A very simple "safe pointer" class that confirms
```

```cpp
// that a pointer points somewhere before it is used.
//
// The template parameter T specifies the base type of the pointer.
//
// Note: This class is for demonstration purposes only.
// It is intended only to illustrate the overloaded -> operator.
// A safe pointer class suitable for real-world use needs to be
// more sophisticated and more resilient.
//
template <class T> class safe_ptr {
  T *ptr;
public:
  safe_ptr() { ptr = 0; }

  // Overload -> so that it prevents an attempt to use a null pointer
  // to access a member.
  T *operator->() {
    if(!ptr != 0) throw bad_ptr("Attempt to use -> on null pointer.");
    else return ptr;
  }

  // Overload the unary pointer operator *.  This operator prevents
  // a null pointer from being dereferenced.
  T &operator*() {
    if(!ptr) throw bad_ptr("Attempt to dereference null pointer.");
    else return *ptr;
  }

  // Conversion from safe_ptr to T *.
  operator T *() { return ptr; }

  T *operator=(T *val) { ptr = val; return ptr; }
};

int main()
{
  // First, use safe_ptr on an integer.

  safe_ptr<int> intptr;

  // Generate an exception by trying to use a pointer
  // before it points to some object.
  try {
    *intptr = 23;
    cout << "The value pointed to by intptr is: " << *intptr << endl;
  } catch(bad_ptr bp) {
    cout << bp.msg << endl;
  }

  // Point intptr to an object.
  intptr = new int;

  // Now the following sequence will work.
  try {
```

```
      *intptr = 23;
      cout << "The value pointed to by intpr is: " << *intptr << "\n\n";
    } catch(bad_ptr bp) {
      cout << bp.msg << endl;
    }

    // Now, use safe_ptr on a class.

    safe_ptr<myclass> mcptr;

    // This sequence will succeed.
    try {
      mcptr = new myclass(100, 200);
      cout << "The values of alpha and beta for mcptr are: "
           << mcptr->alpha << " and " << mcptr->beta << endl;

      mcptr->alpha = 27;
      cout << "New value for mcptr->alpha: " << mcptr->alpha << endl;
      cout << "Same as (*mcptr).alpha: " << (*mcptr).alpha << endl;

      mcptr->beta = 99;
      cout << "New value for mcptr->beta: " << mcptr->beta << "\n\n";
    } catch(bad_ptr bp) {
      cout << bp.msg << endl;
    }

    // Create another myclass pointer, but don't initialize it.
    safe_ptr<myclass> mcptr2;

    // The following assignment will throw an exception because
    // mcptr2 points nowhere.
    try {
      mcptr2->alpha = 88;
    } catch(bad_ptr bp) {
      cout << bp.msg << endl;
    }

    delete intptr;
    delete mcptr;

    return 0;
}
```

The output is shown here:

```
Attempt to dereference null pointer.
The value pointed to by intpr is: 23

The values of alpha and beta for mcptr are: 100 and 200
New value for mcptr->alpha: 27
Same as (*mcptr).alpha: 27
New value for mcptr->beta: 99

Attempt to use -> on null pointer.
```

Options and Alternatives

Be careful when overloading ->. Pointers are already a troublesome feature for some programmers. If you overload -> in a confusing, counterintuitive manner, you will simply destructure your code and make it difficult to maintain. In general, you should overload -> only when creating a custom pointer type. Furthermore, your custom type should look, act, and feel like a normal pointer. In other words, its operation should be transparent and its use consistent with a built-in pointer. Of course, your pointer type may perform additional checks or implement a custom memory management scheme, but it should work like a normal pointer when used in a program.

In some cases, you may find that C++ already provides the pointer type that you want. For example, an often-overlooked class provided by the standard C++ library is **auto_ptr**. An **auto_ptr** automatically frees the memory it points to when the pointer goes out of scope. See *Use auto_ptr* for details.

Overload new and delete

Key Ingredients		
Headers	**Classes**	**Functions**
		void operator delete(void *ptr)
		void operator delete[ ](void *ptr)
		void *operator new(size_t size)
		void *operator new[ ](size_t size)

Newcomers to C++ are sometimes surprised to learn that **new** and **delete** are considered operators. As such, it is possible to overload them. You might choose to do this if you want to use some special allocation method. For example, you may want allocation routines that automatically begin using a disk file as virtual memory when the heap has been exhausted. Or, you might want to use an allocation scheme based on garbage collection. Whatever your need, it is relatively easy to overload these operators, and this recipe shows the process.

Step-by-Step

Overloading **new** and **delete** involves the following steps:

1. To overload **new** for single objects, implement **operator new( )**. Have it return a pointer to a block of memory that is large enough to hold the object.

2. To overload **new** for arrays of objects, implement **operator new[ ]( )**. Have it return a pointer to a block of memory that is large enough to hold the array.

3. To overload **delete** for a pointer to a single object, implement **operator delete( )**. Have it release the memory used by the object.

    4. To overload **delete** for a pointer to an array of objects, implement **operator delete[ ]( )**. Have it release the memory used by the array.

Discussion

Before we begin, an important point needs to be made. The **new** and **delete** operators can be overloaded globally or relative to a specific class. When overloaded globally, the new versions of **new** and **delete** replace the default versions when allocating memory for the built-in types and for any class that does not provide its own overload of **new** and **delete**. Unfortunately, this can sometimes cause undesirable side effects. For example, third-party code might use **new** and **delete**, and this use could be incompatible with the overloaded versions. For this reason, I do not recommend overloading **new** and **delete** globally, except in the rare cases. Instead, I recommend overloading **new** and **delete** on a class-by-class basis. When **new** and **delete** are overloaded by a class, they are used only when allocating memory for objects of the class. This eliminates the potential for side effects outside the class. This is the approach used by this recipe, and the discussion that follows assumes that **new** and **delete** are being overloaded relative to a class through the use of member functions.

    There are two basic forms of **new** and **delete**. The first is for allocating and releasing single objects. The second is for allocating and releasing arrays of objects. Both forms can be overloaded, and both are described here. We will begin with the forms that allocate and release single objects.

    Here are the general forms of **new** and **delete** overloaded for single objects:

```
// Allocate memory for an object.
void *operator new(size_t size)
{
  // Allocate memory for the object and return a pointer to
  // the memory. The size in bytes of the object is passed in size.
  // Throw bad_alloc on failure.
}

// Release previously allocated memory.
void operator delete(void *ptr)
{
  // Free memory pointed to by ptr.
}
```

The *size* parameter will contain the number of bytes needed to hold the object being allocated. This is the amount of memory that your version of **new** must allocate. (**size_t** is a **typedef** for some form of an unsigned integer.) The overloaded **new** function must return a pointer to the memory that it allocates, or throw a **bad_alloc** exception if an allocation error occurs. Beyond these constraints, the overloaded **new** can do anything else you require. When you allocate an object using **new** (whether your own version or not), the object's constructor is automatically called.

    The **delete** function receives a pointer to the region of memory to be freed. It must release the previously allocated memory back to the system. When an object is deleted, its destructor is automatically called. It is important that **delete** be used only on a pointer that was previously allocated via **new**.

If you want to be able to allocate arrays of objects using your own allocation system, you will need to overload **new[ ]** and **delete[ ]**, which are the array forms of **new** and **delete**. Here are their general forms:

```
// Allocate an array of objects.
void *operator new[ ](size_t size)
{
  // Allocate memory for the array and return a pointer to it.
  // The number of bytes to allocate are passed in size.
  // Throw bad_alloc on failure.
}

// Delete an array of objects.
void operator delete[ ](void *ptr)
{
  // Free memory pointed to by ptr.
}
```

When allocating an array, the constructor for each object in the array is automatically called. When freeing an array, each object's destructor is automatically called. You do not have to provide explicit code to accomplish these actions.

Example

The following example overloads **new** and **delete** for the **three_d** class. Both the object and the array form of each are overloaded. For the sake of simplicity, no new allocation scheme is used. Instead, the overloaded operators will simply invoke the standard C library functions **malloc( )** and **free( )**. The **malloc( )** function allocates a specified number of bytes and returns a pointer to them. It returns null if the memory cannot be allocated. Given a pointer to memory previously allocated by **malloc( )**, **free( )** releases the memory, making it available for re-use. In general, **malloc( )** and **free( )** parallel the functionality of **new** and **delete**, but in a less streamlined fashion.

```
// Overload new, new[], delete, and delete[] for the three_d class.
//
// This program uses the C functions malloc() and free()
// to allocate and release dynamic memory. They require the
// header<cstdlib>.

#include <iostream>
#include <cstdlib>
#include <new>

using namespace std;

// A class that encapsulates 3-dimensional coordinates.
class three_d {
  int x, y, z; // 3-D coordinates
public:
  three_d() { x = y = z = 0; }
```

```
    three_d(int i, int j, int k) { x = i; y = j; z = k; }

    // Set the coordinates of an object after it is created.
    void set(int i, int j, int k) { x = i; y = j; z = k; }

    // Overload new and delete for three_d objects.
    void *operator new(size_t size);
    void operator delete(void *p);

    // Overload new[] and delete[] for three_d arrays.
    void *operator new[](size_t size);
    void operator delete[](void *p);

    // Let the overloaded inserter be a friend.
    friend ostream &operator<<(ostream &strm, three_d op);
};

// The three_d inserter is a non-member operator function.
ostream &operator<<(ostream &strm, three_d op) {
    strm << op.x << ", " << op.y << ", " << op.z << endl;

    return strm;
}

// Overload new for three_d.
void *three_d::operator new(size_t size)
{
    void *p;

    cout << "Using overloaded new for three_d.\n";
    p = malloc(size);
    if(!p) {
        bad_alloc ba;
        throw ba;
    }
    return p;
}

// Overload delete for three_d.
void three_d::operator delete(void *p)
{
    cout << "Using overloaded delete for three_d.\n";
    free(p);
}

// Overload new[] for three_d arrays.
void *three_d::operator new[](size_t size)
{
    void *p;

    cout << "Using overloaded new[] for three_d.\n";
    p = malloc(size);
    if(!p) {
        bad_alloc ba;
```

```
      throw ba;
    }
    return p;
}

// Overload delete[] for three_d arrays.
void three_d::operator delete[](void *p)
{
    cout << "Using overloaded delete[] for three_d.\n";
    free(p);
}

int main()
{
    three_d *p1, *p2;
    int i;

    // Allocate a three_d object.
    try {
      p1 = new three_d (10, 20, 30);
    } catch (bad_alloc xa) {
      cout << "Allocation error for p1.\n";
      return 1;
    }

    cout << "Coordinates in the object pointed to by p1: " << *p1;

    // Free the object.
    delete p1;

    cout << endl;

    // Allocate a three_d array.
    try {
      p2 = new three_d [10]; // allocate an array
    } catch (bad_alloc xa) {
      cout << "Allocation error for p2.\n";
      return 1;
    }

    // Assign coordinates to three of p2's elements.
    p2[1].set(99, 88, 77);
    p2[5].set(-1, -2, -3);
    p2[8].set(56, 47, 19);

    cout << "Contents of a dynamic three_d array:\n";
    for(i=0; i<10; i++) cout << p2[i];

    // Free the array.
    delete [] p2;

    return 0;
}
```

The output is shown here:

```
Using overloaded new for three_d.
Coordinates in the object pointed to by p1: 10, 20, 30
Using overloaded delete for three_d.

Using overloaded new[] for three_d.
Contents of a dynamic three_d array:
0, 0, 0
99, 88, 77
0, 0, 0
0, 0, 0
0, 0, 0
-1, -2, -3
0, 0, 0
0, 0, 0
56, 47, 19
0, 0, 0
Using overloaded delete[] for three_d.
```

Options and Alternatives

C++ supports a "no-throw" version of **new**. This option makes **new** act like it did in early versions of C++ in which it returned null if memory could not be allocated. (Modern versions of C++ throw a **bad_alloc** exception when **new** fails.) You can create overloaded versions of the no-throw alternative by using these forms of **operator new( )** and **operator new[ ]( )**:

```
// Nothrow version of new.
void *operator new(size_t size, const nothrow_t &not_used)
{
  // Allocate the memory for the object. If successful, return a
  // pointer to the memory. Otherwise, return null.
}
```

```
// Nothrow version of new[ ].
void *operator new[ ](size_t size, const nothrow_t &not_used)
{
  // Allocate the memory for the array. If successful, return a
  // pointer to the memory. Otherwise, return null.
}
```

The type **nothrow_t** is defined in **<new>**.

When using the no-throw version, specify the object **nothrow** in the call to **new** and watch for a null return value, as shown here:

```
ptr = new(nothrow) int;
if(!ptr) {
  cout << "Allocation failed.\n";
  // handle the failure ...
}
```

The **nothrow** object is an instance of **nothrow_t** and is provided by **<new>**.

Overload the Increment and Decrement Operators

Key Ingredients		
Headers	**Classes**	**Functions**
		ret-type operator++( )
		ret-type operator++(int *not_used*)
		ret-type operator−−( )
		ret-type operator−−(int *not_used*)

As it relates to operator overloading, the ++ (increment) and the − − (decrement) operators generate the most questions. Although neither is difficult to overload, it is easy to get it slightly wrong, which makes the operator work correctly in some cases, but fail in others. This can result in bugs that are difficult to diagnose. The increment and decrement operators also have two different forms, prefix and postfix, both of which must be overloaded in order for the operators to work correctly in all cases. This recipe shows how to handle these sometimes-troubling operators.

Step-by-Step

To overload the increment and decrement operators using member functions involves these steps:

1. To overload the prefix form of the increment operator, create an **operator++( )** function. Inside that function, increment the invoking object and return the result.

2. To overload the postfix form of the increment operator, create an **operator++(int)** function. Inside that function, create a temporary object that contains the original value of the operand. Then, increment the invoking object. Finally, return the original value.

3. To overload the prefix form of the decrement operator, create an **operator−−( )** function. Inside that function, decrement the invoking object and return the result.

4. To overload the postfix form of the decrement operator, create an **operator−−(int)** function. Inside that function, create a temporary object that contains the original value of the operand. Then, decrement the invoking object. Finally, return the original value.

Discussion

There are two forms of the ++ and − − operators: prefix and postfix. The prefix form increments its operand and returns the result. The postfix form stores the operand's initial value, increments the operand, and then returns the original value. Both of these forms can be overloaded, and each is overloaded by its own function.

Most often, the increment and decrement operators are implemented as member functions of the class for which they are defined. This is the approach used by this recipe.

However, they can also be implemented by non-member functions, and this is described in the *Options and Alternatives* section for this recipe.

Here are the general forms for **operator++( )** and **operator– –( )** when implemented as member functions. Both the prefix and postfix forms are shown:

```
// Prefix increment
ret-type operator++( ) {
    // Increment the operand and return the result.
}

// Postfix increment
ret-type operator++(int not_used) {
    // Store a copy of the operand's original value.
    // Then increment the operand.
    // Finally, return the original value.
}

// Prefix decrement
ret-type operator--( ) {
    // Decrement the operand and return the result.
}

// Postfix decrement
ret-type operator--(int not_used) {
    // Store a copy of the operand's original value.
    // Then decrement the operand.
    // Finally, return the original value.
}
```

Pay special attention to the *not_used* parameter. It is usually zero and is not normally used within the function. It is simply a way for C++ to indicate which function to call.

There are three keys to correctly overloading increment or decrement:

- You must overload both the prefix and postfix forms.
- When implementing the prefix form, you must first increment or decrement the value and then return the altered value.
- When implementing the postfix form, you must remember to store the initial value and then return that value. Don't accidentally return the altered value.

If you follow these rules, your increment and decrement operators will behave like the built-in ones. Failure to follow them can lead to problems. For example, if you don't overload both the prefix and postfix forms of an operator, then the form you don't overload won't be able to be used. Furthermore, if you don't overload the postfix form, some compilers will report an error if you try to use the postfix operator, and will not compile your program. However, other compilers will simply report a warning and then use the prefix form instead. This will cause the postfix operator to act in an unexpected manner.

Example
The following example overloads increment and decrement for the **three_d** class. Both the prefix and postfix forms are provided.

```
// Overload ++ and -- for three_d.

#include <iostream>

using namespace std;

// A class that encapsulates 3-dimensional coordinates.
class three_d {
  int x, y, z; // 3-D coordinates
public:
  three_d() { x = y = z = 0; }
  three_d(int i, int j, int k) { x = i; y = j; z = k; }

  // Overload ++ and --. Provide both prefix and postfix forms.
  three_d operator++(); // prefix
  three_d operator++(int notused); // postfix

  three_d operator--(); // prefix
  three_d operator--(int notused); // postfix

  // Let the overloaded inserter be a friend.
  friend ostream &operator<<(ostream &strm, three_d op);
};

// Overload prefix ++ for three_d.
three_d three_d::operator++() {
  x++;
  y++;
  z++;

  return *this;
}

// Overload postfix ++ for three_d.
three_d three_d::operator++(int notused) {
  three_d temp = *this;

  x++;
  y++;
  z++;

  return temp;
}

// Overload prefix -- for three_d.
three_d three_d::operator--() {
  x--;
  y--;
  z--;
```

```
    return *this;
}

// Overload postfix -- for three_d.
three_d three_d::operator--(int notused) {
  three_d temp = *this;

  x--;
  y--;
  z--;

  return temp;
}

// The three_d inserter is a non-member operator function.
ostream &operator<<(ostream &strm, three_d op) {
  strm << op.x << ", " << op.y << ", " << op.z << endl;

  return strm;
}

int main()
{
  three_d objA(1, 2, 3), objB(10, 10, 10), objC;

  cout << "Original value of objA: " << objA;
  cout << "Original value of objB: " << objB;

  // Demonstrate ++ and -- as stand-alone operations.
  ++objA;
  ++objB;

  cout << "++objA: " << objA;
  cout << "++objB: " << objB;

  --objA;
  --objB;

  cout << "--objA: " << objA;
  cout << "--objB: " << objB;

  objA++;
  objB++;

  cout << endl;

  cout << "objA++: " << objA;
  cout << "objB++: " << objB;

  objA--;
  objB--;

  cout << "objA--: " << objA;
  cout << "objB--: " << objB;
```

```
    cout << endl;

    // Now, demonstrate the difference between the prefix
    // and postfix forms of ++ and --.

    objC = objA++;
    cout << "After objC = objA++\n  objC: " << objC <<"  objA: "
        << objA << endl;

    objC = objB--;
    cout << "After objC = objB--\n  objC: " << objC <<"  objB: "
        << objB << endl;

    objC = ++objA;
    cout << "After objC = ++objA\n  objC: " << objC <<"  objA: "
        << objA << endl;

    objC = --objB;
    cout << "After objC = --objB\n  objC: " << objC <<"  objB: "
        << objB << endl;

    return 0;
}
```

The output is shown here:

```
Original value of objA: 1, 2, 3
Original value of objB: 10, 10, 10
++objA: 2, 3, 4
++objB: 11, 11, 11
--objA: 1, 2, 3
--objB: 10, 10, 10

objA++: 2, 3, 4
objB++: 11, 11, 11
objA--: 1, 2, 3
objB--: 10, 10, 10

After objC = objA++
  objC: 1, 2, 3
  objA: 2, 3, 4

After objC = objB--
  objC: 10, 10, 10
  objB: 9, 9, 9

After objC = ++objA
  objC: 3, 4, 5
  objA: 3, 4, 5

After objC = --objB
  objC: 8, 8, 8
  objB: 8, 8, 8
```

Options and Alternatives

Although using member functions to overload the increment and decrement operators is the most common approach, you can also use non-member functions. You might want to do this when overloading the operators relative to an enumeration, or when you are defining increment and decrement relative to a class to which you do not have the source code. Whatever the reason, it is an easy task. The non-member forms of the increment and decrement operators are shown here:

```
// Prefix increment
ret-type operator++(type &op) {
  // Increment the operand and return the result.
}


// Postfix increment
ret-type operator++(type &op, int not_used) {
  // Store a copy of the operand's original value.
  // Then increment the operand.
  // Finally, return the original value.
}


// Prefix decrement
ret-type operator--(type &op) {
  // Decrement the operand and return the result.
}


// Postfix decrement
ret-type operator--(type &op, int not_used) {
  // Store a copy of the operand's original value.
  // Then decrement the operand.
  // Finally, return the original value.
}
```

Notice that the operand is passed via reference. This is necessary to allow the functions to alter the operand.

In general, when you want to increment or decrement an object, overloading the ++ and - - operators is the best approach. In some cases, however, you may find that using functions is better. For example, you can create a function called **inc( )** that increments an object and **dec( )** that decrements an object. You might want to do this when you don't want to alter the value of the object. The **inc( )** or **dec( )** function could just return the new value, but leave the object unmodified. You could also do this by overloading the increment and decrement operators such that they do not alter the operand, but this would make them work in a way that is inconsistent with their normal semantics.

You should be careful when working with legacy C++ programs where the increment and decrement operators are concerned. In older versions of C++, it was not possible to specify separate prefix and postfix versions of an overloaded ++ or - -. The prefix form was used for both. Modern compilers will usually flag a warning in this situation, but it's best not to count on it. It is better to confirm that the increment and decrement are properly overloaded. If they are not, you need to upgrade them.

Create a Conversion Function

Key Ingredients		
Headers	Classes	Functions
		operator *target-type*( )

Sometimes, you will want to use a class object in an expression involving another type of data. Although overloaded operators can provide a means of doing this, sometimes, all that you really want is a simple type conversion from the class type to the target type. To handle these cases, C++ lets you create a *conversion function*. A conversion function automatically converts a class type into the target type. This makes the conversion function one of C++'s most useful features. Unfortunately, it is also one of its most overlooked features. This recipe shows how to create a conversion function. In the process, it sheds some light on this often-ignored capability.

Step-by-Step

To create a conversion function involves these steps:

1. To provide a conversion from a class type to a target type, add a conversion function to the class. A conversion function is based on the **operator** keyword, as described in the discussion that follows.
2. Inside the conversion function, convert the object into the target type.
3. Return the result, which must be a value compatible with the target type.

Discussion

A conversion function makes use of the **operator** keyword. The general form of a conversion function is shown here:

```
operator target-type( ) {
    // Create a value that contains the conversion.
    return value;
}
```

Here, *target-type* is the target type that you are converting your class to, and *value* is the outcome of the conversion. The object being converted is passed through **this**. Conversion functions return data of type *target-type,* and no other return type specifier is allowed. Also, no parameters may be included. A conversion function must be a member of the class for which it is defined. Conversion functions are inherited and they may be virtual.

Once you have created a conversion function, an object of its class can be used within an expression of the target type. This means that it can be operated on through operators (without having to overload them), as long as the expression type is the same as the target type of the conversion function. Furthermore, a conversion function lets you pass an object as an argument to a function as long as the parameter type is the same as the target type. These are powerful features, which can be obtained with almost no programming effort.

The best way to appreciate the power of a conversion function is to work through an example. Assume the **three_d** class shown here:

```
class three_d {
  int x, y, z; // 3-D coordinates
public:
  three_d() { x = y = z = 0; }
  three_d(int i, int j, int k) {x = i; y = j; z = k; }

  // ...
};
```

You can create a conversion to **int** by adding the following function as a member:

```
operator int() { return x + y + z; }
```

This converts a **three_d** object into an integer that contains the sum of the coordinates.

Assuming the above conversion, the following sequence is now valid:

```
three_d objA(1, 2, 3);
int result;
result = 10 + objA;
```

After this executes, the result will contain the value 16 (10 + 1 + 2 + 3). Because 10 is an **int** value, when **objA** is added to it, **operator int( )** is automatically invoked on **objA** to supply the conversion.

Example

The following example puts into action the preceding discussion. It creates a conversion from **three_d** to **int**. It then uses that conversion to use a **three_d** object in an integer expression and to pass **three_d** objects as arguments to functions that specify an integer parameter.

```
// Create conversion functions for three_d.

#include <iostream>

using namespace std;

// A class that encapsulates 3-dimensional coordinates.
class three_d {
  int x, y, z; // 3-D coordinates
public:
  three_d() { x = y = z = 0; }
  three_d(int i, int j, int k) { x = i; y = j; z = k; }

  // A conversion to int.
  operator int() { return x + y + z; }
```

```
  // Let the overloaded inserter be a friend.
  friend ostream &operator<<(ostream &strm, three_d op);
};

// The three_d inserter is a non-member operator function.
ostream &operator<<(ostream &strm, three_d op) {
  strm << op.x << ", " << op.y << ", " << op.z << endl;

  return strm;
}

// Return the negation of v.
int neg(int v) {
  return -v;
}

// Return true if x is less than y.
bool lt(int x, int y) {
  if(x < y) return true;
  return false;
}

int main()
{
  three_d objA(1, 2, 3), objB(-1, -2, -3);
  int result;

  cout << "Value of objA: " << objA;
  cout << "Value of objB: " << objB;
  cout << endl;

  // Use objA in an int expression.
  cout << "Use a three_d object in an int expression: ";
  result = 10 + objA;
  cout << "10 + objA: " << result << "\n\n";

  // Pass objA to a function that takes an int argument.
  cout << "Pass a three_d object to an int parameter: ";
  result = neg(objA);
  cout << "neg(objA): " << result << "\n\n";

  cout << "Compare the sum of the coordinates by use of lt(): ";
  if(lt(objA, objB))
    cout << "objA less than objB\n";
  else if(lt(objB, objA))
    cout << "objB less than objA\n";
  else
    cout << "objA and objB both sum to the same value.\n";


  return 0;
}
```

The output is shown here:

```
Value of objA: 1, 2, 3
Value of objB: -1, -2, -3

Use a three_d object in an int expression: 10 + objA: 16

Pass a three_d object to an int parameter: neg(objA): -6

Compare the sum of the coordinates by use of lt(): objB less than objA
```

Options and Alternatives

You can create different conversion functions to meet different needs. For example, you could define conversions from **three_d** to **int**, **double**, or **long**. Each will be applied automatically, as determined by the type of the conversion needed.

In some cases, instead of using a conversion function, you can achieve the same result (but not as easily) by overloading the operators that you will be using. For example, in the preceding example, you could overload the + for operations involving **three_d** objects and integers. Of course, this would still not allow a **three_d** object to be passed to a function that uses an **int** parameter.

Create a Copy Constructor

Key Ingredients		
Headers	**Classes**	**Functions**
		classname (const *classname* &*obj*)

One commonly overlooked but incredibly important feature of C++ is the *copy constructor.* A copy constructor defines how a copy of an object is made. Because C++ automatically supplies a default copy constructor for a class, not all classes need to define one explicitly. However, for many classes, the default copy constructor is insufficient, and its use will lead to trouble. This is because the default copy constructor creates an identical copy of the original. If an object holds a resource, such as a pointer to memory or a file stream object, then if a copy is made, that copy will also point to the same memory or attempt to use the same file. In cases like this, problems are soon to follow. The solution is to define an explicit copy constructor that duplicates an object, but avoids the potential trouble. Towards this end, this recipe describes how to create a copy constructor and reviews the circumstances under which it is needed.

Step-by-Step

To create a copy constructor involves these steps:

1. Create a constructor for the class that takes only one parameter, which is a reference to the object being copied.
2. Inside the copy constructor, copy the object in a way compatible with the class.

Discussion

Let's begin by examining the problem that a copy constructor is designed to solve. By default, when one object is used to initialize another, a field-by-field copy of the original is made. For scalar fields (which includes pointers), an identical, bitwise copy of the field results. Although this is perfectly adequate for many cases—and often is exactly what you want to happen—there are situations in which an identical copy should not be used. One of the most common is when an object uses dynamically allocated memory. For example, assume a class called **myclass** that uses dynamically allocated memory for some purpose and that a pointer to this memory is held in a field. Further assume that this memory is allocated when an object is constructed and freed when its destructor executes. Finally, assume a **myclass** object called **A**, which is used to initialize **B**, as shown here:

```
myclass B = A;
```

If an identical copy of **A** is made and assigned to **B**, then instead of **B** holding a pointer to its own piece of dynamically allocated memory, **B** will be using the same piece of memory as **A**. This will almost certainly lead to trouble. For example, when **A** and **B** are destroyed, the same piece of memory will be freed twice! Once for **A** and then again for **B**.

A similar type of problem can occur in two additional ways. The first occurs when a copy of an object is made when it is passed as an argument to a function. This object goes out of scope (and is destroyed) when the function returns. The second occurs when a temporary object is created as a return value from a function. As you may know, temporary objects are automatically created to hold the return value of a function. This temporary object goes out of scope after the expression containing the function call finishes. In both cases, if the temporary objects act on a resource, such as through a pointer or an open file, then those actions will have side effects. In the case of **myclass**, this would result in the same block of memory being freed two or more times. Clearly, such a situation must be avoided.

To solve the type of problems just described, C++ allows you to create an explicit *copy constructor* for a class. The copy constructor is called when one object initializes another. All classes have a default copy constructor, which produces a member-by-member copy. When you define your own copy constructor, it is used instead.

Before we continue, it is important to understand that C++ defines two distinct types of situations in which the value of one object is given to another. The first is assignment. The second is initialization, which can occur in three ways:

- When one object explicitly initializes another, such as in a declaration,
- When a copy of an object is made to be passed to a function, or
- When a temporary object is generated (most commonly, as a return value).

The copy constructor applies only to initializations. The copy constructor does not apply to assignments.

The most common general form of a copy constructor is shown here:

classname (const *classname* &*obj*) {

    // Body of copy constructor.

}

Here, *obj* is a reference to the object on the right side of the initialization. It is permissible for a copy constructor to have additional parameters as long as they have default arguments defined for them. However, in all cases, the first parameter must be a reference to the object doing the initializing. This reference can also be **const** and/or **volatile**.

Again, assume a class called **myclass** and an object of type **myclass** called **A**. Also assuming that **func1( )** takes a **myclass** parameter and that **func2( )** returns a **myclass** object, each of the following statements involves initialization:

```
myclass B = A;  // A initializing B
myclass B(A);   // A initializing B
func1(A);       // A passed as a parameter
A = func2();    // A receiving a temporary, return object
```

In the first three cases, a reference to **A** is passed to the copy constructor. In the fourth, a reference to the object returned by **func2( )** is passed to the copy constructor.

Inside a copy constructor, you must manually handle the duplication of every field within the object. This, of course, gives you a chance to avoid potentially harmful situations. For example, in **myclass** just described, the new **myclass** object could allocate its own memory. This would allow both the original and the copy to be equivalent but fully separate objects. It also avoids the problem of both objects using the same memory because freeing one object's memory would not affect the other. If necessary, the memory could be initialized to contain the same contents as the original.

In some cases, the same problems that can occur when making a copy of an object also occur when one object is assigned to another. The reason is that the default assignment operator makes a member-by-member, identical copy. You can avoid problems by overloading **operator=( )** so that you handle the assignment process yourself. See *Operator Overloading Basic Techniques* for details on overloading assignment.

Example

The following demonstrates the copy constructor. Although very simple, it clearly shows when a copy is and is not called. (A practical use of the copy constructor is shown in the Bonus Example that follows.)

```
// Demonstrate a copy constructor.

#include <iostream>
using namespace std;

// This class declares a copy constructor.
```

```
class sample {
public:
  int v;

  // Default constructor.
  sample() {
    v = 0;
    cout << "Inside default constructor.\n";
  }

  // Parameterized constructor.
  sample(int i) {
    v = i;
    cout << "Inside parameterized constructor.\n";
  }

  // Copy constructor.
  sample(const sample &obj) {
    v = obj.v;
    cout << "Inside copy constructor.\n";
  }
};

// Pass an object to a function. The copy constructor
// is called when a temporary object is created to
// hold the value passed to x.
int timestwo(sample x) {
  return x.v * x.v;
}

// Return an object from a function. The copy constructor
// is called when a temporary object is created for the return value.
sample factory(int i) {
  sample s(i);
  return s;
}


int main()
{
  cout << "Create samp(8).\n";
  sample samp(8);
  cout << "samp has the value " << samp.v << endl;

  cout << endl;

  cout << "Create samp2 and initialize it with samp.\n";
  sample samp2 = samp;
  cout << "samp2 has the value " << samp2.v << endl;

  cout << endl;

  cout << "Pass samp to timestwo().\n";
```

```
    cout << "Result of timestwo(samp): " << timestwo(samp) << endl;

    cout << endl;

    cout << "Creating samp3.\n";
    sample samp3;

    cout << endl;

    cout << "Now, assign samp3 the value returned by factory(10).\n";
    samp3 = factory(10);
    cout << "samp3 now has the value " << samp3.v << endl;

    cout << endl;

    // Assignment does not invoke the copy constructor.
    cout << "Execute samp3 = samp.\n";
    samp3 = samp;
    cout << "Notice that the copy constructor is not used "
         << "for assignment.\n";

    return 0;
}
```

The output is shown here:

```
Create samp(8).
Inside parameterized constructor.
samp has the value 8

Create samp2 and initialize it with samp.
Inside copy constructor.
samp2 has the value 8

Pass samp to timestwo().
Inside copy constructor.
Result of timestwo(samp): 64

Creating samp3.
Inside default constructor.

Now, assign samp3 the value returned by factory(10).
Inside parameterized constructor.
Inside copy constructor.
samp3 now has the value 10

Execute samp3 = samp.
Notice that the copy constructor is not used for assignment.
```

As you can see, the copy constructor is called when one object initializes another. It is not called during assignment. One other point: the statement

```
    sample samp2 = samp;
```

can also be written as

```
sample samp2(samp);
```

Both forms result in the copy constructor being used to create a copy of **samp**.

Bonus Example: A Safe Array that Uses Dynamic Allocation

The preceding example clearly showed when a copy constructor is and is not called. However, it did not illustrate the type of situation in which one is needed. This example does. It demonstrates the necessity of the copy constructor by developing another implementation of a "safe array," which is an array that prevents boundary overruns and underruns. The approach used here relies on dynamically allocated memory to hold the underlying array. As you will see, this technique requires an explicit copy constructor to avoid problems.

Before we begin, it is useful to contrast this approach with the one shown in *Overload the Subscripting Operator [ ]* earlier in this chapter. In that recipe, the example created an array type called **safe_array** that encapsulated a static array that actually held the elements. Thus, each **safe_array** was backed by a full-length static array. As a result, if a very large safe array was needed, the resulting **safe_array** object would also be very large because it would encapsulate the entire array.

The version developed here uses a different approach. Called **dyn_safe_array**, it dynamically allocates memory for the array and stores only a pointer to that memory. This has the advantage of making the safe-array objects smaller—much smaller in some cases. This makes them more efficient when they are passed to functions, for example. Of course, it takes a bit more work to implement a safe array that uses dynamic memory, because both a copy constructor and an overloaded assignment operator are needed. Like **safe_array** shown earlier, **dyn_safe_array** overloads the subscripting operator [ ] to allow normal, array-like subscripting to access the elements in the array.

The **dyn_safe_array** class is generic, which means that it can be used to create any type of array. The number of elements in the array is passed as a non-type argument in its template specification. Its constructor then allocates sufficient memory to hold the array of the desired size and type. A pointer to this memory is stored in **aptr**. The destructor for **dyn_safe_array** automatically frees this memory when an object goes out of scope. Otherwise, because the [ ] is overloaded, a **dyn_safe_array** can be used just like a normal array.

When one **dyn_safe_array** is used to initialize another, the copy constructor is called. It creates a copy of the original object by first allocating memory for the array and then copying elements from the original array into the newly allocated memory. This way, each object's **aptr** points to its own array. Without the copy constructor, an identical copy of a **dyn_safe_array** would be made, which would result in two objects having **aptr**s that pointed to the same memory. Among other potential troubles, this would result in an attempt to free the same memory more than once when the objects go out of scope. The copy constructor prevents this.

The same type of problem that the copy constructor prevents can also occur when one **dyn_safe_array** object is assigned to another. To avoid this problem, the assignment operator is also overloaded so that the contents of the array are copied, but the dynamically allocated memory used by each object remains separate.

One last point: The copy constructor and the overloaded assignment operator display a message each time they are called. This is simply for illustration. Normally, neither would generate any output.

```cpp
// A generic safe-array class that prevents array boundary errors.
// It uses the subscripting operator to access the array elements.
// This version differs from the approach used in the recipe:
//
//      Overload the Subscripting Operator []
//
// because it allocates memory for the array dynamically rather
// than statically.
//
// An explicit copy constructor is implemented so that a copy
// of a safe array object uses its own allocated memory. Therefore,
// the original object and the copy DO NOT point to the same
// memory. The assignment operator is also overloaded for the same
// reason. In both cases, the contents of the array are copied so
// that both the original array and the copy contain the same values.

#include <iostream>
#include <new>
#include <cstdlib>

using namespace std;

// A generic safe-array class that dynamically allocates memory
// for the array. The length of the array is passed as a non-type
// argument in the template specification.
template <class T, int len> class dyn_safe_array {
  T *aptr;  // pointer to the memory that holds the array
  int length; // number of elements in the array
public:

  // The dyn_safe_array constructor.
  dyn_safe_array();

  // The dyn_safe_array copy constructor.
  dyn_safe_array(const dyn_safe_array &obj);

  // Release the allocated memory when a dyn_safe_array object
  // goes out of scope.
  ~dyn_safe_array() {
     delete [] aptr;
  }

  // Overload assignment.
  dyn_safe_array &operator=(const dyn_safe_array<T,len> &rh_op);

  // Use the subscripting operator to access elements in
  // the safe array.
  T &operator[](int i);
```

```
  // Return the size of the array.
  int getlen() { return length; }
};

// This is dyn_safe_array's constructor.
template <class T, int len>
  dyn_safe_array<T, len>::dyn_safe_array() {

  try {
    // Allocate the array.
    aptr = new T[len];
  } catch(bad_alloc ba) {
    cout << "Can't allocate array.\n";
    // Take appropriate action here. This is just
    // a placeholder response.
    exit(1);
  }

  // Initialize the array elements to their default value.
  for(int i=0; i < len; ++i) aptr[i] = T();

  length = len;
}


// This is dyn_safe_array's copy constructor.
template <class T, int len>
  dyn_safe_array<T, len>::dyn_safe_array(const dyn_safe_array &obj) {

  cout << "Using dyn_safe_array's copy constructor to make a copy.\n";

  try {
    // Allocate an array of the same size as the
    // one used by obj.
    aptr = new T[obj.length];
  } catch(bad_alloc ba) {
    // Take appropriate action here. This is just
    // a placeholder response.
    cout << "Can't allocate array.\n";
    exit(1);
  }
  length = obj.length;

  // Copy contents of the array.
  for(int i=0; i < length; ++i)
    aptr[i] = obj.aptr[i];
}

// Overload assignment so that a copy of the array is made.
// The copy is stored in an allocated memory that is separate
// from that used by the right-hand operand.
//
template<class T, int len> dyn_safe_array<T, len> &
```

```
dyn_safe_array<T, len>::operator=(const dyn_safe_array<T, len> &rh_op) {

  cout << "Assigning one dyn_safe_array object to another.\n";

  // If necessary, release the memory currently used by the object.
  if(aptr && (length != rh_op.length)) {

    // Delete the previously allocated memory.
    delete aptr;

    try {
      // Allocate an array of the same size as the
      // one used by rh_op.
      aptr = new T[rh_op.length];
    } catch(bad_alloc ba) {
      // Take appropriate action here. This is just
      // a placeholder response.
      cout << "Can't allocate array.\n";
      exit(1);
    }
  }

  length = rh_op.length;

  // Copy contents of the array.
  for(int i=0; i < length; ++i)
    aptr[i] = rh_op.aptr[i];
    return *this;
}

// Provide range checking for dyn_safe_array by overloading
// the [] operator. Notice that a reference is returned.
// This lets an array element be assigned a value.
template <class T, int len> T &dyn_safe_array<T, len>::operator[](int i)
{
  if(i < 0 || i > length) {
    // Take appropriate action here. This is just
    // a placeholder response.
    cout << "\nIndex value of " << i << " is out-of-bounds.\n";
    exit(1);
  }
  return aptr[i];
}

// A simple function for demonstration purposes.
// When called, the copy constructor will be used
// to create a copy of the argument passed to x.
template <class T, int len>
  dyn_safe_array<T, len> f(dyn_safe_array<T, len> x) {

  cout << "f() is returning a copy of x.\n";
  return x;
}
```

```
// This is a simple class used to demonstrate an array of objects.
// Notice that the default constructor gives x the value -1.
class myclass {
public:
  int x;
  myclass(int i) { x = i; };
  myclass() { x = -1; }
};

int main()
{

  // Use the integer array.
  dyn_safe_array<int, 5> i_ar;

  for(int i=0; i < i_ar.getlen(); ++i) i_ar[i] = i;
  cout << "Contents of i_ar: ";
  for(int i=0; i < i_ar.getlen(); ++i) cout << i_ar[i] << " ";
  cout << "\n\n";

  // To generate a boundary overrun, uncomment the following line:
//  i_ar[19] = 10;

  // To generate a boundary underrun, uncomment the following line:
//  i_ar[-2] = 10;

  // Create a copy of i_ar. This will invoke dyn_safe_array's copy constructor.
  cout << "Create i_ar2 and initialize it with i_ar. This results\n"
       << "in dyn_safe_array's copy constructor being called.\n\n";
  dyn_safe_array<int, 5> i_ar2 = i_ar;
  cout << "Contents of i_ar2: ";
  for(int i=0; i < i_ar2.getlen(); ++i)  cout << i_ar2[i] << " ";
  cout << "\n\n";

  // Create another safe array for integers, but don't assign
  // it any values. This means that its elements will contain
  // their default values.
  cout << "Create i_ar3.\n";
  dyn_safe_array<int, 5> i_ar3;

  cout << "Original contents of i_ar3: ";
  for(int i=0; i < i_ar3.getlen(); ++i)  cout << i_ar3[i] << " ";
  cout <<"\n\n";

  // Now, pass i_ar3 to f() and assign the result to i_ar:
  cout << "Now, this line will execute: i_ar3 = f(i_ar);\n"
       << "This will result in the following sequence of events:\n"
       << "   1. dyn_safe_array's copy constructor is called to make a\n"
       << "      copy of i_ar that is passed to the x parameter of f().\n"
       << "   2. The copy constructor is called again when a copy\n"
       << "      is made for the return value of f().\n"
       << "   3. The overloaded assignment operator is called to\n"
       << "      assign the result of f() to i_ar3.\n\n";
  i_ar3 = f(i_ar);
```

```
cout << "Contents of i_ar3 after receiving value from f(i_ar): ";
for(int i=0; i < i_ar3.getlen(); ++i)  cout << i_ar3[i] << " ";
cout << "\n\n";

cout << "Of course, dyn_safe_array works with class types, too.\n";
dyn_safe_array<myclass, 3> mc_ar;
cout << "Original contents of mc_ar: ";
for(int i=0; i < mc_ar.getlen(); ++i) cout << mc_ar[i].x << " ";
cout << endl;
mc_ar[0].x = 9;
mc_ar[1].x = 8;
mc_ar[2].x = 7;
cout << "Values in mc_ar after setting them: ";
for(int i=0; i < mc_ar.getlen(); ++i) cout << mc_ar[i].x << " ";
cout << "\n\n";

cout << "Now, create mc_ar2 and then execute this statement:\n"
     << "    mc_ar2 = f(mc_ar);\n\n";
dyn_safe_array<myclass, 3> mc_ar2;
mc_ar2 = f(mc_ar);
cout << "Contents of mc_ar2 after receiving f(mc_ar): ";
for(int i=0; i < mc_ar2.getlen(); ++i) cout << mc_ar2[i].x << " ";
cout << endl;

return 0;
}
```

The output is shown here:

```
Contents of i_ar: 0 1 2 3 4

Create i_ar2 and initialize it with i_ar. This results
in dyn_safe_array's copy constructor being called.

Using dyn_safe_array's copy constructor to make a copy.
Contents of i_ar2: 0 1 2 3 4

Create i_ar3.
Original contents of i_ar3: 0 0 0 0 0

Now, this line will execute: i_ar3 = f(i_ar);
This will result in the following sequence of events:
    1. dyn_safe_array's copy constructor is called to make a
       copy of i_ar that is passed to the x parameter of f().
    2. The copy constructor is called again when a copy
       is made for the return value of f().
    3. The overloaded assignment operator is called to
       assign the result of f() to i_ar3.

Using dyn_safe_array's copy constructor to make a copy.
f() is returning a copy of x.
Using dyn_safe_array's copy constructor to make a copy.
Assigning one dyn_safe_array object to another.
```

```
Contents of i_ar3 after receiving value from f(i_ar): 0 1 2 3 4

Of course, dyn_safe_array works with class types, too.
Original contents of mc_ar: -1 -1 -1
Values in mc_ar after setting them: 9 8 7

Now, create mc_ar2 and then execute this statement:
   mc_ar2 = f(mc_ar);

Using dyn_safe_array's copy constructor to make a copy.
f() is returning a copy of x.
Using dyn_safe_array's copy constructor to make a copy.
Assigning one dyn_safe_array object to another.
Contents of mc_ar2 after receiving f(mc_ar): 9 8 7
```

Options and Alternatives

As explained in the discussion, the most common form of copy constructor has only one
parameter that is a reference to an object of the class for which the copy constructor is
defined. However, it is permissible for a copy constructor to have additional parameters as
long as they have default arguments. For example, assuming the **dyn_safe_array** class, the
following declaration specifies a valid copy constructor:

```
dyn_safe_array(const dyn_safe_array &obj, int num = -1);
```

Here, the **num** parameter defaults to –1. You could use this constructor to allow only the
first **num** elements of the new **dyn_safe_array** to be initialized by the first **num** elements of
obj. The remaining elements can be given a default value. When **num** is –1, the entire array
is initialized by **obj**. This version of the copy constructor could be written like this:

```
// If num is not -1, initialize the first num elements of a safe array
// using the value from obj. The remaining elements get default values.
// Otherwise, initialize the entire array with the elements from obj.
template <class T, int len>
  dyn_safe_array<T, len>::dyn_safe_array(const dyn_safe_array &obj,
                                         int num) {

  cout << "Using dyn_safe_array's copy constructor to make a copy.\n";

  try {
    // Allocate an array of the same size as the
    // one used by obj.
    aptr = new T[obj.length];
  } catch(bad_alloc ba) {
    // Take appropriate action here. This is just
    // a placeholder response.
    cout << "Can't allocate array.\n";
    exit(1);
  }
  length = obj.length;

  // Copy contents of obj, up to the number passed via num.
```

```
// If num is -1, then all values are copied.
if(num == -1) num = obj.length;

for(int i=0; i < num; ++i)
  aptr[i] = obj.aptr[i];

// Initialize any remaining elements with their default value.
for(int i=num; i < length; ++i)
  aptr[i] = T();
}
```

You could use this constructor as shown here:

```
dyn_safe_array<int, 5> i_ar2(i_ar, 3);
```

Here, the first three elements of **i_ar** are used to initialize the first three elements of **i_ar2**. The remaining elements are given a default value, which for integers, is zero.

As explained in the discussion (and demonstrated by the **dyn_safe_array** class in the Bonus Example), if you need to implement a copy constructor, you often also need to overload the assignment operator. The reason is that the same issues that necessitate the copy constructor will also be present during assignment. It is important to not overlook assignment.

Determine an Object's Type at Runtime

Key Ingredients		
Headers	**Classes**	**Functions**
<typeinfo>	type_info	bool operator==(const type_info &*ob*) const
		bool operator!=(const type_info &*ob*) const
		bool before(const type_info &*ob*) const
		const char *name( ) const

In polymorphic languages such as C++, there can be situations in which the type of an object is unknown at compile time because the precise nature of that object is not determined until the program is executed. Recall that C++ implements polymorphism through the use of class hierarchies, virtual functions, and base class pointers. Since a base class pointer can be used to point to an object of the base class or *any object derived from that base*, it is not always possible to know in advance what type of object will be pointed to by a base pointer. This determination must be made at runtime, using runtime type information (RTTI). The key feature that enables this is the **typeid** operator. For some readers, RTTI and **typeid** are well-understood features, but for others, they are the source of many questions. For this reason, the basic RTTI techniques are described by this recipe.

Step-by-Step

To identify an object's type at runtime involves the following steps:

1. To obtain the type of an object, use **typeid(***object***)**. It returns a **type_info** instance that describes *object*'s type.

2. To obtain a **type_info** instance for a specific type, use **typeid(***type***)**. It returns a **type_info** object that represents *type.*

Discussion

To obtain an object's type, use the **typeid** operator. It has two forms. The first is used to determine an object's type. It is shown here:

typeid(*object*)

Here, *object* is an expression that describes the object whose type you will be obtaining. This can be the object itself, a dereferenced pointer, or a reference to the object. **typeid** returns a reference to a **const** object of type **type_info** that describes the type of *object*. The **type_info** class is declared in the **<typeinfo>** header. Therefore, you must include it when you use **typeid**.

The **type_info** class defines the following public members:

const char *name( ) const

bool operator==(const type_info &*ob*) const

bool operator!=(const type_info &*ob*) const

bool before(const type_info &*ob*) const

The **name( )** function returns a pointer to the name of the type, represented as a null-terminated string. For example, assuming some object called **obj**, the following statement displays the type name of the object:

```
cout << typeid(obj).name();
```

The overloaded **==** and **!=** provide for the comparison of types. The **before( )** function returns true if the invoking object is before the object used as a parameter in collation order. (This function has nothing to do with inheritance or class hierarchies.)

The second form of **typeid** takes a type name as its argument. It is shown here:

typeid(*type-name*)

Here *type-name* specifies a valid type name, such as **int**, **string**, **vector**, and so on. For example, the following expression is perfectly acceptable:

```
typeid(int).name()
```

Here, **typeid** returns the **type_info** object that describes **int**. The main use of this form of **typeid** is to compare an unknown type to a known type. For example,

```
if(typeid(int) == typeid(*ptr)) ...
```

If **ptr** points to an **int**, then the **if** statement will succeed.

The most important use of **typeid** occurs when it is applied through a pointer of a polymorphic base class. In this case, it will automatically return the type of the object being pointed to. Recall that a base class pointer can point to objects of the base class or to an object of any class derived from that base. In all cases, **typeid** returns the most derived type. Therefore, if the pointer points to a base class object, then the base class' type is returned. If the pointer points to a derived class object, then the derived class' type is returned. Thus, **typeid** lets you determine at runtime the type of the object that is being pointed to by a base class pointer.

References to an object of a polymorphic class hierarchy work the same as pointers. When **typeid** is applied to a reference to an object of a polymorphic class, it will return the type of the object actually being referred to, which may be of a derived type. The circumstance where you will most often make use of this feature is when objects are passed to functions by reference.

If you apply **typeid** to a pointer or reference to an object of a non-polymorphic class hierarchy, then the base type of the pointer is obtained. That is, no determination of what that pointer is actually pointing to is made.

Example

The following program demonstrates the **typeid** operator. It creates an abstract class called **two_d_shape** that defines the dimension of a two-dimensional object, such as a circle or a triangle. It also specifies a pure virtual function called **area( )**, which must be implemented by a derived class so that it returns the area of a shape. The program creates three subclasses of **two_d_shape**: **rectangle**, **triangle**, and **circle**.

The program also defines the functions **factory( )** and **sameshape( )**. The **factory( )** function creates an instance of a subclass of **two_d_shape**, which will be a **circle**, **triangle**, or **rectangle**, and returns a **two_d_shape** pointer to it. The specific type of object created is determined by the outcome of a call to **rand( )**, C++'s random-number generator. Thus, there is no way to know in advance what type of object will be generated. The program creates six objects. Since any type of figure may be generated by a call to **factory( )**, the program relies upon **typeid** to determine which type of object has actually been made.

The **sameshape( )** function compares two **two_d_shape** objects. The objects are the same only if they are of the same type and have the same dimensions. It uses **typeid** to confirm that the objects are the same type.

```
// Demonstrate runtime type id.

#include <iostream>
#include <cstdlib>

using namespace std;

// A polymorphic class that encapsulates two-dimensional shapes,
// such as triangles, rectangles, and circles. It declares a
// virtual function called area(), which derived classes overload
// to compute and return the area of a shape.
class two_d_shape {
protected:
  double x, y;
public:
  two_d_shape(double i, double j) {
    x = i;
```

```
    y = j;
  }

  double getx() { return x; }
  double gety() { return y; }

  virtual double area() = 0;
};

// Create a subclass of two_d_shape for triangles.
class triangle : public two_d_shape {
  public:
    triangle(double i, double j) : two_d_shape(i, j) { }

    double area() {
      return x * 0.5 * y;
    }
};

// Create a subclass of two_d_shape for rectangles.
class rectangle : public two_d_shape {
  public:
    rectangle(double i, double j) : two_d_shape(i, j) { }

    double area() {
      return x * y;
    }
};

// Create a subclass of two_d_shape for circles.
class circle : public two_d_shape {
  public:
    circle(double i, double j=0) : two_d_shape(i, j) { }

    double area() {
      return 3.14 * x * x;
    }
} ;

// A factory for objects derived from two_d_shape.
two_d_shape *factory() {
  static double i = (rand() % 100) / 3.0, j = (rand() % 100) / 3.0;

  i += rand() % 10;
  j += rand() % 12;

  cout << "Generating object.\n";

  switch(rand() % 3 ) {
    case 0: return new circle(i);
    case 1: return new triangle(i, j);
    case 2: return new rectangle(i, j);
  }
```

```
    return 0;
}

// Compare two shapes for equality. This means that their
// types and dimensions must be the same.
bool sameshape(two_d_shape *alpha, two_d_shape *beta) {

  cout << "Comparing a " << typeid(*alpha).name()
       << " object to a " << typeid(*beta).name()
       << " object\n";

  if(typeid(*alpha) != typeid(*beta)) return false;

  if(alpha->getx() != beta->getx() &&
     alpha->gety() != beta->gety())  return false;

  return true;
}

int main()
{
  // Create a base class pointer to two_d_shape.
  two_d_shape *p;

  // Generate two_d_shape objects.
  for(int i=0; i < 6; i++) {
    // Generate an object.
    p = factory();

    // Display the name of the object.
    cout << "Object is " << typeid(*p).name() << endl;

    // Display its area.
    cout << "    Area is " << p->area() << endl;

    // Keep a count of the object types that have been generated.
    if(typeid(*p) == typeid(triangle))
      cout << "    Base is " << p->getx() << " Height is "
           << p->gety() << endl;

    else if(typeid(*p) == typeid(rectangle))
      cout << "    Length is " << p->getx() << " Height is "
           << p->gety() << endl;

    else if(typeid(*p) == typeid(circle))
      cout << "    Diameter is " << p->getx() << endl;

    cout << endl;
  }

  cout << endl;

  // Make some objects to compare.
  triangle t(2, 3);
```

```
  triangle t2(2, 3);
  triangle t3(3, 2);
  rectangle r(2, 3);

  // Compare two two_d_objects.
  if(sameshape(&t, &t2))
    cout << "t and t2 are the same.\n";

  if(!sameshape(&t, &t3))
    cout << "t and t3 differ.\n";

  if(!sameshape(&t, &r))
    cout << "t and r differ.\n";

  cout << endl;

  return 0;
}
```

The output is shown here:

```
Generating object.
Object is class rectangle
    Area is 465.222
    Length is 17.6667 Height is 26.3333

Generating object.
Object is class circle
    Area is 1474.06
    Diameter is 21.6667

Generating object.
Object is class rectangle
    Area is 954.556
    Length is 23.6667 Height is 40.3333

Generating object.
Object is class circle
    Area is 2580.38
    Diameter is 28.6667

Generating object.
Object is class triangle
    Area is 776.278
    Base is 29.6667 Height is 52.3333

Generating object.
Object is class circle
    Area is 3148.72
    Diameter is 31.6667


Comparing a class triangle object to a class triangle object
t and t2 are the same.
```

```
Comparing a class triangle object to a class triangle object
t and t3 differ.
Comparing a class triangle object to a class rectangle object
t and r differ.
```

Options and Alternatives

The **typeid** operator can be applied to template classes. The type of an object that is an instance of a template class is determined, in part, by what data is used for its type parameters when the object is instantiated. Two instances of the same template class that are created using different data are, therefore, different types. For example, assume the template class **myclass**, shown here:

```
template <class T> class myclass {
  // ...
};
```

The following sequence:

```
myclass<int> mc_int;
myclass<double> mc_dbl;

cout << "mc_int type is " << typeid(mc_int).name() << endl
     << "mc_dbl type is " << typeid(mc_dbl).name() << endl;

if(typeid(mc_int) != typeid(mc_dbl))
  cout << "The two objects are not of same type";
```

produces the following output:

```
mc_int type is class myclass<int>
mc_dbl type is class myclass<double>
The two objects are not of same type
```

As you can see, even though **mc_int** and **mc_dbl** are objects of **myclass**, their types differ because different template arguments are used.

Use Complex Numbers

Key Ingredients		
Headers	**Classes**	**Functions**
<complex>	complex	T imag( ) const
		T real( ) const

A sometimes overlooked feature of C++ is its support for complex numbers. A complex number contains two components: a real part and an imaginary part. The imaginary part specifies a multiple of *i*, which is the square root of –1. Thus, a complex number is usually represented in this form:

$a + bi$

where *a* specifies the real part and *b* specifies the imaginary part. In C++, complex numbers are supported by the class **complex**. This recipe shows the basic techniques required to use it.

Step-by-Step

To use complex numbers involves these steps:

1. Create one or more **complex** objects. The complex class is generic, and you must specify the type of the components. This will normally be a floating-point type, such as **double**.
2. Perform operations on **complex** objects by use of overloaded operators. All of the arithmetic operators are defined for **complex**.
3. Obtain the real component of a **complex** instance by calling **real( )**.
4. Obtain the imaginary component of a **complex** instance by calling **imag( )**.

Discussion

The template specification for **complex** is shown here:

    template <class T> class complex

Here, **T** specifies the type used to represent the components of a complex number. There are three predefined specializations of **complex**:

    class complex<float>

    class complex<double>

    class complex<long double>

Specifying any other type argument is undefined.

The **complex** class has the following constructors:

    complex(const T &real = T( ), const T &imaginary = T( ))

    complex(const complex &ob)

    template <class T1> complex(const complex<T1> &ob);

The first constructs a **complex** object with a real component of *real* and an imaginary component of *imaginary*. These values default to zero if not specified. The second creates a copy of *ob*. The third creates a **complex** object from *ob*.

The following operations are defined for **complex** objects:

+	–	*	/
–=	+=	/=	*=
=	==	!=	

The non-assignment operators are overloaded in three ways: once for operations involving a **complex** object on the left and a scalar object on the right, again for operations involving a scalar on the left and a **complex** object on the right, and finally for operations involving two **complex** objects. For example, the following types of addition operations are allowed:

   complex_ob + scalar

   scalar + complex_ob

   complex_ob + complex_ob

Two member functions are defined for **complex**: **real( )** and **imag( )**. They are shown here:

   T real( ) const

   T imag( ) const

The **real( )** function returns the real component of the invoking object, and **imag( )** returns the imaginary component.

   The **<complex>** header also defines **complex** versions of the standard math functions, such as **abs( )**, **sin( )**, **cos( )**, and **pow( )**.

Example

Here is a sample program that demonstrates **complex**:

```
// Demonstrate the complex class.

#include <iostream>
#include <complex>

using namespace std;

int main()
{
  complex<double> cmpx1(1, 0);
  complex<double> cmpx2(1, 1);

  cout << "cmpx1: " << cmpx1 << endl << "cmpx2: " << cmpx2 << endl;

  // Add two complex numbers.
  cout << "cmpx1 + cmpx2: " << cmpx1 + cmpx2 << endl;
```

```
// Multiply two complex numbers.
cout << "cmpx1 * cmpx2: " << cmpx1 * cmpx2 << endl;

// Add a scalar to a complex number.
cmpx1 +=   2.0;
cout << "cmpx1 += 2.0: " << cmpx1 << endl;

// Find the sin of cmpx2.
cout << "sin(cmpx2): " << sin(cmpx2) << endl;

return 0;
}
```

The output is shown here:

```
cmpx1: (1,0)
cmpx2: (1,1)
cmpx1 + cmpx2: (2,1)
cmpx1 * cmpx2: (1,1)
cmpx1 += 2.0: (3,0)
sin(cmpx2): (1.29846,0.634964)
```

Options and Alternatives

For programmers who focus on numeric computations, C++ provides more support than one might at first guess. In addition to **complex**, C++ includes the **valarray** class that supports operations on numeric arrays. It also supplies two utility classes called **slice** and **gslice**, which encapsulate a portion (i.e., a slice) of an array. These classes require the header **<valarray>**. In the **<numeric>** header are defined four numeric algorithms called **accumulate( )**, **adjacent_difference( )**, **inner_product( )**, and **partial_sum( )**. All of these will be of interest to the numeric programmer.

Use auto_ptr

Key Ingredients

Headers	Classes	Functions
<memory>	auto_ptr	T *get( ) const throw( )
		T *release( ) throw( )
		void reset(X *ptr = 0) throw( )

C++ includes a class called **auto_ptr** that was designed to simplify the management of dynamically allocated memory. As many readers will know, one of the most troubling aspects of using dynamic allocation is the prevention of memory leaks. One way a memory leak can occur is when memory is allocated, but never freed. The **auto_ptr** class is an attempt to prevent this situation. This recipe describes its use.

Step-by-Step

To use **auto_ptr** involves these steps:

1. Create an **auto_ptr**, specifying the base type of the pointer.
2. Allocate memory using **new**, and assign a pointer to that memory to the **auto_ptr** created in Step 1.
3. Use the **auto_ptr** just like a normal pointer. However, do not free the memory pointed to by the **auto_ptr**. In other words, do not use **delete** to release the memory.
4. When the **auto_ptr** is destroyed, such as when it goes out of scope, the memory pointed to by the **auto_ptr** is automatically freed.
5. You can obtain the pointer held by an **auto_ptr** by calling **get( )**.
6. You can set the **auto_ptr**'s pointer by calling **reset( )**.
7. You can release the **auto_ptr**'s ownership of the pointer by calling **release( )**.

Discussion

An **auto_ptr** is a pointer that owns the object it points to. Ownership of this object can be transferred to another **auto_ptr**, but some **auto_ptr** always owns the object. For example, when one **auto_ptr** object is assigned to another, only the target of the assignment will own the object. When an **auto_ptr** is destroyed, such as when it goes out of scope, the object pointed to by the **auto_ptr** is automatically freed. Because only one **auto_ptr** will own (hold a pointer to) any given object at any given time, the object will only be freed once, when the **auto_ptr** having ownership is destroyed. Any other **auto_ptr**s that may have previously held ownership take no action. This mechanism ensures that dynamically allocated objects are properly freed in all circumstances. Among others, one benefit of this approach is that dynamically allocated objects can be automatically freed when an exception occurs.

The template specification for **auto_ptr** is shown here:

    template <class T> class auto_ptr

Here, **T** specifies the type of pointer stored by the **auto_ptr**.
Here are the constructors for **auto_ptr**:

    explicit auto_ptr(T *ptr = 0) throw( )

    auto_ptr(auto_ptr &ob) throw( )

    template <class T2> auto_ptr(auto_ptr<T2> &ob) throw( )

The first constructor creates an **auto_ptr** to the object specified by *ptr*. The second constructor creates a copy of the **auto_ptr** specified by *ob* and transfers ownership to the new object. The third converts *&ob* to type **T *** (if possible) and transfers ownership.

The **auto_ptr** class defines the =, *, and –> operators. It also defines these three functions:

T *get( ) const throw( )

T *release( ) throw( )

void reset(X *ptr = 0) throw( )

The **get( )** function returns a pointer to the stored object. The **release( )** function removes ownership of the stored object from the invoking **auto_ptr** and returns a pointer to the object. After a call to **release( )**, the pointed-to object is not automatically destroyed when the **auto_ptr** object goes out of scope. The **reset( )** function calls **delete** on the pointer currently held by the **auto_ptr** (unless it equals *ptr*) and then sets the pointer to *ptr*.

Example

Here is a short program that demonstrates the use of **auto_ptr**. It creates a class called **X** that stores an integer value. Inside **main( )**, an **X** object is created and assigned to an **auto_ptr**. Notice how the members of **X** can be accessed through the **auto_ptr**, using the normal pointer operator –>. Also notice how one and only one **auto_ptr** owns the pointer to the **X** object at any given time. This is why only one **X** object is destroyed when the program finishes.

```
// Demonstrate an auto_ptr.

#include <iostream>
#include <memory>

using namespace std;

class X {
public:
  int v;

  X(int j) {
    v = j;
    cout << "Constructing X(" << v <<")\n";
  }

  ~X() { cout << "Destructing X(" << v <<")\n"; }

  void f() { cout << "Inside f()\n"; }
};

int main()
{
  auto_ptr<X> p1(new X(3)), p2;

  cout << "p1 points to an X with the value " << p1->v
       << "\n\n";

  // Transfer ownership to p2.
  cout << "Assigning p1 to p2.\n";
```

```
    p2 = p1;
    cout << "Now, p2 points to an X with the value " << p2->v
        << endl;
    if(!p1.get()) cout << "p1's pointer is now null.\n\n";

    // Can call a function through an auto_ptr.
    cout << "Call f() through p2: ";
    p2->f();
    cout << endl;

    // Assign the pointer encapsulated by an auto_ptr to
    // a normal pointer.
    cout << "Get the pointer stored in p2 and assign it to a\n"
        << "normal pointer called ptr.\n";
    X *ptr = p2.get();
    cout << "ptr points to an X with the value " << ptr->v
        << "\n\n";

    return 0;

    // At this point, the allocated object is freed and
    // its destructor is called. Even though there are
    // two auto_ptr objects, only one owns the pointer.
    // Therefore, only one X object is destroyed.
}
```

The output produced by this program is shown here:

```
Constructing X(3)
p1 points to an X with the value 3

Assigning p1 to p2.
Now, p2 points to an X with the value 3
p1's pointer is now null.

Call f() through p2: Inside f()

Get the pointer stored in p2 and assign it to a
normal pointer called ptr.
ptr points to an X with the value 3

Destructing X(3)
```

Options and Alternatives

Although **auto_ptr** is useful, it does not prevent all pointer problems. For example, it is still possible to operate accidentally on a null pointer. You can use **auto_ptr** as the basis for your own custom "safe pointer" type, however. To experiment with this concept, try using an **auto_ptr** for the **ptr** member in the **safe_ptr** class shown in the Bonus Example in *Overload the –> Operator*.

Another thing that **auto_ptr** does not provide is *garbage collection*. As most readers know, garbage collection is a memory management scheme in which memory is automatically recycled when it is no longer used by any object. Although aspects of **auto_ptr** seem related to garbage collection, such as the fact that allocated memory is automatically released when the **auto_ptr** goes out of scope, garbage collection relies on a fundamentally different mechanism. Currently, Standard C++ does not define a garbage collection library, but the next version of C++ might.

One last point: To pass an **auto_ptr** to a function, I recommend using a reference parameter. I have seen significant differences over the years in the way different compilers handle passing an **auto_ptr** value. Passing a reference avoids the issue.

Create an Explicit Constructor

Key Ingredients		
Headers	**Classes**	**Functions**
	any class	explicit *constructor(type param)*

To conclude this cookbook on C++, I have chosen one of its more esoteric features: the explicit constructor. Over the years, I have been asked several times about this feature because it is frequently used in the Standard C++ library. Although not difficult, it is a specialized feature whose meaning is not universally understood. This recipe describes the purpose of an explicit constructor and shows how to create one.

Step-by-Step

To create an explicit constructor involves these steps:

1. Create a constructor that takes one argument.
2. Modify that constructor with the keyword **explicit**.

Discussion

C++ defines the keyword **explicit** to handle a special-case condition that occurs with a constructor that requires only one argument. To understand the purpose of **explicit**, consider the following class:

```
class myclass {
  int val;
public:
  myclass(int x) { val = x; }
  int getval() { return val; }
};
```

Notice that the constructor for **myclass** has one parameter. This means that you can create a **myclass** object like this:

```
myclass ob(4);
```

In this declaration, the value 4, which is specified in the parentheses following **ob**, is an argument that is passed to **myclass( )**'s parameter **x**. This value is then used to initialize **val**. This is a common form of initialization, and it is widely used in this book. However, there is an alternative, as shown by the following statement, which also initializes **val** to 4:

```
myclass ob = 4; // automatically converts into myclass(4)
```

As the comment suggests, this form of initialization is automatically converted into a call to the **myclass** constructor, with 4 being the argument. That is, the preceding statement is handled by the compiler as if it were written like this:

```
myclass ob(4);
```

In general, any time that you have a constructor that requires only one argument, you can use either *ob(x)* or *ob = x* to initialize an object. The reason for this is that whenever you create a constructor that requires one argument, you are also implicitly creating a conversion from the type of that argument to the type of the class.

If you do not want implicit conversions to occur, you can prevent them by using **explicit**. The **explicit** specifier applies only to constructors. A constructor specified as **explicit** will be used only when an initialization uses the normal constructor syntax. It will not perform any automatic conversion. For example, by declaring the **myclass** constructor **explicit**, as shown here:

```
explicit myclass(int x) { val = x; }
```

the automatic conversion will not be supplied. Now, only constructors of the form

```
myclass ob(27);
```

will be allowed. This form

```
myclass ob = 27; // Now an error!
```

will not be allowed.

Example

The following example puts together the pieces and illustrates an **explicit** constructor. First, here is a program that illustrates the automatic conversion that occurs when a constructor is not modified by **explicit**:

```
#include <iostream>

using namespace std;

class myclass {
  int val;
public:
```

```
  // The following constructor is NOT explicit.
  myclass(int x) { val = x; }

  int getval() { return val; }
};

int main()
{
  myclass ob(4); // OK
  cout << "val in ob: " << ob.getval() << endl;

  // The following statement is OK because of the implicit
  // conversion from int to myclass.
  myclass ob2 = 19;
  cout << "val in ob2: " << ob2.getval() << endl;

  return 0;
}
```

The output is shown here:

```
val in ob: 4
val in ob2: 19
```

As you can see, both forms of initialization are allowed, and both initialize a **myclass**
instance as expected.

The following version of the program adds the **explicit** modifier to the **myclass**
constructor:

```
#include <iostream>

using namespace std;

class myclass {
  int val;
public:
  // Now myclass(int) is explicit.
  explicit myclass(int x) { val = x; }

  int getval() { return val; }
};

int main()
{
  myclass ob(4); // Still OK
  cout << "val in ob: " << ob.getval() << endl;

  // The following statement is in error because the implicit
  // conversion from int to myclass is no longer allowed.
  myclass ob2 = 19;  // Error!
  cout << "val in ob2: " << ob.getval() << endl;

  return 0;
}
```

After making **myclass(int)** explicit, the statement

```
myclass ob2 = 19;   // Error!
```

is now in error and won't compile.

Options and Alternatives

The **explicit** modifier applies only to constructors that require one argument. However, this does not mean that the constructor must have only one parameter. It simply means that any parameters after the first must have default arguments. For example:

```
class myclass {
  int val;
  int another_val;
public:
  explicit myclass(int x, int y = 0) { val = x; another_val = y; }
  // ...
};
```

Because **y** defaults to 0, the use of **explicit** is still valid. Its use prevents the following declaration:

```
myclass counter = 19; // not valid
```

If the constructor *had not* been declared as **explicit**, the preceding statement would have been allowed, with **y** defaulting to 0. Because of **explicit**, the constructor must be explicitly invoked, like this:

```
myclass counter(19);
```

Of course, you can also specify a second argument:

```
myclass counter(19, 99);
```

Index